BIG AND SMALL

BIG & SMALL

A CULTURAL HISTORY OF EXTRAORDINARY BODIES

LYNNE VALLONE

YALE UNIVERSITY PRESS
NEW HAVEN AND LONDON

For information about this and other Yale University Press publications, please contact:

U.S. Office: sales.press@yale.edu   yalebooks.com
Europe Office: sales@yaleup.co.uk   yalebooks.co.uk

Set in Minion Pro by IDSUK (DataConnection) Ltd
Printed in Great Britain by Gomer Press Ltd, Llandysul, Ceredigion, Wales

Library of Congress Control Number: 2017948471

ISBN 978-0-300-22886-1

A catalogue record for this book is available from the British Library.

10 9 8 7 6 5 4 3 2 1

For my parents

CONTENTS

List of Plates   viii
Acknowledgments   xi

Introduction: People Big and People Small   1

Part I   Small Bodies
Introduction: The Little Man   17
1 In the Beginning was Tom Thumb   29
2 The Dwarf in High and Popular Culture   60
3 Staging the Dwarf   103
4 Lilliputians in Blackface   130

Part II   Big Bodies
Introduction: The Monstrous Giant   181
5 Gigantic Mechanical Boy Scouts   191
6 The Obese Girl   224

Afterword: The Human Measure   256

Notes   266
Bibliography   316
Index   330

PLATES

1. Sir Anthony van Dyck, *Queen Henrietta Maria with Sir Jeffrey Hudson*, 1633. Oil on canvas. Courtesy National Gallery of Art, Washington, DC.
2. Attribution to Samuel Root or Marcus Aurelius Root, *P. T. Barnum and General Tom Thumb, c.* 1850. Half-plate daguerreotype. National Portrait Gallery, Smithsonian Institution.
3. Charles Ray, *Family Romance*, 1993. Mixed media. © Charles Ray, Courtesy of Matthew Marks Gallery.
4. Ota Benga, *c.* 1915–1916. Glass-plate negative. Library of Congress, Prints & Photographs Division, LC-DIG-ggbain-22741.
5. Theodor Kerckring, *Opera Omnia Anatomica*, 1717. Courtesy of The New York Academy of Medicine Library.
6. Richard Redgrave, *Gulliver Exhibited to the Brobdingnag Farmer*, 1836. Oil on canvas. Victoria and Albert Museum, London.
7. Nicolaas Hartsoeker, *Éssai de dioptrique*, 1694. © The British Library Board, 537.k.19.
8. Daniel Mytens, *Charles I and Henrietta Maria Departing for the Chase, c.* 1630–1632. Oil on canvas. Royal Collection Trust/© Her Majesty Queen Elizabeth II, 2017.
9. Sir Anthony van Dyck, *Marchesa Elena Grimaldi Cattaneo*, 1623. Oil on canvas. Courtesy National Gallery of Art, Washington, DC.

10. Andreas Alciato, *Emblematum liber*, 1531. © The British Library Board, C.57.a.11.

11. R. B. (Nathaniel Crouch), *Delights for the Ingenious in Choice Emblems*, 1684. © The British Library Board, G.13220.

12. Jacob Cats with John Leighton, *Moral Emblems with Aphorisms, Adages and Proverbs, of all Ages and Nations, from Jacob Cats and Robert Farlie*, 1862. © The British Library Board, 1347.i.21.

13. Frans Pourbus the Younger, *The Infanta Isabella Clara Eugenia and Her Dwarf, c.* 1598–1600. Oil on canvas. Royal Collection Trust/© Her Majesty Queen Elizabeth II, 2017.

14. Alonso Sánchez Coello, *The Infanta Isabella Clara Eugenia and Magdalena Ruíz*, 1585–1588. Oil on canvas. © Museo Nacional del Prado.

15. Diego Rodriguez de Silva y Velázquez, *Prince Baltasar Carlos in the Riding School, c.* 1639–1640. Wallace Collection, London, UK/ Bridgeman Images.

16. Diego Rodriguez de Silva y Velázquez, *Don Baltasar Carlos with a Dwarf*, 1632. Oil on canvas. Museum of Fine Arts, Boston. Henry Lillie Pierce Fund 01.104. Photograph © 2017 Museum of Fine Arts, Boston.

17. Diego Rodriguez de Silva y Velázquez, *Las Meninas o La Familia de Felipe IV*, 1656. Oil on canvas. © Museo Nacional del Prado.

18. Charles S. Stratton and his father, *c.* 1845. Daguerreotype. The Barnum Museum, Bridgeport, CT, EL 1988.067.001.

19. Currier and Ives, *"What is It?"*, 1860–1865. Hand-colored lithograph. Collection of the Shelburne Museum, gift of Harry T. Peters, Jr., Natalie Peters, and Natalie Webster, 1959–1967. Shelburne Museum, Vermont.

20. Matthew Brady Studio, *Mr. and Mrs. "General Tom Thumb" in their Wedding Costume*, 1863. Albumen silver print. National Portrait Gallery, Smithsonian Institution.

21. William Edgar Geil, *A Yankee in Pigmy Land*, 1905. © The British Library Board, 010095.de.48.

22. Ota Benga, Louisiana Purchase Exposition, 1904. Photograph. American Museum of Natural History Library, #299134.

23. Illustration by Hugh Lofting from *The Story of Doctor Dolittle*, copyright 1920 by Hugh Lofting; copyright 1948 by Josephine

Lofting; centenary edition 1988 copyright by Christopher Lofting. Cotsen Collection of Children's Books, Princeton University.

24. Illustration by Hugh Lofting from *The Story of Doctor Dolittle*, copyright 1920 by Hugh Lofting; copyright 1948 by Josephine Lofting; centenary edition 1988 copyright by Christopher Lofting. UCLA Special Collections.

25. François Place, *The Last Giants*, 1992. © CASTERMAN.

26. Lewis Hine, *Leo, 48 inches high. 8 years old*, 1910. Black and white photograph from the records of the National Child Labor Committee. Library of Congress, Prints and Photographs Division, National Child Labor Committee Collection, LC-DIG-nclc-01892.

27. Lewis Hine, *Rhodes Mfg. Co., Lincolnton, N.C. Spinner*, 1908. Black and white photograph from the records of the National Child Labor Committee. Library of Congress, Prints and Photographs Division, National Child Labor Committee Collection, LC-DIG-nclc-01345.

28. Louise Lentz Woodruff, *Science Advancing Mankind*, 1933. Postcard. Larry Zim World's Fair Collection, Archives Center, National Museum of American History, Smithsonian Institution.

29. Graham Kaye, illustrator. Cover design of *Tom Swift and His Giant Robot* by Victor Appleton II. New York: Stratemeyer Syndicate, 1954. From *Tom Swift and His Giant Robot* by Victor Appleton II with illustrations by Graham Kaye. © 1954 by The Stratemeyer Syndicate. Reprinted with the permission of Simon & Schuster Books for Young Readers, an imprint of Simon & Schuster Children's Publishing Division.

30. Juan Carreño de Miranda, *Eugenia Martínez Vallejo, vestida (clothed)*, c. 1680. Oil on canvas. © Museo Nacional del Prado.

31. Juan Carreño de Miranda, *Eugenia Martínez Vallejo, desnuda (naked)*, c. 1680. Oil on canvas. © Museo Nacional del Prado.

32. Maxime Du Camp, *Westernmost Colossus of the Temple of Re, Abu Simbel*, 1850. Salted paper print from paper negative. The Metropolitan Museum of Art, New York. Gilman Collection, Gift of the Howard Gilman Foundation, 2005.

ACKNOWLEDGMENTS

How did I come to write this book, who helped, and why did it take me so long? These are the questions (well, the first two, at least) that I often ask when I turn, invariably, to the acknowledgments pages in any academic book that I pick up. It's where I'm likely to find stories—an addiction of mine—and maybe some people whom I know. Here's the story of my book—a story that cannot be told without many thank yous along the way.

This book is about bodily size. When I was in graduate school in the 1980s, "alterity" was a hot topic. We were taught to recognize and appreciate how race and class and gender impacted the texts we read and analyzed. For the most part, I found this approach to be eye-opening and rewarding; everything I read seemed to be illuminated through considerations of these positions. The cosmos shifted when male, for example, was no longer universal, when "identity politics," so called, became a way of interpreting the world around us and the people (and characters) in it. We know the world through size, as well. That's perspective, sure—the "human measure" we're attracted to—but paying close attention to bodily size difference is akin to race and class and gender: everything that always has been right in front of us looks/feels new.

As a grown-up who locates one aspect of her readerly identity in children's books, who transformed an early love of literature into an academic career teaching, reading, and writing about children's literature and culture, I have always been intrigued by the relationships between adult and child. It took me some years before I realized that in addition to age difference, size difference, being big or being small, played an important role in that interest. And I was off, studying miniatures and giants of various kinds, in literature and in life, from the seventeenth century and from yesterday.

This almost anthropological and sociological, as well as literary and cultural and visual analysis, took many years to write and I have many institutions, organizations, colleagues, friends, and family to thank for their part in assisting *Big and Small* and for supporting me.

I began this work while a member of the Department of English at Texas A&M University. *Big and Small* was supported through a sabbatical semester overseen by Dean Charles Johnson and encouraged by two different department heads, J. Lawrence Mitchell and Paul Parrish. Larry Mitchell deserves special recognition as an early champion of children's literature studies in general and my work, in particular. I appreciate his many years of good advice and admire his dedication and hard work on behalf of all of his faculty members. My academic and personal life was greatly enhanced by the intelligence, companionship, and good cheer of many colleagues and students who were also great friends. Mere words are inadequate to express my thanks to Dennis Berthold, Sara Day, Susan Egenolf, Sonya Sawyer Fritz, Marian Eide, Kate Kelly, Pam Matthews, Amy Montz, Claudia Nelson, Larry Reynolds, Jim Rosenheim and Laureen Tedesco for the gifts of their friendship. I miss all y'all very much.

My move from Texas A&M University to Rutgers University—Camden, required a departmental shift as well as an institutional one, a shift that impacted *Big and Small* in significant ways. Inspired by the vision and determination of Dean Margaret Marsh, in 2007 Rutgers University—Camden became the first Ph.D.-granting department of Childhood Studies in the nation. The multidisciplinary nature of the study of children and childhood and the department we created to assist in this work helped to transform my teaching and research. My brilliant colleagues in Childhood Studies—Meredith Bak, Sarada Balagopalan, Kate Cairns, Dan Cook, Dan Hart, Wenhua Lu, Susan Miller, and Lauren Silver—have impacted my thinking and writing and have made the mutual "childhood studies project" immensely rewarding and fun. My partner in crime, Dan Cook, who made the decision to "jump" to Childhood Studies at the same time I did, makes me laugh and through his dedication reminds me why this work is important. I have had the honor of teaching many terrific graduate students over the years. I wish to acknowledge former doctoral students Lara Saguisag, Deborah Valentine, and Nyeema Watson, in particular—smart and dear friends who are extending the vision of childhood studies in multiple arenas. I am also grateful to Dean Kris Lindenmeyer, a stalwart supporter of childhood studies, and to Rutgers University's sabbatical leave program which funded a year's research leave and two Research Council grants in support of this project. I would also like to acknowledge and extend my appreciation for the assistance given to me by my former graduate assistant, Patrick Cox, who helped with the bibliography and other research tasks. I and my colleagues benefit daily from the assistance of our secretary, Joann Schroeder, who was immensely helpful to me when I was working on obtaining permissions, in particular.

The Children's Literature Association has assisted *Big and Small* through its congenial and intellectually stimulating conferences and through the award of a Faculty Research Grant. I would like to thank my many colleagues and friends from the children's literature/history of childhood scholarly community—those who attend the ChLA and International Research Society for Children's Literature and Society for the History of Childhood and Youth conferences—who have patiently listened to numerous presentations on giants and miniatures over the years and who have asked important questions along the way. I offer my gratitude to scholars who have invited me to give talks about *Big and Small* at their universities: Peter Hunt from the University of Cardiff, Wales; Julia Mickenberg from the University of Texas; Kimberley Reynolds and Matthew Grenby from Newcastle University, UK; Bengt Sandin from the University of Linköping, Sweden; Astrid Surmatz from Linnaeus University (formerly Växjö University), Sweden; Laureen Tedesco from East Carolina University.

I would also like to thank the poets Jay Curlin and James Richardson for their willingness to see their words in my book (and permission, in Jay Curlin's case). I am honored to be able to include them. Grateful acknowledgment is made to Copper Canyon Press for permission to reprint James Richardson's "Big Scenes." I wish to extend my appreciation to the anonymous readers of the manuscript for their insights, comments, and suggestions; I was humbled by their enthusiasm for this project.

Numerous librarians offered their time and invaluable expertise to me as I worked to obtain permission to reproduce many of the images in the book. Big thanks are owed to Dr. John Boneham, Reference Specialist in the Rare Books and Music Collection at the British Library; Vibiana Cvetkovic, Head of Access and Collection Services at Rutgers University—Camden; Dr. Andrea Immel, Curator of the Cotsen Children's Library, Princeton University; Arlene Shaner, Historical Collections Librarian at the New York Academy of Medicine; Adrienne Saint-Pierre, Curator of the Barnum Museum. James D. Keeline generously shared with me his deep knowledge of the publication history of the Stratemeyer Syndicate and set me on the right path when I had nearly given up hope of finding the current copyright holder.

And finally, my most personal acknowledgments: I am deeply appreciative of my many friends who, through their generosity, kindness, and unflagging support, have made the long process of writing this book more enjoyable. In particular, I would like to thank Matthew Grenby, Colin and Olena Heywood, Gordon MacMullan, Lissa Paul, and especially Peter Hunt, for the affection, laughter, good conversation and community they have shared with me over the years. I have been, quite simply, the most favored author in the world to have Robert Baldock as my long-time editor. From our first meeting in London some time ago (let's just say pre-Y2K), it was clear to me that Robert was a giant in the publishing industry. I wasn't sure how I had become so lucky as to have him in my corner. His encouragement, clear-eyed guidance, and wise counsel have improved my books and his boundless generosity and friendship have changed my life.

To my closest friend, Kim Reynolds, who lives three thousand miles away in real life, but who appears digitally in my computer almost every day, I could not have written this book without you. You read every word of the manuscript as I revised it, commented insightfully and shared every doubt and delight along the way. When I walk the path of gratitude, I hold your hand.

This book is dedicated to my parents, John and Phyllis Vallone. I recognize that this gesture is very small in the face of my big debt to them. Wise, unselfish, loving, supportive and always fun to be with, they are my heroes. My children, Max Vallone Marchitello and Rosalie Vallone Marchitello, have grown well out of their teens through the writing of this book. Their combination of intelligence, wit, and playfulness makes them perfect companions. Both social justice advocates, I learn something new from them every day and I could not be prouder of them. And to Howard Marchitello who has always been my very first and very best reader as well as my greatest advocate and partner, the biggest thank you of all. You are the champion of this book and of my life. *Big and Small* is yours as much as mine.

Acknowledgments are not the same thing as apologies, yet somehow I feel the need to express my regrets at the length of time it has taken me to write this book. I'm not sure to whom I am making apology, exactly, or why. But I'm glad *Big and Small* is done; it has been a great ride.

INTRODUCTION
People Big and People Small

This book asks questions about scale, extraordinary bodies, and matters of size as they inform what we do, how we think, and what we think about. Put simply, this book argues that size, as a crucial marker of difference often overlooked, informs human identity and culture—as do race, gender, and class. Size difference is both a fact of nature and a central organizing principle of culture (western culture in particular). We categorize people, objects, and ideas according to how big they are, or how small. We use human scale to judge normality, goodness, and beauty, as well as to assign preciousness and otherness. Thus, the book argues, adult perceptions of size and scale significantly impact our ways of thinking, feeling, and constructing the world around us. To help illustrate this point, consider the practices of seventeenth-century scientists in their quest to prove the existence and purpose of unseen yet imagined objects: beings of immense or tiny size. The invention of those complementary instruments, the telescope and the microscope, allowed the first intimate looks at very large bodies—Galileo's moons of Jupiter illustrated in *Starry Messenger* (1610), for example—and parts of very small bodies—"Head of an Ant" or "Teeth of a Snail" described by Robert Hooke in *Micrographia* (1665). The attempt to comprehend the truly large focuses the gaze ever upward and outward toward the heavens and the desire to see the hidden, the very tiny thing, draws us down to contemplate the formerly invisible. In either scenario, our response to the exaggerated object is inflected not only by the wonder of discovery and the drive to understand what it means, but also by the anxieties that attend bodies out of scale with our own. In other words, we asked, what might giant celestial bodies tell us about the order of things or minuscule parts and particles tell us about the beginnings of life? Historically, we have both desired and feared the answers to these questions. Anxieties about big and small bodies closely align with concerns about the origins, and ultimate destination, of all bodies—whether celestial, animal, or human. In ascribing values to those bodies that challenge us—the very big and the extra small—we also seek reassurance in the ordinary, the norm. In these pages I explore the lives and contexts of those with extraordinary bodies, from the seventeenth century to the present day, through examinations of the literature, art, scientific discourses, everyday life and performance that create the meanings attached to big and small bodies, both real and imagined. These ways of thinking and acting may be called philosophical, aesthetic, epistemological, ethical. Indeed, it is necessary to inhabit all of these spheres (although not all at the same time), in order to see and comprehend how important our relationships to size and scale are to human creativity, behavior, and emotion. As humans, it is perhaps wholly natural to set the human norm as our most reliable and comfortable form of measure.

Thus, implicit in thinking about size is thinking about human bodies as the measure of being "in" or "out" of scale. For many adults, the so-called "average," size may not affect their lives in any notable way. Others, those taller, shorter, or wider than the typical adult man or woman, may find that their size presents daily challenges. The shelf is too tall to reach the desired book, the theater rows are positioned uncomfortably close together for long legs, the chic clothing store carries few on-trend items in large enough sizes. In addition to these annoyances, for still others whose height or girth is significantly different from those perceived to be adult and "normal"—the dwarf, the giant, the obese, the child—rude stares, insensitive comments and regular physical discomforts may make it difficult *not* to think about size virtually all the time. *Big and Small* considers, in part, examples of out-of-scale persons throughout modern history. The stories we tell and pictures we paint not only offer glimpses into their lives and times, but also focus attention on our obsessions with size difference. As a class, children are chronically small and many of the details of their lives are determined by their relationship to the larger adults around them. Thus, children—as both lived and constructed beings—and childhood play a very important role in this study.

Andrew Solomon suggests in *Far From the Tree: Parents, Children, and the Search for Identity*, his book about parents raising children very different from themselves whether through disability, mental illness, or criminal behavior, among other attributes, that "difference unites us. . . . The exceptional is ubiquitous; to be entirely typical is the rare and lonely state."[1] While Solomon's provocative statement that "difference unites us" may well be true, just as accurate are less inclusive and egalitarian aspects of the human condition and human nature: a fascination with difference, an inability to look away, the eager use of difference to stand for otherness, the exploitation of big and small for political purposes. I would argue that all of these motivations unite us as well.

Although it does not follow a specific theoretical paradigm or model, *Big and Small* engages a variety of disciplines, discourses, and methods in an attempt to understand the complex social identities, power relations, constructions, and cultural categories of the miniature and the gigantic. Confronting size and scale is an epistemological challenge as well as an aesthetic one: this book asks what can we learn about the world, about ourselves, through size difference? How is size difference valued, appreciated, or feared? How might our affective engagement with extraordinary bodies lead us to ethical insights? My discussions of big and small are primarily concerned with bodies both imaginary and real: thumblings, dwarfs, pygmies, giants, children, robots, and the obese. I am particularly curious when these figures overlap, as in the case of the obese child and the giant robot or when the figures of the miniature and the giant collide, as we often find in folklore and children's books, as well as at court or in performance spaces. I find my big and small subjects in literature, art, and life in the distant past as well as the present moment, in both European and American contexts. Notions of big and small have been debated in scientific theory, folklore, religious doctrine, public policy, alchemy, sociology, literature high and popular, art, and politics. These discourses are both visual and textual: much of my analysis is indebted to the ways that big and small bodies have been interpreted in words and in pictures. Figures from very different times, places, and positions come together to focus our attention on the ideologies of size. Yet it is the lives of real people with extraordinary bodies that have intrigued me the most while researching this book. Getting to know and to attempt to tell their stories represents, for me, some of the most meaningful aspects of this study.

Difference, Otherness, Diversity

People are afraid of difference. Scrutinizing size difference is like paying close attention to other markers of difference such as race, gender, class, and age. When you give size difference its due, the world shifts. Some of the unbalance comes from who is doing the looking and who is being looked at, of course, but acknowledging bodily size difference as real, as an historical truth, and as an everyday occurrence can also be uncomfortable if the difference feels "weighty." "I don't see race," some people say with a superior air. Setting aside the dubiousness of that claim, however, it is even more difficult to defend not noticing the extraordinary bodies of a dwarf, an NBA player or even a young child. If the relationship between those with the "majority" bodies and everyone else is primarily characterized by anxiety, then categorizing "us" and "them" quickly follows. Interest in maintaining as wide a gulf as possible between "us" and "them," whether the divide comes from race, size, religion, gender, sexuality, nationality, or social class, has historically been very strong. Swift's *Gulliver's Travels*, a biting satire on the weakness, sloth, and savagery of human nature and culture, revealed the disgusting Yahoos to be "us." The widespread and enduring negative reactions to Swift's book (first published anonymously to acclaim in 1726) in the eighteenth century through the Victorian period—during which time the book became established as a text for juveniles—underscore the threatening nature of either recognizing the western white man's failures or acknowledging the humanity, dignity, and equality of "others." William Makepeace Thackeray, for one, blasted *Gulliver's Travels* in 1851 by transforming its author, a literary giant, into a folktale monster: "Mr Dean has no softness, and enters the nursery with the tread and gaiety of an ogre. . . . As for the humour and conduct of this famous fable, I suppose there is no person who reads but must admire; as for the moral, I think it horrible, shameful, unmanly, blasphemous; and giant and great as this Dean is, I say we should hoot him."[2] Thackeray transferred his disgust with the brutish Yahoos to Swift himself. Similarly, Charles Darwin, whose theory of evolution by natural selection has often been misinterpreted as collapsing categories of animals with humans, suffered ridicule from the moment his ideas became widely known. Attempting to explain the complex, abundant, and diverse animal and plant species found throughout the world, Darwin's theories, first published in *On the Origin of Species* (1859)[3] and later expanded in *Descent of Man* (1871), undergird the ever-changing map of human origin and evolution. Even today, many Americans reject "Darwinism" due to their misunderstanding of its tenets and implications. In fact, Darwinism does not argue that humans are descended from apes, nor is its acceptance irreconcilable with a belief in a creative deity.

Thus, one aspect of the desire to deny evolution is to preserve a kind of human "exceptionalism" that privileges humanity over other life forms and establishes an "us" that can be contrasted with "them." Yet, differences also *attract*: in terms of size, for example, we are captivated by the tiny, and love and need the small in multiple ways. When race enters the nexus of size difference and scale, the meanings of the miniature both conform to ideological presuppositions of primitiveness, helplessness, and childlikeness, and, just as importantly, inform larger issues of big and small, adult and child. This book aims to focus attention on reactions to and representations of the anomalous body as a particular site of difference. In *Gulliver's Travels*, Swift, of course, focuses closely on physical size and scale as metaphors for intelligence, corruption, power, and beauty. Our dismissal of the anomalous body, our disgust or fear of the extraordinary or anomalous body, as well as our ongoing fascination with size difference are all cultural symptoms of an unease with difference.

This cultural symptom has both a long history and a western perspective. Classical authors such as Herodotus and Pliny the Elder wrote about exotic races of giants and miniatures almost wholly different from ordinary humans. As literary critic Felicity Nussbaum points out, in the eighteenth century many believed that human abnormality stretched to include racialized others as well as those out of scale physically. Race, size, and "unnatural" hot climates, combined and blurred so that the giant as well as the African were set outside of "us" to become the exotic "other." According to Nussbaum, "Mutant forms are, like race, given geographic specificity; often indicative of a species apart, abnormality is relegated to intemperate climates. The defective, then, are easily intermingled and made synonymous with the racialized since dwarfs, giants, and blacks together composed 'deformed races.' "[4]

This is not to say that we are not also in awe of difference. The great theorist of size difference—both big and small—is Edmund Burke (1757) who locates extremes of size among the sublime:

> Greatness of dimension is a powerful cause of the sublime. . . .
> However, it may not be amiss to add to these remarks upon
> magnitude; that, as the great extreme of dimension is sublime,

so the last extreme of littleness is in some measure sublime likewise; when we attend to the infinite divisibility of matter, when we pursue animal life into these excessively small, and yet organized beings, that escape the nicest inquisition of the sense, when we push our discoveries yet downward ... we become amazed and confounded at the wonders of minuteness; nor can we distinguish in its effect this extreme of littleness from the vast itself.[5]

As Burke suggests, proportion can mitigate the disconnect and distrust that otherness so often elicits. Stuart Little, E. B. White's heroic man-mouse, though never truly child-like (his tantrums are of the more typically adolescent variety), fascinates those around him because his tiny, yet perfect, mouse-like body functions in a balanced inversion with his outsized intellectual and physical abilities. For example, when serving as a substitute teacher for a classroom of children, Stuart refutes a student's put-down that he is "too small" to serve as "chairman of the world" saying, " 'Size has nothing to do with it. It's temperament and ability that count.' "[6] In fact, the book suggests that his proportionate small size presents no bar to Stuart's fitness as a leader, sportsman, philosopher, or traveler.

Some miniatures—unlike other anomalous bodies—benefit from the glow of the "cute effect." In her study of freakery, Lori Merish comments on the power of cute to quiet difference's noise: "Cuteness aestheticizes the most primary social distinctions, regulating the (shifting) boundaries between Selves and Others, cultural 'insiders' and cultural 'outsiders,' 'humans' and 'freaks.' "[7] Certainly, small children partake of the cuteness effect; cuteness implies preciousness and encourages protection. And children are certainly "other" in many ways, both us and "not-us." Their perfection as miniature created beings whose creation is invisible (in most cases) seems mystical and magical. We know where babies come from, of course, yet their coming seems, every time, miraculous. The mysteries of reproduction and the politicization of the figure of the child is a primary focus of my first chapter.

While Americans, in particular, have become used to the idea of "diversity" as code language indicating non-white "race" and non-male gender used, in positive ways, to bring awareness and hopefully redress to historical inaccuracies in curricula and unfair hiring practices, among other areas of potential exclusion, size is generally left out of the diversity pool. Or it may be that we have simply overlooked size as an aspect of human diversity. Andrew Solomon's important book and the cultural phenomenon of reality television programming both work to address small size as a kind of difference—though perhaps for different purposes. Solomon pays particular attention to parents in his book and comments that "Whether they like it or not, parents of dwarf children often feel they must display their families as emblems of diversity."[8]

Miniatures and Monsters

As I discuss in the chapters that follow, various scientific disciplines and quasi-scientific theories have attempted to explain big and small bodies. These include alchemy, reproductive science, evolutionary biology, psychology, and anthropology. In chapter one, "In the Beginning was Tom Thumb," I discuss how these narratives of various kinds of discovery and adventure—illuminated by experiment, the microscope, observation or by travel—all attempt to see and know the previously unseen—the small. In chapters two and three—"The Dwarf in High and Popular Culture" and "Staging the Dwarf," I discuss "dwarf discourse" as represented in paintings and emblem books as well as expressed through the performances of individual dwarfs from history such as Charles Stratton and Jeffrey Hudson. Chapter four, "Lilliputians in Blackface," describes how nineteenth-century European colonists "discovered" African pygmies and their stories and images informed judgments made about small persons. I discuss how the pygmy Ota Benga was caught up in the new science of anthropology at the turn of the century. In the second part to the book I turn from the miniature to the giant.

If, as I argue in part one of this book, the racialized miniature functions as our cultural gigantic—a figure freighted with burdens of nostalgia, longing, guilt, and anxiety—so, too, has the figure of the giant been made to carry a heavy load of fantasies and desires. We imagine the multiply reproduced and reproductive miniature as copies, clones, seemingly endlessly replicable in vaguely "ethnic"-sounding multiples—clans, tribes, sets, and classes.[9] The giant, by contrast, stands alone, looming in relief above the landscape, in the mind's (closed) eye, as in a nightmare or horror movie. The threat of the giant's brethren lurks as well—could there be more where it came from? But how? Their immensity makes them impossible to hide. The miniature swarms, emerges from the earth, the deep forest, the clouds above, and just as swiftly disappears. The powerful giant, however, is fixed, grounded, solid, and above all, visible. When he enters the social realm, the giant's exaggerated size types him as a monster. Victor Frankenstein's eight-foot-tall creation bemoans his fate as a pariah, a monster, when he realizes that his "speech" and his appearance put him outside of human society: " 'When I looked around, I saw and heard of none like me. Was I then a monster, a blot upon the earth, from which all men fled, and whom all men disowned?' "[10] Whether a literal or metaphorical monster, the giant must be destroyed, acculturated, or pushed to the margins in order to balance the destabilizing force his presence unleashes.

By our monsters we shall be known, and by interrogating our monsters we shall perhaps come to know ourselves. "We live in a time of monsters," Jeffrey Jerome Cohen insists in the preface to his edited collection of essays *Monster Theory*.[11] Cohen's examples of real and created monsters range from angry dinosaur movies such as the *Jurassic Park* series, to the so-called "abnormal" serial killer Jeffrey Dahmer (who ate his victims rather than simply killed them), from the demonization of lesbian, gay, and transgender citizens, to the proliferation of support groups for Americans abducted by aliens. This late-twentieth-century monster mania has extended into the twenty-first century. The monsters who abide with us today include faceless international "terrorists," humanized creatures such as the transformed King Kong and Grendel who star in film and opera respectively, and adult predators who attempt to gain access to unsuspecting youth by posing as teens on social networking sites such as Facebook.[12] We create monsters that both delight us with their remoteness (no one really expects to meet a velociraptor) and terrify us by their nearness (through their embodiment of our deepest fears and anxieties). For example, in post-9/11 America, fears of terrorist acts "at home" are very common and easily exploited by self-serving politicians who elevate the personal dangers of failing to wage "the war on terror" (risking the loss of the so-called American way of life) and downplay the physical dangers of failing to fix the health care system, halt or slow global climate change, or clean the air and waterways. No matter the extreme unlikelihood of death or injury due to terrorism (especially in comparison with disease and accidents), the international terrorist has nevertheless been granted an oversized portion of fear in the national psyche. Terrorists—monsters—have also become part of "us." As Cohen argues, "the monster is difference made flesh, come to dwell among us. In its function as dialectical Other or third-term supplement, the monster is an incorporation of the Outside, the Beyond—of all those loci that are rhetorically placed as distant and distinct but originate Within."[13] We first give birth to our monsters, energetically reject them, and then encourage them to inhabit the margins of "normal." For without the monster, how do we determine who belongs where?

"Monsters," David J. Skal suggests in his foreword to the anthology *Speaking of Monsters*, "are slippery, ever-adaptive metaphors, but above all, they are natural teachers and teaching tools. Monsters demonstrate things, usually of the cautionary kind."[14] As this book suggests, the didactic potential of the monster, the giant, is often connected to anxieties about gender. Chapter five, "Gigantic Mechanical Boy Scouts," argues that in the mid-twentieth-century era of scientific utopianism the giant mechanical man—the robot—informed the creation of an ideal masculinity and the notion of the perfectible body. The book's final chapter, "The Obese Girl," considers the clash that occurs when obesity, childhood, and femininity collide. The monstrous aspects of the giant robot and obese girl, both related to fears of "othered" bodies, lead us to multiplying anxieties over the future of the human body, anxieties with us in the present moment as we struggle with and celebrate advances in mechanical engineering, artificial intelligence (AI), computer programming, and genetic engineering. What will the body become? Will we need bodies in the future? How might genetic engineering and perhaps AI help us to respond to the frailties of the human body?

While from this complex mix of questions few definitive answers have emerged, the artistic imagination is a good place to look for new ideas about exceptional bodies. Art and science, Suzanne Anker and Dorothy Nelkin argue in their book *The Molecular Gaze: Art in the Genetic Age* (2004), unite in genetics: "Since the late 1980s, a stream of visual artists have entered [the cultural discourse of genetics] initially through identity politics in the form of 'body art' and more recently through molecular models. Their work comments on issues of identity, normality, and authenticity raised by the daunting new imaging technologies and the possibilities of germ-line transformation."[15] Identity and normality, in particular, and their relation to personhood and to the body are key concepts in this book. Size, once again, becomes important to this conversation about science and art, both in the littleness of DNA molecules, the cells of reproduction, the unseen hand of God-the-maker and in the bigness of mutation, of monstrosity and God-the-destroyer. Both genetic mutation and size manipulation have a lot in common: both can produce "monsters" and both take us back to questions of selfhood and identity, asking, "what is human?" "what is normal?" Visual art is intimately connected to notions of human scale and, as some contemporary artists have demonstrated, uniquely able to generate "monsters." Let us take one example, cited and illustrated in Anker and Nelkin: the American artist Charles Ray's *Family Romance* (1993) (see Plate 3).

Ray often plays with scale in his sculptures, enlarging human and animal figures or machines to great size. In *Family Romance*, a nuclear family of mother, father, son, and daughter stand naked with clasped hands, gazing blankly forward. Although there is nothing of the toy about them, the almost aggressively lifelike figures embody the creepiness of dolls. What is shocking about the approximately half-life-size mannequins, however, is that all of the family members are the same height. The children are giants or the parents are miniatures. Anker and Nelkin comment, "The viewer is confronted with the possibility that if these children are to reach adulthood, they would be giants—in effect, monsters in a side show. Have these children been engineered with growth hormones to turn them into the desired offspring? Does a dysfunctional society create a dysfunctional family?"[16] I would add to these questions, why does the human body out of scale stand for "dysfunction" at all?

And as this introduction has sketched, ranging through time and place, historicizing size difference as expressed in representations, epistemologies, ideologies, and persons, raises many more questions with which to grapple. One question might ask how I selected the big and small bodies, the texts, images, and ideas under discussion. Certainly there is much left out and one is bound to be disappointed that, for example, leprechauns and their folklore or comic book superheroes such as the Incredible Hulk—or any number of other big and small bodies—are not analyzed in these pages. My perhaps not wholly satisfactory response to such disappointment is that in many cases I felt chosen by my extraordinary subjects rather than choosing them: Jeffrey Hudson, Charles S. Stratton, Ota Benga and Barbara and their fascinating, heavily documented and objectified life stories took hold of my imagination. Their contexts were each so different from the others and yet each has a particularly incisive story to tell about size. All "victimized," perhaps, by their bodies but also triumphant in their individuality and after-lives.

As a scholar of children's literature it felt natural to me to become a kind of anthropologist of the miniature races that populate children's books—thumblings, Borrowers, Lilliputians, minpins, fairies, elves, brownies, Oompa-Loompas. Reading images of the dwarf figure—as well as actual dwarfs—over time and emblematically, teases out how the other is defined and circumscribed through size and circumstance. Thinking about small bodies of the everyday drew my eye to the real-life miniatures created by religious leaders and politicians: the fetus, embryo, and stem cell. The requirements of an ethical response to size difference provide another key concern of this study. It bears witness to the devastating legacy of the colonized pygmy and other racialized miniatures, as well as its resistance, in popular culture stereotypes of savagery and minstrelsy. I consider scientific utopianism as an American identity project of the mid-century in which the beneficent promise of the world of tomorrow is hailed through the giant robot and the "moral" science of progress. I question the digital revolution as one aspect of such progress. Even obesity, characterized by most health professionals as causing unequivocally negative physical effects, may be contextualized within our constructions of childhood and girlhood and the debates we wage about bodies big and small. I hope that this book will provide an opportunity for associative "play" among ideas, texts, pictures, events, experiments, and relationships I have not considered here. If so, I will have achieved one of my aims in writing about extraordinary bodies in western culture.

Ultimately, *Big and Small: A Cultural History of Extraordinary Bodies* is a political book in which I reveal my political positions—not in any party-specific or doctrinaire way, I hope, but as deeply felt beliefs. How could it be otherwise? The book first emerged from my long-term research in children's literature and culture—realms in which big and small bodies abound. I came to understand that we may look to the powerful and potent symbiotic and symbolic relationships between big and small as a means to understand not only children's literature, but also how and why we construct the world around us. These are political and politicized acts. I ask that we pay attention to them.

PART I

SMALL BODIES

INTRODUCTION
The Little Man

The first section of this book takes up various "little man" theories expressed over time in reproduction science, literature (emblems and folktales), alchemy, and popular entertainment. As I discuss in the general introduction, for Edmund Burke and for many other theorists of scale, only proportionate size anomalousness provides pleasure. Disproportionate humanity, for Burke, invokes disgust, while imagining a miniature man inspires wonder:

> There is a dwarfish size of men and women, which is almost constantly so gross and massive in comparison of their height, that they present us with a very disagreeable image. But should a man be found not above two or three feet high, supposing such a person to have all the parts of his body of a delicacy suitable to such a size, and otherwise endued with the common qualities of other beautiful bodies, I am pretty well convinced that a person of such a stature might be considered as beautiful; might be the object of love; might give us very pleasing ideas on viewing him.[1]

I consider three such "pleasing" miniature men from different centuries and countries in detail in this book: the court dwarf

Jeffrey Hudson; P. T. Barnum's most famous performer, General Tom Thumb; and the Congolese pygmy, Ota Benga.

Consider the following images of these figures.

Jeffrey Hudson (1619–1681) is depicted with his queen, Henrietta Maria (consort of Charles I), in a magisterial portrait by van Dyck (1633) (see Plate 1).

Charles Stratton (1838–1883), known world-wide as "General Tom Thumb," is shown with his promoter P. T. Barnum soon after, as a young child, he began performing at Barnum's American Museum in 1842 (see Plate 2).

Ota Benga, brought from Africa to be displayed at the 1904 St. Louis World's Fair as a member of the pygmy exhibit, was photographed at the Bronx Zoo in 1906 where he was essentially incarcerated with the monkeys and apes (see Plate 4).

As different as these images of "little men" may be, however, a number of elements as well as ideas about race and gender unite them: youth (Stratton is about 6 and Hudson is 14), monkeys, patronage, costume, performativity, masculinity, portraiture, otherness, freakishness, civility, savagery. And, of course, size. Hudson and Stratton, like other dwarfs across time, were from childhood compelled to perform tricks of mimicry for the satisfaction of curious onlookers in awe of their tiny bodies and supple minds. Yet the very distinctiveness of their bodies seems to provide insight into "extra-physical" concerns: questions over the origins of the self and anxieties about the ultimate fate of the body and soul after death. As significant as their tiny bodies, these real-life Tom Thumbs also served to illustrate a certain legibility that begged to be interpreted by those who watched them, listened to tales about them, or read accounts of their lives. Variously described as written forms—as emblem, epitome, index, or dictionary—Hudson, Stratton, and other human "miniatures" were reduced further into performing man's abstract or summary in order to encourage religious humility or to create commercial value. In this way, too, the miniature's small size and perfected body strongly link him/her to children who in childhood both resemble their ultimate form—men and women—and remind adults of a lost past. In a 1628 miniature book by John Earle that provides brief essays delineating various characters such as "A discontented Man," "An upstart Knight," "A Shop-Keeper," and "A Plodding Student," among many others, the "childe" is described as "a man in a small Letter."² Earle goes on to write, "His father hath writ him as his owne little story, wherein hee reads those days of his life that he cannot remember; and sighs to see what innocence hee has out-liv'd."³

In his American context, the pygmy Ota Benga, too, was forced to occupy a position of "lostness"—that is, to embody the idea of the "missing link" connecting the animal to the "primitive" human. For the scholars of the new discipline of anthropology, Ota Benga's extreme short stature, sharply filed teeth, native clothing, dark skin, and perceived savagery made his pairing (and housing) with the chimpanzee a "simple" matter of categorization rather than exploitation.

I offer these brief glimpses of some of the animating figures of this study by way of introducing its interests in the small body. My considerations of the miniature have been especially indebted to the work of Carolyn Steedman, Susan Stewart, and Patricia Pace, scholars who have contributed a great deal to the discussion of tininess and small bodies and their greater cultural meanings. Stewart explores the "personification" of childhood via the miniature as metaphor.⁴ While Stewart largely ignores children's literature, Pace's work focuses on the role of the miniature in children's books; in particular, she considers Mary Norton's *Borrowers* series (from *The Borrowers*, 1952, to *The Borrowers Avenged*, 1982). Pace links the small bodies of her miniature characters to the lived experience of children: "In the *Borrowers* series, bodies are lived in miniature and under scrutiny, as children's lives and children's bodies so often are."⁵ Steedman's fascinating historical "reconstruction" of the idea of the self and interiority by way of the figure of the child Mignon represents one version of the history of the importance of smallness to social and cultural development.⁶

Steedman needs the child Mignon and her child's body to tell her story of small, commenting, "Sometimes [in writing her book *Strange Dislocations*] it seemed to me that what I was really describing was *littleness* itself, and the complex register of affect that has been invested in the word 'little.' "[7] For my purposes in historicizing the ideas and questions surrounding big and small bodies, I also require the assistance of the figure of the child, as well as children's literature. Children's literature offers a path into the story of big and small in unique and useful ways. Introducing her article on the *Borrowers*, Pace elegantly encapsulates the breadth of children's literature's importance:

> Like myth and folklore, fiction written for children is an imaginative enactment of our personal and cultural origins, our perceived identity, our psycho-sexual orientation, and of language—teleological projects which are deeply inter-twined. To write for the child is to reconstruct and re-present the child's body, to particularize the experiencing body-self at different stages of development. To write for the child is inevitably to situate the (child's) body in relation to some text, to cultural notions of child/adult, boy/girl, author/reader, experience and innocence.[8]

Pace and Steedman, among other scholars of miniature beings, focus their attention on female miniatures, such as Mignon, Thumbelina, feminized fairies and the like. The miniature is often gendered as fragile, precious, and delicately beautiful—all characteristics typed feminine. Other obvious miniatures, such as dolls, key objects in the material culture of childhood, are so closely associated with femininity and training to become mothers that they may be considered miniatures of girlhood itself. The dwarf performer Lavinia Warren was almost as famous as her husband, General Tom Thumb; her measurements, clothing, and sexuality were all topics of interest to the nineteenth-century American public. However, in this study I have chosen to focus on the especially masculine and phallic attributes of the tiny body in life as well as in literature. This attention, I believe, brings us closer to an understanding of an important yet overlooked aspect of the cultural construction of the small in history, literature, and art.

Children's literature informs my reading of the figures of Ota Benga, Charles Stratton, and Jeffrey Hudson in multiple ways. For example, chapter two on "dwarf discourse" focuses on the figure of the dwarf in early modern to nineteenth-century emblem books, including many emblem books created for child readers. This chapter also reads in depth van Dyck and Velázquez paintings of seventeenth-century court dwarfs such as Jeffrey Hudson. Chapter three considers Charles Stratton and the dwarf body alongside contemporary young adult books that feature dwarf protagonists. An important aim in chapter four about Ota Benga is to examine the developing ethics of the big and small relationship from a postcolonial context as it is described in children's literature.

As I referenced above, the historian Carolyn Steedman identifies the child as critical to the development of the self and the notion of interiority in the late eighteenth to early twentieth centuries, an idea that resonates today: "The idea of the child was the figure that provided the largest number of people living in the recent past of Western societies with the means for thinking about and creating a self: something grasped and understood: a shape, moving in the body . . . something *inside*: an interiority."[9] While westerners are likely to feel most connected to modern-era Western ideas about the symbolic uses of childhood, we may also learn from ancient and non-western societies, as well.

For example, a brief consideration of an ancient Inca ritual festival involving children provides a point of access here between notions of smallness, "interiority," and the connections formed between them and hidden worlds. In the Inca *capac hucha* festival, children between the ages of six and ten, selected for their beauty, were taken from their villages, "married," and then returned not as children but as miniature adults who had earned the right to receive the gifts and attire appropriate for the newly wedded. Once returned, they were intoxicated and buried alive in specially constructed graves. In considering this festival in his book *The Art of Small Things*, John Mack argues that this sacrifice represented not closure, but opening up: "The evidence is that [the children] did not, in Inca perception, lose their lives. Their fate was to set the world to rights, to institute a new cycle or order, and to move on to join the ancestors at appropriate points in the sacred landscape . . . ." He continues, commenting that the young children's size and their physical perfection were key to the links made between sacrifice and bringing the unseen, in a metonymic way, to this world: ". . . smallness was a visualization that was as close to the efficacious world of the unseen as could be attained. The world of small was not among the least but among the most significant of created things. Through the sacrifice of children, new worlds and renewed possibilities were opened up to the deceased and the living alike."[10] This festival unites, and equates, beauty with small size, and the divine with childhood.

I am interested in some of the ways that children have been and continue to be caught up in scientific and pseudo-scientific discourse and the arguments over Darwin's theories, evolutionary thinking, and a politics of exclusion and difference. For example, some of Darwin's skeptics, sometimes called "young earth creationists," have taken their disagreement to the US courts; they fight to interrupt the teaching of evolution in American public schools and to insert creationism, or its cousin, "intelligent design," into the curriculum as a viable competing "theory" with evolution.[11] The continuing debates over human evolution affect children—not only through the children's books of an earlier time that describe racial hierarchies and access notions of heritable savagery and primitivism, but also through attempts to influence public school curricula. In the section on education, the 2016 Republican Party platform opens a statement about the place of the Bible in high schools with a stunning premise: "A good understanding of the Bible being indispensable for the development of an educated citizenry, we encourage state legislatures to offer the Bible in a literature curriculum as an elective in America's high schools."[12]

Yet, sometimes children come out "on top," as it were, as members of races of the small. Cultural critic Marina Warner reminds us that Darwin's mid-Victorian theory of natural selection had been informed by the folktale world in which children—the Grimm Brothers' Hansel and Gretel, for example— represent the "fittest": these tales "[proclaim] the resilience and the eventual emergence of the small as supreme. This frame of mind will eventually lead to Darwin's insight into natural selec- tion and the survival of the most adaptable—the tricksters who dominate through intelligence and bravery."[13] Certainly, fanta- sies of dominance and fears of "others" along with admiration for the cleverness and affection for the tiny all coalesce within the flexible and resolute figure of the miniature and find expres- sion in scientific discourse as well as in examples of popular culture such as folklore.

Dwarf, Pygmy

In this project I am interested in probing the cultural, social, and psychological needs accounting for the prevalence of the dwarf figure in so many different artistic and pop-cultural outlets, given that the genetic, hormonal, or skeletal disorders that produce a dwarf child (who may have one of many medical conditions that result in dwarfism) remain rare.[14] To make a crude and unscientific observation, the average person is much likelier to "meet" a dwarf on a screen (large or small), museum wall, or within the pages of a book, than in daily life.[15]

Dwarfs are othered in ways beyond their small size. Unlike differences coded by sexual preference or race, for example, the dwarf cannot choose to "pass" as anyone other than a dwarf. In addition, the dwarf is a figure who exists both in the real and in the imaginary worlds. As Solomon notes, "the relentless visibility of dwarfs is amplified by their iconic place in fairy tales as supernatural beings, a burden not shared with any other disability or special-needs group."[16] The potential impact of this "dual identity" is quite extraordinary.

Some dwarfs—and, I should say, some parents of dwarfs—choose to undertake radical action against dwarfism through limb-lengthening treatments. These require surgeries, bone-severing, debilitating pain, and extreme patience. Yet, through such treatments a dwarf can grow out of dwarfhood. In *Dwarf: A Memoir* (2012), Tiffanie DiDonato recounts her childhood and early adulthood as she undergoes limb lengthening. DiDonato is quite upfront about her reasons for putting herself through the torments that resulted in the extension of her arms and legs and that enabled her to grow 14 additional inches to reach the height of 4 foot 10 inches, the official (according to the Little People of America) minimum height of a non-dwarf: "I was ready to do what it took to get the life that I wanted. I was ready to fight and go to war against dwarfism."[17] For Tiffanie, her pre-surgery dwarf body/identity was a foe to be vanquished: "She was everything I hated. She was my enemy."[18]

In the memoir DiDonato expresses surprise at the backlash she received as she celebrated her post-surgery triumph over dwarfism. As she puts it, "I wanted more for myself, more out of life, so I changed my body to that end. I'd never given any thought to what the 'dwarf community' might think about that. But here I was being judged, as if I'd gone against some sacred order of Dwarfdom."[19] As an outsider to dwarfism, my response to DiDonato's anger must be understood within that context. Yet, it certainly seems willfully ignorant not to understand the view that "curing" dwarfism through growing devalues its essential nature or to find it insulting to consider the small body hateful and an enemy. This perspective could easily offend those who embrace their natural bodies and do not find them to be abnormal. But to ignore the extra challenges presented by dwarfism—those to which Solomon refers as well as others—is equally short-sighted, it seems to me (I am not intending to make an awkward pun here!).

Historically, the dwarf body has been encumbered and marked by its categorization as not quite human. In his study of the uses of power in the realms of culture and aesthetics, Yi-Fu Tuan provides a short history of the ancient and enduring treatment of dwarfs as pets and fools, arguing that "Human pets are people whom their self-designated superiors regard as powerless, not fully human, and in some ways entertainingly peculiar."[20] This connection between the dwarf and comedy has long-standing roots in human culture. Solomon quotes Woody Allen, who once joked that "dwarf" is among the four funniest words in English and concludes, "To be in your very essence perceived as comical is a significant burden."[21] This burden lies at the heart of Oscar Wilde's tragic dwarf character in his children's story, "The Birthday of the Infanta" (1891). The dwarf, brought from the forest to entertain the Infanta and her birthday party guests, responds with adoration to the young princess's delighted laughter at his antic dancing. His feelings of love and purpose are short-lived, however, as once he is confronted by his "monstrous" image reflected in a mirror, the dwarf realizes that the Infanta does not admire him but mocks him; he falls into despair and dies at her feet, much to her disgust.[22] The tragicomic nature of Wilde's dwarf and many dwarf characters from literature, folklore, and visual art highlights, in Susan Stewart's phrase, "the essential theatricality" of all miniatures.[23]

A central concern in this project is to address the discourses of racial difference that mesh with ideologies of size difference and come to rest in particular on the figure of the African miniature, the "pygmy"—as well as on other "native" and racialized miniatures. By "racialized" I mean that color, primitiveness, and savagery are emphasized and critical to the construction of the miniature. A word about vocabulary: although "pygmy" is "entirely a Western construct,"[24] as Kairn A. Klieman reminds us in her book about the Bantu and Batwa in west central Africa, as well as being inexact, unscientific, and anachronistic as a label, the term continues to be resonant. Because the word "pygmy" remains part of English vernacular and was in widespread use from Classical times through the twenty-first century, it would be difficult to trace the history of the role of the miniature as racialized other within western culture without using this term. Exploring the *idea* of the pygmy as we find it expressed in various sites including children's literature, travelogues, performance arenas such as world's fairs, dime museums, and zoos interests me the most. Klieman argues that the idea of the pygmy has obsessed and fascinated the western world: "the power of the idea [of the pygmy] lay in its role as a common-place referent to the non-Western or nonhuman other, one that was readily and freely evoked by both the masses and intellectuals alike."[25] The "idea of the pygmy" is related to the "invented [American] Indian"—that is, selective narratives of "Indianness" constructed by anthropologists, advertising campaigns, dramatized performances, and popular literature, among other communication venues. The American Indian, too, has been targeted as an object of miniaturization in children's literature, film, and other media.[26]

It's difficult to separate the history of the colonialist and racist idea of the pygmy as miniature "other," from the creation of early twentieth-century children's literature, given the prevalence of the figure in kids' books. Children's literature provides a particularly sensitive instrument both for reflecting core cultural values as well as for radically challenging them. Hence, even in late twentieth-century children's books, the figure of the pygmy—or its metonymic counterpart, the Lilliputian, Native American, or Celt, to name a few incarnations from recent children's books—remains visible in revisions of older texts and in awkward textual apologias. However, the idea of pygmy may also be challenged, as radical new visions of the racialized other emerge in conversation with the complicated nexus of racial and size difference. The pygmies, and other racialized miniatures, provide irresistible moving targets for competing fantasies of lack and excess, childlikeness and gravitas, need and independence. As I have suggested before, how we conceive of and treat "our" miniatures uncovers and reveals "us" as we attempt to discover "them."

But not so fast. A twenty-first-century example of a collision between discovery, miniatures, race, and fantasy complicates this us/them divide: in late 2004, a scientific find enormously significant to the history of human evolution and development was announced to the world. As reported in the journal *Nature*, a team of Australian and Indonesian paleo-anthropologists unearthed the sub-fossilized remains of a human dwarf species on the remote Indonesian island of Flores.[27] A near-complete skeleton of a three-foot-tall adult female who had died approximately 18,000 years ago was found among the remains of six to seven other individuals whose bones range in age from 95,000 to 12,000 years old. The implications of this discovery for understanding the evolution of *Homo sapiens* are profound since scientists had previously theorized that *Homo erectus* had "crowded out" pre-human (that is, upright walking) species 160,000 years ago. It now appears that Flores hominins may be their descendants. Thus, the discovery of a relatively recent human dwarf species—nicknamed "Hobbits"—casts doubt upon the accepted chronology of the development of modern humankind, as well as providing information on the evolution of dwarfism in human "cousins."[28] Once again, as this introduction suggests, we often think of the miniature as "other," distinct, remote, and fantastic—as the Hobbit moniker attests—so it may be surprising to learn, as this find appears to demonstrate, that the miniature is, in fact, "us."

In the Beginning Was Tom Thumb

In chapter one, I explore the intricacies of the Tom Thumb figure as expressed over time and in a multiplicity of venues. This analysis helps me to illustrate one aspect of my project's larger argument about size and scale: the miniature functions as a linchpin figure, standing as a figuration of "the child" at the boundary of self and other, youth and age, freighted with symbolic meanings and yet lightened by perceptions of vulnerability and fragility. Certainly, the infamous little man, Tom Thumb, plays an important role in the history of the miniature in western culture, forming, in Susan Hancock's phrase about the miniature's symbolic resonance, "the heart of a culture's collective engagement with 'otherness.' "[29]

Both the Tom Thumb tale and the Tom Thumb trope begin with the twin ideas of conception—first the wish for a child that is imagined to be excessively small (the greater the desire, the smaller the child may be who satisfies that desire) and then his actual birth. The thumbling's mysterious birth and tiny size focus attention upon the most secret, inner workings of the body and the domestic arrangements of the family to which he is made to belong. As Stewart comments, referring to Charlotte Yonge's description of the infant Tom in her *The History of the Life and Death of the Good Knight Sir Thomas Thumb* (1855), "The miniature has the capacity to make its context remarkable; its fantastic qualities are related to what lies outside it in such a way as to transform the total context."[30] Thus, given his minuteness, Tom's clothing, bedding, and physical needs reveal the marvelous in the quotidian. It might appear that the intense scrutiny and attention that the miniature requires would also encourage an ever-contracting view pinpointing the miniature's simulacral world and erasing the world of "normal" scale. Yet, the reader's experience of the miniature, I believe, is the opposite: the character literally moves beyond domestic confines to succeed in a wider sphere. Tom's very eruption into the folk-world not only creates a correspondence with the familiar, as Stewart argues, but also explodes notions of interiority as enclosed or contained by allowing the reader to "see" the miniature in a new way—as an extant expression or metaphor of "before" in action—before birth, before subjectivity, before sight. In this way we might argue that the miniature brings us closer to worlds unseen except in the imagination.

Chapter 1

IN THE BEGINNING WAS TOM THUMB

... indeed what reason may not goe to Schoole to the wise-dome of Bees, Aunts, and Spiders? what wise hand teacheth them to doe what reason cannot teach us? Ruder heads stand amazed at those prodigious pieces of nature, Whales, Elephants, Dromidaries, and Camels; these I confesse, are the Colossus and Majestick pieces of her hand; but in these narrow Engines there is more curious Mathematicks, and the civilitie of these little Citizens, more neatly set forth the wisedome of their Maker ...
　　　　　　　—Thomas Browne, *Religio Medici* (1643)

—in an insect or a flower,
Such microscopic proofs of skill and power,
As hid from ages past, God now displays,
To combat atheists within modern days.
　　　　—William Cowper, *Tirocinium: or, a Review of Schools*
　　　　　　　　　　　　　　　　　　　(1784)

Who is Tom Thumb? Why, everyone knows that he's no bigger than a man's thumb!

This obvious, if tautological, response to naming Tom Thumb's identity fixates, quite naturally, on his size, yet only partially answers the question about his meaning. And the question is not as silly as it might first appear, given that the figure of Tom Thumb has presented varying qualities to audiences over time and in many different contexts. Once upon a time, this miniature boy became a valiant knight errant in King Arthur's court. Another boy, of similar stature but lustful and over-confident, attempted to ravish the queen. Yet a third thumbling found success as an instructor, teaching children their letters and moral lessons in words of few syllables. Thaumlin, or Little Thumb of the Northmen hails from Scandinavia; Svend Tomling is Danish and the "Daumerling" represents the Germanic thumbling character. Thumblings also appear in the Eastern folk literatures of India and Japan. "Tom Thumb" himself is resolutely English.

Although in the sixteenth century thumbling tales were well known in English folk legend and in traditional European stories originating from oral narratives, it wasn't until the seventeenth century that the tale was made popular in chapbook form, elevating the small hero to "the undisputed champion of an Englishman's childhood."[1] Indeed, Tom Thumb stories featuring an adventuresome, antic minute character are among the earliest and best-known tales printed in English. Considered to be the first printed Tom Thumb story, Richard Johnson's 1621 40-page pamphlet, *The History of Tom Thumbe, the Little, for his small stature surnamed King Arthurs Dwarfe: Whose Life and adventures containe many strange and wonderfull accidents, published for the delight of merry Time-spenders,* laid the groundwork for subsequent tales in English.[2]

Numerous named and anonymous authors contributed their versions of the tale to the growing list of variants, and Tom Thumb's notoriety grew. Beyond hack writers and those trading on the Tom Thumb myth, popular and respected authors such as Henry Fielding in the eighteenth century, and Dinah Mulock Craik and Charlotte Yonge in the nineteenth, also fell under the thumbling spell and adapted the Tom Thumb tale for adult and child audiences. The multivalent Tom Thumb offers a fascinating glimpse into the history of English folklore as well as a look at how a global icon may be transmitted and adapted to changing cultural values. The flexible tale stretches to include many variations on the theme of the life and death of a child born the size of a man's thumb.

However, the Tom Thumb figure cannot be confined to stories alone. Both enigmatic and energetic, the Tom Thumb figure is simply too marvelous and capacious a character, a type and a trope, to remain between the borders erected by narrative. Like other characters such as Cinderella, Robin Hood, or even Romeo and Juliet who have successfully breached the boundaries of comedy, adventure, or tragedy to appear in popular and consumer culture, the Tom Thumb figure may be found in other media such as films about shrinking bodies and reality television programming (in the fascination with dwarf families) or in greeting cards and tea towels that feature vaguely Victorian fairies. Unlike these characters from folklore, legend, and Shakespeare's works, however, Tom Thumb's impact may be felt in the sober realms of science and religion, as well as in popular culture, as I discuss below.

How and why does Tom Thumb dance delicately on the divide between faith and science? The epigraphs to this chapter by the seventeenth-century philosopher and doctor Sir Thomas Browne and the eighteenth-century poet and hymnodist William Cowper offer one clue. Both were deeply religious men whose relationship with God consumed their thoughts and writing and both spent some time thinking about how tiny things ought to lead one to acknowledge the greatness of God. In Browne and Cowper, anxieties about the apparent unimportance of those tiny beings beneath our feet or in the air, or the surprising discoveries of the microscope are expressed either through conspicuous absence or through the attention paid to the evidence of God's intention and power that the extremely small make visible: that is, Browne's "wisedome of [the insects'] Maker" and Cowper's defiance of the atheist's denial of God. The yoking of scientific discovery aided by new technologies with crises or celebrations of religious belief may be found in literatures of both childhood and science as well as in cultural events of the modern west, more generally.[3] In this chapter I will explore how the Tom Thumb character, or "little man," figures within constructions of identity and origins and how he highlights anxieties over the relationship between divine intention and scientific inquiry as it emerged from the early modern period through the twenty-first century.

Indeed, the concern with size and scale has not diminished over time or with the advent of new science. In the face of "old faith," anxieties about our relationship to the super-small remain. I have gestured toward one example of what I mean when I say that constructions of the miniature profoundly affect how we think and what we do: the political maneuvering that spotlights specific children—such as those born as a result of embryo implantation—and pits them against proponents of human embryonic stem cell (hESC) research derives, in part, from the greater cultural and literary context of the struggles and subversions of the relationship between big and small in which Tom Thumb plays a part. This particular struggle has a long history: for example, Theodor Kerckring's 1717 illustration of early fetal development clearly shows the embryo as a complete but miniature child (see Plate 5).[4]

A strong connection may be made between Tom Thumb, early theories of reproduction, and embryo adoption made possible today by assisted reproductive technologies. Thinking about the ethics and intentions of embryo adoption or hESC research leads to questions about how we are made, how identity is formed, what makes us human and where God belongs in these existential matters.[5] These are the same questions that attach so easily to Tom Thumb. What can "Tom Thumb" tell us about the origins of life or the meanings of death? A lot.

The Tom Thumb Trope

Broadly speaking, a "trope" is an umbrella term covering metaphor, metonymy, synecdoche and other figures of thought. It is a condensed form that plays with literal sense in an effort to expand and enhance how language can reflect experience. Typically, a trope stands for an idea that is both common and complex, although a trope is quite a bit more interesting than this formulation seems to suggest. For example, a kitchen table is not a trope—it is a thing—but the *trope* of "the kitchen table" represents much more than the thing itself: it calls to mind the nexus of family and ordinary domestic discourse combined with homely virtues such as hospitality and loyalty. In the political sphere, the question may be asked how a proposed policy might fare "around the kitchen table." The Tom Thumb trope, by contrast, arises from imagining the meanings of the small, from universal ideas and desires rather than from the behaviors associated with a physical object. These particular ideas and desires coalesce around "conception"—both in the sense of a construction that reflects a certain notion (here, in particular, the powerful drive to attempt to understand and to control our origins) as well as in the literal meaning of fertilization. Both aspects of conception refer to the beginnings of things known but unseen. At its most essential, the Tom Thumb trope invokes the potency of the small.

More specifically, I have identified three traditions within the Tom Thumb trope that relate in different ways to "conception": these are reduction, reproduction, and redaction. The first, reduction, focuses on the figure as a distillation of mankind; in textual form, Tom Thumb represents *"multum in parvo,"* or "much in little," a recurring concept that helps to explain the powerful nature of the miniature. I discuss *multum in parvo* in detail in the following chapter about the figure of the dwarf and "dwarf discourse." In the current chapter I am especially concerned with reproduction.[6] In this aspect of the trope, the Tom Thumb figure functions as phallus or fetus, small yet powerfully symbolic objects with clear links to conception. The reproductive tradition within the Tom Thumb trope is typically located in medieval and early modern alchemical recipes for creating the "homunculus," or in scientific treatises about discoveries in, and theories of, sexual reproduction. The phallic nature of Tom Thumb is also explored in folklore. The reproductive Tom Thumb plays a role, too, in later European literature such as bawdy tales or burlesque drama featuring the tiny man. The redactive tradition within the trope repudiates the reproductive or sexual Tom Thumb by reconceiving his nature, through recasting him as an ideal Christian gentleman. The redactive impulse provides an alternative version of the tale considered to be especially suitable for young readers and is thus found most readily in children's literature. These three traditions have operated sequentially or sometimes simultaneously from the medieval period forward. Finally, in addition to the historical, literary, and scientific iterations of the trope that I have sketched above, the Tom Thumb trope has been and continues to be exploited through the political hijacking of the discourse surrounding controversial practices such as hESC research and embryo adoption.

Why has Tom Thumb been such a figure of fascination? To return to reproduction: in most Tom Thumb tales, the thumbling's birth is a matter of magic and parthenogenesis. Tom Thumb is born, variously, as a result of a professed wish, an eclipse of the sun, fairy intervention, or Merlin's intercession. His enigmatic birth and his tiny size mark him as a potentially dangerous other, yet Tom Thumb's mysteries seem only to increase his attractiveness and secure his place within the cultural imaginary. Given that the figure offers a delightfully protean sensibility easily exploited for a variety of symbolic purposes, there are many ways to interpret Tom Thumb's ontological meaning. His synecdochal qualities, for example, reflect his generative nature in two ways: his very name as well as his size suggests the opposable thumb—a physical attribute of the primate—as representative of the entire man (and perhaps "mankind" as well). And in an inverse synecdoche in which the whole stands for a part, Tom Thumb's miniature body also gestures toward what is ordinarily hidden by clothing or by flesh: phallus, or embryo, or even sperm. In the 1621 version of the Tom Thumb tale mentioned above, Tom's phallic and fetal nature is made clear in Merlin's prophecies of the bonelessness and premature birth, respectively, of the child who is destined to fulfill the desires of the Plowman and his wife: "Ere thrice the Moone her brightnes change,/A Shapeless child by wonder strange,/Shall come abortiue from thy wombe,/No bigger then thy Husbands Thumbe."[7]

Although this interpretation may seem utterly singular, or even perverse, phallic and embryonic thumblings and their brethren are easily spotted outside of folklore if you know where to look; discourses of discovery present one such promising location. From the primordial soup of alchemy, early embryology, and the scientific and literary discourses of the fifteenth, sixteenth, and seventeenth centuries, a variety of mysterious Tom Thumb figures, including the homunculus, fetus, and spermatozoa, emerged. Each of these contributes to the reproductive strain of the Tom Thumb trope. Specifically, these "little men" are all characterized by a "genetics" of size. The tiny, chimerical Tom Thumb—in genetics, a chimera is an organism combining two or more genetically distinct tissues—yokes seemingly antithetical elements together (such as comedy and tragedy) in his multiple roles as trickster, performer, warrior, lover, and in his metonymic representation as both phallus and fetus.[8] The thumbling character encourages us to consider the human life cycle, from generation through gestation to birth, youth, and manhood.

As Perrault's *le petit Poucet*, Tom functions as the trickster hero of the entertaining tale, saving his brothers' necks, and triumphing over his adversary, the gigantic ogre. As the tale begins, tiny Tom is an unlikely savior—the youngest, smallest, and "stupidest" of the woodcutter's seven children. We are told that seven-year-old Tom is nearly mute; he is also the shrewdest of the brothers. After outwitting the ogre's attempts to slit their throats in the night, Tom steals his precious seven-league boots (a symbol of masculine authority) and usurps the giant's place in his own household, controlling his wife and tricking her out of all their riches. But if tiny Tom is a hero in the high stakes game of economic survival, his success story is also a tale of patriarchal mastery and his dominance over the ogre represents, in part, a triumph within masculine competition for power and

status. Indeed, Perrault's Tom masters, in Patricia Pace's formulation, both language and sexual identity: controlling his destiny
and rescuing his brothers, the once-mute Tom is then able to
speak.[9] And while female Tom Thumb figures from literary fairy
tales and children's literature easily come to mind—Andersen's
Thumbelina and Norton's Arrietty Clock, for example—the
ancient figure of Tom Thumb, in his many incarnations as trickster, knight errant, hero, bawdy rogue, and messenger, is both
male and sexually mature. By masterminding the deaths of the
ogre's progeny, duping his wife, stealing his wealth and placing
the symbol of his dominance (the seven-league boots) upon his
own feet, Tom effectively cuckolds the ogre.

By purloining both the ogre's sexual and economic power,
the tiny, phallic Tom replaces the clumsy, hoarding, gluttonous
ogre with a hero of modern style: sharp-witted, loyal to the
crown, and politically savvy. Typically, in the second part of the
tale, Tom is welcomed at court and given a job: "For not only did
the king pay him handsomely to carry orders to the army, but
many ladies at the court gave him anything he asked to get them
news of their lover . . . ."[10] The tale suggests that Tom is paid for
his messenger work, perhaps with sexual favors, and certainly
with sexual knowledge. At this point in this example of a well-
known Tom Thumb tale, Tom has traveled far beyond the
boundaries of the woodcutter's cottage and forest to succeed
through "marvelous acts of manhood" in a civilized world
replete with codes of conduct, rituals, and nationalist concerns.[11]

Certainly the Tom Thumb character's tiny size, coupled with
his physical perfection as a specimen of masculinity, stands as
his most wondrous quality. Indeed, all three traditions within
the Tom Thumb trope—reduction, reproduction, and redaction—draw our attention particularly to the male body through
the concentration of masculinity found there. In publicly
performing masculinity, virility, and fertility on a small scale, the
miniature often unwittingly invites laughter and wonder. Proud
thumblings reject such treatment and resist being contained by
either ridicule or awe. Gulliver, for example, frustrated by the

limitations his size imposes upon him while living in a land of giants forced to play entertainer, concludes, " 'How vain an attempt it is for a man to endeavour doing himself honour among those who are out of all degree of equality or comparison with him.' "[12]

The "incomparable" nature of the miniature man leads to philosophizing on what the very small reveal about their actual complement, the ordinary man. Demonstrating Stewart's point that "the miniature appears as a metaphor for all books and all bodies,"[13] a pamphlet from 1844 describes the dwarf Charles S. Stratton ("General Tom Thumb") as ". . . one of nature's *indices*, in which the principal features of the race may be looked at with one glance, without turning over interminable folios to see 'what man is made of.' " The pamphlet continues, "[General Tom Thumb] is a sort of mental and physical concentration—a chemical synthesis, in which manhood has been *boiled down* . . . the cube-root of a creation."[14] Similarly, in a long article about her courtship and marriage, Lavinia Warren, Stratton's 32-inch-tall "symmetrical wife," is described as a "dictionary of beauty and sweetness."[15] We return, by way of these excessive texts of praise, to the genetics of size. The real-life examples of miniatures performing the book of life serve as reminders of God's dominance over humans—a hierarchy that alchemy, embryology, and the discovery of sperm, can appear to threaten.[16] A useful literary example of this tension, not surprisingly, comes from *Gulliver's Travels*: in determining Gulliver's origins, the Brobdingnagians do not invoke God, but Nature. Gulliver is a "Tom Thumb," a little man of mystery.

The Homunculus and his Discontents

Accidentally left ashore on the island of Brobdingnag, Gulliver swiftly realizes that once again he has stumbled upon a proportionate world vastly out of scale with his body (see Plate 6).

To his dismay, Gulliver finds himself to be a "Lilliputian" in a land of giants and monsters: he is amazed to see corn rising

40 feet in the air, men as tall as spire-steeples, and cats three times larger than oxen.[17] Soon after his capture, the King of Brobdingnag gathers a group of philosophers and scientists to examine the tiny being and determine his origin, species, and characteristics. Before settling upon *lusus naturae*, or "sport of nature," the puzzled sages hypothesize a number of different identities for Gulliver.[18] A discarded theory proves most fruitful for my discussion of the reproductive tradition of the Tom Thumb trope: one Brobdingnagian gentleman suggests that Gulliver is a living "embryo or abortive birth" somehow expelled from the womb.[19]

Like Tom Thumb, for the Brobdingnagians, Gulliver's birth is both mysterious and uncanny; he is familiar and unique.[20] Yet, since "uniqueness" fails to provide a satisfying theory within the scientific method of hypothesis and experiment, a rational reason to explain Gulliver's existence was required. The theory of the living embryo or fetus could explain his tiny size and even his perfect form.[21] In this way, Gulliver's body size supplied one answer to questions about origins, interiority, and pre-birth at issue for anyone interested in the "truth" afforded by scientific inquiry.

Although the learned Brobdingnagians ultimately reject the embryonic explanation for Gulliver's existence, the idea was not so far-fetched or alien in the early eighteenth-century society in which Swift conceived and wrote *Gulliver's Travels* (1726). From antiquity onward, both naturalists and theologians on the one hand, and occultists, on the other, persistently searched for clues that would unlock the enigma of human origins, life before birth (which, it was hoped, would reveal the secrets of generation and perhaps lead to the creation of new life), and the nature of humanity. The "homunculus"—or "little man"—was one theory used to explain such reproductive mysteries. Both the medieval alchemists interested in generating life and later scientists dedicated to understanding reproduction, found the concept of the homunculus to be a fertile source of inspiration for their related projects.[22] The anxieties attendant upon the hidden or obscure—

what is unknown about creation, identity, and the participation of God in both—as well as the fears of and fascination with "deformity" and difference, are perfectly expressed in the iconic figure of the living thumbling—the homunculus.

Medieval and early modern alchemists, most famously Paracelsus (1493–1541), devised "recipes" for the creation of "homunculi," little men no taller than 12 inches in height that required neither God nor woman as participants in their birth. Paracelsus first outlined the multiple steps necessary to create a homunculus in his *De Natura Rerum—The Nature of Things* (1572):[23]

> Let the semen of a man putrefy by itself in a sealed cucurbite with the highest putrefaction of the horse stomach[24] for forty days, or until it begins at last to live, move, and be agitated, which can easily be seen. At this time it will be in some degree like a human being, but, nevertheless, transparent and without a body. If now, after this, it be every day nourished and fed cautiously with the arcanum of human blood, and kept for forty weeks in the perpetual and equal heat of the venter equinus, it becomes thencefold a true living infant, having all the members of a child that is born from a woman, but much smaller. This we call a homunculus; and it should be afterwards educated with the greatest care and zeal, until it grows up and starts to display intelligence.[25]

Although Paracelsus's plan for creating homunculi was debated and widely disparaged as heretical—both during his lifetime and well afterward[26]—later scholars took up the homunculus quest and produced their own recipes for the creation of little men. To cite just one example, in 1638 Laurens de Castelan, some fifty years after *The Nature of Things*, published his thoughts on another form of the homunculus, the mandrake, a plant with roots in the shape of a man.[27] Popular belief held that the mandrake—which grows in soil fertilized by hanged men's semen spilled on the ground in their last convulsions or, in other versions, it's the urine from innocent men hanged for theft that produces a generative mixture—would become a miniature human once pulled from the ground by a black dog, cleaned and given milk and honey and sometimes blood to eat and drink. Once animated, the homunculus's job was to protect its owner.[28]

Paracelsus's rather astonishing recipe for the generation of the homunculus concludes with an assertion of the kinship between homunculi and supernatural creatures of an exaggerated scale— giants and dwarfs—well-known from folklore: ". . . although up to this time [knowledge of the creation of homunculi] has not been known to men, it was, nevertheless, known to the wood-spirits and nymphs and giants long ago, because they themselves were sprung from this source; since from such homunculi when they come to manhood are produced giants, pygmies, and other marvelous people, who get great victories over their enemies, and know all secrets and hidden matters."[29] Thus, we see that the link between the folklore world and the fantasies and desires of the "real world" touch and mingle in the figure of Tom Thumb, Homunculus.[30] Indeed, Paracelsus's description of the special abilities of the homunculus—as warrior and spy—seem, as I have noted, to inform in particular the specifics of the Tom Thumb trope as manifest in stories based on folklore (such as Perrault's "le petit Poucet"), and in children's tales.

The embryo, another kind of homunculus, remained a mostly mysterious being in the early modern period through the eighteenth century.[31] The Brobdingnagian's theory of Gulliver-as-embryo reminded eighteenth-century readers of the wonders of science that persistently inquired into the interior nature of things and made it a practice to reveal and uncover, sometimes for the first time, the hidden. What is hidden, of course, is often very, very small and also taboo. Gulliver was briefly considered to be a performing embryo or fetus, thus recovering and reconstituting or reorienting the reader to reconsider the secret and hidden as both natural and illustrative. The uses to which these hidden beings were put, however, were increasingly mutable. Some years after Swift, in yet another eighteenth-century satire, Laurence Sterne's *The Life and Opinions of Tristram Shandy* (1759–1767) the inside becomes visible, and the taboo a matter of comedy, through the activities of a little man: Tristram Shandy's unfortunate homunculus.

Sterne's experimental novel emphasizes the hidden and the original—aspects of the Tom Thumb trope as I have been describing it—by taking the autobiographer's burden of narrating the beginning of life to an absurd, if technically accurate, point of origin: conception, the "key" to the trope. The novel opens with Shandy's parents and their clumsy lovemaking which, at the critical moment, causes "the animal spirits" to be "scattered" and "dispersed."[32] As Shandy relates in the second chapter, this ill-advised start to his pre-born life was an affront to the rights and status of the recently discovered and scientifically significant homunculus:

> The HOMUNCULUS, Sir, in how-ever low and ludicrous a light he may appear, in this age of levity, to the eye of folly or prejudice;—to the eye of reason in scientifick research, he stands confess'd—a BEING guarded and circumscribed with rights:—The minutest philosophers . . . shew us incontestably, That the HOMUNCULUS is created by the same hand,—engender'd in the same course of nature,— endowed with the same loco-motive powers and faculties with us . . . . He may be benefited, he may be injured,—he may obtain redress;—in a word, he has all the claims and rights of humanity . . . .[33]

Indeed, Shandy's homunculus is a puny fellow—"his muscular strength and virility worn down to a thread"[34]—whose weaknesses, Shandy opines, were transferred to him.[35] Sterne's satiric theory of the rights of sperm, and his reliance on the trials of reproduction to communicate clues about identity, will turn out to have a long literary and cultural half-life.

The alchemical and spermatic homunculus traced in Sterne belongs to the comic tradition within the reproductive strain of the Tom Thumb trope. In this tradition, the miniature's lusty and phallic nature is exploited and the appetites of the body emphasized. Tom's tiny size makes him an analogue for the phallus and for the appetitive body in a variety of ways. In folktale variants he is often consumed as food and thus satisfies the hunger of others. In these acts of ingestion he also penetrates other bodies (such as the cow, the miller, the salmon, the giant, etc.). The bawdy and scatological strain of the Tom Thumb trope's sexual and reproductive aspect plays an integral role in many of the chapbook versions of the tale, such as *Tom Thumbe, His Life and Death* (1630), in which Tom is eaten by a cow, travels the alimentary canal and is shat upon the ground. Or, *The Life and Death of Tom Thumb* (1810) in which Tom, who desires to see foreign parts, travels to the Country of Eagles and lives in the pocket of the cruel giant Grumbo, eating the bread the giant stored there and using one corner of the pocket for a toilet. Tom's lusty nature gets him into trouble in *The Famous History of Tom Thumb* (1750). He chooses the queen as the object of his desires and plots to ravish her while she sleeps. Because he is so small, lying down with the sleeping queen in her bower, he feels sure of successful penetration: "But now approaching to the place,/Of his desired haven,/Not fearing the least disgrace,/By eagerness was driven." When the queen awakens and loudly protests against his behavior, Tom merely rises and laughingly makes a "jest."[36]

Along with ancient oral and chapbook Tom Thumb variants, Henry Fielding's Tom Thumb was a likely inspiration for Sterne's homunculus some thirty years later and for subsequent versions of the story featuring bawdy jokes for which the tiny masculine body provides the vehicle. Fielding's popular farce burlesque about the eponymous thumbling was first produced in 1730 as *Tom Thumb*, and revised and expanded into *The Tragedy of Tragedies; or the Life and Death of Tom Thumb the Great* the following year.[37] In the short play—an afterpiece—Fielding used the disparity of Tom's small size in comparison with the greatness of his deeds (and the "tragedy" of the multiple murders at the end of the play), to parody heroic drama, and satirize contemporary politics.[38]

Tom Thumb's masculinity and virility are emphasized and ridiculed throughout the drama—a woman took the role during the first run of the play[39]—as Tom is a figure both desired and desiring: the giant-killing warrior rides triumphantly into the court of King Arthur, beloved by the frivolous Princess Huncamunca as well as by her mother, the jealous and scheming queen (in *Tragedy of Tragedies*, the giant Glumdalca is also in love with Tom). The farce is filled with sly, bawdy jokes about sexual intercourse, adultery, and the wedding night.[40] It is not only Tom Thumb's tiny size that type him as a homunculus, but also his unusual bodily composition—rumor has it that he is formed from a "Lump of Gristle.[41] This bonelessness and the courtship plot of the drama mark him as both spermatic and phallic, an absurd "hero" whose fertility, the parson prophesies, should be prodigious: "Long may they live, and love, and propagate,/Till the whole Land be peopled with *Tom Thumbs*."[42]

Another comic version of the phallic Tom Thumb may be found in an unlikely place: a children's picture book. William Steig's *The Toy Brother* (1996)[43] a late twentieth-century version of the homunculus tale, offers a different view of the genetics of size and accesses the Tom Thumb trope to delight the child reader, winking and nodding to the alchemical and then comedic history of the homunculus that I have been sketching. Apprenticed to his father, Magnus Bede, a famous alchemist— perhaps a playful reference to Albertus Magnus, the medieval Dominican cleric famous for advocating the coexistence of science and religion—young Yorick (the name, of course, of Sterne's parson in *Tristram Shandy*) looks down upon his little brother, Charles, and scorns his childish games and pastimes.[44] In spinning a tale of family rivalry, Steig's picture book version of the homunculus making his way in the world uses exaggeration, rather than bawdy or crude jokes, for comic effect. His father reminds Yorick that he's "still no alchemist"[45] and warns him to stay out of the lab, but Yorick, who has alchemical delusions of grandeur, immediately gets himself into trouble by shrinking to the size of a mole. Confronted with this unlucky accident, the family pulls together to protect and minister to the needs of the miniature child. Eventually the alchemist is able to "transmogrify" his son back to his full height.[46]

Wit and dark humor seem to follow the homunculus wherever he goes. Simon Mawer's novel for adults, *Mendel's Dwarf* (1999), combines many spermatic moments with the tragedy of small size—his protagonist, the geneticist Benedict Lambert, is a bitter dwarf, an Everyman who seeks to unlock the genetic mystery of creation and identity. As an adolescent, Lambert examined his own sperm under a microscope and contemplated his conception, seventeen years earlier: He muses, in a flashback, " 'Was my future research determined then [as I scrutinized the sperm], just as my future life had been determined seventeen years before, when a sperm such as one of these nosed its way up my mother's fallopian tube and encountered a wandering, wondering ovum with its delicate cumulus of follicular cells?' "[47] For Lambert, the genetics of size is a curse he has suffered. For Olympia McGurk, the hunchback albino dwarf narrator of Katherine Dunn's novel *Geek Love* (1989), by contrast, physical difference is celebrated and exploited. To create a family of genetic "freaks" for display at their traveling carnival, Olympia's mother willingly ingests various chemicals and drugs prepared by her husband and exposes herself to the hazards of radiation and insecticides. Although many stillbirths and miscarriages result (each preserved in a glass jar), the McGurks successfully produce a number of living children with genetic abnormalities and physical impairments. As an adult reflecting back on her life, Olympia thinks, with pride, "They [spectators] thought to use and shame me but I win out by nature, because a true freak cannot be made. A true freak must be born."[48]

How are we to distinguish between "made" and "born" or to rank them in importance or legitimacy? The characters Benedict Lambert and Olympia McGurk find meaning in the knowledge that science provides or the "truth" that the genetically different child embodies. The "true freaks" of Dunn's novel, created by purposeful acts of sabotage, may be reconciled with "nature" (to the extent that a character may be considered "natural"), as Olympia asserts, because she is born, not made. That is, she has not been hand-crafted like a machine; instead she and her siblings are ultimately formed by chance, aberration being one aspect of the natural. Literature, of course, is informed by real life. One actual example of natural "difference" aided by chemical intrusion may be found in the thalidomide tragedy. The drug was revealed to be teratological—a word from biology that means to create "monsters."[49] During the 1950s and until 1961, mothers in Europe and elsewhere willingly took thalidomide to "cure" morning sickness. After thousands of women gave birth to severely damaged infants, many without limbs, the drug was pulled from the market. The number of miscarriages and still-births linked to thalidomide are unknown, but it is conjectured that for every living thalidomide baby born—upwards of 10,000 world-wide—ten affected babies died.[50] Although it may seem a stretch to link the two, assisted reproductive technologies—IVF, for example—also requires willful, manipulative acts and sometimes these acts result in live births. Money was made—and continues to be made—in both situations, one in which the results tended toward heartache and the other tending toward happiness. In both cases, babies may be born as a consequence of, or in spite of, meddling in "God's business." One might argue that morning sickness was not a disease to be cured and that in the 1950s and early 1960s, pregnancy itself was treated as pathological.[51] "Test tube" babies and thalidomide babies: both are experiments in the tradition of the Tom Thumb trope.

Into the mysteries of conception that *Gulliver's Travels*, *Tristram Shandy*, *Mendel's Dwarf* and *Geek Love* consider, and even Steig hints at, the microscope intrudes. In life science studies (as opposed to alchemical belief or folklore), the Tom Thumb trope is indebted to the work of the Dutch naturalist and pioneer of microscopic research, Anton van Leeuwenhoek (1632–1723).[52] Leeuwenhoek discovered sperm, which he called

"spermatic animalcule," in 1677; the "animalcule" was understood to be an early form of the fetus. (The Dutch physician and
anatomist Regnier de Graaf had discovered the ovarian follicle
in 1672, the same year that Theodor Kerckring reported to the
Royal Society his observation of the " 'first lineaments of a
child' " in a three-to-four-day-old embryo extracted during
the autopsy of a woman.[53]) These discoveries gave rise to the
mid-seventeenth-century theory of embryological development
known as "preformation" or "preformationism." Roughly, this
theory held that God animated all the organisms of all the
species of the world during the six days of creation and contained
them within each other in increasingly smaller sizes, much like
a series of Chinese boxes or Russian nesting dolls. Generation,
then, was an "unfolding" from the parents' sexual organs of an
already created, and infinitesimally small, life-form that needed
merely to grow big. Preformation recognized the primal efforts
of the Creator, thus avoiding the difficulties faced by proponents
of other scientific theories of embryo development in which
God appeared to have little involvement, such as epigenesis (the
systemic growth of the embryo from undifferentiated matter).[54]

The important role of the microscope in the rise of preformation theory will be obvious here. Eggs, and later sperm
(Leeuwenhoek's "adventurers"), were discovered by use of this
magnifying equipment and gave rise to competing theories
within preformationism: the "ovists," such as the seventeenth-
century English physician William Harvey, believed that God
had encased all life within the ovaries;[55] the "spermists" (or
"animalculists") such as Leeuwenhoek, considered the testes to
be the location of the beginning of life. Leeuwenhoek argued at
the end of the seventeenth century that " 'the foetus proceeds
only from the male semen and the female only serves to feed and
develop it.' "[56] In *Making Sex: Body and Gender from the Greeks to
Freud*, Thomas Laqueur comments that the divide between
ovists and spermists was often ideological in nature: "among the
main arguments against the animalculists was that God would
never have devised so profligate a system that millions of

preformed humans had to die in each ejaculation so that one might, on occasion, find food for growth in the egg."[57] While a minority of preformationists were animalculists, my interest in the history of the homunculus lies with the spermists, as once sperm cells were discovered in semen, the little man once again reared his head. Most famously, in 1694, Nicolaas Hartsoeker published his observations of the spermatozoon, and illustrated them with the image of a tiny, preformed homunculus curled up in the sperm head, waiting to grow into an embryo (see Plate 7).[58]

The Child's Tom Thumb, Reproductive Science, and the Politics of Size

How did the homunculus, the fabricated little man whose role was to protect his creator, the animating force encased in each sperm cell, grow up to become the beloved figure of Tom Thumb? In particular, how was Tom Thumb rehabilitated from black magic, bawdy humor, and human reproduction to become a hero of didactic children's tales? The answer, I believe, lies in redaction: a self-conscious shift from Tom Thumb's physical masculinity—his sexuality and reproductive capacity—to a character-driven masculinity. These two forms of the miniature man are not as distinct as may be perceived at first glance: in both the homunculus and the child's Tom Thumb, masculinity is emphasized. As William Newman comments, the homunculus, "created without any feminine matter, [serves] as a magnification of the intellectual and heroic virtues of masculinity."[59] In didactic tales for the young, the genetics of size that informed the Tom Thumb trope in alchemical discourse, folklore, seventeenth-century scientific discoveries, eighteenth-century literature (and ultimately contemporary novels for adults) are downplayed or erased once the Tom Thumb figure has been returned to childhood and instruction.

Children's books—especially those from the nineteenth century—had little to do with anxieties about origins or metaphysical questions, given their firm belief in an ordered and stable world controlled by a present and living God. Indeed, many books of science were written for the purpose of leading children to just such a world view, as the subtitle to the children's book *The Wonders of the Microscope* (1808) makes clear: *An Explanation of the Wisdom of the Creator in Objects Comparatively Minute: adapted to the Understanding of Young Persons.* The anonymous author celebrates the microscope for its ability to introduce reasons to praise God: "The microscope discovers to the attentive observer new worlds, in which he beholds, in miniature, all that can excite his wonder, and lay claim to religious reverence."[60] The large, fold-out illustrations depict portions of insects such as the leg and foot of a fly or the entirety of very small creatures such as a flea. These illustrations make visible the insects' intricate bodies as seen through a microscope. Interpreting these images for young readers, the author asserts that there can be no fear attached to the microscope, for "apply the microscope to whatever of [God's] works we will, nothing is to be found but beauty and perfection. If we examine the numberless species of insects that swim, creep, or fly around us, what proportion, exactness, uniformity, and symmetry shall we perceive in all their organs!"[61]

In addition to the opportunities provided by the microscope to worship the Creator in new ways, microscopic technologies also enhanced the communication of sensual knowledge. According to Catherine Wilson in *The Invisible World: Early Modern Philosophy and the Invention of the Microscope*, innovations in educational methods that promoted learning by the senses helped influence the seventeenth-century European scientific revolution. Wilson notes that Comenius, along with Samuel Hartlib in England, helped to "connect reformed pedagogy and methodical science in the utopian imagination."[62] In his educational treatise *The Great Didactic* (1657), Comenius writes, " 'Everything visible should be brought before the organ of sight, everything audible before that of hearing . . . the truth and certainty of science depend more on the witness of the senses than on anything else.' "[63] We can see, then, how the Tom Thumb figure, through his connection with the tiny and previously hidden, is a pedagogically apt teacher, functioning as a kind of emissary between the worlds of big and small. Not surprisingly, in works for the young such as Mrs. Barwell's *The Novel Adventures of Tom Thumb the Great, Showing How He Visited the Insect World and Learned Much Wisdom* (1838), Tom Thumb pops up at the juncture I've been examining between children's books, miniatures, religious doctrine, and scientific inquiry.[64] All of Tom's knowledge from the insect world, both experiential learning and moral lesson, can be summed up in the philosophy of life that concludes the narrative: "Here then is the end of my reasoning; all that is done leads to good; but to arrive at this good, there is much danger, evil, pain, and death; but there is also more pleasure, beauty, good news, and life. To be content, and to submit in the hope of better times, is then a duty."[65]

Participating in the same redactive effort demonstrated by Mrs. Barwell's book, Charlotte Yonge, in her 142-page extended tale entitled *The History of the Life and Death of the Good Knight Sir Thomas Thumb* (1855), "rescues" Tom Thumb the homunculus from the burlesque tradition.[66] While relying upon the same literal and cultural source texts that inform all nineteenth-century adaptations, Yonge transforms Tom's masculine body (phallic, spermatic, scatological) into a discursive ideal masculinity predicated upon Christian duty and notions of a loyal, gallant, and honest English national character.

In her preface, Yonge cites Fielding, in particular, as responsible for the vulgarization of the nursery hero's history and creating the need for a didactic retelling.[67] Yonge's story is specifically located and contains well-known characters: Tom Thumb is born "on the borders of a forest not far from the mountains of Wales" to a goodly peasant woman and her husband, Owen, whose happy life, Merlin comments, could leave nothing to be desired.[68] The tale proceeds, maintaining many conventional plot details such as the deep desire for a child, even a thumb-sized one; Merlin's intercession; the ingestion by the cow; service at King Arthur's court, and death by a spider—but adds an overlay of Christian commentary upon each event. Thus, Tom's unusual size causes concern that he may be bewitched and that the fairy gifts might be packaged with pagan strings attached, connecting Tom to fairyland forever. Just as the illustration of the flea's proportion and uniformity in *The Wonders of the Microscope* encourages thoughts of the goodness of God, the tale's priest concludes that the beauty and symmetry of the infant Tom's body communicates his purity. The priest "hallow[s] him as a Christian" and pronounces the miniature's life's work to be internal struggle—quite different from the economic striving of "le petit Poucet" or the political maneuvering of many of the chapbook Tom Thumbs—to struggle, that is, "to overcome the Imp and draw forth the Christian."[69]

Tom's internal conflict is made visible in the events, misfortunes, and successes the miniature boy/man experiences throughout his life. His lessons are clearly delineated for the benefit of young readers: Tom becomes "wiser for his mishaps, and began to see that though the elves might make all seem winning and full of pleasance for a time, they would only lead him into trouble when he followed their freaks . . . ."[70] His service to King Arthur aids his development into an ideal gentleman and loyal Briton. Queen Guenever vies with her husband for Tom: directly echoing earlier thumbling tales—through repudiation—as, when coaxed by the queen to " 'sleep on velvet, and eat manikin comfits, and carry . . . sweetest messages, and hearken when . . . pages and damsels gossip their secrets together,' " Tom turns the queen down. He refuses to live life as a lazy eavesdropper. King Arthur agrees with this decision, concluding that " '. . . manfulness lies in the spirit, not the height.' "[71] Tom is also awarded an order of knighthood for his bravery, honesty, and loyalty to King Arthur—nostalgic symbol of a lost Britain. Even when caught in a spider's web facing certain death, he refuses to be released by fairy magic: " 'Better honourable death as a Christian than such a life as thine,' " he retorts to the fairy Puck.[72]

The honorable, thus tragic resolution of the struggle for Tom's soul represents the conflict each sinful child reader undergoes in daily life. Although very small in size, Tom's fortitude in the face of temptation and his willingness to die rather than accept magical aid, types him as a model of exemplary masculinity and Christian duty. Yonge's story is also a self-conscious attempt to link Tom Thumb with the heroic and romantic past of Arthurian Britain. King Arthur features in many Tom Thumb variants, and here Yonge explicitly connects Arthur's return and Britain's rise with Tom: "Some say that whenever good King Arthur shall return from Avallon to reign again over Britain, Sir Thomas Thumb will return also, and again sit by his side and guard his signet-ring."[73]

Leaving aside the child's Tom Thumb for a moment, I would like to return to the kernel at the heart of the Tom Thumb trope—the potency of the small. As I have suggested, the trope is characterized by imagined and literal aspects of "conception": that is, both by action—the beginning of life—and by thought. In contemplating the little man, the two combine as anxiety about origins, delight in discoveries and yet fear, in some, of imagining a world without God, if God is lost in the process of seeing the hidden, of knowing more than is good for us. These fears about the genesis of identity and subjectivity and the creation of life remain with us today. In considering the homunculus in particular, it is clear that the *genetics* of size have been co-opted by a *politics* of size. Today's "homunculi"—the embryo and fetus— have been manipulated into performing as reborn Tom Thumbs. In this climate, the "small" are promoted over the "big."[74] Discussing fetal imagery, Lauren Berlant argues that the fetus, once made visible, enlarges and engulfs the maternal body: "When the fetus became available to photography, making 'life' miraculous in a new way, it came to occupy a new scale of existence, often taking up an entire frame like a portrait. In the process of becoming bigger, it pushed the externally visible bodies involved in reproducing it outside the family picture . . . ."[75] The Right-to-Life movement (as it is called in America) consistently

employs—sometimes explicitly—the methods of the reproductive strain of the Tom Thumb trope (that is, making the hidden
visible and conferring an identity upon it), in its arguments
against the practice of abortion and against hESC research. In
her 1997 biography of her father, Jérôme Lejeune, a French
geneticist, professor of medicine and director of the Institute for
the Pre-born, Clara Lejeune makes an almost preformationist
argument. She writes, "[an embryo] is a little man. It is not a mass
of tissue; it is not a little chimpanzee; it is not a potential person."[76]
Among his many positions, Jérôme Lejeune became the president of an institution to assist mothers-to-be—the name of this
institution? The Tom Thumb Houses.[77]

Lejeune's "little man" assessment is clearly an aspect of the
contemporary Tom Thumb trope, as is "fetal personhood," a
theory of rights that has been tested in American courts. The
following is an example of what may occur when the little man is
pitted against his bigger mother: in 2008, an Alabama woman,
Amanda Kimbrough, tested positive for methamphetamine after
her premature infant died within minutes of his birth. The
district attorney charged her with chemical endangerment of a
child, a class A felony, six months after the baby's death. A swift
trial resulted; Kimbrough pleaded guilty and she was sentenced
to ten years in prison (the minimum sentence, given that the
infant had died). She was released on appeal bond in 2011.[78]
Much controversy has ensued. Groups such as the ACLU,
Planned Parenthood, and the American Congress of Obstetricians
and Gynecologists have taken a keen interest in Kimbrough's
case and in the precedent in favor of the fetus that it and other
adjudicated cases of child endangerment bestowed on pregnant
women seems to set. Personhood USA is another group with an
abiding interest in Kimbrough's case and chemical-endanger-
ment laws applied to fetuses. The group originated in 2008 and is
led by Keith Mason; according to their website, its primary goal
is to "serve Jesus by being an Advocate for those who can not
[sic] speak for themselves, the pre-born child. We serve by
starting/coordinating efforts to establish legal 'personhood' for

pre-born children through peaceful activism, legislative efforts and ballot-access petition initiatives."[79] If Personhood USA succeeds, and the fetus's right to personhood is established under law, then the fetus would be granted, as Sterne predicted for the homunculus, the same legal right to redress that the mother enjoys. According to a 2010 RAND report, in the years between 1973 and 2003, over 300 violent attacks (including arson, shootings, murder, bombing, and acid) were made against abortion providers.[80] While many state propositions have been defeated—either before or after getting on the ballot—the intended consequences of the proposed rules would have a wide effect if adopted: Mississippi's defeated Proposition 26, for example, would not only have outlawed abortion, but also hESC research, some cancer treatments for a pregnant woman if the fetus could be endangered, and even some forms of birth control. In December 2016, Governor John Kasich (R-Ohio) vetoed a so-called "Heartbeat Bill" passed by the Ohio Legislature. This bill would have forbidden any abortion (even in cases of rape or incest) after a fetal heartbeat could be detected (at about 6 weeks of pregnancy when many women are not aware that they are pregnant). He then immediately signed a measure banning abortions after 20 weeks, a law which may be unconstitutional.[81]

And there's more: in an extension of the ongoing abortion "war," hot debates over the rights of the embryo, as, perhaps, Sterne foretold in his satire on sperm, have ensued in America and around the world. These debates sometimes escalate into violence, as the shooting deaths of Dr. Barnett Slepian in 1998 and Dr. George Tiller in 2009, both abortion providers—as well as three people at a Colorado Springs Planned Parenthood in 2015 make clear. The 2016 Republican Party Platform, a good indicator of that party's beliefs, unqualified by its viability, health, or the health of its mother, states "[the] unborn child has a fundamental right to life which cannot be infringed."[82] As the fetus—and now embryo—is elevated into "iconic superpersonhood," in Berlant's phrase,[83] all perspective becomes distorted. The visible potential child is invested with the saturated meanings of childhood itself. John R. Gillis maintains that "the image of the foetus provides all these qualities that western culture has projected onto childhood since the mid-nineteenth century. In effect, the womb has become the Garden and the foetus the latest little angel . . . ."[84]

Ah, angels. When Snowflakes appeared in the Rose Garden in September, 2004, many called it a miracle. These twenty-one Snowflakes did not melt in the heat of the media glare trained on their unusual gathering, but toddled about the Rose Garden lawn, or were carried in their parents' arms. Many Snowflakes were kissed or held by President Bush and Capitol Hill lawmakers who were eager to proclaim an abiding interest in protecting them. Some Snowflakes even wore tee-shirts that asserted, "This embryo was not discarded."[85] "Snowflake children" were once frozen, fertilized eggs—"spares" created for infertile couples enrolled in *in vitro* fertilization programs but not used by them. These microscopic pre-embryos were eventually thawed, implanted into "adoptive" mothers and grew into embryos, fetuses and eventually live children. Children born in this manner are called "Snowflakes"—the name is registered by the American Nightlight Christian Adoptions Agency because each child is unique, like a snowflake (and because, I suspect, each one was derived from a frozen test tube zygote[86]). The Nightlight Christian Adoptions Agency, established in 1959 and the first organization to promote embryo adoptions, refers to frozen embryos in its mission statement: "Committed to life—unborn babies being carried by young women in an unplanned pregnancy, embryos awaiting the opportunity to be born . . ."[87] While in power, the Bush administration helped to publicize the Snowflakes through media events and grants to programs that promote embryo adoption.[88]

Snowflake children play an especially photogenic and charming role in the ongoing debate over human embryonic stem cell research waged within the intersecting arenas of politics, media, and public opinion.[89] A stem cell's potency and value derive from its ability to grow into any organ of the body. hESC research uses undifferentiated stem cells extracted from fertilized

human eggs in order to further its work on the science of embryology that, it is hoped, will provide cures or treatments for devastating illnesses such as Parkinson's, diabetes, and cardiovascular
disease. Indeed, the range of eventual therapeutic uses for embryonic stem cells has yet to be entirely mapped. However, despite the
exciting potential for fresh, effective defenses against, or responses
to, disease, the use of embryonic stem cells in medical research
has been severely curtailed in the past, derailing possible scientific
breakthroughs. President Bush's executive order of 2001 banned
federal funding for research that would destroy embryos for their
stem cell lines or for any other reason. Although President Obama
lifted this ban in March 2009 by his own executive order, two days
later he signed the Omnibus Appropriations Act, 2009, containing
the so-called Dickey–Wicker Amendment that forbids the use of
tax dollars to support hESC research. The history behind this
amendment goes back to the Clinton administration and the
fears, in the aftermath of successful animal cloning experiments,
that cloning humans was imminent. The Dickey–Wicker amendment was first included in the appropriations bill for the
Department of Health and Human Services in 1996 and was
added as a rider to the annual appropriations bill for the
Department of Health and Human Services until the Obama
administration did away with it in 2011.[90] Although an August
2012 decision by the D.C. Circuit Court affirmed the legality of
federal funding for hESC research, the political machinations
over the use of embryos in medical research are far from over.[91]

And for obvious reasons. The ethical issues surrounding the
status, purpose, and ontology of the human embryo are indeed
complex. A fertilized egg can be best characterized as *potential*
and it is within this characterization and the terminology that
surrounds it that politics, medical ethics, religion, and philosophy
collide: the embryonic stem cell (present only in fertilized eggs)
has the potential to grow into the various organs needed by the
body or those affected by disease; the fertilized human egg has
the potential to grow into a child. These uniquely worthy ends
are at odds with each other since each stem cell extraction

destroys the fertilized egg. Proponents of hESC research, such as medical professionals and patient advocates, accept the truth that in order to conduct the experiments that might save many lives in the future, the living tissue that comprises fertilized eggs must die in the present. Opponents of hESC research maintain that any fertilized egg destruction is the death of a proto-person and thus these experiments break ethical codes and religious laws requiring the protection of human life. While it may be difficult for the average person to imagine a fertilized human egg with any specificity (how large is it? What color is it? Can it move?), or to have feelings for them as a "class" or a "people," just about everyone appreciates a baby and considers adoption to be a social benefit.[92] Enter a flurry of Snowflakes wearing tee-shirts. Snowflake "adoption" puts a cute face on the faceless embryo. By highlighting "adoption" (as opposed to "donation") and linking this social value to the debate over hESC research, the Religious Right effectively puts the past in opposition to the future, or the adult with Parkinson's (who represents the past) against the toddler in his mother's arms (who symbolizes the future). Or, another way to imagine this match-up is between big and small: the grown-up big is pitted against the vulnerable small.

When angelic Snowflake children, those former embryos— specifically named "tiny unborn children" or even "microscopic Americans" by conservatives, putting them squarely in the homunculus camp[93]—are displayed, they unwittingly partici-pate in the best tradition of the performing dwarf, the sideshow entertainer, the visible homunculus, and the captive Tom Thumb figure. We've come full circle back to Paracelsus and preforma-tionism: these Snowflakes function as created homunculi, meto-nymically representing the embryos they once were, but as babies clasped in their adoring parents' arms, performing an identity—innocent, pure, vulnerable—that, their very visibility seems to suggest, was always already there. In this politicized climate, the power of the smallest is very strong indeed.

Yet, even a quick look into the history of science confirms that in the past, it was possible for the new science and the old religion to coexist. From Hooke's *Micrographia* (1665) in the seventeenth century through Paley's early nineteenth-century refining of John Ray's *Wisdom of God in the Creation* (1691) in *Natural Theology* (1802), and even in the debates that ensued in the aftermath of Darwin's *On the Origin of Species* in 1859, both God and the hidden or nearly unseen play crucial roles in negotiating questions of origins.[94] For some, however, God's handiwork may no longer be perceived on the microscope slide. The dwarf geneticist protagonist of *Mendel's Dwarf* who spends his life working to isolate the gene mutation that causes achondroplasia, the most common form of dwarfism, directly acknowledges that there is no room for God in the science of reproduction: "Once upon a time the mystery [of the secret of life] was enshrined in the tabernacle on the altar, in a sliver of wafer. Now it lies, stripped open for mankind to read, in a poly-acrimide denaturing gel."[95] Nevertheless, even at the moment of elevating science's supposed clarity over divine mystery, Benedict Lambert unites Creator and created in twinned acts of reading and of storytelling. By reciting the talismanic words that begin our stories, "Once upon a time," and at the same moment insisting that the secret of life is textual and its meaning revealed through reading ("stripped open for mankind to read"), Lambert actually blurs the line between the sacred and the scientific he was at pains to demarcate. Lambert's assessment reminds us that acts of creation are also stories, and stories are always open to interpretation. Or to inspiration. John Mack concludes his illustrated disquisition on the art of small things with a similar thought: "If seeing is believing, then *not* seeing may be even more so. Where our eyes can no longer penetrate, or can barely distinguish the outlines of things, sight gives way to insight . . . ."[96]

The poet Jay Curlin is likewise inspired by the relationship between science and faith, the power of the imagination and the juxtaposition of big and small—perhaps even by the Tom Thumb trope. In his poem "The Evidence of Things Not Seen" (2012), Curlin uses the language of scientific discourse ("evidence," "hypothesize"), discovery ("the 'Higgs boson' ") and technology ("the lens"), to compare human sight and its abilities with the selfsame abilities of "the eyes of faith."[97]

> How strong the lens, how keen the eyes
> To see what we hypothesize,
> To watch so small a thing in motion
> As what we've christened the 'Higgs boson,'
> A tiny, massive thing that passes
> For what can best explain the masses
> Of other things we cannot see
> But somehow, nonetheless, must be.
> A thing so small is surely cute,
> Though weirdly shaped, perhaps hirsute,
> And just as real as any wraith
> Imagined with the eyes of faith.[98]

Curlin's poem concludes with an interesting idea, one related to Browne and Cowper, who both find the beneficent hand of God in the tiny. In our era of distrust between the Religious Right and science, however, Curlin suggests something perhaps more radical than anything Browne or Cowper conclude: that the *a priori* "realness" of the unseen bodies of religious devotion may in fact assist us in the work of abstract science which similarly asks for belief. We may take the information provided by one set of "eyes" already trained to see the invisible, to help another set find "tiny massive" things—objects that both confirm our awareness of how much we still don't know and encourage us in seeking ever further. In other words, science needs faith.

As I hope that this chapter has shown, it is not surprising to find the Tom Thumb trope informing debates over the beginnings of human life and the struggles that ensue when big uses small to promote political agendas. When a folktale father wishes for a child no bigger than his thumb and receives his desire through a fantastical intercession on his behalf, or when a Snowflake mother adopts an embryo external to her body in the hopes that a different—yet no less fantastic—feat will enable a child to emerge *from* her body, we've entered the world of magical science, a world in which, as the Tom Thumb trope makes clear, God and science, alchemy and faith, big and small, uneasily reside. Wishes are made and sometimes they are granted. The world of wishes is Tom Thumb's world, and one, we have seen, we live in today, a world of marvels over which Tom Thumb, that protean man of mystery, also presides.

Chapter 2

THE DWARF IN HIGH AND POPULAR CULTURE

In chapter one I discussed how, over centuries, thumbling characters and their counterparts such as homunculi, sperm, and embryo have cartwheeled through both the folk imagination and the scientific/political imaginary embodying various theories about identity and reproduction and how they have helped to assuage anxieties attendant upon these mysteries along the way. The size differential between the "manikin" Tom and his milieu (parents or ogre figures), between cells of reproduction (ovum and sperm) and the embryo, between the fetus and the infant, or the child and the adult, not only highlights the power of tiny figures to stand for big ideas, but also focuses our attention on the special qualities of the little to contain or personate the big: thumbling as man, embryo as child, stem cell as baby.

One of the central questions this chapter asks is: what does the dwarf mean? Not to himself, of course, but as a cultural sign or marker of something other, or something more, than small size. After finding dwarfs virtually "everywhere," I have realized that the dwarf figure is a particularly capacious representation of the engaging and didactic power of oxymoronic pairings, and that dwarf figures have been used to teach and to spur the imagination for centuries—as this chapter will discuss. Differences fascinate us—it's hard to look away—but they also worry us. The dwarf figure, and the dwarf "discourse" that attempts to "explain" him, can help us confront this anxiety of difference. While drawing attention to the typical human scale through his small body, at the same time the dwarf relieves the tensions that result when like and unlike, tragedy and comedy, big and small, adult and child, high and low status, are combined or set next to each other. He does this by promising something, or someone, new. The dwarf has been defined simultaneously as both man *and* not-man (as a man-like ape or a child-like man), big *and* small (in the motto *multum in parvo*—"much in little") tragic *and* comic (or tragicomic). In this way, the dwarf body also suggests the erasure of difference. Yet, in order to have this effect, the dwarf must be highly visible.

As a site of difference, the dwarf body persistently attracts attention when pictured or displayed—something that both Diego Velázquez and P. T. Barnum knew well. Yet, it would be misleading to suggest that the dwarf figure functions solely in the visual realm. The "dwarf" has significant verbal or textual identities as well as pictorial ones. For example, "dwarf" is a term of classification used as shorthand to denote small size within a like group of larger size; both plants and animals have been deliberately bred into dwarf varieties (such as dwarf sunflowers or dwarf rabbits) as a means to enhance versatility (not all gardens can accommodate towering sunflowers) or desirability (full-grown dwarf rabbits resemble cute baby rabbits). But we also seem compelled to use "dwarf" as a term of comparison that combines or unites opposites for purposes of description. To imagine such a textual dwarf, consider Pluto. Official categories assigned by the International Astronomical Union (IAU) to very large heavenly bodies such as stars and planets include dwarf designations. Stars may be classified as dwarfs of different colors such as red and white (the different colors denote size, luminosity, and density) and planets may also be "dwarf." Pluto was demoted to dwarf planet status in 2006 when the IAU definition of "planet" was refined. Pluto is a dwarf planet both because of its mass and because of its location in the Kuiper Belt, surrounded by other astral objects such as asteroids.[1] How could something so resolutely related to physicality and taking up—literally—space, such as a dwarf planet, be "textual" rather than visual, in nature? Pluto cannot be seen because it is at the same time too big *and* too small. Pluto is invisible to the naked eye, yet its enormous size makes it so out of human scale that it would be impossible to take it in all at once even if one could encounter it. In other words, while Pluto's dwarf status is related, in part, to size, its status as an object of immensity makes its dwarf nature oxymoronic, a figure of speech, and draws attention both to the ways that we *see* and the ways that we *say, read,*and *write,* difference.

Interestingly, the story of how Pluto was named connects size and textuality with childhood, topics I explore in this chapter. In 1930, amateur astronomer Clyde W. Tombaugh, based at the Lowell Observatory in Flagstaff, Arizona, conclusively identified a ninth planet in the solar system. Excited by this good news, which expanded the known universe and provided a distraction from earthly problems, people from around the world suggested various names for the new planet. Naming rights belonged to the Lowell Observatory, yet nothing submitted impressed its astronomers as suitable. Nothing, that is, until the observatory's director received a telegram from Herbert Hall Turner, a professor of astronomy at the University of Oxford. One of his friends, Falconer Madan, a retired librarian at the Bodleian Library, had brought him a most promising name—Pluto—and a charming story along with it. While scanning the papers at breakfast, Madan happened to inquire of his eleven-year-old granddaughter, Venetia Burney, her thoughts on the naming question. A devotee of Greek and Roman mythology—from which most astral names hail—Venetia suggested the Classical god of the underworld, ruler of the dark, as appropriately describing the tiny new planet so far away. The Lowell Observatory astronomers agreed, pleased that the name stayed true to tradition and honored at the same time—via the first two letters of the planet's name—the observatory's founder, Percival

Lowell, who had died in 1916. Young Venetia received a five pound note from her grandfather once they heard the news of Pluto's selection by the observatory.

The links between the dwarf planet Pluto and a bookish child may seem wholly accidental or incidental, but I have noticed that where visual and textual examples of the dwarf emerge, the child cannot be far behind. And so it is that we find both child and dwarf, visual and textual, united in one person in the historical figure of Jeffrey Hudson, also known as "the Queen's dwarf." Although the life of the seventeenth-century Englishman may seem far removed from Arizona's Lowell Observatory and the naming of Pluto in 1930, "dwarf discourse"—the way that we talk about and represent the dwarf in his various guises—helps to illuminate the contexts surrounding both. Dwarf discourse shaped Jeffrey Hudson's life and helped to spur an afterlife for the tragicomic figure. Indeed, the life of Jeffrey Hudson encapsulates all of the issues at play in this chapter: words, pictures, performances.

The Queen's Dwarf

In early November, 1626, George Villiers, the 1st Duke of Buckingham and favorite of two successive monarchs—James I and Charles I—hosted a number of lavish banquets at York House, his grand London dwelling. These events honored King Charles I and his young queen, Princess Henrietta Maria of France. By playing to his strengths as host, Buckingham attempted to burnish his tarnished image through this series of sumptuous banquets: though in the good graces of the king, he was almost universally reviled elsewhere (in less than two years he would be murdered by a disgruntled lieutenant of the English army).[2] Seventeen-year-old Henrietta Maria, for one, was locked in a series of conflicts both with her rival, Buckingham, and with her new husband. The ambassador Marshal de Bassompierre, who had known Henrietta Maria since she was an infant, had lately been sent to England by the King of France, Henrietta

Maria's brother, to try to heal the breach between the recently wed pair. Offering spectacular entertainments, multiple courses, music, and gifts, the handsome and charming Buckingham attempted to woo his honorable company. The most dramatic gift of all was reserved for the young queen, a lover of lapdogs, songbirds, and monkeys: from an enormous pastry emerged a perfectly proportioned seven-year-old boy, Jeffrey Hudson, only 18 inches tall.[3] The compliment was accepted, smiles exchanged between rivals and, to mark the tiny child's new "owner," he was renamed the "Queen's Dwarf."

Especially notable and apropos for my discussion below is the fact that when he was introduced to the queen and assembled aristocrats, not only was Jeffrey Hudson very small in stature, he was also very young in years: a little, little boy transformed into a manikin pie or the filling for a "starry gazey" pastry. In this instance, however, the pie was filled with upright child instead of whole fishes or blackbirds—yet at the same time the stunt reminds us both of the gaping fish heads found in the Cornish dish and the image of birds singing for royalty from the nursery rhyme. In this dramatic true-life scene, Hudson's escape from the pie also calls to mind the mishaps of the folktale hero Tom Thumb and prefigures tiny Gulliver amidst the giant Brobdingnagians. How did the youth Jeffrey Hudson come to be enclosed in a pie and given to the queen, little more than a child herself?

Hudson was born in 1619 in Oakham, Rutland County (the smallest county in England), a son of the butcher and slaughterer John Hudson. One of Hudson senior's employments was to organize bull-baiting entertainments for his patron, the Duke of Buckingham, whose great hunting lodge, Burley on the Hill, overlooked Oakham. Not surprisingly, once the small size and slow growth of John Hudson's son became apparent, news of the unusual child spread rapidly and eventually a curious Duchess of Buckingham requested a meeting. Accordingly, the seven-year-old Hudson arrived at Burley with his father. The Duchess was enchanted with the miniature child and invited him to become a member of her household. Refusal of the offer was not a viable option for the Hudsons, and so young Jeffrey was removed from his family. This change was not to last long, however, as soon afterward the duke gave Hudson to the queen by way of the pregnant pie, a presentation designed to surprise, invoke awe, and create the greatest obligation between giver and recipient. It is not clear, however, whether the gift himself, the young dwarf, was consulted as to his opinion of the exchange.

By all accounts Henrietta Maria dearly loved Jeffrey Hudson and he remained in the queen's service for eighteen years.[4] Both his dramatic rise and the subsequent tragic twists that dogged him seem to shadow the fate of his master and mistress and the court that became his new home. Sharing the Catholic faith with the queen, Hudson lived for many years as her cosseted pet, secluded from the hurly-burly of the outside world;[5] yet his fortunes, like those of the exiled queen and the executed king, would later fall to what would have seemed to be, in 1626, almost unimaginable depths. Handsome and popular, Hudson was thoroughly absorbed into life at court and his presence there was both well-documented and rewarded. Most notably, Hudson was painted by van Dyck and by other artists, made the subject of some minor poetry, cast in court masques and eventually named a Captain of Horse. While life within the court presented its own center of petty politics and intrigue for Hudson and everyone in it, outside of this self-absorbed world, dangerous turmoil reigned and bitter resentments grew stronger each year that the King refused to convene Parliament (1629–1640). Ultimately, Charles's battles with Parliament over religion, taxes, and the (im)balance of power culminated in the formation of opposing armies and, in 1642, the onset of the Civil War. This turn of events necessitated the removal of the Queen and her court (including Hudson) to the Netherlands. While Henrietta Maria returned to England in the early part of the war, fore-knowledge of an attempt to take her hostage forced the Queen again to flee in 1644. France would become her primary residence for the remainder of her life (though she made an extended four-year visit to England in 1660 for the Restoration when her son, Charles II, was crowned). Within a year of their flight, Hudson found himself in trouble after killing a man in a duel. Banished from the court-in-exile—as dueling was illegal in France and he had killed a man who had influential friends— Hudson was next captured by Barbary pirates and sold into slavery in North Africa. After twenty-five years he was rescued and returned in 1669 to Oakham, the place of his birth, where he lived for a number of years before seeking royal preferment in London in 1678. There he was imprisoned as a wave of anti-Catholic hysteria and suspicion swept through the capital in the aftermath of the "Popish Plot." Hudson was released two years later and died in 1681.

Jeffrey Hudson died in obscurity. Yet he was not entirely forgotten after his death: the earliest account of Hudson's life appeared in 1662 in a compendium volume, *The Worthies of England*, by Thomas Fuller and in 1684 James Wright published a brief sketch of Hudson's life in his *The History and Antiquities of the County of Rutland*. Indeed, Hudson's fame has grown— albeit slowly—over the years. Hudson makes an appearance in Walter Scott's *Peveril of the Peak* (1822), set during the reign of Charles II. *Giants and Dwarfs* (1868), a compendious mid-Victorian history of persons of exaggerated size from antiquity to the present, by Edward J. Wood, introduces Hudson as "the famous dwarf." In the twentieth and twenty-first centuries, Jeffrey Hudson has inspired both a beer and a full-scale biography (the latter, by Nick Page, although a serious and well-researched treatment of Hudson's life, is printed in a rather gimmicky small size).[6] While these posthumous representations of Jeffrey Hudson help to immortalize him as a tragicomic historical novelty, the first "branding" of "the Queen's dwarf" actually began during his lifetime—not only in his being gifted to the young queen via the pie—but also through pictorial and textual commentaries. These commentaries, intended for elite audiences, centered on interpreting what littleness meant in the context of "greatness." By "greatness" I mean, in part, the disconnect that exists between the physical stature of the dwarf and other people—even short people such as the King and Queen. However, "greatness" here also indicates rank and prestige; Hudson's milieu, the royal court, was a site in which the aristocracy was located and concentrated as well as displayed for the masses through various methods of cultural communiqué.

Among other artistic and ceremonial sites of the seventeenth century such as court masques, portraiture and poetry were conventionally used as powerful means for the communication of lessons about nobility and authority, or their lack. Certainly, in Jeffrey Hudson's case, the most eloquent method by which his unusual body size was exploited for delivering such messages may be found in portraits both penned and painted. These outlets for representing Hudson's ambivalent status—as dwarf and as "member" of the royal household (as much as pets and slaves were also aligned with royalty)—make plain the visual and textual identities that I suggest are so often linked to the dwarf figure. To take painting first: *Queen Henrietta Maria with Jeffrey Hudson* (1633), by the Flemish master Anthony van Dyck, celebrated court painter to Charles I, arguably represents the most significant visual portrait we have of Hudson (see Plate 1).

E. H. Gombrich, in his delightful introduction to art history *The Story of Art* (1950), credits van Dyck with creating a sympathetic and appealing artistic record of the court of Charles I, "with its defiantly aristocratic bearing and its cult of courtly refinement."[7] Van Dyck, well known to aristocratic art patrons as a portraitist of the first rank, relocated to London in 1632 at the request of Charles I and accepted the position of "Principal Painter in Ordinary to their Majesties." The elegant and cultured van Dyck, whose technically brilliant, refined and sensitive portraits thrilled his royal patrons, was kept furiously busy painting pictures of the people who made up the insular world of the court and aristocracy (not all of whom would remain loyal to the king through the years of unrest leading up to Civil War). Except for a few trips to the Continent, the artist remained in England and in his position as court painter until his death in late 1641, at the age of 42. Once van Dyck entered the scene, his dramatic and fresh style quickly eclipsed his predecessors at the English court, most notably Daniel Mytens. Considering the style of Mytens's large painting *Charles I and Henrietta Maria Departing for the Chase* (*c.* 1630–32), Graham Parry notes, "all the elements of the subject are accommodated in the same foreground plane, which is awkwardly integrated with the landscape behind (see Plate 8). The nature of the subject demands motion here, but everything is static—even the dog jumping off the terrace seems suspended in mid-air."[8]

Indeed, Karen Hearn, curator of the 2007 "Van Dyck & Britain" exhibit at the Tate, notes that *Queen Henrietta Maria with Jeffrey Hudson* successfully reworks the image of Henrietta Maria and some of the themes of Mytens's work—among them the purity of the queen—of a few years prior.[9] For her part, the queen was so pleased with the new court painter that she had one of Mytens's portraits of her royal person overpainted in the style of van Dyck.[10]

As reflected in the famed painting *Charles I and Henrietta Maria with their two eldest children, Prince Charles and Princess Mary* (1632), also known as "The Greate Peece," by the 1630s the king and queen were united in familial and marital harmony (Buckingham's death proved to be a catalyst in this regard).[11] Van Dyck's *Queen Henrietta Maria and Jeffrey Hudson* flatters the queen, dressed in elegant riding attire, suggesting both a beauty and height that she did not quite possess. Most analyses of the painting, understandably, focus on the figure of the queen and the iconography of the orange tree, crown, and monkey. While interpretations vary slightly, the architectural elements (column and dais) and crown suggest royal authority; the orange tree, chastity and purity and her maternal lineage; and the small monkey represents the base, animal nature of humanity.[12]

Thus, the figure of the queen is surrounded by objects representing her station, nature, and maternity, lofty elements that mark the painting as subtly allegorical as well as personal—the king had commissioned the portrait as a gift not long after van Dyck arrived in England.[13] Her more quotidian interests, including a love of small creatures, are symbolized by the inclusion of the monkey, Pug. Why might Jeffrey Hudson also have been included in van Dyck's early, and, some say, most beautiful portrait of Queen Henrietta Maria? One answer is that Hudson figured as another of the "objects" of the queen's daily life. He was, quite literally, a familiar face. A loved member of the queen's household, Hudson appears in other paintings of the royal family, notably Mytens's *Charles I and Henrietta Maria Departing for the Chase*, referred to above.[14] In this enormous piece, Hudson is again off to the right side of his royal mistress (the viewer's left), and again nearly out of the frame of the painting's composition. The king and queen stand stiffly, with eight hounds in various postures at their feet, sharing the foreground. Hudson holds the collar and leash of two straining dogs; his hunting costume resembles that worn by the king. The gaze and attitude of the largest hound, set behind Hudson—only partially visible in the painting—is mirrored by a smaller dog emerging from the lower right-hand corner. Notably, a small monkey rides this dog. Yet the monkey is rarely commented upon, as the painting is often cut off in reproduction so that the monkey is not visible. Also mirroring Hudson is the diminutive (although nearly twice Hudson's height) black stable-groom in "primitive" dress who holds the bridle of Henrietta Maria's horse.[15] In this second instance of a human/animal dyad, the figure is behind the larger animal, as opposed to Hudson who stands in front of the big hound. The monkey on the back of the dog is another example of a human/animal dyad, as the monkey suggests human qualities.

I offer this description of the Mytens work and Hudson's position within it in order to add an element absent from the conversation concerning van Dyck's *Queen Henrietta Maria with Jeffrey Hudson* as a reconsideration of *Charles I and Henrietta Maria Departing for the Chase*. Van Dyck's reworking of Mytens's group portrait, I believe, offers a cogent comment about the exotic "other" in the Caroline court. In both *Charles I and Henrietta Maria Departing for the Chase* and *Queen Henrietta Maria with Jeffrey Hudson,* the dwarf figure is paired with an exotic other: in the former work, his other is the black servant and in the latter, it is the monkey. Owning and displaying non-indigenous pets as well as servants was fashionable with elites during the Caroline era, and Henrietta Maria's entourage, in particular, included dwarfs, dogs, natives, and monkeys.[16] Although van Dyck is credited with helping to introduce into European portraiture the vogue for representing black servants with their masters in, for example, an early painting from his Italian period, *Portrait of Marchesa Elena Grimaldi, wife of Marchese Nicola Cattaneo* (1623), *in Queen Henrietta Maria with Jeffrey Hudson* neither the young black stable-groom nor the dogs appear, even in this image of the queen presumably about to ride or perhaps hunt.[17]

Rather, for van Dyck, both the African servant and the animals of Mytens's work (in particular, the fluffy white pup directly at the queen's feet bound not for the chase but for the queen's lap) coalesce into one unstable being, the monkey.

Size as well as race and ontology is a crucial element here—in the early modern period, as John Knowles reminds us, it was "unclear whether apes [were] men in the making or unmaking"— because, I argue, size indexes age as well as authority or its lack.[18] So much smaller than the regal figures who are the ostensible subjects of each work, the black stable-groom behind the high-stepping horse is clearly a youth, as is the page holding the red umbrella over the imperious Marchesa Elena Grimaldi (see Plate 9).[19] Van Dyck has reconceived and reargued both Mytens's painting and his earlier portrait of an imperial female figure by condensing the exotic African "other" and animal—subordinates to royal majesty and to humanity (so it was believed by some)— into the form of the marmoset upon which Henrietta Maria rests her hand in a caress as well as a gesture of dominance and ownership. Though an ape, he is a tiny one, able to sit on the dwarf's shoulder. Significantly, the little monkey (and his metonym, the black boy) is closely associated with the little man.

The connection between dwarf and ape (and especially pygmy and ape, as I discuss in chapter three) was long considered in fabular, emblematic, and scientific traditions to be a close one: both creatures "approximate" mankind as imitation or aspiration. But in this case, the little man is a child.[20] Van Dyck's portrait of the pretty dwarf as pet is clearly a portrait of the dwarf as apish or not quite human.[21] Yet the work is also a portrait of the construction of seventeenth-century childhood.

Jeffrey Hudson looks like a child in the painting: he is diminutive in relation to the queen and, although fourteen years old at the time the portrait was painted, his round facial features and wispy fair hair suggest a much younger child. A truly young child would be depicted wearing a child's clothing: at this time, very young boys and girls wore dresses and caps essentially indistinguishable from each other—see van Dyck's 1637 *The Five Eldest Children of Charles I* in which the Princess Royal (six years old) and James, Duke of York (four years old) wear similar garments; the Prince of Wales, aged seven years, wears breeches. Yet Hudson's apparel, the cut of his spurred boot, gauntlet, and breeches mimics a man's hunting costume, as we see in Mytens's painting of the royal couple before embarking on the hunt. Hudson's sophisticated dress is one clue that his size does not tell the entire story about his identity and relationship to the queen.

To return to the question I raised earlier, what is Jeffrey Hudson doing in this portrait? A compelling, if less obvious answer than his membership in the queen's household is that the dwarf child in particular unites small size, subordination, and "otherness"—that is, his figure reflects the position of the child in relation to adult authority—and thus the portrait makes an argument about childhood as well as one proclaiming the queen's purity and majesty. Hudson is dressed in the sumptuous scarlet associated with privilege and wealth—a color also worn by the two eldest princes in *The Five Eldest Children of Charles I*. Yet unlike Charles and Henrietta Maria's actual children in "the Greate Peece"—the future king and princess royal—Hudson does not touch, nor is touched by, the queen. He belongs to the queen and appeals to her—in both senses of the word—but he is not like her.[22] The savage nature of ordinary children, those not of royal or noble birth, was understood to be a fact of nature and one that could be overcome in one way only: through growing up into, especially, a white man of a good or good-enough social class. The ape and the dwarf, separately, may only aspire to such heights of humanity. The dwarf wearing a monkey becomes an icongraphically perfect representation of the liminal status of the child-in-the-making. There's more. An especially key aspect of the queen's majesty in this era of the aggressive profession of the divine right of kings—a portion of which Henrietta Maria shared as consort to the king and mother of the future king—lies within her maternal relationship to the English people. Gazing intently at the queen, in an attitude of obedience and loyalty associated both with dependent childhood and dependent subjecthood, young Hudson, in figure and in fact, is a body subject to the queen's towering maternity. Knowles concludes his analysis of this painting by returning to the relationship between size and power: "... Henrietta Maria, almost a giant, gazes out serenely and asserts her dominion ...."[23] Henrietta Maria is indeed represented as statuesque in this portrait: one means by which this argument is made in paint is that in color, proportion, and height, the vertical embroidery down the front of her gown reflects the narrowly fluted column rising behind her and out of the frame. My point is that size matters in another way in this celebrated painting: in the figure of the liminal dwarf we find united child and not-child, animal and man, servant and savage, a tiny, necessary other to monarchy's "greatness."

Thus far I have discussed in some detail visual arguments made about Jeffrey Hudson, "othered" figures of small stature as well as childhood itself. Similar arguments about the meanings attached to size may be found in the few texts written about Hudson during his lifetime; however, unlike the van Dyck and Mytens paintings that tend to place Hudson within the greater court or with Henrietta Maria, poetry about the "queen's dwarf" typically linked him with the king. For example, John Taylor's poem marveling at the "three wonders" of the Caroline court—the dwarf Jeffrey Hudson, the giant porter William Evans, and the 151-year-old man Thomas Parr—is dedicated to Charles ("The Old, Old, Very Old Man," 1636). A more significant work of praise for Hudson—yet similarly turning on jokes about littleness—is the miniature gift-book entitled *The New Yeare's Gift by Microphilus* (1636). The work was first a private one, but so admired at court that it was soon-after published. Page suggests that *The New Yeare's Gift* was likely commissioned by Henrietta Maria and written by Thomas Heywood, the author of short essays on the "three wonders" attached to a print engraving of the figures in one frame.[24]

As its name implies, *The New Yeare's Gift* was originally meant as a small token in the tradition of gift-giving to servants and courtiers on the occasion of the new year (March 25th in the Julian calendar—which England followed until 1752). Not surprisingly, Jeffrey Hudson cannot be mentioned in print without referencing his small stature. Thus, the poem celebrates Hudson's exceptional wit, virtue, and the "greatnesse of his spirit" when considered in the context of his small body. Yet, there's another issue at play here: Hudson's physical size difference is repeatedly compared to textual "size" as both big *and* small, or *multum in parvo*. The book asserts a "Lady Parvula" as the commissioner of the work ("parvula" means small or little). In her dedication, Hudson is described both as an "Epitome of Nature" and as a "compleat compendium of a Courtier"[25]—that is, something condensed and someone expansive at the same time. Both "epitome" and "compendium" have textual meanings. Page reminds us that in the seventeenth century "epitome"—a word used more than once to describe Hudson—meant "condensed record or representation in miniature."[26] Significantly, the Latin couplet used as a caption to the Martin Droeshout engraving of Hudson added to the second edition of *The New Yeare's Gift* translates as "Gaze on with wonder, and discerne in me/The abstract of the world's Epitome."[27]

Itself a short text, this motto uses textual metaphors—
"abstract" and "epitome"—to describe how the dwarf body
functions as a symbol of the essence of mankind. The choice
of "abstract" is an interesting one in the seventeenth-century
context since the word carried many meanings, including
"summary" or "abridgement" of a document—creating smaller
out of big—as well as being a synonym for the definition of
"epitome" cited above. In other words, the now rare meaning
of "abstract" found in this didactic message regarding Jeffrey
Hudson includes a "person or thing regarded as encapsulating
in miniature, or representing the essence of the characteristic
qualities or features of something much larger" (*OED*). The
picture of Hudson is meant first to draw the reader's gaze and
then to inspire a sense of awe at the "double miniaturization"
Hudson represents as the summary of man's essential nature.
And the content of that nature? Hudson's small size in comparison with the ordinary-sized man is analogous to human
littleness in the face of God's greatness. At this textual juncture,
the king himself enters in order to be compared with both man
and God as a reminder of what he owes to each (his compassion
in the first case and his fealty in the second). The image of the
courtier dwarf communicates a warning, or *memento mori*, to
the king: "So little dwarfs (boyes in proportion though perchance
men in discretion) being about a Monarch, though silent, yet
their very persons are a voice crying; *Rex memento te esse
minimum*: O King remember how thou art little, borne like others
little, to teach thee to heaven humility, to Earth, humanity."[28] The
emblematic nature of the dwarf body represented in both image
and text, as we have seen in the story of Jeffrey Hudson—and the
generic form of the emblem itself as both a picture and a short
text—is the essence of dwarf discourse to which I will now turn.

The Emblematic Dwarf

A few defining words about emblems are in order: the emblem is
a hybrid literary form with its roots in sixteenth-century Italy

and Germany. In his *Emblematum liber* (1522; the first illustrated edition was published in 1531), the famous Italian legal scholar Andrea Alciato (or Alciati) created the emblem book by combining adages and epigrams and added, at the request of his publisher, woodcut pictures to make the whole easier to understand for those lacking adequate knowledge of Latin and Greek.[29] The book, published in Germany, was very successful and served as a model for others to come, both on the Continent and in England. The three-part structure of motto–picture–poem, however, was codified in the work of subsequent authors, such as Georgette de Montenay in her *Emblems ou Devises Chrestiennes* (1571) and Geffrey Whitney's *A Choice of Emblemes* (1586). Alciato also set the standard for the presentation in which each emblem is featured on a new page, beginning with motto and picture and then verse text following. The emblem's purpose, and that of the emblem book more generally, was to impart a social, spiritual, or moral lesson and to be read and interpreted as a manual for future behavior. Stories from Classical mythology were mined for their wisdom, but turned to Christian ways of thought through the combination of pictura–inscriptio–subscriptio.[30] As Charles Moseley notes, the emblem's text and picture are equally important in "the aim to teach a moral truth so that the memory will grasp it not as a mere formula but—this is important—as an experience, which will be a guide to understanding and conduct."[31]

This description of the look and purpose of the emblem may seem fairly abstract without a concrete example. To that end, consider an emblem from Alciato's *Emblem Book*, starting with the inscription: "Quae supra nos nihil ad nos", or, What is above us is nothing to do with us."[32] A more colloquial translation reads, "What lies above us is none of our business."[33] The woodcut illustration shows a man lying beneath a blasted tree with an enormous bird perched upon him pecking at an exposed internal organ (see Plate 10).

The six-line poem is translated from the Latin by Moseley as follows:

Prometheus, hanging forever on his Caucasian rock, has his liver torn asunder by the claw of the holy bird [the eagle of Zeus] and would certainly wish in his disgust he had not made mankind. And, disgusted with the men of clay, he curses the torch lit with the stolen fire. The breasts of those far-seeing men who are keen to know the circumstances of heaven and the gods are gnawed by various worries.[34]

Even if one finds the story of Prometheus and his punishment clear from this image (illustrations from other editions—and there are many—that show Prometheus's chains provide a helpful clue missing here) and the verse useful in illuminating how Prometheus's story was read symbolically as a warning to mankind about overreaching in the desire for knowledge, it may be difficult for a reader to put all three together. In the picture, we see Prometheus in torment, and if one knows the story, one knows this punishment resulted from his disobedience to Zeus and his protection of humanity. The motto tells us that the hierarchy between gods and men is absolute, and the poem links Prometheus's physical pain resulting from the eagle gnawing at his flesh with a metaphorical, psychological pain described as "worries." So, what's the moral lesson? It might appear to be "stay in your place and be content" or "beware pride"—but a more sophisticated reading, such as the one offered by Moseley, below, requires a deeper knowledge than many readers possess today of the myth of Prometheus, Latin, and the contemporary iconography of the eagle:

The verse looks straightforward but is not. Prometheus's suffering was ultimately ended by Hercules, and both were benefactors of mankind and accorded divine honours: the winning of wisdom is accompanied by pain, but ultimately its noble goal receives divine recognition. Thus it is only ironically that the emblem invites us not to seek for wisdom; for the eagle which tears is also a bird of good omen (there is a pun on this sense of *praepes* [winged]) and is the messenger of Zeus.[35]

Oh. As I hope that this brief example of one sixteenth-century emblem makes clear, one must not be too concerned if its "answer" did not spring readily to mind without a gloss or commentary for assistance in its interpretation. Sixteenth- and seventeenth-century emblems are very difficult for modern readers to grasp (even in translation): not only are the sign systems far removed from our visual vocabulary today, but also the turns and complexities of the poems may provide more puzzlement than clarity. But this was the case for many contemporary readers as well. Moseley argues that the emblem "is a deliberately clever creation, purposely subtle and difficult, demanding resourcefulness, intelligence and an awareness in its readers of the complex nature of their own perception."[36] Elizabeth See Watson concurs that the condensed nature of the visual and verbal components of the emblem add to the interpretative sophistication of the form: "When to the brevity of the adage was joined one small picture and one (usually) short poem in the new miniature genre of the emblem, the potential for interpretation of meaning grew correspondingly in breadth."[37] Perhaps Rosalie L. Colie's firm conclusion about the self-conscious difficulty of the emblem may provide comfort to the modern reader: ". . . far more than the adage, the emblem mimics the theory of the hieroglyph, a presentation of the truth veiled, to be understood only by the initiate or the piercing reader."[38]

Colie's "piercing reader" would be tested in reading emblems throughout the heyday of the emblem book in sixteenth- and seventeenth-century Europe and England, as well as in interpreting other artistic forms of the early modern era writ large that include the emblem in one way or another. The masque, painting, poetry, and fable, through their use of metaphor as a means to communicate abstraction, each contain aspects or traces of the emblematic, a form of great power and perseverance.[39] Indeed, the emblem tradition did not conclude in the seventeenth century: during the Romantic era and into the nineteenth century, a revival of the emblem may be glimpsed in the illustrated poetry of William Blake, the symbolic poetry of Coleridge and in many works for children. Today, in more prosaic fashion, ubiquitous product logos with mottos similarly participate in the symbolic mode of communication found in early and later emblem books. For example, the Nike "swoosh," with its energetic sweep reminiscent of Mercury's winged sandals, coupled with the exhortation "just do it"—a motto informed both by the concept that failing to exercise is a particularly *moral* failing and that exercise may be equated with success and "winning"—is an emblem as universally recognized as the sunflower, which always turns its face to the sun (as should the soul to God), would have been in Shakespeare's or Jeffrey Hudson's day.

To return, once again, to Hudson: the miniaturized, condensed, essential nature of an "epitome," as described in *The New Yeare's Gift* about Jeffrey Hudson, may remind us of the emblem itself—given the miniature and didactic nature of both. Congruencies between the emblem and the figure of the dwarf form the basis of my argument about the emblem genre as informing "dwarf discourse." Both the emblem and the dwarf are forms that may be understood as signs and texts simultaneously; that is, so often the dwarf character (whether actual, as in the case of Jeffrey Hudson, or imagined) is both pictured and inscribed, with mottos or labels mapped onto its figure. Indeed, reading emblematically helps us to interpret the dwarf in his many guises and roles throughout history. The verbal nature of Hudson is plainly communicated through the textual metaphors and writing that surrounded him during his lifetime and which remain today. His relationship to the work of the emblem is directly described in *The New Yeare's Gift*: dwarfs are "accounted *emblematically* necessary, to denote those who desire to approach neere Princes ought not to be ambitious of any Greatnese, but [ought] to acknowledge all their court-lustre is but a beame of the Royall Sunne their Master."[40] This statement, which functions like the motto of the emblem, reminds readers of the court dwarf's low position in relation to the king and of the gratitude and loyalty owed to the monarch. The message, while ostensibly confined to the figure of the court dwarf, may be extended to reach the king's ordinary subjects who also ought to recognize their rightful inferior place and exercise proper conduct toward their ruler. As I have suggested above, *The New Yeare's Gift* itself includes an emblem in the old style: the Latin caption underneath the Droeshout engraving of Hudson— "Gaze on with wonder, and discerne in me/The abstract of the world's Epitome"—promotes a moral message about human littleness.

While images of, and poems about, dwarf characters were not especially common in early modern emblems or those from the eighteenth or nineteenth centuries, for that matter, the dwarf figure appears in popular emblem books by Alciato, Father Cats (the seventeenth-century Dutch moralizing poet and statesman Jacob Cats who successfully brought emblems to a wider audience) and "R. B." (the pseudonym of Nathaniel Crouch, a late seventeenth-century English bookseller and amateur historian).[41] In two of the three emblems from this set of authors/compilers, the emblem's meaning about the dwarf figure relates closely to the idea that one should understand one's place and status and not attempt to change either. This lesson is inextricably connected to size in which the powerful figure (whether pictured or imagined) is larger than is typical and the upstart or even inhuman figure is much smaller than what is considered to be "normal."

To take Alciato first: emblem LVIII incorporates elements of the Greek myths about the labors of Hercules and his battle with the pygmies, a race of tiny people mentioned in the writings of Homer, Pliny, Herodotus, and Aristotle.[42] Depending on the edition of Alciato's emblems, the image variously depicts a giant sleeping with a club in his hand surrounded by a tribe of tiny warriors or a giant crushing the amassed miniature fighters. The motto, "*in eos qui supra vires quicquam audent*" (which may be translated as "against those who dare anything beyond their strength"), read with the picture clearly links bodily size with the futility of attempting to confront those with great power: the audacious—and stupid—warriors are described as "pigmies" and "dwarves," while the powerful is the mighty Hercules. This emblem was included and adapted by English emblematist

Geffrey Whitney in his *Choice of Emblemes* (1586). In the first stanza of Whitney's translation of the poem, the pygmies are called "foolishe dwarffes" whose "force was all too smalle"[43] and the second stanza reminds readers that the metaphors of size and strength are related to social status as well as to intelligence: "This warneth us, that nothinge paste our strengthe/Wee shoulde attempe: nor anie worke pretende,/Above our power: lest that with shame at lengthe/Wee weakelinges prove, and fainte before the ende./The pore, that strive with mightie, this doth blame:/And sottes, that seeke the learned to defame."[44]

Alciato's conceit in which humans of small size stand in for powerlessness, for false ambition and for foolishness is repeated in an example from *Delights for the Ingenious, in above Fifty Select and Choice Emblems, Divine and Moral, Ancient and Modern* (1684), a late seventeenth-century emblem book compiled by "R. B." (hereafter referred to by his actual name, Nathaniel Crouch).[45] Like Jacob Cats before him (although a compiler and collector rather than a distinguished poet and moralist), Crouch popularized the emblem for the ordinary reader, uniting entertainment with usefulness.[46] Crouch was an inveterate borrower of material (in his histories) and method. By the latter point about "method" I mean that Crouch adopted the fortune-telling game made popular by George Wither in his *A Collection of Emblemes* (1635). Crouch, like Wither before him, created a kind of toy book out of *Delights for the Ingenious* through a paper volvelle (or wheel) and pointer attached by string to the back of the book. Upon the wheel 56 equal partitions are drawn, like slivers, and each "piece of the pie" is given a number, from one to 56. Players take turns spinning the pointer and determining which number it lands upon and then reading the corresponding emblem out loud to the other participants, making special note of the moral as something that the reciting player needs to hear in particular. Thus, the lottery leavens the serious aspect of the emblem form without dispensing with the moralizing aspect entirely by creating a game out of discovering an emblem (and lesson) meant for each player.

In his introductory poem to the reader, Crouch anticipates and deflects any criticism that might be launched against his work for bringing a game of chance together with the serious work of the emblem.[47] He asserts, "This Game occasions not the frequent crime/Of swearing, or misspending our time,/Nor loss of money, for the Play is short,/And every Gamester winneth by the sport . . . ."[48] Following Wither, a few of the emblems are labeled "M" beneath the lottery number and after the text. This indicates that the emblem is suited for men only, and if a woman lands on this number she must take another turn.

One such "masculine" emblem is VIII, the dwarf emblem (see Plate 11). In this emblem, the dwarf figure pictured is not proportionate, but a big-headed and small-limbed little man. In this way, the character is unlike the perfectly formed Jeffrey Hudson. Although I am hazarding a guess here, I find it likely that Hudson was a figure known to Crouch, a successful bookseller and historian whose inexpensive, easy-to-read books about the monarchy, past and present, contained as many facts as possible to divert the common reader. The illustration certainly references the styles of fifty years before the publication of *Delights for the Ingenious*, as the dwarf pictured is a perfect Caroline courtier, complete with doublet, breeches, plumed hat, and van Dyck beard (although his large ruff harks back to a slightly earlier age). Other important elements of the picture include the twisted limbs of the dwarf, suggesting deformity, a bird in flight over his shoulder, and the large oval mirror in front of which the character stands, on stilts. In other ways, too, the emblem, through its motto and poem, calls to mind the messages about size and self that Jeffrey Hudson's tiny body next to the royal and beastly (especially the monkey) elicited in both the paintings and poetry discussed above. The motto, "Quid si sic?" asks "What if you wish so"? And the couplet, condensing the message of the whole, reads, "Though he endeavor all he can,/An Ape will never be a man."[49] Here we have dwarf and monkey brought together again and set apart from the human. The opening of the poem reinforces the idea of the futility and ignominiousness of men who attempt to "look big" and be more than they are: "What though an *Apish-Pigmy* in attire,/His Dwarfish Body *Gyant-like* array?/Turn *Brave*, & get him *Stilts* to seem the higher?/What would so doing handsome him, I pray?/Now surely such a Mimick sight as that,/Would with excessive laughter move your Spleen,/Till you had made the little *Dandiprat*/To lye within some Auger-hole unseen."[50] The poem concludes by invoking the laughter and scorn such figures cloaked in both fine clothes and pretense to virtue must call forth: "For when to gross *Unworthiness*, Men add/Those dues which to the *Truest-worth* pertain;/Tis like an Ape, in *Human Vestments* clad,/Which when most fine, deserveth most disdain:/And more Absurd, those Men appear to me,/Then this *Fantastick Monkey* seems to thee."[51] In other words, the dwarf figure is used once again to signify, in visual and textual fashion, the tragicomic mode of helpless and hapless striving to become more than one's birth (and body) allows.

The bird in flight offers another clue to this emblem concerning the negative consequences due to those who indulge in overweening ambition. The eagle is a key avian symbol that recurs in emblem books throughout the centuries. In two additional emblems from *Delights of the Ingenious* the bird pictured is identified as an eagle. Reminding us of the eagle's classical role as Zeus's messenger and good omen, Emblem XVII's eagle helps the virtuous man to heaven; and similarly, in Emblem XLIV, the eagle assists man in elevating his thoughts to God.[52] Other examples of the eagle icon, in this case for young readers, may be found in John Huddlestone Wynne's *Choice Emblems, Natural, Historical, Fabulous, Moral and Divine, for the Improvement and Pastime of Youth* (1772). In Wynne's emblem XXVIII, "on ambition," the child reader learns that "the Eagle has ever been reckoned an emblem of ambition";[53] the pictured eagle's "ambition" to move a log chained to his leg is considered sheer lunacy and a false ambition. If we take eagle symbolism in the aggregate, then, it's clear that the eagle's ambition may be either sacred or profane. To return to Crouch: the eagle on the wing in his dwarf emblem is a reminder of an ambition that is outsized and thus immoral and underscores the overall meaning of the emblem against "aping" or mimicking those one resembles but may never reach. English emblem authors and collectors such as John Bunyan in the seventeenth century; Wynne in the eighteenth century; and Richard Pigot, who translated and adapted Jacob Cats's popular early seventeenth-century Dutch emblems for Victorian readers, found the didactic emblem to be an obvious and useful format for the instruction of young readers. The title page of Wynne's *Choice Emblems* quotes lines from Goldsmith, playing, yet again, with the notion of *multum in parvo*, here in terms of the salutary effect of the miniature form of the emblem on the youthful mind: "Say, should the philosophic mind disdain/that good, which makes each humbler bosom vain?/Let school-taught pride dissemble all it can,/These *little things* are great to *little man.*"[54] Mindful of their appeal to child readers, as one might expect, "little men," that is, children, are much more plentiful as child characters in emblem books designed for young readers than they are in works for learned and adult readers. Similarly, the short stature and low status, as compared to that of adults, and the underestimation that children may face, is metaphorically alluded to in emblems that, rather than focusing on overweening pride or the powerlessness of the small, grant a greater acknowledgment of the child's abilities. For example, in the emblem of the gnat and the lion, the enormous lion is sorely troubled and blinded by the tiny stinging gnat. The moral poem concludes, "There's neither man nor brute so great/But, like the Lion pictur'd here,/May learn to rue the wrath and hate/Of that which seem'd too small to fear."[55]

In Jacob Cats's moral emblems, small size is not limited to the symbolic child; a little man/dwarf figure makes his appearance in an elegantly illustrated Victorian edition. The illustrations, by Adrian van de Venne, first accompanied the 1618 Dutch Folio edition of Cats's work. Van de Venne's illustrations may be distinguished from the general field of early modern and eighteenth-century emblem *picturae*—which tended to be simple woodcuts—through their fine detail and elaborate decorations. Indeed, van de Venne's illustrations of Cats's work are said to have influenced Joshua Reynolds who, when learning the art of drawing as a child, studiously copied them.[56]

The "dwarf" emblem actually features two hunchbacks, but the illustration and verse make clear that they are, in fact, coded as dwarfs (see Plate 12). In this emblem, the reader is exhorted to recognize and resist a negative aspect of human nature: we see others' faults much more easily than our own. This ugly truth is metaphorized literally as the hump upon the figures' backs: "the hunchback sees not his own hump, but he sees his neighbour's."[57] Interestingly, although both figures are squat and disfigured by their humps, this is where the congruence between the two ends. The mocking man's plain dress, hat, short sword and missing teeth signal a lower status compared to his elegantly dressed "neighbor." Not only is his hump smaller than his aggressor's, but the smiling, strolling man sports the slashed doublet, long sword, cloak and plumed hat of nobility. The reader's attention is brought to bear upon the grimacing, pointing man: "Yet he himself; the Jeerer, what is he?—?/A crooked Dwarf, mis-shap'd from head to toe."[58] While the similarly aristocratically dressed dwarf figure in the 1684 *Delights for the Ingenious* is typed and "othered" as a hideous figure to be scorned for his mimicry and vanity, van de Venne's strutting nobleman dwarf (the illustration perhaps functions as a marker of a bygone age of male dress that would appear ridiculous to mid-Victorian child readers), is credited as being, in effect, "one of us." Finally, the lesson reminds youth that a person's true worth will never be revealed by externals such as clothing, shape, or size: "Look not in scorn upon thy brother's shape,/If nature chose to vary it from thine;/For though it may resemble more the Ape,/It may have Light within far more divine!"[59] Here, although the connection between the dwarf and ape remains close, quite unlike the other emblems under discussion in which the dwarf/ape plays a role, this moral asserts that appearance is a poor indicator of virtue and should not be used to judge character.

Yet, in each instance, the tiny, deformed, not-quite-human or homely figure is used symbolically to point out an imbalance in human nature or conduct. In the miniature world created by each emblem, the "ugly" behavior outgrows better nature and overwhelms it. Such imbalances—which the dwarf as both out of size (too small) and a man at the same time helps to make visual—are resolved in the didactic poem and motto which themselves offer an important (or big) lesson through a condensed visual and textual unit. The emblems that feature the dwarf figure as representing an ape, "pigmy," foolishness, pride, vanity, or un-Christian behavior rest, in part, upon oxymoron and paradox, two devices essential to the didactic symbolic pictures of the emblem tradition. Referring in particular to Achille Bocchi's *Symbolicarum Quaestionum de Universo Genere* (*Symbolic Questions*, 1555), but helpful in considering emblems through time, emblem scholar Elizabeth See Watson comments, "In the texts of the emblems . . . the most common topics involve the play of opposites: greatest/smallest, one/many, wisdom/ foolishness, war/peace, and the oxymorons of love."[60] The dwarf is the perfect symbol for the emblem form itself as his very body suggests the paradox of both man and not-man (or almost-man) at the same time and the oxymoronic meaning of *multum in parvo*, much in little.

As I have suggested through my reading of one aspect of van Dyck's *Queen Henrietta Maria and Jeffrey Hudson,* another symbolic use to which the dwarf is put both textually and, especially, visually, is indebted both to the idea of *multum in parvo* and to questioning notions of childhood. That is, the dwarf also stands as a kind of mid-point figure in the human development spectrum from child to adult. Once again, the dwarf is a figure of imbalance used to resolve the tensions that surround differences. The Puritan John Bunyan points to the conflation of size, age, and agency in his preface "to the reader" in his *A Book for Boys and Girls: Or, Country Rhimes for Children* (1686—better known as *Divine Emblems: or Temporal Things Spiritualized*, the title given to the book in the eighteenth century).[61] Bunyan acknowledges that attempts to teach children by talking down to them or treating them like adults in understanding will fail because children's interests are different from those of men and women. The "thunder-bolts" of knowledge and morality shot at children by "ministers" and others of the past miss their mark every time: "these Dwarfs they touched not."[62] Bunyan calls children "dwarfs" in a good-humored way, as a kind of joke, but I believe that a serious message about childhood underlies such usage, a message we have glimpsed in van Dyck's work and will explore in greater detail through the masterpieces of his contemporary, the celebrated Spanish court painter, Diego Velázquez.

Framing the Dwarf

I would like to introduce considerations of dwarf/child pairings in the art of Velázquez by asking how gender impacts manifestations of dwarf discourse found in the visual and literary cultures of early modern through eighteenth-century Europe. To help me in this regard, I turn to a portrait of another early modern royal figure and her dwarf, *The Infanta Isabella Clara Eugenia and Her Dwarf* (*c.* 1598–1600) by Frans Pourbus the Younger (see Plate 13).

The context surrounding the creation of the portrait as well as a number of its formal elements reminds us of van Dyck's *Queen Henrietta Maria and Jeffrey Hudson*: the portrait of Isabella Clara Eugenia, by birth an infanta of Spain and Portugal and by marriage an archduchess, whose distinguished lineage includes members of the House of Hapsburg, the French royal family, as well as the Medici, was given as a diplomatic gift to James VI of Scotland in 1603 on the occasion of his accession to the throne as James I of England.[63] Some thirty-odd years later, the official portrait *Queen Henrietta Maria and Jeffrey Hudson* was also designated as a gift (although the intended recipient is unknown today). *Archduchess Isabella Clara Eugenia* ultimately ended up in Charles I's collection of fine art. Van Dyck may well have been inspired by the composition of this painting in creating his commentary on the young Henrietta Maria—a centrally placed, imposing and elegantly dressed woman, flanked to the figure's right with a dwarf to whom she gestures, and to her left with an allegorical object signifying status. In *Henrietta Maria*'s case, this object is the crown (she was never actually crowned, but the sign of the monarchy establishes her position as queen) and in *Isabella*'s, the object is the large red chair—not a throne, but an indicator that she may sit in the presence of royalty.[64] The female subject of the painting gazes directly at the viewer, a gentle smile barely tugging at her lips. And then there is the dwarf. Unnamed, the dwarf figure is partially hidden by Archduchess Isabella's voluminous gown. She holds a tiny glove in her tiny hand and appears to clasp the back of Isabella's skirt. This gesture establishes the dwarf's physical connection to Archduchess Isabella as she, too, gazes calmly toward the viewer, unlike Jeffrey Hudson, whose anxious glance is all for his queen.

Not only does the overall triangular shape in the placement of her arms and width of the hooped skirt of the little dwarf mimic the bell-like angle of Isabella's stiff embroidered dress over the conical Spanish farthingale, but the facial features of the two females in the contours of the jaw, nose, eyes, and lips are also remarkably similar. The family resemblance is such that one might mistakenly take the dwarf to be Isabella Clara Eugenia's child—even given the slightly jarring note that a womanly face on a small body produces. It is within the depicted relationship between the sitters—large and small—that gender plays one part, I believe, in shaping the dwarf discourse represented by this portrait. There is little body, bold gesture or movement in portraits of noble women of the period. The "body" depicted is face and hands alone, unlike portraits of men in which the shape of the leg may be emphasized, or a martial stance or contemplative position. By contrast, female figures framed in official portraits are confined by the dress and deportment of gentility. This is the case for the female dwarf figure as well as for her mistress. Along with the body, conventions of female clothing also combine the two into one figure of nobility and its privilege. Gender helps to create the archduchess and dwarf as a matched set, like with like.

The connection between the two female figures, however, is not simply one of the small feminine figure mirroring the larger figure. Their relationship, I suggest, is one of "chiasmus," a term from rhetoric, taken broadly, that identifies a pattern of reversal. A famous example of literary chiasmus is Keats's phrase, "Beauty is truth, truth beauty" ("Ode to a Grecian Urn," 1819). The term "chiasmus" is named for the Greek letter chi (X); symbolically the X represents chiasmus in visual form. The power within the chiastic turn comes not only from surprise and sometimes humor, but also from the tension that holds the X, or pattern, together. Although chiasmus is typically considered a rhetorical figure, we may find chiastic relationships within other art forms, including visual art.

Chiasmus functions in this portrait in two ways: in terms of composition and narrative. To take the latter first, why might the figure of the female dwarf have been necessary to tell the story of the Archduchess for a royal audience? As suggested earlier, the presence of exotics including dwarfs in aristocratic house-holds was a convention of early modern Europe, demonstrating cosmopolitanism and status. However, other elements might have performed the same role in denoting Isabella's character and interests in Pourbus the Younger's painting. The female dwarf, I suggest, provides an important foil for the archduchess, highlighting in both her similarity to her mistress and in the reversal of that similarity—held in tension within the painting— the archduchess's womanly dignity and maturity.

Compositionally, it is easy to map Xs upon the figures given that their waists appear pinched in contrast to the illusion of wide hips created by the farthingales. These visual Xs ground the figures within the painting via the exaggerated skirts and frame the faces by way of the cartwheel lace ruffs each woman wears. In addition to the structural chiasmus found in the position and shape of the figures, recurring patterns of opposites and reversals may be found in the use of color, ornament, and size. For example, the archduchess is dressed in white overlaid with rich embroi-dery, including the fleur-de-lis, denoting French royalty (on her mother's side), while the dwarf is in black and her dress is decorated with bands of simple chevron design. Interestingly, the patterns of the fleur-de-lis symbols and the chevrons are both right-side-up and inverted in the cloth. The reversal of dark and light coloration may be glimpsed in each woman's complexion: the dwarf's glowing white skin stands in contrast to Isabella's darker complexion. (Better reproductions of the painting in color make Isabella's olive skin tone evident, an aspect of her appearance that had at times been remarked upon by her contemporaries). Size reversal is centered within the figure of the dwarf whose childlike size belies her woman's age. The patterns of reversal and opposition found in these differences in coloration, ornamentation, and size are highlighted in the objects centered in each woman's chest—cross and rosette—the location of the central joint of the Xs we may imagine mapped upon the figures. That is, the cross, a devotional piece worn by the Catholic Isabella Clara Eugenia as a sign of faith and concern with the next life contrasts with the flower—an element of the natural world—worn on the breast of the dwarf. The earthly and ephemeral status of the plucked flower contrasts with the enduring and stable symbol of everlasting life. The dwarf's "crown" of flowers, a feminine ornament of childhood, may be compared with the archduchess's elaborate bejeweled tiara, a sign of the continuity and gravitas of royal dynasty. Ultimately, in the painting *Archduchess Isabella Clara Eugenia and Her Dwarf*, no matter the age of the dwarf handmaid, the chiastic relationship between the two figures positions the female dwarf figure as an antithesis of the archduchess. While they share a gender, the significant difference in size, coloration, and ornamentation between the figures confines or frames the dwarf within the sphere (or crisscross) of "childhood," a childhood she will not outgrow due to her subordinate status, stature, and gender, thus emphasizing the womanly nature and maturity of the female aristocrat who is the subject of the painting.

An earlier portrait of Isabella Clara Eugenia and a dwarf, this one by court painter Alonzo Sánchez Coello, favorite of Philip II,

The Infanta Isabella Clara Eugenia and Magdalena Ruiz (1585–1588), helps me to make a more general point about age and dwarf discourse and to serve as a transition to a discussion of the dwarf subject in the royal portraits of Diego Velázquez (see Plate 14). While there is much to say about this painting, I will focus on the dwarf figure who, unlike any of the other dwarf portraits or emblems under discussion, is elderly and stands to the left of the painting's subject (on the viewer's right). The noblewoman, in a now familiar gesture, puts out a firm hand in benevolence or even blessing, while gazing directly at the viewer. Our friend the monkey makes another appearance, this time in the arms of the aged servant. Contrasting colors, headwear, and size once again emphasize the difference between the imposing figure and the female dwarf whose age reminds the viewer of the conclusion of life and end of beauty as well as stressing the vitality of the haughty infanta. Into old age Isabella Clara Eugenia will surely go, yet this portrait seems to suggest at the same time—by way of the dwarf as "other" (here in terms of age, size and in relation to the quasi-human monkeys which she cradles)—the heights of majesty the aristocracy could both attain and sustain.

Isabella Clara Eugenia was a member of the House of Hapsburg, the dynastic European family whose power, wealth, and influence—primarily consolidated through intermarriage (marriages between first cousins and uncles–nieces was common)—was used to "defend" Christianity from Islam and Catholicism from Protestantism in kingdoms across the Continent, including Austria, Hungary, Bohemia, Spain, Portugal and the Holy Roman Empire. The house was split into two major lines, Hapsburg Spain (the senior line) and Hapsburg Austria (the junior line). In 1623, Philip IV, King of Spain and Portugal and Ruler of the Spanish Netherlands, the son of Philip III and his wife, Margaret of Austria (also of the House of Hapsburg), invited the young painter Diego Velázquez to enter his household and serve as court painter. Velázquez would be associated with the Hapsburgs, documenting the king, the royal family, other important courtiers, and Spanish court life in general, for the rest of his career. Svetlana Alpers maintains that Velázquez's position as a courtier cannot be separated from his role as the primary painter for the king: "His performance as an artist was that of a courtier. His painting was a merging of the two roles."[65] Indeed, Velázquez ultimately became very close to the king and was named to a succession of important offices that integrated him fully into the inner circle of courtiers surrounding the monarch, culminating with his appointment as Chamberlain of the Royal Palace. In the year before his death he was invested with the Order of Santiago (a Christian military-religious order of knights), an honorary knighthood and elevation of his social status that he had long coveted.

Europe's greatest Baroque painters, of which Velázquez is surely one, of course, are made, not born, trained through apprenticeship and travel. Like van Dyck, and many other painters, Velázquez was influenced by the celebrated master Peter Paul Rubens. They met in 1628 or 1629 when Rubens visited the Spanish court on a diplomatic mission. An admirer of Caravaggio, Velázquez had never been to Italy and that lack in his education needed addressing. Thus, upon the advice of Rubens and with royal permission, in 1630 he traveled to Italy to study the great masters. Soon afterward, Velázquez returned and established his unique style of color, brushwork, and naturalism for the glory of the Spanish court. Velázquez is credited with having a very sensitive brush and an abiding interest in telling the stories of the various courtiers who sat before him. As Alpers remarks, "He paints the royal dwarfs with the same interest as he paints the king."[66] Part of Velázquez's job, in the tradition of court painters across the European courts throughout the sixteenth and seventeenth centuries, was to immortalize the children of the reigning king and queen, in particular the heir apparent. The impetus driving the remarkable proliferation of these royal portraits, as we have seen in the case of van Dyck and the children of Charles I and Henrietta Maria, was the need to provide visual assertions of the health and future of the monarchy. Accordingly, early in his career at court, one of Velázquez's primary employments was to paint the very young heir to the throne, Prince Baltasar Carlos, in the context of dynastic succession.

A good example of such a painting may be found in *Prince Baltasar Carlos in the Riding School* (*c.* 1639–1640) (see Plate 15). In this layered composition, figures appear in the middle ground while the background is dominated by one of the imposing towers that formed part of the Buen Retiro palace, Philip IV's suburban Madrid "pleasant retreat" set amidst an enormous garden park.[67] There is no mistaking the subject of the painting, however; the ten-year-old Prince Baltasar Carlos sits his mount with supreme confidence, gazing directly at the viewer. The horse and rider fill the entire lower left-hand quadrant of the painting. Their great size miniaturizes the adult men, including the Master of the Hunt and the Count Duke of Olivares, powerful advisor to the king, behind him and to his left. Philip IV and his first wife, Isabella of Bourbon, are mere miniatures in the background, standing with others on a balcony and watching their son ride. Baltasar Carlos is depicted as a skilled rider able to perform the classical dressage movement known as "levade" in which the horse balances briefly on its hind legs, its front legs raised to a 30–35 degree angle.[68] Dressage airs such as levade and pesade developed from military training exercises and the fact that the young prince is shown engaging in such feats of horsemanship helps to affirm his fitness for a future role as king and commander. Indeed, Baltasar Carlos appears as solid as the tower of the Buen Retiro itself. The heir apparent and the monarch's palace combine into one symbol of enduring power and prestige. Baltasar Carlos's mastery over his horse, his Hapsburg ancestry clearly shown in his facial features, mirrors the political control the ruling family enjoys and seeks to sustain. The painting communicates a direct message: Prince Baltasar Carlos is invested with the confidence of his father and the hope of the nations he will rule and, though still a child, he is ready to rise to the greatness that should be his destiny, given his birth.[69]

As we have seen in other European court paintings from the Baroque period, the figure of the dwarf often accompanies such allegories of present or future "greatness." *Prince Baltasar Carlos in the Riding School* is no exception and provides my first example of child-and-dwarf in Velázquez's portraiture. Tucked behind the rearing horse but on the same plane as the men who serve the king and his heir (Olivares, the Master of the Hunt, and the prince's valet) stands the dwarf, often identified as Sebastián de Morra.[70] The presence of the dwarf is curious. This figure is in shadow and wedged between the luxurious sweep of the horse's magnificent tail on one side and the frame of the painting on the other. Why paint the dwarf into such a tight spot on the canvas, creating what appears to be an awkward pictorial afterthought?

Before I attempt to address this question, other puzzles worth consideration surface in this painting. Both Baltasar Carlos and Morra, if the figure is indeed Sebastián de Morra, face the viewer—like Olivares on the opposite side of the painting—and all three of these figures wear inscrutable expressions. What might each party be thinking? A wide gulf separates the prime minister and the prince, and an even greater distance exists between the prince and his parents, who gather on a different plane altogether. Size and scale juxtapositions in which the most powerful body in the image—the king—is among the very smallest and the child by far the largest figure, create a kind of destabilizing oscillation between big and small and, more importantly, adult king and child prince.[71] Who is masterful here? While Alpers reminds us, quite rightly I believe, as the later dwarf portraits demonstrate, "A resistance to social distinctions seems part of [Velázquez's] way of painting," the court dwarf seems to owe his forced presence not simply to verisimilitude (Checa argues that this painting does not refer to a specific moment in time) or to convention.[72] Rather, the dwarf performs necessary work in helping to establish what size and age mean in the heated context of the Spanish court and its anxieties about succession. Once again, the figure that mediates between a body in transition and its aspiration or inevitable status—in this case, between the king who is and the child who is destined to replace him (rather than between monarch and monkey or between beauty and old age)—is the dwarf. In this painting, dwarf and child unite through composition and brushstroke. For example, dwarf and child are connected through the color red via the red band around the dwarf's hat and his red sleeves and the crown prince's light red sash. More significantly, the dwarf figure blends with the horse itself. Although the dwarf is not actually standing right behind the horse, the perspective suggests that the dwarf and the horse/ rider form one chimerical being. We have seen this combination of animal, child, dwarf—in different iterations—in van Dyck's portraits of Jeffrey Hudson and in emblems for young readers. In each case arguments about becoming or embodying an ideal are made—whether that ideal is to grow into adulthood, into reason, humanity or majesty—and require the interplay of age, size, and difference. In order to be crowned king, Prince Baltasar Carlos must simply outlive his father. However, in order to become fully regal he must assume mastery over both horse and dwarf, certainly, and he must also internalize the "difference" that the dwarf represents in this context (social inferiority, obligation, insignificance) and become "large," both physically and politically. The king worked very hard on this last point, raising his son's stature by increasing his future dominions: while a teenager, Baltasar Carlos was made prince of the kingdoms of Aragón, Gerona, Valencia, and Navarre.

Yet, the glory for Baltasar Carlos, for the Hapsburg dynasty, promised by this painting, failed to materialize. Prince Baltasar Carlos died of smallpox in October 1646, just before his seventeenth birthday. The death of Philip IV's only son and heir destroyed the hopes for the succession. Given his wife's death a few years earlier, and the loss of the crown prince, the king would be forced to marry quickly in an attempt to secure a new male heir.[73] While history shifts at this point away from Baltasar Carlos, our interest in him remains. Baltasar Carlos's intertwined history with the figure of the dwarf does not conclude with this Velázquez painting or with his death. Both the early *Don Baltasar Carlos with a Dwarf* (1632) and Velázquez's most celebrated painting, *Las Meninas* (1656), play crucial roles in the articulation of what I have called dwarf discourse.

To take the portrait of Baltasar Carlos as a toddler first: certainly great joy attended his birth in October 1629 (see Plate 16). The heir to the throne was celebrated in a ceremony held on March 7, 1632 in which the nobles of Castile swore allegiance to the nearly two-year-old. *Don Baltasar Carlos with a Dwarf* was painted in commemoration of that event.[74] This canvas is the first of Velázquez's dwarf paintings and, as such, offers a unique view of the value and depth of interest that Velázquez and the royal family invested in their court dwarfs. Most intriguing for me is the fact that this official portrait of dynastic succession includes a dwarf figure as a competing subject with the royal child.

In many ways this is a very conventional portrait of royalty. The prince is framed by opulent drapery; to his left a plumed hat of the kind the king wears rests on a plush tasseled pillow. Drapery, pillow, and patterned carpet are in shades of rich red. The prince wears an armor collar ("gorget"); general's sash, also in red; and clasps a general's baton, clear symbols of his future as king and military leader. His left hand rests on the intricate hilt of a dagger or sword hidden under his sash. His costume is elaborately embroidered in gold and his neck and wrists are encircled with delicate lace. Each accessory and every element of his dress's ornamentation draws attention to his rank and his future role. The dress itself, however, and his pink-cheeked cherubic face, round eyes, and wispy fair hair, all indicate a very young child. Rather than jarring, this clash between baby and majesty charms and invites the viewer's smile.[75]

The painting is a double portrait, and any interpretation of it must account for the additional small figure below Baltasar Carlos (the prince stands on a carpeted step). This figure is a female dwarf who fills the lower left-hand corner of the frame and who may herself be a child (her identity is unknown).[76] Her dress is dark but elegant; she wears a simple flared collar, choker beads and a white linen apron. She looks back at the prince, her eyes straining in their corners, in an expression reminiscent of the anxiety we see on Jeffrey Hudson's face as he looks at Henrietta Maria in *Queen Henrietta Maria with Jeffrey Hudson*, painted the very next year by van Dyck. The dwarf holds a jeweled rattle in one hand and an apple in the other (Jeffrey Hudson holds a pear); most commentary considers the shapes of these objects as reflecting the orb and scepter of the monarch.[77] As the female dwarf is turning her back to the prince and keeping the toys from him, it is reasonable to read the painting's message as Baltasar Carlos is not meant to play but to rule.

What other messages might this painting convey? The prince is elevated and centered; dwarf figures, when they accompany the nobility, are virtually always framed and contained by the portrait's corners.[78] Certainly, the baby prince's royalty contrasts with the dwarf's role as servant and perhaps pet or playmate. It is an attractive conceit for a child prince to associate with an older but same-sized companion. Unlike *Prince Baltasar Carlos in the Riding School* which juxtaposes large and small figures of differing levels of authority in order, in part, to question those levels of authority, the bodies in *Don Baltasar Carlos with a Dwarf* are essentially of equal height and dimension. The realization that the second figure in the painting is not another toddler but either a dwarf child or young adult (certainly the figure's chubby cheeks and plump lips—while much coarser than the fine features, delicate curls, and rosebud mouth of the prince—suggest youth) causes the viewer to pause and perhaps spend more time parsing the portrait's symbols.[79] The presence of another very young child in the portrait—a reasonable choice might have been the son of Antonia de Ipeñarrieta y Galdós, a member of Baltasar Carlos's staff, whose portrait with her son Luis was also painted by Velázquez—would have detracted from the unique status of the painting's primary subject. Given the authority granted by size, an adult, even an adult with permission to sit in the presence of royalty, might also have unbalanced the painting's statement about Baltasar Carlos's future. This portrait is an intimate portrayal of the power of potential—the future—to cloak the delicacy and vulnerability that attach to dependency and small size; to childhood, in other words. To repeat: "all" that Baltasar Carlos must do in order to become King of Spain is to survive his father. However, the likelihood of his growing out of his youth was low: Philip IV fathered twelve legitimate children by his two wives. From these twelve, only three outlived their father: Maria Theresa (the king's last child with his first wife, Elizabeth), Margarita Theresa, and Charles II (the latter two children with his second wife, Mariana).While the infant and child mortality rate in seventeenth-century Spain, along with the rest of Europe, was no doubt high, generations of Hapsburg inbreeding certainly weakened the offspring of Philip IV. At the time of the portrait's creation, all four of Baltasar Carlos's siblings had predeceased him. By tempering the anxieties of this world in the absent presence of the Castilian noblemen and the king himself, it is the dwarf, in this context of the toddler prince receiving homage from his most highly placed subjects, who fills the frame of the situation appropriately. The portrait ignores the past and declares its truth: the prince will grow up to wield the general's baton and sword in defense of Spain. Don Baltasar Carlos with a Dwarf enlists the dwarf's help as a contrastive "shadow" of childhood, and makes a strong statement in support of Baltasar Carlos's destiny, particularly in the face of the great odds against his success.

Hopes are not so much expressed as aggressively asserted in this portrait, and knowing that they come to naught makes looking at Don Baltasar Carlos with a Dwarf rather poignant. By contrast, Diego Velázquez's Las Meninas (1656; "The Maids of Honor"), celebrated for its ambition, intricacy, and mystery, explores the royal family from a primarily domestic, rather than dynastic, perspective—although the former heir to the throne lingers even here, in the anxiety over the collapsing Spanish court (see Plate 17).

Looking at Las Meninas is an altogether more dizzying prospect than looking at the stiffer and more formal Don Baltasar Carlos with a Dwarf. The enormous canvas is crammed with people, paintings, gestures, reflections, an animal, an artist. For all of the crowded foreground and middle ground, however, the painting also communicates a sense of expansiveness: much of it depicts the empty air above the figures' heads. This visual record of Philip IV's family is so well known that it is almost silly to describe it, but here goes: in the immediate left-hand foreground stands an enormous stretched canvas that reaches nearly to the ceiling of a spacious and deep room in the Alcazar Palace, with paintings lining the walls. In the opposite foreground a large dog lies resting. The five-year-old Infanta Margarita Theresa stands in the center of the middle ground, her white-blonde hair and dress shine; she is attended by two young maids of honor who kneel and bend toward her. Two dwarfs surround the dog and the young male dwarf kicks or caresses the oblivious pet. Velázquez himself has stepped back from his painting and considers the subject of his painting or perhaps the viewer, while two adult attendants converse behind the grouping of children. In the background, one of Philip IV's chamberlains exits the room and in a framed mirror on the far wall behind the assembled party we see the reflection of the king and queen.

What makes this painting so special? The king valued the painting and its artist so much that he had the cross of the Order of Santiago painted on Velázquez's breast after his death in August 1660. (Velázquez had earned this position, with some effort, in late 1659.) The painting was praised by contemporary artists and art historians—Luca Giordano's oft-repeated remark that the canvas represents the "theology of painting" may stand in for all early appreciations of the work. Today, Las Meninas enjoys a reputation as one of the most important paintings of all time.

There's certainly much to talk about. The first puzzle, of course, is the subject of the enormous painting behind which Velázquez stands. Is it the Infanta? The king and queen? The very painting that becomes Las Meninas? Checa considers the masterpiece to be a painting in defense of painting, an argument addressed to the king: that he should support the importance of the office of the painter and his work.[80] Critics also discuss the conversation between the mythological paintings hanging on the walls of the Alcazar Palace and the subjects of *Las Meninas* (in life, these were themselves copies after Rubens and other Flemish painters by Juan Bautista del Mazo, Velázquez's son-in-law and assistant). Then there is the importance of the self-portrait, the issue of dynastic succession once again, the "modern" techniques of broad brushstrokes and sharp accent strokes, among other topics.[81] Whether we consider individual aspects of its artistry or the painting as a whole, the work never fails to fascinate. López-Rey sums up the painting's power well: "There is in *The royal family* a starry interplay of ambivalences, with one slant spanning the gulf between the realm of painting and the realm of reality, another underscoring both the Infanta's regal bearing and her childish charm, a third offering a luminous view of Philip's forlorn Court, and yet another making vivid at one and the same time the compass of Velázquez's world—his circumstance—and the might of his brushstroke."[82]

Amidst these "ambivalences" and conundrums live the dwarfs. Certainly, *Las Meninas* is also a painting about the court dwarf and his/her relationship with childhood. The tragic youth Baltasar Carlos, in whose former rooms the painting is set, haunts *Las Meninas* through his conspicuous absence that has, in fact, instigated the reconfiguration of the royal family on display in the painting. The meanings of dwarf/child are also inverted here: the baby's contrived performance of masculine power and great ambition played against his dwarf's tiny stature and toys in *Don Baltasar Carlos with a Dwarf* is replaced in *Las Meninas* by his half-sister's seemingly unselfconscious embodiment of "natural" childhood and femininity attended by other delicate and/or small beings—young handmaids and dwarfs.

There is nothing particularly surprising about the inclusion of the dwarfs Maribárbola and Nicolasito (the playful Nicolas Pertusato) in this portrait of the royal family and court life—as we have seen, Velázquez regularly painted dwarf figures in groups as well as solo subjects. See, for example, the portrait of Francisco Lezcano, intended as decoration, along with other dwarf portraits, for the rehabilitated and refurbished hunting lodge, Torre de la Parada. In her study of images of childhood in art, Erika Langmuir finds only stark differences in this relationship—not only in *Las Meninas* but also in *Don Baltasar Carlos with a Dwarf* and in Baroque court dwarf paintings as a genre: "When we strip away all the bustling incidentals, we find once more, as in the *juramento* portrait of little Baltasar Carlos, the traditional Spanish duo of prince and dwarf, the ideal and its malformed counterpart."[83] Lara R. Bass, too, reads the child and dwarf as essentially foils for each other: "In the case of *Las Meninas*, it is not so much size that is contrasted as beauty—Maribárbola is the imperfect twin of the infanta at the center."[84] Is the contrastive relationship between royal child and dwarf servant the only way to read their association or that between dwarf and nobility more generally? Certainly, stark juxtapositions of size, gender, status, and authority, as this chapter has demonstrated, populate seventeenth-century portraits of aristocrats and dwarfs. However, assessing these comparisons as simply glorifying the noble and denigrating the dwarf reduces the pairings, or groupings, in the case of *Las Meninas*, to just one note and ignores the complexities of the dwarf figure and of court life. In this reading, the viewer, too, is channeled to only one way of looking at the dwarf, at childhood, and size, one in which "normality" is made to disavow difference—as if there was anything "normal" or typical about any royal family or monarchy.

Maribárbola's gaze is one of the puzzles that has intrigued art historians and admirers of the painting alike. While Velázquez, the infanta and the chamberlain all look forward, Maribárbola's gaze is projected outward, direct and unwavering, undisturbed by any object or person attracting her attention (as the canvas in front of him would engage Velázquez who is pictured in the act of painting, or as the vessel of water offered to Margarita Theresa would distract the princess). Maribárbola is not painting, kicking, attending, conversing, or exiting. She just stands and looks. This quietude links the dwarf figure with the reflected king and queen and infanta who similarly present stillness. If we are drawn to interpret this triumvirate symbolically—as the painting encourages—and perhaps playfully, then taken together the three (if we consider the royal couple as one figure) may be considered to function emblematically. These are the figures in the painting that engage most directly with the viewer or that represent the viewer—in the case of the king and queen, who stand outside the canvas and presumably look in. Like the emblem, the paradoxical *Las Meninas* requires the participation of the reader/viewer in order for meaning to be made. Indeed, Alpers defines *Las Meninas*, in contrast to most court paintings, as "a viewer's picture" with "direct address to the viewer."[85] The painting's theatricality also links it to the emblem tradition. Karen Pinkus calls the emblem "a play acted out briefly on a two-dimensional stage, often by a player in costume."[86] Certainly, *Las Meninas* is a piece of theater, encompassing both domestic and dynastic drama within its frame.[87]

So far, so emblematic, but what about the defining characteristic of the emblem, its three-part structure of picture–motto–poem? The infanta must be the picture (the central image of the painting and the figure drawing together the concerns of both motto and poem); the king and queen, the motto (offering a condensed yet broadly applied message to the picture); and the dwarf Maribárbola, the poem (elaborating the picture and motto). The infanta represents the perfect embodiment of childish feminine beauty and its promise of future fecundity. She is pink and white and gold and holds the hopes of the Hapsburgs in her elegant farthingale's skirts. The motto, represented by the king and queen, could be read as something like "the righteousness and regality of the dynasty resides in this living expression of love." And Maribárbola? She explains *and* complicates, in her small woman's body and through her cool shared gaze with the viewer, the motto and picture. Certainly, as the infanta's physical double, Maribárbola's heavy features, shadowed complexion, and dark, plain dress contrast unfavorably with the light, bright jewel of the princess. This juxtaposition supports the claim by the picture and motto that the infanta is unlike all others and embodies the appropriate vessel for the continuation of the monarchy. In this way, Maribárbola explains the picture and motto through the extreme difference her dwarf body expresses. However, the poem "continues" through her direct address to the viewer, troubling the notion that "ugliness" is her only characteristic. As I have suggested above, the dwarf typically performs two actions at once, as *multum in parvo* makes clear. Her counter-narrative is that the way into the painting, into the dramatic setting that is the Spanish court, indeed, into the future is through the dwarf who ultimately erases differences of size and status through her individuality and clear-eyed knowledge of the family. Maribárbola, too, holds the entire history of the royal family in her intimate, knowing gaze and adds to the emblem by asking the viewer, "What do you think of the painting's message?"

Certainly I understand that this reading is a bit perverse as there are no words in the painting and the textual reading must be inferred. Yet it's the "starry interplay of ambivalences," as López-Rey so aptly puts it that encapsulates the discursive and enduring powers of *Las Meninas*. Typically, the emblem author, the "voice" behind the emblem's "truth," allows the picture–motto–poem to speak the moral while he or she remains hidden. In this case, Velázquez is the "author" of the emblem and of the painting. It is his vision of the royal family, of childhood and of the people who make up the Spanish court that is communicated here and he asserts his authorship through the performative self-portrait, showing the artist at work creating art. Words, pictures, performances, as we have seen, unite in the emblem, this painting, and in dwarf discourse more generally.

Chapter 3

STAGING THE DWARF

Still harping on dwarfs? Well, yes: the capacious dwarf offers many insights into the negotiations of big and small and the meanings of each—so much so that there is more to say about the dwarf figure in the context of performance, in particular. The performative dwarf provides a crucial insight into the cultural constructions of the dwarf figure more generally and one that follows naturally from my discussion of visual and verbal aesthetics of dwarf discourse. Dwarfs and children—real and imagined—emblems, Baroque old master portraits, all gather within the frames of performativity. Although chapter two considers in depth the actual circumstances of one famous dwarf from the past, Jeffrey Hudson, as well as the myths and mysteries that surround him, my primary interest there was in exploring representations of the dwarf figure. In this chapter, my focus shifts to related topics. That is, suggesting a way of experiencing the history of dwarfs in performance, the essential theatricality of dwarfs in the more recent past, and the importance of performance in children's literature that features dwarf characters, all provide a way of understanding how the small body is made to perform ideas about celebrity, freakery, and identity, among others.

Thus far my discussion of the dwarf figure has resided primarily in early modern Europe and within the royal court, and in the aesthetic realms of emblem and painting. My further exploration of dwarf discourse will continue with the ideas already on the table and expand to enter the nineteenth through twenty-first centuries in the theatrical context provided by the American dime museum; circus and television programming; as well as in children's literature, a genre in which dwarf characters often appear in performance spaces. My first particular concern will be with the celebrity dwarf, a figure anticipated both in the history of Jeffrey Hudson and in Velázquez's dwarf portraits. López-Rey reminds us that Velázquez's treatment of the dwarf in his portraits resisted reducing them to jokes or ideals: "Velázquez's approach to the clowning of dwarfs and jesters was, indeed, stoic; the pictorial stresses which he masterfully used in portraying them emphasize the sitters' human nature, cloddish, enduring, individual."[1] The individuality and singularity of a performing dwarf from the nineteenth century such as General Tom Thumb was a key aspect of his celebrity.

Although the performing dwarf was particularly prevalent in the nineteenth century and earlier, the recent past and present moment similarly construct the dwarf figure as theatrical. What makes the dwarf body "performative"? That is, why is theatricality or performativity inscribed onto the dwarf body at all? In his history of the American freak show and of the relationship between disability studies and "freakery," Michael M. Chemers invokes Goffman's theory of stigma as "spoiled identity" and argues that the response of the stigmatized to ostracism or discrimination is performative in nature.[2] The freak show is one form of social interaction that forces a confrontation between "normates" and those stigmatized due to disability.[3] Disabilities studies scholar Jim Ferris notes, "Through the staging of stigma, freakery focuses our attention on certain assumptions about the human body that we usually take for granted; so profoundly do we take them for granted that we usually don't even know they exist!"[4] This focus links closely to curiosity and to entertainment. While the freak show's golden age is long past, we continue to ask those we name as "others"—including dwarfs, who enact a host of identities—to perform on various stages, including film and television. Well-known examples of scenes featuring dwarf actors from popular culture include Munchkinland in the MGM technicolor fantasy *The Wizard of Oz* (1939) and the opening sequence of the long-running ABC television series *Fantasy Island* (1978–1984) in which the character played by Hervé Villechaize embodied the "mini-me" fashion of a small man juxtaposed with a similarly dressed big man.[5] More recently, the Home Box Office (HBO) television series (2010–present) based on George R. R. Martin's *Game of Thrones* novels features Peter Dinklage as Tyrion Lannister, a main character in the fantasy adventure.

In the elite world of the court, displayed for a coterie audience, the dwarf could be figured as *memento mori*, child, pet, or jester. The gulf between the court dwarf's low status and the lofty nature of the monarchy or aristocracy that his small size or disproportion suggests is often exploited in pictorial representations of the relationship between "high" and "low" even as the dwarf pictured assumes a place beside nobility or royalty. By contrast, in the vulgar world of popular entertainment—staged for "the people"—similarities are often emphasized between the dwarf's body—particularly when proportionate—and, importantly, his desires, and the bodies and desires of his audience. In children's literature featuring a dwarf character, readers are invited to share or inhabit the dwarf perspective, the dwarf's way of knowing. In these works, too, as we shall see, the dwarf character is linked with performativity over and over again.

Inheritors of Jeffrey Hudson and the dwarfs of van Dyck and Velázquez, the nineteenth-century American performing dwarfs such as Charles Stratton and Lavinia Warren became internationally known personalities whose reputations spread far beyond rarefied European courts and palace hallways, although they were known there, too. Just a little boy when he was first put on display, "General Tom Thumb," as Stratton was called as a tip of the hat to the popular folktale thumbling, like Crown Prince Baltasar Carlos with his sword and baton, was burdened with the trappings of adulthood while very young. Brought from the sideshow to center stage, Stratton's performances as a miniature man reflect a particular construction of size indebted to curiosity about difference as well as a celebration of *same* that result in the creation of the celebrity dwarf. In the parlance of freak show sociologist Robert Bogdan, Stratton performed in the "high aggrandized mode" which imbues the performer with "status-enhancing characteristics," as opposed to the "exotic mode" that emphasized the strange anomalousness of the freak.[6]

General Tom Thumb

The story of General Tom Thumb must be told in concert with the history of the most important man in his life, Phineas Taylor Barnum, the showman who made Tom Thumb both famous and wealthy. The figure of Barnum and his role as impresario forge a link between my two discussions of the dwarf in high and popular culture. Regarding dwarf discourse in the emblem tradition, as we will recall, in the tripartite emblem structure the "impresa" is the motto, drawing together the picture and poem in condensed form. The Italian word *impresa* is linked to "impresario," the word for a man who organizes public entertainments. Barnum owned that appellation, certainly, and endowed it with a certain flair to boot. As a promoter of sideshows and exhibits, one of Barnum's jobs was to craft "mottos" describing his human oddities. These advertisements were designed to tease and teach his potential audience members how to read and understand the acts he presented. For example, Tom Thumb was the "distinguished man in miniature;"[7] Joice Heth, an elderly African-American woman, was "George Washington's nurse;" the microcephalic "Zip" was a "man monkey" or (unbelievable as this seems today), a "what-is-it?"[8] The impresario distills the essence of the performer's incongruity and proclaims it through descriptors or mottos crafted to attract attention and pique curiosity.

In late 1842, the year of General Tom Thumb's "discovery," Barnum was the manager of the American Museum in New York City, the infamous entertainment palace that featured sideshow "freaks," such as giants and bearded ladies; a picture and statue gallery; a lecture hall for theatre and presentations; live animals; and displays of ingenious recent inventions and mechanics, among many other exhibits.[9] The five-story building was located at the corner of Broadway and Ann Street in the same neighborhood as the fancy Astor House hotel; City Hall; and Delmonico's, the best restaurant in the city. Banners and posters decorated the exterior of the building labeled, in enormous letters, "Barnum's American Museum." P. T. Barnum had a gift for concocting ideas that would entice visitors across the social classes to his museum—multiple times—and for relieving them of their money. As Lillian Craton notes, "science and medicine legitimated bodily spectacle" in the Victorian era. By way of his human "specimens," Barnum certainly took advantage of burgeoning interests in anthropology, Darwinian theory, and artifacts of world cultures.[10] Throughout his long career he was shameless in promoting his museum, circus, and traveling exhibits. While his American Museum brought "legitimate" educational and scientific exhibits to the masses, he also bent the truth, manipulated audiences and exploited his employees. Yet, at the same time he enabled a higher standard of living than most of the "curiosities" could have earned outside of the performance arena. This is one point that Robert Bogdan makes in his study of the freak show: "some [of the human exhibits] were exploited, it is true, but in the culture of the amusement world most human oddities were accepted as showmen."[11] Barnum became as famous as the acts he promoted and many associated him with the idea of the museum itself.[12] Barnum also possessed great charm, wit, and resilience—all of which came in handy as he experienced dramatic ups and downs over the course of his lifetime.

Barnum was forever on the lookout for new specimens and exhibits. In November, 1842, while visiting his brother in

Bridgeport, Connecticut, Barnum was introduced to Charles Sherwood Stratton, a child who had been born a large infant but who had stopped growing after five months. He stood only 25 inches high and weighed a mere 15 pounds (see Plate 18).

The blond-haired boy was healthy, smart, and handsome, proportionate in every way. Barnum was both charmed and intrigued by the commercial possibilities presented by this miniature literally dropped into his lap. Although he had some concerns that young Stratton would begin growing, Barnum was certain that the dwarf would draw paying customers. Barnum convinced Charlie's parents to allow him to train the child and to exhibit him at the American Museum for a four-week period, proposing three dollars per week as payment.[13] The humbug commenced immediately, as Barnum changed Charlie's name, age and nationality in order to emphasize his tiny size (a two-foot-tall eleven-year-old seemed more unusual than a tiny almost-five-year-old), foreignness, and to whip up greater excitement about the coming rare attraction: "P. T. Barnum of the American Museum, Broadway at Ann Street, is proud to announce that he has imported from London to add to his collection of extraordinary curiosities from all over the world, the rarest, the tiniest, the most diminutive dwarf imaginable—TOM THUMB, ELEVEN YEARS OLD AND ONLY TWENTY-FIVE INCHES HIGH, JUST ARRIVED FROM ENGLAND!!!"[14] Barnum added the honorific "General" to Tom Thumb's name and Charlie Stratton was no more. His original four-week run was extended again and again until "Barnum" and "Tom Thumb" became virtually conjoined.

Over the next three decades, General Tom Thumb was a star attraction both at home and abroad as a representative of Barnum's American Museum and later the traveling Barnum and London Circus. Within the first weeks of making the dwarf's acquaintance, Barnum was delighted to learn that Stratton could sing in a high treble. His rendition of "Yankee Doodle Dandy" would become a perennial favorite with audiences around the world, functioning as a kind of theme song for the diminutive

American. His early act included skits, songs, living tableaux (posing as Ajax, Cincinnatus, Hercules, and Samson) and dialogues with the master of ceremonies. The child worked extremely hard, starring in two performances a day—at 3 p.m. and 7 p.m.—and in between he could be found in the Hall of Living Curiosities with the giants, armless man, a 350-pound fat boy, jugglers, and fire eaters.[15] This hard work was rewarded with an adoration that other "freaks" did not receive.[16] Indeed, Lehman comments in his 2013 biography of Stratton that "he may have been America's first international celebrity."[17] Stratton's shows were so popular in New York and other Eastern seaboard cities that in April 1843 Barnum was able to buy the American Museum at last and to plan for ways to garner new audiences for his celebrity dwarf. The natural next step was to take General Tom Thumb back to the place of his birth, as Barnum's advertisements had named it, that is, back to the Old World. On January 18, 1844, the six-year-old child sailed to England with Barnum and his parents, ready to dazzle the European nobility with his songs, witty repartee, and impersonations.

Once in England Stratton's Yankee heritage was restored (again to emphasize his novelty). After a disappointing run in Liverpool, Barnum took Tom Thumb and his entourage to London where a series of exclusive levees heightened the desire to see the little star. For General Tom Thumb had become fashionable, delighting the nobility—as he had plebeian American viewers—with his anomalous size and entertaining ways. Eventually, to the relief of the Americans, the General was summoned to Buckingham Palace to meet Queen Victoria, fulfilling Barnum's boast and the putative purpose of the trip. As Barnum notes in his autobiography, after visiting the Royal Family, Tom Thumb became even more popular with all classes of people: "The British public were now fairly excited. Not to have seen General Tom Thumb was voted to be decidedly unfashionable. . . ."[18] The money continued to pour in, averaging about $500 per day while he was exhibited at the Egyptian Hall in Piccadilly.[19]

"Freaks," or "very special people," were exhibited for their abilities to generate money. Barnum, for example, charged 25 cents admission for the American Museum—children were half-price—and was a shrewd enough businessman to spend money in order to make it. In their first trip to England, Barnum made sure to house the General and his family at an exclusive address, to dress him in finery, and to court the titled and influential before taking Tom Thumb to the masses. While volume was ever a businessman's friend, "quality" was the first necessary ingredient in Barnum's recipe for financial success with General Tom Thumb. General Tom Thumb, through his status as a gentleman and as one of the elite, provides a clear example of what Bogdan calls the "aggrandized" performer.

Tom Thumb would visit Queen Victoria multiple times. While his purpose was to entertain royalty and the aristocracy and thus encourage the punters to pay to see him, he was also feted himself, and over the course of his first trip to various European countries he was inundated with costly gifts by members of the nobility and various heads of state. General Tom Thumb had become an international celebrity whose picture was often in the paper, whose likeness was made into paper dolls, snuffboxes and chocolate figures, and whose existence inspired musical compositions and theatrical entertainments (*Hop O' My Thumb*, commissioned by Barnum, was originally written for Charles Stratton).[20] Even the gifts themselves, his tiny carriage and other accessories, became famous and popular exhibits. By the time Barnum and General Tom Thumb returned to America in 1847 after three successful years abroad, the dwarf child's family was very rich and he was one of the most recognizable figures in the west. He would continue to travel the world with Barnum and without him, visiting Europe often, as well as Australia, Japan, China, India, and Egypt, until his death in 1883 at forty-five years of age.

In his performances, the actor General Tom Thumb displayed a multitude of talents and attitudes that delighted his audiences and won him many fans. He was both man and boy, serious and comic, professional and plaything. Unlike the "freaks" of the side-show, however, Tom Thumb's incongruities were never distortions. Or his particular distortions—the fact that for many years he was a very young boy and then adolescent when performing as an adult through smoking, mimicking adult heroes and villains, kissing female members of the audience, etc.—were pleasing rather than frightening.[21] Certainly, as adver-tisements to his entertainments proclaimed, key to Tom Thumb's success was that he was "perfectly symmetrical in all his propor-tions, and graceful beyond belief."[22] As Burke foretold, General Tom Thumb's miniature perfection reassured audiences rather than alarmed them and his performances elicited admiration and wonder rather than cruel stares and mocking laughter. While exceedingly small and thus different, the General was also "natural" in the way that the bearded lady, dog-faced boy or Zip (also known as the "What-Is-It?") were not, even as Tom Thumb's stylized and "civilized" character was punctuated by his elaborate and formal costumes.[23] By contrast, Zip's humanity was questioned by setting him in nature, as the Currier and Ives illus-tration demonstrates (see Plate 19).

Even the giants, with whom Tom Thumb was often exhibited in order to highlight the outsized or undersized aspects of each, suggested a more challenging oddity than did Tom Thumb. Although the giants, too, were natural—if too large—their size has no obvious corollary. By contrast, we are very familiar with tiny humans—they are called children.

As I suggested in my reading of Jeffrey Hudson in van Dyck's portraiture, the perfectly formed dwarf indexes notions of child-hood as well as the idea of *multum in parvo*. In analyzing Tom Thumb's great appeal, Neil Harris comments that he was ". . . the perfect man-child, the perpetual boy, appealing to all ages and conditions."[24] Susan Stewart calls him "the epitome of the enchanted and enchanting, the toylike child."[25] Certainly General Tom Thumb's size gestures toward childhood but his act was predicated on audiences finding that the frisson between child and man created an interesting *performance*.[26] This connection between Tom Thumb and childhood is made explicit in the description of the General as "SMALLER THAN ANY INFANT that ever walked alone!" in an 1848 advertisement from the *Brooklyn Eagle.*[27]

If Charles Stratton had been a typically sized boy when he began his association with Barnum, he would have been nothing more than talented and precocious. However, as a minute being whose every action emphasized his curious stature, Stratton's act was endearing and awe-provoking to audiences that cut across the social classes.[28] Unlike Jeffrey Hudson and other court dwarfs who moved in rarefied circles, Stratton's purpose was not only to highlight who and what he was not (a "normal" man), but also to be admired for what he was: a skilled entertainer who charmed through clever exploitations of the incongruity of his small size. In fact, General Tom Thumb didn't have to *do* anything at all to be entertaining. In 1845, within his first European tour, Barnum took General Tom Thumb to Paris where he again found a ready audience. There, the editor of the *Journal des Débats* met the young performer and encouraged his readers to attend one of Barnum's shows. The aspect of Tom Thumb's performances that this editor found to be the most impressive was artlessness. That is, the mere fact of the miniature man (just seven years old at this moment, but resembling "adulthood" in both appearance and behavior) was entertainment enough for this viewer:

> We prefer to see Tom Thumb when he appears in the character of a gentleman. He takes out his watch and tells you the hour, or offers you a pinch of snuff or a cigar, each of which are corresponding with his size. He is still better when he sits in his golden chair, crossing his legs and looking at you with a mocking air. It is then he is most amusing. He is never more inimitable than when he imitates nothing, when he is himself, for no one resembles him.[29]

Notably, the editor considers Tom Thumb to be a gentleman not in fact, but in character. Ultimately, the tiny General's feats of strength, boasts, and impersonations of heroes of old—Hercules, etc.—revealed him to be a punning marvel of domesticated and emasculated "manhood." To give just one representative example of what I mean: during his first London season, in an hour's entertainment for the Baroness Rothschild, wife of the head of the powerful banking firm, Tom Thumb's opening remarks played on the mismatch between his size and his sense of importance: " 'I am only a *Thumb*, but a good *hand* in a *general* way at amusing you, for though a *mite* I am *mighty* and against all rivals can bear off the palm' " (etc.)[30] Tom Thumb's bluster coupled with his littleness calls to mind the humorous and endearing qualities of a child imitating his elders through costume and/or speech acts. In General Tom Thumb Barnum created a performance featuring a young dwarf designed both to highlight the charming childlikeness in the performer and to appeal to his female audience. In his dwarf performers Barnum self-consciously solicited the maternal affection and protective instinct for small bodies and appreciation of their cute appearance. As Lori Merish notes, "In the performances of these diminutive prodigies, the cute emerged as a site for feminine identification as well as a strategy for domesticating (the) Otherness (of 'freak,' of child), annexing the Other to the Self."[31] In other words, Tom Thumb was allied and aligned with the feminine and the innocently childlike (in the Victorian era, the child was particularly typed as feminine). For those who cooed and applauded General Tom Thumb, he was primarily a figure of impotence, cute and clever, but only approximating a "real" man.

These observations about Tom Thumb as a dwarf and as a curiosity are supported by the evidence presented by aspects of his performances, audience reception and by the patronizing treatment he received from Barnum and the press; yet, the charming qualities that attach to his size and talents neither diminish the power that emerges from the cute nor negate the General's masculinity.[32] Ultimately, General Tom Thumb, rather like the bawdy Tom Thumbs of the burlesque tradition, was all man. Indeed, theatre historian Michael Chemers comments upon the General's "remarkable erotic magnetism."[33] Consider this: besides his very existence, the most memorable thing about Tom Thumb was his participation in a ritual that marks the heart of heterosexual manhood—marriage. Tom Thumb's wedding in 1863 to another of Barnum's performers, the 32-inch dwarf Lavinia Warren, became the New York City event of the year, perhaps even the decade, and infamously pushed the Civil War off the front pages of the newspapers (see Plate 20).[34]

Not surprisingly, Barnum exploited the courtship, wedding, and marriage of two of the dwarfs in his employ. Lavinia Warren, four years younger than Charles Stratton, joined Barnum's museum in 1862 when she was twenty years old. Like Stratton, Warren was a "midget," as proportionate dwarfs were often called. Declarations of her beauty were indexed to this fact. In an article from the *New York Times* in December 1862, Warren is called "very beautiful, and exceedingly symmetrical, a remarkably well developed, and an absolutely choice specimen of feminine humanity."[35] This aspect of her size made her particularly attractive as Stratton's future mate. The tiny couple became, in the viewers' imagination, spurred on by Barnum, the "mimic miniature Adam and Eve," a "matched pair" and destined for each other.[36] In a pamphlet entitled *Sketch of the Life, Personal Appearance, Character and Manners of Charles S. Stratton, the Man in Miniature, known as General Tom Thumb, and his wife, Lavinia Warren Stratton*," presumably written by Barnum for advertising purposes, Warren is described as "entirely free from deformity and every drawback that would give pain to the spectator."[37] Also like Stratton, she was born to parents of typical size. Lavinia's youngest sister, Minnie, who also joined Barnum and acted as a wedding attendant with Commodore Nutt, another of Barnum's dwarfs (tinier than Stratton and a competitor for Warren's affections) was more diminutive than the bride.

In the weeks preceding the ceremony, Barnum made sure the press coverage of the impending nuptials of the "Loving Lilliputians" was unrelenting. Lavinia Warren's levees were attended by upwards of 20,000 people in the days before the ceremony.[38] General Tom Thumb's letter to Lavinia's father requesting his permission to marry her was published in the *New York Times* and the following week the result of the request— permission granted—was reported there as well.[39] By the time the wedding took place, on February 10, 1863 at the fashionable Grace Church in Manhattan, wedding fever was high.

Invitations to the NYC event were coveted as the wedding guest list formed a veritable "who's who" of that city's social elite, including General Ambrose Burnside, Vanderbilts and Astors, among other notables. Immense crowds gathered to see the wedding procession and remained outside the reception venue, the Metropolitan Hotel, where Charles Stratton addressed the assembly from a balcony. Tickets were sold for the reception where the enormous wedding cake and gifts were displayed. The celebrated Matthew Brady served as wedding photographer. While the dwarf wedding certainly presented a "feel good" story to a population in the midst of a national crisis, not everyone was in favor of the "Barnumfication" of a sacred ritual. Members of the church who were displaced from their pews protested their ouster. In advance of the ceremony, the author of a *Brooklyn Eagle* opinion piece entitled "Marriage a la Barnum" commented, ". . . when Mr. Barnum brings the church and its solemn rites into his show business, he outrages public decency. . . . We are surprised that the clergy, or representatives of so respectable a body as the Episcopal Church should, for a moment, allow themselves to be used by this Yankee showman to advertise his business; or that a Bishop should allow himself to be exhibited like the Albino, or the What is it."[40] Proponents and detractors of the wedding alike, however, understood it to represent a prime example of Barnum's ability to put on an entertaining and unique show.

Certainly some of the excitement surrounding the event had to do with its visual spectacle and the novel juxtaposition of the excesses of the event with the tiny size of most of its elements— bride and groom and attendants, clothing, accessories, trousseau, and gifts (many of which were miniatures, including a miniature silver-plated sewing machine, a set of parlour furniture, a set of church service books mounted in gold and a miniature silver horse and chariot by Tiffany and Co.).[41] The audience's responses to the wedding-as-performance was likely rather complicated given that the ceremony is meant to be solemn, invoking lifelong promises and requiring the blessing of both God and man (in the form of the bride's parents and assembled guests), and yet the participants were constructed as curiosities to admire for their pleasing tininess—Look! Little people dressed as a wedding party! How precious! As Rachel Poliquin comments about Tom Thumb weddings and other mock weddings such as those between dolls or fairies, ". . . from delight to the visual erotic, at the heart of every mock marriage is this hazy association between the longing to coddle and the yearning to possess and dominate."[42] In addition, the wedding—that public precursor to sanctioned sexual union—of two dwarfs fueled speculation about the physical relationship between a couple both very like and unlike ordinary people.[43] In later years, once the couple had returned to the life of the traveling exhibition, Barnum capitalized on prurient curiosity about the sexual habits of dwarfs and often posed Mr. and Mrs. Stratton with a borrowed baby, proclaiming it to be their own child.

As celebrities, as curiosities, Stratton and Warren not only enacted the roles of bride and groom, husband and wife, they performed these roles for commercial gain from the moment of their engagement when they were once again exhibited in front of huge crowds, through the wedding itself, their honeymoon tour during which they were introduced to President and Mrs. Lincoln at a special party held in their honor, and ultimately as faux parents performing procreation.[44]

The wedding of Charles S. Stratton and Lavinia Warren was a culturally significant event—called, in retrospect, an American Royal Wedding—and it inspired a long-running performance act that, while less popular than in its heyday in the late nineteenth through mid-twentieth centuries, remains today: the Tom Thumb wedding.[45] Just as Stratton and Warren's actual wedding ceremony may have appeared, if one squinted, to be that of two children marrying, Tom Thumb weddings are child performances. The Tom Thumb wedding mimics the wedding of Stratton and Warren through the use of child participants—playing the roles of bride and groom and attendants and often acting as the minister, too. The events were typically staged either as parodies in which the wedding vows were played for laughs or as serious miniaturizations of the entire ceremony in which the intention was to be both charming and solemn.[46] In either case, the Tom Thumb wedding was intended to provide pleasure for both the child participants and their mothers, who would sew elaborate miniature gowns and suits, organize the flowers and prepare the food. Child-appropriate vows—whether humorous or serious—created the play-script and wedding cake the refreshments. Often, tickets were sold to the guests so that Tom Thumb weddings could raise funds for the sponsoring church. Tom Thumb weddings, which survive today primarily in African American churches, unite childhood, performance, and profit—each element a key aspect of Charles Stratton's story and the idea of the performing dwarf more generally. Stewart calls the Tom Thumb wedding "the reproduction of an idealized, or model, wedding on a miniature scale."[47] The Tom Thumb wedding reproduces our fondest hopes for social and cultural significance of the wedding ceremony: commitment, blessing, "normality" and social stability. And it does so in a contained and ritualistic manner. And yet, what is the wedding ceremony if not spectacle and performance?

Let us return to the theatrical nature of the dwarf body, an interpretation ascribed to dwarfs rather than reflecting any innate characteristic of short-statured persons. Such a belief in the theatricality of the dwarf by reason of his small size alone may be found in the *raison d'être* of the nineteenth- and twentieth-century "midget villages" popular in European and American world's fairs and also found at amusement parks such as Coney Island in New York. These villages replicated small town life in miniature, exploiting the exotic nature of the

tiny size of the buildings and people, certainly, but also emphasizing the ordinariness of everyday life within the context of a
performance space.[48] Unlike dwarf performers whose acts were
indebted primarily to contrast and slapstick humor, when
General Tom Thumb was on stage alone, or performing his
witty repartee, songs, and impersonations, his singular nature
and talents linked him more fully with the audience than in the
case of dwarf clowns. Betty M. Adelson notes about circus dwarfs
that as tiny oddities they *"exist only in relation to others."*[49] There
is no doubt that Tom Thumb's diminutive stature piqued the
curiosity of the crowd, yet at the same time, his individuality and
unique perspective, rather than his "freakishness," formed the
greater part of his charm. His "stigma" was negotiated in such a
way that his tiny ordinariness formed the basis of his celebrity.
As Neil Harris suggests about the young performer, "crowds
identified with him, rather than against him."[50]

We find a similar relationship between the dwarf child
character and the reader in many children's books featuring
dwarf protagonists. Although dwarf characters may remain
stuck in positions of a kind of exalted otherness indebted to
their talents as much as their singular size—rather like Charles
Stratton himself—their narratives given from the dwarf perspective tend to orient the literary works toward a position in which
"spoiled identity" does not construct or contain the protagonist's
dwarf identity. While performance remains a key trope in dwarf
children's literature and in recent television programming as
well—even in comic serials—dwarf characters and dwarf reality
show that actors "perform" the everyday as much as the exotic.

The Dwarf Perspective in Children's Literature

In her brief overview of literature highlighting dwarf characters,
Betty M. Adelson comments that within the general burgeoning
of dwarf books there has been a dramatic increase in such books
written for children in particular.[51] Typically, they feature dwarf
children. While it is not my purpose here to offer a similar

survey of dwarf literature, a consideration of Oscar Wilde's moral fairy tale mentioned in the introduction to this book offers both a way into my discussion of the dwarf perspective in children's books and a contrast to later works for the young. My exploration of dwarf children's literature will be bookended by two tales featuring the court dwarf: "The Birthday of the Infanta" by Oscar Wilde (1891), and *Jepp, Who Defied The Stars* by Katherine Marsh (2012).

"The Birthday of the Infanta," loosely based on members of the House of Hapsburg, is a dark fairy tale reminiscent in its tragic conclusion of the works of Hans Christian Andersen and the contrast between beautiful and grotesque bodies found in Dickens.[52] The story relates the sorrow of the King in perpetual mourning for the mother of the Infanta, and the joy of the beautiful princess on her special day. Elaborate entertainments are staged for her pleasure and that of her young guests: a sham bullfight, Italian puppet play, African juggler and snake charmer, and gypsy musicians, among other exotic performances. The final and funniest act, however, is the dancing Dwarf lately discovered living in the nearby cork forest: "when he stumbled into the arena, waddling on his crooked legs and wagging his huge misshapen head from side to side, the children went off into a loud shout of delight, and the Infanta herself laughed so much . . . ."[53] The Infanta is so delighted with his dancing that she throws him the beautiful white rose adorning her hair, an ironic gesture of favor the young Dwarf misunderstands to be a declaration of love. He falls in love with the Infanta and imagines her returning to his forest home with him.

Unbeknownst to the Dwarf, his most amusing quality is his "complete unconsciousness of his own grotesque appearance." This gift of unconsciousness is soon taken from him, however, as he wanders into the palace in search of the Infanta and discovers a mirror.[54] The Dwarf is horrified to learn that the ugly misshapen monster he sees in the mirror is he: "When the truth dawned upon him, he gave a wild cry of despair, and fell sobbing to the ground. So it was he who was misshapen and hunchbacked, foul to look at and grotesque."[55] After siesta, the Infanta and the child guests come upon the Dwarf writhing and beating the earth in his anguish and they laugh at his "acting" which is " 'funnier still,' according to the Infanta and almost as good as the puppets' acting 'only of course not quite so natural.' "[56] When the Dwarf finally stops sobbing and lies still, the Infanta demands that he dance for her, unaware that he is dead. When informed that the Dwarf will never dance again and that he has died of a broken heart, the cruel child proclaims, "For the future let those who come to play with me have no hearts.' "[57]

"The Birthday of the Infanta" is a cautionary tale. The naïve Dwarf had been generous in his performance and affectionate to the children who had laughed at him. Fully integrated into his forest home, he was a talented friend of nature and accepted by the birds and lizards. As a natural child, a feral child, he was a stranger to the artifice of court society, social hierarchy and human cruelty. While he recognized the physical beauty of the Infanta and was disgusted by his own ugliness, he did not understand that the exterior of a person does not reflect his or her inner worth. This is the lesson for the reader to learn as he/she identifies with the maligned dwarf. The Infanta's insensitivity and stupidity is particularly revealed when she declares the puppets—jointed objects controlled by strings and the puppet master—to be more "natural" in their movements than the Dwarf's outpouring of genuine anguish. His authentic grief is contrasted with the overweening sorrow of the King who refuses to perform his royal duties after his wife's death, to the detriment of his kingdom and his daughter. Ultimately, Wilde's dwarf character is akin to Velázquez's dwarf portraits in which the featured subject gazes directly at the viewer, requesting recognition and deserving reciprocity.

The search for love is a key plot element in dwarf children's literature. Wilde's Dwarf learns that the beautiful white rose the Infanta threw to him was not a symbol of the purity of her affection, but a mockery of chivalric love tokens. His horror at being an object of derision—he has not entertained the children so much as been enslaved by their laughter—results in his death from a broken heart. The Infanta's rejection of love—she has been well-schooled by her father and sycophantic courtiers—reveals her soulless nature and points out the need for a more humane way to treat difference and to encourage friendship and love. Certainly there is no possibility for mutual love in the tainted, unnatural, and overwrought world of the court.

Both *Little Little* by M. E. Kerr (1981) and *Jepp, Who Defied the Stars* by Katherine Marsh (2012) focus on romantic love, but other dwarf books highlight the quest for love and understanding between friends or within the dwarf community. Lisa Graff's *The Thing About Georgie* (2006) is middle-grade novel about an achondroplastic fourth-grader who negotiates the ups and downs of friendship and his fears about becoming a big brother to a sibling who will one day grow taller than he. *Trudi and Pia* (2003), a picture-book version of characters from Ursula Hegi's novel for adults, *Stones from the River* (1994), is told from the perspective of dwarf characters who seek relationships within the dwarf community.[58]

Not surprisingly, performance figures in both *The Thing About Georgie* and *Trudi and Pia*. *The Thing About Georgie* contains dual perspectives: a first-person narrative by an unnamed speaker who is not revealed until the book's conclusion and a third-person omniscient narrative that tells the story of the dwarf Georgie in the context of his increasingly fraught relationship with his best friend, Andy, and the impending birth of a new sibling. As Georgie becomes estranged from Andy, his in-class tormenter, an unpopular girl named Jeanie, is assigned as his partner in a project on the American presidents. "Jeanie the Meanie," as everyone calls her, is both cruel, at times, and misunderstood. In the midst of doing research about their topic, Abraham Lincoln, which Jeanie manifestly refuses to do, Georgie looks for a book in the school library, *Little in a Big World*. This book about dwarfs had never been checked out of the library before, but Georgie can no longer find it on the shelf. Georgie has mixed feelings about the fact that every other time he looked no one had taken the book out: "It kind of stank to know that no one wanted to learn about him, but in a weird way it made him feel a little more normal too, like maybe he wasn't different enough that people thought they *should* learn about him."[59] Jeanie signs Georgie up to perform in the fourth-grade play about the presidents. Much to Georgie's horror, she signs him up to play their topic, Abraham Lincoln, America's tallest president. Yet Jeanie alone is sensitive to Georgie's unhappiness and loneliness. She creates an elaborate Abe Lincoln costume for Georgie that involves her father's suit, multiple coffee cans, and gloved rulers that create arms and hands. His stand-out performance wins over the crowd. By the novel's conclusion Georgie has made two new friends, Jeanie and Russ, the new kid Andy befriends, while he keeps his oldest friendship. His anxiety over his sibling's impending birth and his own inadequacies as a dwarf who cannot play a musical instrument—his musician parents' earliest wish for him—dissipates in part as a result of his successful comic performance. He and Jeanie, revealed to be both the "I" of the novel and the student who reads *Little in a Big World* and provides facts about being a dwarf in the first-person narrative, make plans to try out for fifth-grade drama the following year. Georgie's talents are not confined to acting—the book takes pains, through Jeanie's direct address, to expand Georgie's identity beyond "dwarf" and failed musician (his wrist and back problems make playing musical instruments too difficult)—yet his character, once again, finds additional acceptance through the stage. Can this stereotype be transcended in children's books about dwarfs?[60]

Trudi and Pia introduces two dwarf characters to the picture book audience: Trudi, an unhappy girl who tries all manner of tricks to try to grow, and Pia, a dwarf and circus animal tamer. Pia's small size emphasizes her skill with the animals: the elephants bow down to her and she places her head into the lion's mouth in safety. Trudi, who feels stifled and overlooked as a dwarf among the ordinary-sized, finds Pia fascinating. She steps forward as if compelled by some unseen force when Pia calls for a volunteer from the audience to help her with a trick. Pia is startled, but tells the audience: " 'It looks like we have a volunteer. From the magic island I call home. The island of the little people, where everyone is our height.' "[61] Together, as the dwarf child and dwarf woman perform, they also construct a story about the magical island of little people. "Between them, they wove the story of an island so glorious that everyone in the audience would have followed them there without question ...."[62] Reminding us of the rose of contention in Wilde's tale, yet transforming the scene into one of mutual love, with a kiss, Pia gives Trudi a huge paper rose she had plucked from the air.

Pia mentors the lonely and alienated Trudi. Trudi seeks out Pia and marvels that in her beautiful blue caravan all the furnishings are sized for dwarf bodies. She mourns the fact that she has never met a dwarf before and that they are scattered everywhere. Pia disagrees and tells her that dwarfs are united both as a community and as members of the wider world: " 'It's called earth,' " she says.[63] As Pia relates tales of the 104 dwarfs she has met in her travels, Trudi begins to understand and value a healthy dwarf perspective: "In that instant she understood that for Pia, being a dwarf was normal, beautiful even. To Pia, long arms were ugly, long legs unsteady. Tall people looked odd, too far from the ground."[64] Refusing to allow Trudi to escape her lonely life and join her in the circus, Pia's final bit of advice could stand as a dwarf children's literature manifesto: " 'Even if I welcomed you,' Pia said, 'it wouldn't change that feeling of being the only one. No one but you can change that.' "[65] As she wraps her short arms around her small body and hugs herself, Pia reminds Trudi that happiness lies in self-acceptance.

Rather than comic, Pia's talents as a circus dwarf lie within acts of courage and imagination. She turns the notion of the performing dwarf clown on its head by emphasizing the dwarf point of view and relegating normates to the sidelines and to ugliness. Although in many ways the theme and narrative purpose are similar to *Trudi and Pia*, M. E. Kerr's satiric and brave young adult novel *Little Little*, written more than twenty years earlier, takes a decidedly different path to promoting dwarf self-acceptance. Kerr is not afraid to engage stereotypes, sketch unlikeable dwarf characters or confront the physical limitations and liabilities of the dwarf body. *Little Little* probes the politics of difference within the dwarf community by creating a love triangle between two "p.f" teens (the acronym Little Little's mother gives "perfectly formed" little people) and an achondroplastic teen. Bogdan's notion of the "aggrandized" performer plays a role, too, as both male suitors of Little Little LaBelle are entertainers, although only one fulfills the "aggrandized" role: Knox Lionel (aka "Little Lion" and "Opportunity Knox") is a "philosopher and con man"[66] who has gained fame as a flamboyant evangelical preacher. Sydney Cinnamon, by contrast, is a popular dancing cockroach for Palmer Pest Control.

The pains of growing up, establishing a mature identity, and finding pride in being different are negotiated through Little Little's family dynamics and the love triangle: both Little Lion and Sydney vie for Little Little's attention. Little Little is cosseted by her parents and grandfather and tormented by her mother's banality and obsession with physical perfection. Mrs. LaBelle indulges this fixation through her participation in TAD, "The American Diminutives," an obvious lampooning of the organization Little People of America (LPA, established in 1957). An alcoholic who writes sentimental verse published in the newspaper, much to Little Little's disgust, Mrs. LaBelle strongly disapproves of Sydney because he is disproportionate: Little Little proclaims, ' "You are all bogged down in p.f.! Sydney Cinnamon has one of the best minds of anyone who's ever sat down at our dinner table and all you see is the tooth that sticks out! . . . The hump, the tooth that sticks out, the twisted leg—you never see anyone's real worth!' "[67] While the rebellious Little Little is attracted to Little Lion and also to the prospect of leaving home through marriage, all of his actions and beliefs are shallow and insincere. Sydney, by contrast, although a "roach," is also a reader and thinker. He charms Little Little with his personality at the same time as the vain and pompous Little Lion runs around on her with another dwarf. Little Little's eighteenth birthday party at which Sydney is scheduled to perform as "the Roach," and Little Lion is expected to propose serves as the novel's crisis. The party is ruined by her rival accidentally on purpose and clearly spells the end of Little Little's romance with the dastardly Little Lion. Sydney remains in town, enrolls in high school and vies with Little Little for the honor of being the best writer in the senior English class. Their romance—between two strong minds—remains to be written.

Rather than skirt or sugar-coat the pervasive assumptions about physical beauty that dominate the world in which dwarfs live, *Little Little* confronts them head on. Sydney takes on the role of cockroach—a universally loathed insect—and transforms it into a popular television act. His fame grows to the extent that he is also given a job as a dancing dragon in the town's new pachinko parlor. Certainly there is more than a little of the freak show performer in Sydney Cinnamon. Yet, as Little Little describes the Roach to her father, " 'Instead of trying to be like everyone else, [Sydney] celebrates being different. He dramatizes it.' "[68] "The Roach" embraces his enfreakment through these roles. Kerr's dwarf fiction highlights the freedom and radical nature of much 1970s and early 1980s fiction.

Jepp, Who Defied the Stars is another young adult novel about making one's own destiny. The story takes us full circle back to the rarefied world of the seventeenth-century court dwarf and some of the characters we met in chapter two: the Infanta Isabella Clara Eugenia and one of her dwarf companions.[69] The character Jepp is also based on an actual figure—a dwarf who formed part of the astronomer Tycho Brahe's household on the island of Hven (or Ven), located in the Öresund strait between Denmark (Zealand) and Sweden (Scania). Recruited from poverty in 1597 to join the dwarf retinue of the Infanta Isabella Clara Eugenia and her husband, Archduke Albert of Austria, Jepp finds that while aspects of his new life are sweet—living with other dwarfs, eating well, sleeping in comfort—his role as court dwarf requires various acts of humiliation, among them jumping out of a pie, à la Jeffrey Hudson. After his attempt to escape the court with a dwarf he has come to love—she had been raped by a courtier and subsequently made pregnant—Jepp is betrayed and taken to Hven and Tycho Brahe. Although he is at first treated again as a fool—one of his duties is to pick up Tycho Brahe's false nose as it constantly falls off Brahe's face—ultimately the literate and curious Jepp is invited to join Brahe's scientific community. He also falls in love with Magdalene, one of Brahe's daughters who is herself an outsider: the commoner daughter of the noble Brahe (his common-law wife was a commoner and while his children were considered legitimate, they could not take his name or inherit property). In addition, she was educated as a student of the classics in a world that did not recognize the intellectual gifts or contributions of women. Jepp thinks about how he and Magdalene are similar: "I suddenly realize why [Magdalene] has always seemed to understand me so well. My fate as a curiosity is not so different than the one she imagines for herself."[70] Their love story, which is based on the belief that one can help to mold one's destiny, that one's fate is not written in the stars and that it is "better to act out of love rather than fear," offers inspiration for the creative and passionate potential to be found when differences are joined.[71] Jepp's thoughts conclude the novel: as he and Magdalene kiss, he thinks, "I care not whether the world thinks us a motley pair . . . . I care not that we face adversity by daring to look upward. For I am no longer on earth but in a heaven of my own making."[72]

In her Author's Note to *Jepp*, Katherine Marsh acknowledges the liberties she has taken with the historical record. Very little is known about Jepp, for example, and Magdalene Tygesdatter never marries. She also discloses that her interest in writing a dwarf character was influenced by her childhood fascination with Velázquez's dwarf portraits and that she based Jepp's pie exploits on Jeffrey Hudson's life.[73] So much of contemporary dwarf discourse emerges from these early antecedents that function as inspiration to tell dwarf stories as well as impetus to change the narratives from exploitation to stories of everyday life. For example, in the successful reality television show *Little People, Big World* (TLC, 2006–2010) featuring the Roloff family, the camera—the show itself—creates a performance space, and while curiosity about the differences that size makes as a family goes about its business clearly draws viewers, each episode's dramatic arc tends to come from the conflicts and accommodations that arise for the very short as they lead ordinary lives. The can-do attitude that the family adopts in order to meet its challenges provides the motivation for viewers to watch. The Roloffs are particularly interesting because they are a "mixed" family: the parents are dwarfs, as is one of their twin boys, while their other three children are ordinary-sized.[74] Certainly the family members have become celebrities—their pumpkin farm outside of Portland, Oregon is a popular tourist destination— yet not celebrities entirely in the mode of Charles Stratton. Stratton's greatest legacy is the cultural ritual of the Tom Thumb wedding. By contrast, Amy Roloff and her husband Matt are both motivational speakers, and Amy Roloff has founded a charity, the Amy Roloff Charity Foundation, dedicated to assisting non-profit organizations in raising money for kids who face a variety of challenges that emerge from their social, emotional, mental, and physical difficulties.

While American children's literature and documentaries or even reality shows make clear their inheritance from the focus on the dwarf individuals of the seventeenth-century court and portraiture, most television programming links closely with the freak show legacy of comedy and mockery, even as celebrity dwarfs are featured in quasi-heroic or tragicomic roles. Thus, if the Roloffs in their domestic drama may be said to function within the "high aggrandized mode" of dwarf performances, emphasizing the similarities between the dwarf and the non-dwarf, much television programming and comedy show routines—for example, both the comedian Chelsea Handler and radio shock jock Howard Stern have had dwarf sidekicks—focuses on the tragicomic mode of most dwarf performances.[75]

As I suggested above and in the previous chapter, the dwarf body is both like and unlike the typically sized—and thus he is often a tragicomic figure. The tragicomedy of the dwarf figure communicated in early modern emblems, for example, may also be glimpsed in a contemporary example of dwarf comedy, performance, and art (I use that term loosely here) mimicking life. The British entertainer and director Ricky Gervais's television series *Life's Too Short* (which aired in Britain in 2011 and in the US in 2012; the show was canceled in 2013) features Warwick Davis, a very short actor who plays a man who runs a talent agency for "little people," much as Davis does in real life. Davis has called the series "mainstream" and described the show as " 'about a person, not necessarily somebody who's short .... He's a desperate man, and as he gets more desperate, he makes more mistakes.' "[76] While it is undoubtedly true that a businessman's struggles are largely the same no matter one's height, much of the humor of the series and the panic of the main character, as the title makes abundantly clear, were connected to Davis's size and those of the actors he attempts to place in performance roles.

Bogdan's theory of the "status-enhancing characteristics" inherent in the performances of General Tom Thumb as he mimicked adult preoccupations and enacted a precociousness that engaged with the audience's sympathies and curiosity might also be linked to childhood itself. That is, childhood, too—in particular, white middle-class childhood—confers status. Some of this status comes from the appealing vulnerability of the child and the fleeting nature of childhood. Tom Thumb's greatest years as a performer were in his youth and in the ritual of marriage (a ceremony typically associated with the young and with potential rather than age). His enduring fame may be found in a children's performance act—the Tom Thumb wedding. Other celebrity dwarfs such as Jeffrey Hudson are remembered for their childhoods, too. In Hudson's case, the "famous dwarf" is best known for both the pie and the status-enhancing royal portrait with Queen Henrietta Maria. In her discussion of dwarf characters and the concept of "littleness" in the works of Charles Dickens, Craton writes about the evil dwarf Quilp's pursuit of Little Nell: "In the prospect of their marriage, the reader sees the collision of two common themes in Dickens's images of littleness: the seductive appeal of the performing dwarf, and the potential exploitation of the child."[77] In addition to these fascinating aspects of littleness that attach to the dwarf body in performance and in emblematic and allegorical visual representations of the child dwarf in particular, in some venues—especially in young adult (YA) fiction—we also find agency and healthy identity formation that suggests developments in dwarf discourse away from freakery and exploitation even while performance remains a pervasive space for the creation of dwarf identity within western culture.

Chapter 4

LILLIPUTIANS IN BLACKFACE

"Queer Little Freaks"[1]

As we have seen, in his various ventures creating eye-catching exhibits and performances as well as collecting specimens and curiosities, P. T. Barnum delighted in putting incongruous persons and objects side by side. In uniting the big and the small, civilized and savage, comic and tragic, Barnum emphasized and exploited the spectacular nature of each. Barnum's most famous performer, General Tom Thumb, was notable not only for his tiny size and perfect proportions, but also for his gentlemanly qualities, his refinement and good taste. And, although Barnum employed other dwarfs who were similarly fashionable, General Tom Thumb was considered to be uniquely talented. Tom Thumb's popularity certainly reflected this general assessment. By contrast, Barnum's displays of native peoples from around the world engaged with their "generic" qualities as exotic, savage, and primitive. While both dwarf and pygmy, for example, performed otherness for the crowds, the aboriginals were not considered as individuals at all but as physical reminders of the idea of inferior races.

In this chapter I will first trace the ideologies of race and colonialism that construct the miniature as "a race apart." Along the way I will also expand upon the true story of Ota Benga, introduced in the first pages of this book, who captivated New York in the early twentieth century and inspired different retellings of his life. In this cultural history of big and small bodies I am keenly interested in analyzing the often fraught relationship once "small" is typed as inferior. My primary focus is in examining the developing ethics of the big and small relationship as it is described in children's literature in a postcolonial context. Within discourses of size, discovery, whiteness, and cultural dominance, the "idea of the pygmy," as well as the racialized savage "other," have played crucial roles in the construction of nineteenth- and twentieth-century children's literature and culture. The adaptations and revisions of the racialized miniatures' stories, in particular, highlight not only confrontations between big and small bodies, but also those between authenticity and nostalgia for a mythic past, as well as the tensions that arise when attempts at revision approach erasure and forgetting.

The same desire for knowledge about origins and the unseen that drove seventeenth-century experiments with lenses, leading to the invention of the early microscope, may be found in the work of those who sought to confront and anatomize miniature beings from far-off lands. Both folklorists and scientists theorized or denied the existence of miniature races of people—in particular, pygmies—that had so captured the human imagination since Classical times in Homer, Aristotle, and Pliny. One example of an attempt to locate the meaning of the pygmy—is he a man or is he a monkey?—may be found in the late seventeenth-century work of Edward Tyson, physician and Fellow of the Royal Society. In 1699 Tyson published his most famous book, *The Anatomy of a Pygmy*. Tyson's treatise, the first detailed exploration of the anatomy of an anthropoid ape, also aimed to add to medical knowledge about human structure by dissecting and anatomizing apes and monkeys. This was a position first advanced by the European comparative anatomists Galen in the second century and later Vesalius, some thirteen centuries later. Though he calls it an "orang-outang," a common misapplication at the time, the animal that Tyson anatomized was a chimpanzee. Tyson's philosophical purpose in undertaking the anatomy was to prove that the pygmies described by Classical authors were not small humans, but apes and monkeys: "That the Pygmies of the Antients were a sort of Apes, and not of the Humane Race, I shall endeavour to prove in the following Essay. And if the Pygmies were only Apes, then in all probability an Ape may be a Pygmie; a sort of animal so much resembling Man, that both the Antients and the Moderns have reputed it to be a Puny Race of Mankind, call'd to this day, Homo Sylvestris, the Wild Man; Orang-Outang, or a Man of the Woods . . . ."[2]

Tyson relegated all stories from the past, as well as contemporary first-hand accounts of small people including "Little Men," the "Pygmæn Men," the "Black Men," and "Men with Dogs' Faces," to the realm of fancy. In the late nineteenth century, after exploration and European colonial expansion had definitively revealed the existence of very short statured people around the globe, Bertram C. A. Windle edited and reintroduced Tyson's work (in a limited edition of sixty copies) in order to refute Tyson's conclusions and to allow Aristotle and Pliny their "revenge."[3] Windle's particular focus in his introduction is the inverse of Tyson's dismissal of "Fabulous and Romantick Stories": in this contribution to the new "science" of folklore that emerged in Europe in the nineteenth century, he enters a conversation with other folklorists to help account for the origin of the belief in fairies and the persistence of fairy tales, using the existence of pygmy people throughout the world as one kind of evidence.

From Tyson in 1699 through the late nineteenth century, "scientific" discourses of anatomy, folklore, and evolution informed the conversation about origin, "progress," and "civilization" that became essential both to colonialist ideologies of conversion and commerce and to children's literature and culture of the early twentieth century. The explicit link between the idea of the pygmy and a children's literature intended for (white) children is based on assumptions of immaturity and inferiority in both the African (or any racialized miniature) and the "child"—

an idea reminiscent of dwarf discourse, as well. Ashis Nandy describes these "adultist" assumptions in this way: "to the extent adulthood itself is valued as a symbol of completeness and as an end-product of growth or development, childhood is seen as an imperfect transitional state on the way to adulthood, normality, full socialization and humanness. . . . Much of the pull of the ideology of colonialism and much of the power of the idea of modernity can be traced to the evolutionary implications of the concept of the child in the Western worldview."[4] Indeed, as Carole G. Silver notes, for some Victorian ethnologists organizing a hierarchical scale of human evolution, the Pygmy represented the lowest biological human form: ". . . the Pygmy, still lower in the evolutionary chain [than the childlike African "savage"], was a permanent fetus, a case of arrested development."[5] We might call the Pygmy a kind of Tom Thumb figure. Children's literature, with its focus on improving and instructing the child reader, thus mirrors colonialist activities meant to "develop" the African continent into a collection of modern Europeanized colonies.

As well as being a kind of fetal Tom Thumb figure whose status is unclear, the pygmy was also understood within a freak show mentality of collecting curiosities or as characters from folklore, or even as toys. Colonial missionary narratives and travel books that punctuate their tales of trial and conquest, wonder and conversion, with descriptions, drawings, and photographs of pygmy "others," even if not written explicitly for children, illustrate well the relationship between children's literature and the idea of the pygmy. The Englishman Captain Guy Burrows, whose colonialist travelogue *The Land of the Pigmies* (1898) concludes with a letter from the King of the Belgians, Leopold II, who calls the Congolese pygmies he encounters during his three-year posting (1894–1897) in Africa "queer little freaks."[6] The first-person colonial narratives tend to infantilize the pygmy people, transforming them into children or even fairies or Lilliputians in a manner suggestive of Windle. A good example of this fairy effect can be found in William Geil's

armchair traveler's book *A Yankee in Pigmy Land* (1905) (see
Plate 21). Geil fetishizes the central African pygmy as the greatest
"trophy" of his journey. He gushes, "At last I saw a real Pigmy!
And I managed to photograph him! Later on we met two more
pigmies!"[7] Once he regains his composure, his more typical wry
tone resumes and Geil frames his interaction with the Congo
Free State African in terms specifically related to the subordinate status of childhood, a convention of colonialist discourse
that understands the colonial encounter as bringing "maturity"
to the native populations through the example of "civilization."
For Geil, this young African, a chief's son, contains all of the
qualities of a folktale trickster: he is "bewitching," "elfin," and a
member of "a *race* of Tom Thumbs."[8]

Ruth B. Fisher, a British Catholic stationed in Uganda from
1900, calls her mission field "Pigmy-Land," an obvious nod to
"fairyland."[9] Naming whatever region of Africa they visit as
"Pygmyland" seems to be a kind of universal response of western
missionaries and travel writers. Fisher is more respectful in her
approach to the short-statured native people she encounters—
she protests against making them into objects of display (a
tragic commercial enterprise that I will discuss below): "The
pigmies themselves are worthy of a better lot than to be carried
off by a traveler and be made a show for the sordid curiosity of
holiday crowds"[10]—and recounts the long history of pygmies as
described by Herodotus. Yet she also comments on the lack of
physical and moral progress the people have made throughout
their history.[11]

Those late nineteenth-century and early twentieth-century
westerners in Africa who write about pygmy people—
missionaries, travel-writers, explorers, colonialists—picture
through words and (often) photographs these tiny dark-skinned
"others" for their audiences at home. Extending Daniel
Headrick's thesis described in *The Tools of Empire*, Paul S.
Landau argues that photography—as well as the Gatling gun,
steamship, and quinine—functioned as a "tool of the empire":
"As racial ideologues accommodated Charles Darwin's theory

of evolution to their way of thinking, the concerns of physical anthropology were joined to the power of photography in order visually to 'type' indigenes in Australia, Africa and Asia."[12] These images play an integral role in defining pygmies as a "species" rather than individual humans. Often an identified white person—the I and "eye" of the book—will be photographed with a "tribe" or group of anonymous persons.

Not only the dominant size of the white colonialist is emphasized in these photographs, but also the stark contrast between the "exceptional" westerner and the unknown Africans. After the Boer War, John Buchan, the prolific Scots author, editor, war correspondent and Governor-General of Canada, spent time in South Africa as a government administrator. In his book *The African Colony* (1903), Buchan wrote: "Mentally [the African] is as crude and naïve as a child, with a child's curiosity and ingenuity, and a child's practical inconsequence. Morally he has none of the traditions of self-discipline and order which are implicit, though often in a degraded form, in white people. In a word, he cannot be depended upon as an individual save under fairly vigilant restraint."[13]

While misleading in a different way, the ideal of the Noble Savage inverts the judgment of the African as degraded and degenerate and offers a counter-narrative to the negative portrayals of native people found in the travelogues of Buchan, Fisher, and Geil. The well-known idea first promoted by Montaigne and Jean-Jacques Rousseau had its detractors, as well. Charles Dickens's infamous essay "The Noble Savage," published in *Household Words* in 1853, lampooned the myth.[14] In *The Poor Indians: British Missionaries, Native Americans, and Colonial Sensibility* (2004), Laura M. Stevens notes the relationship between the idea of the Noble Savage and the related ideology she describes as "the poor Indians." Stevens comments, ". . . the figure of the poor Indian borrowed much from the noble savage, whose moral simplicity was used to set off Europeans' contrasting hypocrisy. Ultimately, though, these figures oppose each other. Poor Indians are defined through their need for the very things that noble savages do not need, Christianity and European civilization."[15] Missionaries writing about pygmies in Africa tend to subscribe to the "poor Indian" mythology much more than to the ideal of the Noble Savage.

While providing for the poor African's "needs," Anglo-American missionaries and travelers described virtually everything about Africa as strange, difficult, or dangerous for the westerner. In Geil's opinion, "a light skin is fatal to those who live in tropical countries,"[16] and the native people themselves are perceived to be threatening. The pygmy tribes, although their small size is continually noted and marveled at in a patronizing way, as I've described above, are also credited with skills in hunting and fighting. According to Geil, when in their home, though they may be considered to be "jolly miniatures," they are also "Nimrods," an allusion to the biblical mighty hunter, Noah's great-grandson.[17]

"Little Burnt Faces": Myths of Africa and Nineteenth-Century Spectacle[18]

In western children's literature of the late nineteenth and early twentieth centuries, Africa is generally described using the language of knowledge and discovery. Jan Nederveen Pieterse interrogates this Eurocentric view in *White on Black: Images of Africa and Blacks in Western Popular Culture* (1992), arguing that "the journeys of exploration did not simply produce 'knowledge,' they were also large-scale operations in myth-making, and they unfolded in a kind of western 'tunnel vision' that was to culminate in European colonialism."[19] In books for Euro-American children, "the dark Continent"—so-called by white Europeans and Americans even into the 1950s—and its inhabitants were described and dissected for educational and sometimes religious purposes.[20] For example, in a biography of David Livingstone (1813–1873) written as part of the "Heroes of the Cross" series of children's books (published in the 1950s by a British publisher with imprints in America, Australia,

Canada, and New Zealand), colonialist ideologies of mapping, penetrating, and patronizing pervade the story of the Scots medical missionary who traveled through much of Africa during the mid-nineteenth century. The narrator directly addresses the (white) reader at a number of different moments, situating Livingstone as an explorer whose presence in Africa appeared to create Africa: "Now you know a pioneer is a man who goes where other people have never been."[21] After Livingstone reaches the Zambezi River Falls, and names it for Queen Victoria, the narrator comments, "Still, a man who first discovered such a wonderful sight as the Victoria Falls had some right to be just a little tiny bit vain. Don't you think so?"[22] Livingstone meets many native people—described in the text as savages, and labeled according to their "color" and size: "Not all of the natives that Livingstone saw were black. Some of them were little brown people called Bushmen. And they were very clever, too."[23]

The tiny and "clever" Bushmen (a popular term still in use to describe southern African peoples such as the San, Khoi, or Batwa), exotic figures whose "discovery," along with that of the Congo pygmies, reinforced theories of social evolution and racialized human classification systems, were widely associated with ancient myths of Pygmies, or dwarf people.[24] Travel literature and photographs only whetted the appetites of curious westerners to see the African "fairies." In fact, once discovered in the nineteenth century, the African pygmies were not left alone but put on display. For western audiences, this displacement changed the emphasis of their meaning from childlike merry hunters in need of civilizing and Christianizing, to captive "savages" performing the "idea of the pygmy" in traveling exhibits, museums, world's fairs and even zoos. There is more than a touch of the commercialism and exploitation of blackness found in blackface minstrelsy within the spectacle of nearly enslaved pygmies and other aboriginal people performing as miniature exotics for white audiences. As the era of minstrelsy waned in America through the latter half of the nineteenth century (though popular in Britain, minstrelsy was primarily an entertainment export), colonialist expansion in Africa, Australia, and South America steadily increased. As we have seen in chapter three, venues for exhibiting native people in costume, such as Barnum's American Museum and less celebrated dime museums, burgeoned in late Victorian America and Britain.[25] Indeed, "the little burnt faces," as Geil calls the Congo pygmies he meets, who are made to dance, stage fights, and construct traditional crafts, are treated as Lilliputians in blackface, although the face they put on does not come from burnt cork, but from performing primitivism, performing Africa in miniature, within the context of the ideologies of scientific inquiry, white supremacy, freak show and exploitation of the small.

Roslyn Poignant argues in *Professional Savages: Captive Lives and Western Spectacle* (2004) that the displacement and display of aboriginals in the late nineteenth century heralded spectacle as an integral part of modernity: "as [spectacle] was configured in the fairgrounds, circuses, exhibition halls, theatres and museum spaces."[26] According to Annie E. Coombes, the organizers of European exhibitions created powerful myths about Africa through the "exhibitionary narratives" of black performers in simulated villages or in dramatic re-enactments of white/black conflict that relied upon a "rhetoric of 'objectivity' and 'authenticity.' "[27] Colonial ideologies of racial hierarchies, belief in teleological western progress, and an early form of "edutainment" coalesced around the figure of the "savage" in what Poignant calls the "show-space"—"a cultural space that is both a zone of displacement for the performers and a place of spectacle for the onlookers."[28] In 1882, Barnum sent a letter to several hundred consulates and towns throughout the world, seeking agents to carry out his desire to collect "specimens of uncivilized peoples" for an exhibit at his traveling show. Barnum's interest in pygmies was in direct line with his success with General Tom Thumb and other dwarf performers. Barnum was keen not only to assemble what were understood to be the world's races, but also to highlight factors of "extraordinary peculiarity" such as size, talent, and deformity.[29] The pygmy, in Barnum's and others' estimation, was thus doubly attractive, representing both a "degenerate" race and extreme size difference.

Given this intense interest in exotic tribespeople, it is not surprising that they would be featured at one of the world's foremost show-spaces—the World's Fair. Members of small-statured peoples from the Congo were displayed, along with other native people from around the globe, as an educative ethnological exhibit at the 1904 World's Fair, held in St. Louis, Missouri.[30] Also known as the Louisiana Purchase Exposition (celebrating the centennial of the Louisiana Purchase which doubled the size of the United States at the time it was acquired from France), the World's Fair in St. Louis was America's largest and most successful, attracting over 18 million visitors to the nearly 1,300-acre fairgrounds during its seven-month run. Millions of children, paying 25 cents for the privilege, attended the fair and were awed by the Pike—the mile-long midway (from which the phrase "coming down the Pike" originated)—as well as by the animal shows, ice-cream, twice-daily re-enactments of the Boer War, and "villages" of some 1,200 native peoples from around the world. These indigenous people included Eskimos, Filipinos, the Ainu from Japan, South Americans, Native Americans from over fifty different tribes, and a number of tribal or family groups from Africa, including pygmies from the Congo.[31] The fair organizers wished to emphasize not only the future by way of commercial and industrial innovations and discoveries in mechanics and technology, but also the human past, and for this, the theories of a new science—anthropology—were relied upon to construct a narrative of human triumphalism.[32]

Samuel Phillips Verner, African explorer and sometime missionary, was the primary collector of Africans for the St. Louis Fair. Phillips Verner Bradford, Verner's grandson, argues that the reasoning behind his grandfather's task in helping to assemble the Africans for display at the St. Louis World's Fair was to make the case that human evolution could be traced in native African people:

Under Dr. W. J. McGee [the head of the Anthropology Department of the Fair], special agents of the fair were dispatched to the four corners of the Earth. Their mission, McGee wrote, was to assemble "representatives of all the world's races, ranging from smallest pygmies to the most gigantic peoples, from the darkest blacks to the dominant whites." Anthropology wanted to start with "the lowest known culture," and work its way up to man's "highest culmination." This "highest culmination" was plainly the culmination symbolized by the exposition itself, a culture moving rapidly from the "Age of Metal" into the "Age of Power."[33]

This colonialist narrative of progress, of black and white, and big and small, coalesced in the figure of one man, the pygmy Ota Benga.

Ota Benga and Children's Literature

When Verner, dispatched to Africa by the Head of Anthropology of the St. Louis World's Fair, first met Ota Benga in the spring of 1904, the young African was in desperate straits. While he had been away from his camp for several days hunting an elephant, the Force Publique, native "tax collectors" for King Leopold II, came upon Ota Benga's camp and demanded ivory. The pygmies had none to give, and in retaliation most of the inhabitants of the camp, including Ota Benga's family, were slaughtered. When Ota Benga returned to his camp, he was captured and brought to a slave market. There Verner found the grieving man and bought him for a pound of salt and a bolt of cloth. Ota Benga was perfect for Verner's purposes: he was tractable, tiny (about 4 foot 8 inches in height), and looked exotic. Perhaps it was because Ota Benga's world had been irrevocably destroyed that he agreed to travel to America.[34]

The pygmy exhibit at the World's Fair was very popular (see Plate 22). Ota Benga was singled out as a cannibal and his pointed teeth, in particular, elicited strong reactions from the audience. Visitors wishing to see Ota Benga's teeth had to pay an additional 5 cents. Although Ota Benga's true feelings have not been documented, once the Fair was open, Verner wove a tale that emphasized Ota Benga's gratitude toward him and delight in leaving Africa and coming to America. During his months on display in the ethnographic exhibit of the Fair, Ota Benga and the others were jeered at and hit with mud pies as they shivered in the cold (they were made to wear native costume inadequate to the weather conditions). The pygmies were also forced to participate in the anthropological athletic games. After the conclusion of the Fair, Ota Benga went back to Africa with Verner who, true to his word, returned the Africans to the Congo Free State. According to a 2002 short documentary made about Ota Benga's life, the nine pygmies who were part of the World's Fair exhibit were given $8.35 as a group payment when the Fair closed.[35] While in Africa, Ota Benga married among the Batwa and accompanied Verner on his subsequent travels collecting African animal specimens. After his wife's death from a snake bite, Ota Benga returned to America with Verner and, in 1906, along with a poisonous snake and a chimpanzee, ended up at the New York Zoological Gardens, also known as the Bronx Zoo.

For almost two weeks in late summer, Ota Benga was a guest of the zoo, allowed to wander around and visit the animals and the zoo director, who often had a message for him from Verner. But a trap of "Darwinism, Barnumism, pure and simple racism"[36] was laid for Ota Benga in the Bronx Zoo as he became a prisoner of the Monkey House. As Bradford and Blume comment flatly about this time period in Ota Benga's life, "He didn't have to do much. He just had to be short and black."[37] To emphasize the evolutionary point that humans and primates share a common ancestor—and the outrageous assertion that some humans are more closely related to monkeys than others—Ota Benga was exhibited with the orang-utan.[38] This view was not unique to American anthropologists: the aforementioned Captain Burrows, an English officer with the Force Publique (the group that had massacred Ota Benga's first wife and children and band), argued in 1898 that pygmies function outside of time and history and thus have not ascended very high on the evolutionary ladder: "The low state of their mental development is shown by the following facts. They have no regard for time, nor have they any records or traditions of the past; no religion is known among them, nor have they any fetich [sic] rights; they do not seek to know the future by occult means, as do their neighbors; in short, they are, to my thinking, the closest link with the original Darwinian anthropoid ape extant."[39] Although the focus here is on "anthropological reductionism," we are not far from Tyson's 1699 anatomical theory conflating the chimpanzee with the pygmy.[40]

Ota Benga was an overnight international sensation: his new address was reported all over the world and children and their parents flocked to the zoo. On one Sunday, 40,000 people visited Ota Benga's exhibit.[41] Yet controversy over Ota Benga's incarceration and display with apes quickly arose. A delegation of African American Baptist ministers, led by the Reverend James H. Gordon, superintendent of the Howard Colored Orphan Asylum in Brooklyn, protested Ota Benga's role at the zoo. Gordon declared, " 'Our race, we think, is depressed enough . . . without exhibiting one of us with the apes. We think we are worthy of being considered human beings, with souls.' "[42] After a month of record attendance at the zoo, continual press coverage, and concomitant with Ota Benga's escalating hostility toward the crowds of people who gathered to watch and taunt him, Ota Benga was released from the zoo by Verner (still his "owner") and remanded to the custody of the Reverend Gordon and the orphan asylum.[43] Once again, through his misplacement at the orphanage, the repository of children, Ota Benga was considered to be something other than a man; he was merely small. And Ota Benga never really fit in with the children or took to academic pursuits. He worked as a farm laborer at the Asylum's agricultural facility on Long Island and eventually drifted away from the orphanage.[44] In 1910 he left the New York City region for good and settled in Lynchburg, Virginia, in a well-established black community surrounded by a bountiful countryside. He wore pants, had his teeth capped, learned to speak English and even converted to Christianity. Yet he spent most of his time in the woods hunting. If he ever considered returning to Africa he could neither afford the steamship ticket nor call upon Verner for assistance since he had disappeared from Ota Benga's life. On March 20, 1916, Ota Benga stole a revolver and shot himself in the chest. After years of being ignored, in death he made the papers once again.

Bradford and Blume ask, "Who was Ota Benga? Elf, dwarf, cannibal, Wildman, savage loose in the metropolis, beyond ape but not quite human, stunted, retarded, incomplete . . . —these are among the contemporary descriptions of him."[45] In life and in death, Ota Benga was a miniature "other" burdened with ideologies of social evolution, racial hierarchies, and primitivism. As the early twentieth century western world's most famous African, a modern-day Friday living out a contemporary Robinsonnade-cum-minstel show, Ota Benga became a symbol of colonized "Africa" for the white world, another specimen to be exhibited.[46] At the same time, I suggest, Ota Benga's literary afterlife symbolizes the obsession with the miniature—in particular, the racialized miniature—that constructs a powerful motif traceable in Anglo-American children's adventure stories from the 1920s forward.

Given the pervasive associations made between Africans and comedy in the nineteenth and early twentieth centuries, it is dismaying, yet not surprising, that caricatures of Africans are replicated in adventure tales such as the Doctor Dolittle series of novels, first published in the 1920s, by the Anglo-American author Hugh Lofting (1886–1947).[47] Lofting's books, set in the first part of the nineteenth century,[48] were innovations of nineteenth-century boys' tales of derring-do and conquest made popular by authors such as R. M. Ballantyne (1825–1894), G. A. Henty (1832–1902), Rider Haggard (1856–1925) and Edgar Rice Burroughs (1875–1950). Romances such as Haggard's, for example, helped to create a context for interpretations of Africa as backward and exotic, an "undiscovered" land that helped (white) boys to become men and, as such, these books—and later Lofting's—advanced powerful imperialist statements that reached a wide audience.[49] In his popular books combining plots of voyage and discovery with domestic comedy, Lofting leavened the conventional adventure story with gentle social commentary, an unlikely hero, and a fantastic premise. Hugh Walpole proclaimed in 1923 that in Lofting a successor to those giants of the nursery—Charlotte Yonge, Juliana Horatia Ewing, Mrs. Gatty and Lewis Carroll—had been found.[50] Yet, as many critics since have noted, although Lofting wrote movingly against cruelty to animals, he also, as Donnarae MacCann argues, "was apparently an unwitting originator of regressive, racially biased children's books."[51]

Some of Lofting's illustrations in the first book in the series, *The Story of Doctor Dolittle* (1920), underscore the kind of "missing link" evolutionary thinking that emerges from anthropological theorizing about pygmies such as Ota Benga. In the illustration, a gigantic top-hatted Doctor Dolittle takes the pulse of a tiny monkey that stands upon a steamer-trunk (a symbol of colonialist domination through travel and "discovery") wearing native costume very similar to Ota Benga's (see Plate 23). (Lofting had been a railway engineer in West Africa before the First World War and would have been familiar with some forms of African dress.) The tiny monkey appears as a pygmy figure in the act of being rescued by the white doctor whose top hat, enormous hands, and pocket watch all confer authority and superiority.[52] We can contrast this image with one of Ota Benga's official Bronx Zoo photographs in which he is holding a chimp. Zoo officials, who quite religiously kept records and photographs of all of their animals, did not know how to classify a human being; they solved the conundrum by posing Ota Benga with a chimpanzee and filing the photograph with the primate records.[53]

Lofting located the miniature racial other in his characterizations of the comic and foolish young African character, Prince Bumpo, whom Doctor Dolittle and his animal companions meet

1. *Queen Henrietta Maria with Sir Jeffrey Hudson* (1633) by Anthony van Dyck is a magisterial portrait of the young queen, featuring a favored member of her household: the court dwarf Jeffrey Hudson as a child.

2. P. T. Barnum with a young Charles S. Stratton, one of Barnum's most popular performers, in his role as the smartly dressed General Tom Thumb, *c.* 1850.

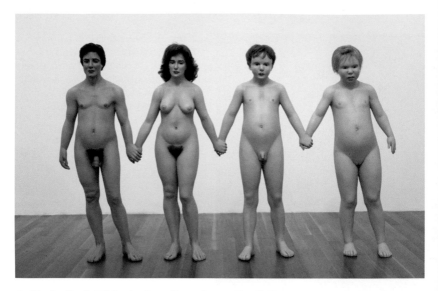

3. Charles Ray's 1993 mixed-media sculpture *Family Romance* presents a mystery to the viewer: are the children giants or the parents miniatures?

4. The Congolese "pygmy" Ota Benga was photographed with a chimp in 1906 while he was an inhabitant of the Bronx Zoo. Ota Benga's presence in the orangutan exhibit was widely reported and visitors flocked to the zoo during the month of his incarceration. After protests by a delegation of African American Baptist ministers, he was released to the Howard Colored Orphan Asylum in Brooklyn.

5. The Dutch anatomist Theodor Kerckring's 1717 illustration of early fetal development shows the embryo as a complete miniature child.

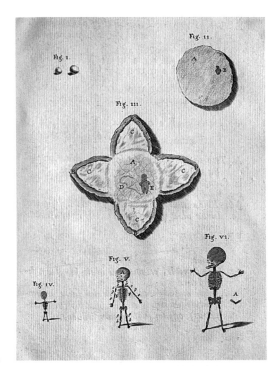

6. Richard Redgrave's painting *Gulliver Exhibited to the Brobdingnag Farmer* (1836) provides a sense of scale not only through the large faces peering at the tiny gentleman, but also by way of the small items gathered on the table around him, including a coin, die, and bee.

230 ESSAY DE DIOPTRIQUE.

que la tête seroit peut-être plus grande à proportion du reste du corps, qu'on ne l'a dessinée icy.

ART. XC.
Ce que c'est
que l'œuf de
la femme, &
comment un
enfant vient
ordinairement
au monde.

Au reste, l'œuf n'est à pro-
prement parler que ce qu'on
appelle *placenta*, dont l'enfant,
après y avoir demeuré un certain temps tout courbé & com-
me en peloton, brise en s'éten-
dant & en s'allongeant le plus
qu'il peut, les membranes qui le
couvroient, & posant ses pieds
contre le *placenta*, qui reste atta-
ché au fond de la matrice, se
pousse ainsi avec la tête hors de
sa prison ; en quoi il est aidé par
la mere, qui agitée par la dou-
leur qu'elle en sent, pousse le
fond de la matrice en bas, &
donne par consequent d'autant
plus d'occasion à cet enfant de
se pousser dehors & de venir
ainsi au monde.

L'experience nous apprend
que beaucoup d'animaux sor-
tent à peu prés de cette maniere

ART. XCI.
Que l'on peut
pousser bien
plus loin cette
nouvelle pen-
sée de la gene-
ration, &
comment.

des œufs qui les renferment.

L'on peut pousser bien plus
loin cette nouvelle pensée de la
generation, & dire que chacun de ces animaux
mâles, renferme lui-même une infinité d'autres

7. Nicolaas Hartsoeker imagined each sperm cell enclosing a minute child in his 1694 *Éssai de dioptrique.*

8. Daniel Mytens's enormous painting *Charles I and Henrietta Maria Departing for the Chase* (*c.* 1630–1632) makes an argument about the exotic other and size through its depiction of the dwarf Jeffrey Hudson, the monkey riding the dog, and the black stable-groom. Along with the flower-strewing cherub above, these exotics frame the opulently dressed king and queen.

9. In *Marchesa Elena Grimaldi Cattaneo* (1623), van Dyck's use of contrastive color—the rich red of the umbrella and the marchesa's cuffs, as well as her pale complexion next to the African servant's dark skin—emphasizes the marchesa's high status. Her exaggerated height in comparison with the black attendant similarly attests to the Genoese aristocrat's stature.

10. In Greek mythology, as punishment for his disobedience to Zeus, the Titan Prometheus is chained to a rock while his liver is torn out by an eagle—the event pictured here by Andreas Alciato in his *Emblematum liber* (1531). Each night, the liver would regrow and the torment would resume by day. It was not until many years had passed that the hero Hercules killed the eagle and rescued Prometheus.

11. The well-dressed courtier dwarf on stilts in R.B.'s emblem book *Delights for the Ingenious* (1684) is mocked for his pretentious attempts to elevate himself.

12. The jeering hunchback in the Victorian edition of Jacob Cats's *Moral Emblems* cannot see his own "faults," symbolized as short stature and disfigurement.

13. Just over seven feet in height, this imposing painting of the Infanta Isabella Clara Eugenia, attributed to Frans Pourbus the Younger (*c.* 1598–1600), was once one of a pair (its companion being a portrait of the Infanta's husband, Archduke Albert). The small figure nestled behind Clara Eugenia is not a child, as some had conjectured in researching the painting's history, but a dwarf.

14. Size, age, status, and species are contrasted in this Alonzo Sánchez Coello portrait of the Infanta Isabella Clara Eugenia (1585–1588). The Infanta holds a miniature of her father, Phillip II, while her dwarf Magdalena Ruiz holds two tiny monkeys. These animals are found in the Portuguese territories of the Amazon, which at the time belonged to Philip following the union of Spain and Portugal in 1580.

15. Through his confident gaze and skilled horsemanship, this hopeful painting *Prince Baltasar Carlos in the Riding School* by Diego Rodriguez de Silva y Velázquez (*c.* 1639–1640) posits a mastery that its young subject never attained, given his early death at almost seventeen years of age. In the painting, the figure of the dwarf, behind the rearing horse, unites with the prince through color, position, and size.

16. Child/dwarf, dwarf/child: Velázquez's 1632 portrait of the only son of King Philip IV of Spain and his first wife, Elizabeth of France, provides the viewer with an oscillating look between the two figures, both small and dependent, yet only one destined for the crown.

17. *Las Meninas* or *The Family of Philip IV* (1656) is Velázquez's masterpiece and one of the most celebrated paintings of all time. In 1692, the Italian Baroque artist Luca Giordano praised this work as the "theology of painting."

18. Charlie Stratton is about seven years old in this daguerreotype (*c.* 1845) taken with his father. By this point, he was already a seasoned performer.

19. William Henry Johnson was born in New Jersey in 1842. Known variously as "Zip the Pinhead," the "Man-Monkey," "The Missing Link," and the "What Is It?," Johnson was a mainstay of Barnum's freak show and performed into his 80s.

20. By virtue of the standing mirror and fireplace mantel that frame Charles Stratton and Lavinia Warren in their wedding attire, this portrait of the celebrity couple showcases both the bride and groom's size and the elegance of the event.

21. William Edgar Geil (1865–1925) was an American Evangelical missionary, explorer, photographer, and travel writer. Although called "America's Forgotten Explorer" today, Geil was well known during his lifetime for his journeys to China, Africa, Australia, and elsewhere around the globe.

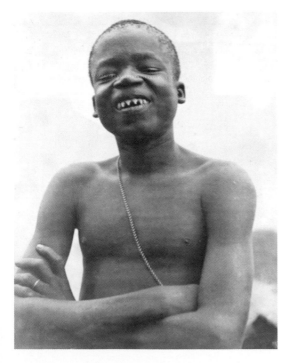

22. Ota Benga was a big draw at the "native" exhibition at the 1904 St. Louis World's Fair. In particular, his sharply filed teeth fascinated visitors as a physical marker of his supposed savagery.

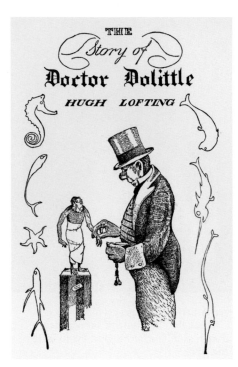

23. In this illustration from Hugh Lofting's first Doctor Dolittle book, *The Story of Doctor Dolittle* (1920), the monkey's small stature, especially in relation to the looming doctor, and his African dress type him as a pygmy.

96   *The Story of Doctor Dolittle*

and began reading the fairy-stories to himself.

Chee-Chee and Polynesia watched him, keeping very quiet and still.

"He began reading the fairy-stories to himself"

After a while the King's son laid the book down and sighed a weary sigh.

24. The illustration of the fairy-tale-reading Prince Bumpo that emphasizes his minstrel qualities was removed from the 1988 Dell Yearling reissue of *The Story of Doctor Dolittle*.

25. While the giants' nakedness contrasts with the tiny Englishman's formal dress, their topknots and his top hat connect the figures. In François Place's tragic tale, *The Last Giants*, however, the similarity in ornamentation is no match for the failure to overcome difference—here imagined in part as extreme difference in bodily size.

26. Lewis Hine captioned this 1910 photograph of the eight-year-old Leo with the child's response to a question about his wages: "No, I don't help me sister or mother, just myself."

27. The National Child Labor Committee (NCLC) was formed in 1904 to investigate and document child labor practices. Lewis Hine was hired by the organization in 1907 and took this photograph of a young spinner in 1908.

28. In *Science Advancing Mankind*, Louise Lentz Woodruff's sculpture featured at the 1933–1934 Century of Progress Exposition in Chicago, the enormous robot guiding the smaller male and female figures forward suggests that the robot's authority is assisted by the power and potential residing in great size.

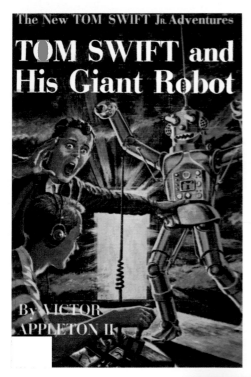

29. In its use of primary colors, characters' dramatic facial expressions, and the prominence of a menacing giant, Graham Kaye's cover design for *Tom Swift and His Giant Robot* (1954) reflects the visual aesthetic of B-movie horror film posters of the 1950s.

30. The child Eugenia Martínez Vallejo, depicted in Juan Carreño de Miranda's portrait (*c.* 1680), is nicknamed "la monstrua"—the monster—for her weight.

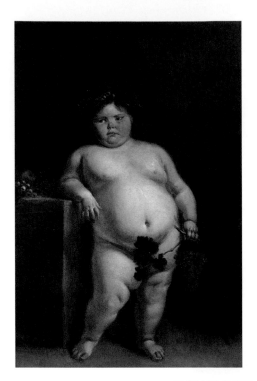

31. Eugenia Martínez Vallejo's body is further revealed in Miranda's companion portrait (*c.* 1680) of the naked child as Bacchus, the Roman god of wine and agriculture.

32. In 1850, Maxime Du Camp used the human figure to establish a sense of the scale and grandeur of the Egyptian colossus most westerners would never see but for the miracle of photography.

when they go to Africa to save the monkeys from a terrible spreading sickness. Bumpo is a recurring character, but he plays his most significant role in *The Story of Doctor Dolittle*. While he is not physically tiny, he is comically figured as a child—naïve and foolish (see Plate 24). Prince Bumpo's childlikeness is also emphasized through his preferred reading material—fairy tales—which he takes to be factual. This characterization of the fairy-tale-reading, childlike black native places Lofting's Bumpo as an inheritor of the ideology that manipulated Africans such as Ota Benga into becoming performative minstrel pygmies. Even his name—Bumpo—is reminiscent of "Tambo," the tambourine-playing endman in blackface minstrel shows. Lofting's illustration of Bumpo, whose features are grossly exaggerated, reading his fairy tales, curled up, head in hand, supports this reading of the childish minstrel performer made familiar by caricatures of Africans and minstrel-show advertisements.

Inflamed by his passion for Sleeping Beauty, whose tale he had read, Bumpo searched widely for her: " 'And having traveled through the world many days, I at last found her and kissed the lady very gently to awaken her—as the book said I should. 'Tis true indeed that she awoke. But when she saw my face she cried out, "Oh, he's black"! And she ran away and wouldn't marry me—.' "⁵⁴ Believing that whiteface alone would increase his chances of success with Sleeping Beauty, Bumpo appeals to the doctor to transform his face into a reversal of blackface (he adds that he will cover the rest of his body with "shining armor and gauntlets of steel, like the other white princes, and ride on a horse."⁵⁵ To Bumpo's delight, the doctor succeeds not only in changing his skin "to the color of snow," but also in altering his eyes, "which had been mud-colored, [to] a manly gray!"⁵⁶ Bumpo is so pleased with his new complexion that he begs to keep the doctor's looking glass (a trope borrowed from "Snow White") in order to look at his face all day long. Bumpo desires another kind of conversion—from "savage" to courtly knight, minstrel clown and cannibal to suitor, from African to European—that is also predicated on a hierarchy of color.⁵⁷

Certainly, the discourse of conversion—of true and false gods, righteousness, patronage, repudiation—is also the language of colonization and of many children's books from the eighteenth century and after. Lofting's "conversion" narrative is meant to be comic, yet the satire is actually focused upon the absurdity of the black youth's notion that he could be equal to the pure-white heroine of a fairy tale. In the second volume of the series, *The Voyages of Doctor Dolittle* (1922), as explanation for why he cannot leave the "Red Indians" who have made him their chief, Doctor Dolittle says, "They are, as it were, my own children—I never had any children of my own—and I am terribly interested in how they will grow up.' "[58] Lofting falls upon the familiar trope of linking native people with children, miniaturizing and patronizing their cultures and values as incomplete and other. As David Steege notes, in the Doctor Dolittle books, "Africa is there to confirm the West's view of itself, not to disturb it."[59]

A decade after Lofting first released his animal fantasy stories, American journalist and travel writer Richard Halliburton began to publish books about his adventures around the world that extend in non-fiction the colonialist thinking about Africa and Africans found in Lofting's novels.[60] These compilations of travel narratives, such as *The Famous Adventures of Richard Halliburton* (1932), were intended for a general readership, yet their popularity with youth led to additional books aimed at children; these texts reworked the material in some of his earlier stories, employed direct address and a self-conscious frame narrative—taking the young reader on a trip to "The Occident" or "The Orient." I would like to examine, in particular, an account of Halliburton's relationship with two African children, published first as "The Two Slaves" in *The Famous Adventures of Richard Halliburton* and then, some six years later, recycled as "The Slave City" in *Richard Halliburton's Second Book of Marvels: The Orient* (1938). These tales represent examples of colonialist appropriations of the racialized miniature for comic and ideological purposes and emphasize the performative aspects of the African child, another kind of racialized miniature.[61]

In the first telling of the tale, Halliburton and his pilot, Moye Stephens, arrive in the West African French colonial city Timbuctoo [sic] by biplane, christened "The Flying Carpet." For centuries, Timbuctoo was a thriving commercial center in the Mali empire run by the Tuaregs, Muslim trans-Saharan trade merchants. In addition to selling salt and gold, Timbuctoo was also a notorious slave market.[62] During their stay, the two travelers were continually annoyed by the bat colonies that roosted in the ceiling mats of the mud houses, and squeaked by day and flew in and out of the windows all night. Halliburton's solution was to buy two slaves to help combat the bats.

As Halliburton relates, "To me, that idea seemed in no way shocking, for both my grandfathers had been slaveowners in Tennessee, and I had been brought up believing in the sanctity of the institution."[63] To his surprise, the only slaves available to Halliburton were "miniatures"—not pygmies, but two ten-year-old children—". . . rather pretty children, judging from Negro standards, and apparently about as healthy as the goats they herded."[64] He bought them for five dollars each. As the new owners of these children, the two men had the privilege of naming them. Going down the alphabet, they considered a number of ordinary Anglo names such as Alice, Eddie, Mabel, and Pat, but settled on pet names instead: Little Eva and Monkey. "Monkey," of course, calls to mind the "missing link" theory relied upon by the scientific and popular press (including children's books) that posits Africans such as Ota Benga as close relatives to primates. But why "Little Eva"?

This section of Halliburton's adventure for young (white) readers corresponds with Lofting's fantasy of childhood reading and complexion-envy, though Halliburton's story is based on fact rather than fiction. "The Two Slaves" represents yet one more use of the conversion narrative—in this case, also inflected by notions of the vulnerability of the child and the small—for colonialist, racist ends. Halliburton alludes to another well-known "fairy tale" of a sleeping/dying white girl: not "Sleeping Beauty," in this case, but Harriet Beecher Stowe's *Uncle Tom's*

Cabin (1852). "Little Eva" is the angelic golden-haired five-year-old daughter of a wealthy plantation owner around whose bedside, as she lies dying, people gather in order to hear her "good news" of God's love. Halliburton's decision to name the enslaved girl "Little Eva" and not "Topsy" (the name of the impish slave girl whose antics were burlesqued in dramatic re-enactments of *Uncle Tom's Cabin* as recently as the early part of the twentieth century) ironically and cynically reverses the two characters' identities so that the enslaved African child becomes the beloved American character. Stowe's Little Eva converts both slave and plantation owner alike through her innocence and perfect faith, and, as Halliburton relates with a relish meant to be comic, Little Eva (with Monkey), true to her name, converts Halliburton and the pilot—into slaves themselves: "Looking after Monkey and Little Eva became a twenty-four-hours-a-day job. Moye was finally driven into remarking that he didn't know who were the slaves—they or we. They were as free and happy as the wind, enjoying life and liberty as they never had before, while Moye and I, the distracted slaveowners, found ourselves more and more shackled with the responsibility of our two little savages."[65] Yet, ultimately, of course, the African Little Eva's "attempts" at converting the white men around her through her innocence, beauty, and affection (she is forever hugging the two men) fail; her story lacks the purposeful and moving "happy" ending provided by Little Eva's death in *Uncle Tom's Cabin*. Though Stowe's Little Eva dies, her purity—seemingly unavailable to her African namesake—is the catalyst for redemption; the Timbuctoo Little Eva's inability to "understand that she was a *slave*"[66] seals her fate, and she and Monkey are taken back to the Tuareg chief. The chief refuses to repurchase the children, but accepts Halliburton's ten-dollar bribe to take them off his hands. In a further indulgence of his ironic "white slave" metaphor, Halliburton declares himself "emancipated" once the children are gone.[67]

What changes were made to this story in its retelling for Halliburton's book aimed at a young readership? In *Richard*

Halliburton's Complete Book of Marvels, published in 1938, the rationalization that slave ownership was a sacred institution has been deleted in favor of a comment meant to put distance between Halliburton and the decision to own slaves. He takes cover under the excuse of "resorting" to local custom.[68] In this version, Halliburton mentions the "long sad journey" many Africans had endured when "Arab overlords" sold them to America.[69] The children are named "Little Eva" and "Monkey," as before, but the emphasis is placed on ordinary child life: descriptions of the children's antics, the pretty red costumes procured for them to wear, and the good "parenting" that Halliburton and Stephens give the children by providing a balanced diet, adequate sleeping arrangements, clean clothing and bedtime rituals. Ultimately, as in the first telling of this series of events, the two men decide that their failures in "slave-training" mean that they cannot keep the children. However, the price of return doubles in this version of the tale: Halliburton must pay the slave trader a bribe of ten dollars for each child. In a direct address to the young reader added to this later book, Halliburton concludes, "You say you'd like to meet Little Eva and Monkey before we go? I'd like to see them again too, but I'm afraid there's no use trying. Several years have passed since I said good-by to them. They are almost grown now, and I have no doubt that they've been sold long ago by their Arab owner to other Arabs somewhere in the vast Sahara. Wherever they are, I hope they have kind masters— and lots of pink soap, and vitamins, and the reddest pants in Africa."[70] When it was in his power to do so, Halliburton does not free the children, nor does he later wish they were no longer enslaved. He converts two young people, who are in fact slaves, to positions of "childhood" that are merely performative and illusory, and transforms the tragedy of their history into what is meant to be a humorous story with commercial overtones. At this point, Halliburton's pity for the children is worthless.

Exploitative conditions circumscribe the idea of the pygmy just as they do the folktale miniature, court dwarf and performative dwarf discussed in the first three chapters. Both the African pygmy and the African child similarly function as incomplete, merry, and unselfconscious beings. Both are quite valuable as performers who display for white audiences the idea of the African pygmy (savage, primitive, and heathen) and "missing link" ideologies. Since he literally owns the children for a time, Halliburton misuses the language of parental responsibility when writing about Little Eva and Monkey. This "colonial" relationship between big and small, owner and "product," ringmaster and entertainer, colonizer and colonized—like the relationships between Verner and Ota Benga, Henrietta Maria and Jeffrey Hudson, P. T. Barnum and Charles Stratton, among many others—are characterized, in part, by unethical manipulations of the small for the pleasure of the big. The mutability of the miniature's many stories—retold in folklore, emblems, myth, early novels (such as *Gulliver's Travels*) and children's literature—attests to the enduring nature of his role as linchpin of complex cultural fantasies about others and origins. The figure of the pygmy not only recalls these same issues, but highlights the ethical dilemmas that arise from the collisions between racist scientific "knowledge," popular imagination, and emerging humanistic sensibilities and postcolonial perspectives that begin to recognize the subjectivity of the other. Within children's literature, responses to these clashes take the form of revision, adaptation, and censorship.

Adapting *Lusus naturae:* The Child and the Eth(n)ics of Size

Let's return to the scene in *Gulliver's Travels* in which the tiny Gulliver is examined by the learned Brobdingnagians. As I discussed in chapter one, the puzzled group of philosophers advance a number of theories to account for Gulliver's littleness. After discarding many different ideas, including living fetus, they determine that he represents a kind of joke: a *lusus naturae,* or "sport of nature." African pygmies and other miniatures, such as the performing dwarf or court dwarf, as well as miniatures within children's literature of the 1930s, '40s and '50s and western culture more generally, are often treated as "jokes" and expected to entertain adults or the "large" (however conceived). Thus, the *lusus naturae* functions as an apt symbol for many representations of the miniature racialized other depicted in children's literature. Yet, within this same period, an ethics of the relationship between big and small was developing. One site for this work can be found in T. H. White's *Mistress Masham's Repose* (1947), an adaptation and extension of Swift's satiric *Gulliver's Travels*. In his particular reimagination of the foundational text of miniaturization/giganticization, White focused upon the exact relationship between big and small that this study, and postcolonial theory and inquiry more generally, remains interested in today.

Although Gulliver is respectful of the well-ordered Lilliputian culture, the frivolous war with the neighboring kingdom of Blefuscu and the ridiculous Big-Endian egg controversy—fought over which end of the egg should first be cracked before eating—spotlights a "childish" and petty national character. Of course, Swift is lampooning British society via the small (read small-minded) Lilliputians in comparison to the "lofty" Gulliver; though his tone is wry throughout the book, White never ridicules the Lilliputian descendants or uses them metaphorically to represent human folly. His interest elaborates an ethics of big and small that, as Joan Bodger noted in 1965, "is the central theme of English children's literature" and could well serve as an inspiration for postcolonial children's literature's exploration of race, authority, and age difference—that is to say, much of contemporary children's literature, as well.[71]

Mistress Masham's Repose was written for Amaryllis Garnett (the infant daughter of White's closest friend, David Garnett), completed in 1944 and published in 1947. White's novel tells the story of a young orphan and her discovery of a community of Lilliputians whose ancestors were stolen from the island of Lilliput after Gulliver's tenure there. Although the tale was a Book of the Month Club selection and has been called a "minor classic" of children's literature, it is not particularly well known today.[72] This is a pity as the book is a fascinating and complex study of interpersonal ethics set within an expanded folktale plot complete with villains, child hero, kindly helper and a miniature race.

White's novel features ten-year-old orphan Maria who lives on an immense dilapidated English estate, Malplaquet, with her governess, Miss Brown. White based Malplaquet on the grounds of Stowe School, where he was once a teacher and later Head of English. The adults in Maria's life, Miss Brown, and Maria's guardian, the vicar, Mr. Hater, are repulsive and unkind. Whenever possible, the lonely and ill-treated Maria slips out of the house and explores the vast grounds, looking for adventure. One day she rows to the tiny island in the middle of the estate's lake and discovers a minuscule baby cradled in a walnut shell. That the miniature is an infant—not a tiny proto-adult such as Thumbelina or Tom Thumb—in possession of a mother who will fight Maria fiercely in order to protect her child, emphasizes White's obsessive attention to realistic details within his remarkable fantasy world. As Martin Kellman notes, in *Mistress Masham's Repose* "we get a masterful recreation of three societies at once, a Utopian one, an eighteenth-century one and an extension of a famous, miniature one, all triumphs of the concrete imagination."[73] The "concrete" nature of White's vision, in fact, provides the perfect backdrop to the important philosophical issues the book raises.

White's interest is in exploring the ramifications of love, and the potent desire to possess the other; he argues that this desire must be suppressed. For her part, Maria is utterly charmed by the tiny people—yet they refuse to behave like toys one might own and play with. After Maria shows her find to the Professor, one of only two friends she has in the world, she complains that mother and child are "no fun."[74] The Professor's heated response exposes Maria's unfeeling behavior: " 'Why should she be fun? Why should she do anything? Why should she eat? Is she yours?' "[75] The theme of ownership and obligation is so strong in the novel, in fact, that White toyed with the idea of titling the book "No Masters, No Slaves."[76] In any colonial relationship, the identities of colonizer and colonized jointly form an unequal power exchange. The Professor would have Maria reject the role of colonizer altogether, and he convinces Maria to return the two to their home and warns her about the dangers inherent in her desire for the little people: Maria might tyrannize and the Lilliputians might fawn; these unhealthy behaviors would transform Maria into a lordly bully and the others into feeble dependents.[77] Although Maria protests, she ultimately returns the Lilliputians, meets their spokesman, the Schoolmaster, and becomes intimately acquainted with the entire community.

Maria learns how the original Lilliputians, at the mercy of one so much bigger than they, had been enslaved and ill-treated. In the eighteenth century the Lilliputians had been captured by the captain who transported Gulliver home and who later returned to Lilliput to collect as many people and animals as possible and exploit them for profit. The Schoolmaster of Lilliput in Exile, who is Maria's teacher in the history and ways of the Lilliputians, relates that, to their captor, " 'our broken and distrackted [sic] People were Creatures not possessed of human Rights, nor shelter'd by the Laws of Nations. Our Cattle were for his Profit, because we could not defend them; our very Persons were an Object of Cupidity, for he had determined to show us in his native Land, as Puppet Shews and Mimes.' "[78] Thus the descendants of the original Lilliputians taken to England have grown to be a secretive and suspicious people for their history was shaped by the tyranny of the big over the small. Maria knows their past, yet still a child, she cannot withstand the allure of attempting to make the tiny into wonderfully animated, perfect, playthings: "Although she was decent, as was shown by her offer to carry the Schoolmaster in the barrel, she was still young. The more she adored and wondered at the doings of her six-inch People, the more she wanted to take control of them. She wanted to play with them, like lead soldiers, and even dreamed of being their queen."[79] Maria compels some of the Lilliputians to playact for her; she chooses a favorite and makes a toy out of him. The people begin to hide when she visits the island. Ultimately, after she puts her favorite into a toy airplane and he is injured, the Lilliputians reject her.

Again, the Professor offers advice in an effort to educate Maria in the ethics of responding to the "other." The Professor reminds her of the difference in point of view between the tiny Lilliputians and a full-grown child: " 'Now, Maria, you must try to look at this from their point of view. It is an exceedingly curious situation. You are a child, but very big; they are grown-up, but very small.' "[80] She asks to choose just a few to play with, but the Professor is stern: " 'If they had given in to you, they would never have been able to call their souls their own, and their economic life would have been upset in order to play at queens and subjects. However nice you were to them, it would have been intolerable.' "[81] As she grows in maturity, Maria comes to marvel not *at* the People—their tiny size, their bodies, their minuteness, that is, what they look like—but who they are as a culture, their "minuscule Oeconomy."[82] One way in which this understanding comes about is through the ritual of gift-giving: "[what Maria] discovered was that it was a mistake for giants to choose small presents for dwarfs. The proper thing for a giant to do was to choose the largest present which a dwarf could possibly use, while the dwarf had to choose the smallest or finest thing which could be of use to the giant."[83] The most welcome and appropriate gift respects the ingenuity of both cultures—big *and* small.

Finally, Maria's guardians discover the secret of the Lilliputians and resolve to capture and display them, kill Maria and frame the Professor for the deed. Their nefarious plans are foiled by the quick thinking and joint cooperation of Maria, the Lilliputians, the Professor and the Cook. All ultimately ends happily, as the Professor replaces Miss Brown as Maria's teacher, her lost inheritance is restored, and the People, Maria, and a few others, live in harmony ever after.

A lesson from *Mistress Masham's Repose*—size corrupts—is one we have seen manifested over and over again in colonialism and in the idea of the pygmy. Once an individual or group discovers that it is "big," and thus someone else is "small," tyranny or patronage can poison the relationship as the big attempts to own or control the small. Yet White's novel also explores the opposite dynamic, the "Napoleon effect": sometimes the small manipulates the large. Certainly this reversal forms an important aspect of the Tom Thumb trickster tales discussed in chapter one, as well as in dwarf children's literature more generally (but is employed less often in children's books about race—certainly twentieth-century books). When the Professor warns Maria that she must not keep the tiny woman and baby he urges her to recognize that her own powerlessness, her "littleness" as a child, could influence her to try to control something smaller than herself, or to prove that she is "great": " 'Well then, Maria, although this is not a fashionable way of going on, nor even a successful one, it is a thing which I believe in—that people must not tyrannize, nor try to be great because they are little. My dear, you are a great person yourself, in any case, and you do not need to lord it over others, in order to prove your greatness.' "[84] The wry and dry narrator reminds the reader of the power that the child possesses:

> "Parents," says the immortal Richard Hughes, who wrote the best book about children that was ever written, "finding that they see through their child in so many places the child does not know of, seldom realize that, if there is some point the child really gives his mind to hiding, their chances are nil."[85]

In siding with the child against adults White shows himself to be a children's book author in the style of Lewis Carroll (in the *Alice* books), E. Nesbit and J. M. Barrie—a position later taken up by authors such as Roald Dahl, Florence Parry Heide and Raymond Briggs—who similarly confront issues of big versus small.[86]

The tragic consequences, within a fictionalized colonial context, of the small lording it over and conquering the great are played out in a prize-winning French picture book, François

Place's *The Last Giants* (originally published in France in 1992 as *Les derniers Géants*, translated by William Rodarmor and published in English in 1993).[87] This postcolonial cautionary tale is illustrated with detailed, delicate, whimsical and small-scale pen and ink watercolor illustrations, reminiscent of Mitsumasa Anno's work, that at times belie the serious and violent events described in the text. In this picture book, a tragedy occurs as a result of the small's tyranny and selfishness. Here, the small represents the mind—"civilized," the "scientific," and the "intellectual"—and the large embodies the ideal of the Noble Savage which focuses on the body in nature: artless and sensual. The book is a kind of fable, yet another rewriting of *Gulliver's Travels*, and travel and adventure books such as Halliburton's and the Doctor Dolittle series, in which the western and "civilized" world comes into contact with exaggerated racialized others. In this case, however, there are giants, rather than miniatures, as the "others" of extraordinary size.

The 75-page, text-heavy picture book (a detailed illustration that reflects the plot is framed on every other page) is told by a first-person narrator, the fictional nineteenth-century English explorer and scientist, Archibald Leopold Ruthmore (his second name, of course, reminds us of King Leopold II of Belgium, one of Africa's most notorious and successful colonizers). On September 29, 1849, Ruthmore sets off on an expedition to Burma to find the Land of the Giants. The story is set within the context of colonial commerce and exploration: Ruthmore complains about the price of guides for his expedition and the bonuses he must promise the boldest natives who continue to accompany him, even after others turn back, on the hot, uncomfortable and tortuous trail. The trip is very dangerous: Ruthmore loses men to river rapids and then his entire company to a massacre by a headhunting tribe. Only Ruthmore survives. He continues on his quest, though he is exhausted and nearly starved. Finally, his fool's errand is rewarded and he discovers, in succession, enormous footprints, a giants' graveyard and, ultimately nine living giants, each 40 feet high (see Plate 25).

The half-dead Ruthmore, still sporting his top hat, is treated gently and compassionately by the giants. These beings are remarkable not only for their great size, but also for their beautiful singing voices and the elaborate tattoos that cover their bodies. After being restored by the giants, Ruthmore recounts, " 'They must have taken very good care of me, as not a trace of fatigue remained. To the contrary, I experienced a feeling of total well-being and found it almost normal to be casually rubbing shoulders (as it were) with the sweet-voiced colossi who had welcomed me with such kindness."[88] Ruthmore accepts the position in which most miniatures are placed, that of dependent child: " 'From our very first meeting, the Giants cared for me as they might a child. I remember our first real exchanges during long evenings together. The Giants would spend entire nights calling to the stars, one by one, their voices a chorus of mingled harmonies. The flowing melody was complex and repetitive, a rich tapestry of low, deep notes laced with extended variations, pure high trills, and crystalline flights. It was celestial music, and infinitely subtle.' "[89]

Although Ruthmore comes to appreciate the giants and their mysterious ways of communication, harmony, storytelling, and recording history (through their ever-changing tattoos), he is foremost a man of science—and this self-identity translates into commercial activities, trading in information and knowledge, and using people (the natives and ultimately the giants themselves) in order to elevate his own position in the western scientific community. When Ruthmore returns to England and publishes treatises on this lost race, he is at first laughed at and his findings scorned. Yet the end result of his detailed maps and scientific work is annihilation of the giant "others." By revealing their existence to the curio-hunting world, Ruthmore conquers and exploits the giants as fully as if he had enslaved them. Ruthmore's realization of the consequences of what he has written comes too late to save the giants. Ruthmore's "scholarship" is used by others to locate the giants, kill them, and display their enormous heads as trophies.

Like *Mistress Masham's Repose, The Last Giants* also rewrites *Gulliver's Travels,* warning against the exploitation and oppression of "third worlds" populated by beings of extraordinary size—some of which exist within our midst, others we (westerners) seek and "discover."[90] In these worlds, as Gulliver finds, awe-inspiring miniature and giant others abound, but a cautionary note must be sounded as the knowledge of such others—in literature, as in life—generally results in their destruction. There is no happy ending in Place's book. The tiny can disrupt the Eden of the large just as the large can disrupt the small's paradise. The giants' former perfect happiness—"At night, they celebrated the cycle of the seasons, the pathways of the stars, the always-troubled unions of water, earth, air, and fire. They seemed perfectly and eternally happy"[91]—is torn apart. The giant ape King Kong is another exaggerated "nonwhite" victim of "civilization."[92] Place rewrites the King Kong story to the extent that the remote giants are gentle, nurturing and maternal. Yet these isolated giants are sacrificial victims as much as the sexually frustrated captive Kong. If, famously, "Beauty killed the Beast" in *King Kong*—that is, the old story of racialized sexual desire leading to male disempowerment—the giants' story reveals the rotten underside of "discovery": loss and extinction. Like King Kong and other giants brought down by tiny adversaries, Ota Benga, the Borrowers and other miniatures destroyed by hulking "friends," the death of the freedom and happiness of the racial others is foretold at the moment of their discovery or their displacement.

The Figure of the Pygmy in Postcolonial Apologiae and Revision

Halliburton's cruel treatment of the slave children, recounted in *Richard Halliburton's Complete Book of Marvels,* a book meant to entertain (white) children, tells another version of the Ota Benga story, and trades on the idea of the pygmy we have found to be so pervasive in early twentieth-century children's literature and culture.[93] In this case, Halliburton's descriptions of the lively children mirror the "clever" and comical pygmies who, it is assumed and projected, never fully grow up. Nor are they easy to erase from the history of Anglo-American children's literature, though attempts have been made. In rewriting the past and attempting to revise the future, some children's book authors— with varying degrees of success—have altered the terms that made trading in Africa, the third world, and miniature native people so easy and common in earlier children's books.

For example, in Roald Dahl's well-known and well-loved *Charlie and the Chocolate Factory*, first published in 1964, the Oompa-Loompa characters are clearly constructed as African pygmies: they are described as "pure black" with "fuzzy heads" and no taller than Willy Wonka's knee. When the children exclaim at their color, Wonka explains, " 'Right! . . . Pygmies they are! Imported direct from Africa!' "[94] In later editions, the Oompa-Loompas no longer hail from Africa, but from Loompaland and their skin color has changed to "rosy-white."[95] Yet their need for a warm climate, their tiny size, merry ways, and their love of dancing and singing mark them as the western idea of the pygmy, no matter their skin color. A related "white-washing" occurs in the film *Willy Wonka and The Chocolate Factory* (1971) in which the Oompa-Loompas have orange faces, green hair and wear clownish costumes. However, the revisions made to the Doctor Dolittle books are perhaps the most extreme. In 1988, Dell Yearling republished the books after deleting and revising the most blatantly racist scenes. Each American version is now accompanied by an afterword written by Lofting's son, Christopher, explaining the changes (literally bookending the laudatory Hugh Walpole essay comparing Lofting to Lewis Carroll and others). Although the commentary begins in a passive and equivocating way—"In some of the books there were certain incidents depicted that, in light of today's sensitivities, were considered by some to be disrespectful to ethnic minorities and, therefore, perhaps inappropriate for today's young reader"[96]—the decision was made to change the books. Most significantly, the Prince Bumpo character and his scenes have been altered so that he no longer desires to be white, black characters are no longer referred to by derogatory epithets, and a number of Lofting's drawings have been deleted.

In 1997, Michael Hague collaborated with Patricia and Fredrick McKissack on a new version of *The Story of Doctor Dolittle*. They describe their rewriting of the Prince Bumpo scene thus: "Unfortunately, by having the young man beg Doctor Dolittle to make him white, Lofting expressed the prince's dilemma in a manner that reflected the prevailing racial attitudes of his day, and the positive message [to accept yourself as you are and avoid foolishly trying to make yourself more attractive to others] got lost and confused."[97] Of course, any changes to the original text are themselves controversial because they may well be not only patronizing and political, but also radical erasures of an earlier understanding—we would call it a *mis*understanding—of race and culture. In considering Dell's versions of the Doctor Dolittle tales, critic Anne Collett argues that "the removal of overt signs of racism that leaves a covert racism in place would seem in many ways more 'dangerous' to young readers whose critical responses might well be provoked by words like 'coon' and 'nigger.' "[98] Does the alteration—some call it censorship—of Africa in children's books such as *Doctor Dolittle* and *Charlie and the Chocolate Factory* and even Richard Halliburton, itself participate in a kind of patronizing miniaturizing principle? Yet one more version of the pygmy in the zoo?

Revision may well represent a natural response to troubling children's books. But revision, especially when it takes the form of revising history, comes at a cost. I would like to recall the end of Ota Benga's life. Immediately upon Ota Benga's suicide in 1916, the program to erase history began in a *New York Times* article titled "Ota Benga, Pygmy Tired of America: The Strange Little African Finally Ended His Life at Lynchburg, Va." The author of the obituary blithely altered the events of Ota Benga's life, asserting that he was an employee of the Bronx Zoo and that his job was to feed the "anthropoid apes:" "It was this employment that gave rise to the unfounded report that he was being held in the park as one of the exhibits in the monkey cage."[99] The obituary goes on to state, reversing that old colonialist Rudyard Kipling, "Finally the burden of the white man's civilization became too great for him to bear, and he sent a bullet through his heart."[100]

Ota Benga may well have been "tired of America," but we have not tired of him. Certainly westerners are used to thinking of Africa—and perhaps, "pygmy" peoples as well—as a point of origin, a place from which to go forward. As we have seen, however, in the treatment of Africa and Africans in children's books and American culture, "going forward" was too often translated into damaging ideologies of "progress" and racial hierarchy. Postcolonial theory, by turning a critical eye upon colonialism and listening to the voices of the colonized, highlights the hurtful and ignorant nature of such ideologies and calls for conscious re-examinations of the past. Within children's literature, revision represents one significant aspect of accepting the responsibility to remember and acknowledge the past. As Leela Gandhi comments, "if *postcoloniality* can be described as a condition troubled by the consequences of a self-willed historical amnesia, then the theoretical value of *postcolonialism* inheres, in part, in its ability to elaborate the forgotten memories of this condition."[101] Yet, attempts to erase the past through a clumsy reintroduction of the old ideal of the Noble Savage—another reductive ideology—or a simplistic "apology" for colonial exploitation, or a nostalgic return to an earlier precolonial history, fail to confront the reality of colonialism's effects and essentially superimpose another flat image upon the figure of "pygmy-as-minstrel" or the racialized miniature needing white characters—often children—to restore freedom or mediate danger.

I would like to mention briefly three recent books for children written by British, South American, and American authors, respectively, featuring pygmy characters that attempt to repair the damage of colonialist thinking that reduced the pygmy to folktale trickster, primitive savage, or missing link. *Forest Singer* (1999), a beautiful and well-intentioned picture book written by Sylvia Sikundar and illustrated by Alison Astill, avoids negative stereotypes, and, for the most part, reflects accurately the dwellings, flora, and fauna of the deep forest home of the main character, and provides in an Afterword factual information about contemporary life for African pygmies. Yet the book manages, at the same time, to offer an outsider's patronizing "peace corps" attitude of helpfulness, a conventional didactic plot—practice makes perfect—and a tidy conclusion that treats the pygmy children as exceedingly gullible. The book also attempts too much—combining elements of the folktale, didactic story, and information book—and ends up relying upon myth and metaphor to communicate "pygmies" to white readers. The main character, a young pygmy boy named Mabuti, lives in a mythical place (the "ancient slopes of the Mountains of the Moon") outside of time. His name, "Mabuti" suggests "Mbuti"—the name of an entire pygmy people from the Ituri Forest in the Democratic Republic of Congo. Thus, Mabuti seems to be essentialized into Pygmy.

Isabel Allende's *Bosque de los Pigmies/Forest of the Pygmies* (2005) is the third in her young adult trilogy featuring two teens (one from South America and one from America) whose totemic animals provide mystical powers of shape-shifting, protection, productive trances, and abilities to talk with animals.[102] The teens, Alexander and Nadia, accompany Alexander's journalist grandmother on assignment to Kenya. In the book, Allende acknowledges the complicated politics of contemporary post-colonial Africa. Power vacuums have allowed for unscrupulous Africans to exploit and oppress their own people. The book carefully idealizes the pygmy society in a way that highlights its superiority to white western culture: "[pygmies] had the freest and most egalitarian society on earth. Men and women lived in close companionship, the husbands and wives hunting together and equally sharing in the care of the children. . . . There were no differences between genders or old and young, and the children owed no obedience to the parents."[103] In Africa, the trio is confronted with the corruption and violence of the African forest: the murder of missionaries and the enslavement of the pygmies. Through the course of the novel, the small group of travelers (including one African woman)—led by the teens—free the pygmies, depose the tyrant who had enslaved them and restore the rightful ruler. Although, significantly, the final battle for the fate of the pygmies takes place between the despotic and cruel overlord and the pygmy leader, in fact, it is Nadia and Alexander who save the pygmies and restore order to the deep forest. The teens often "explain" Africa to the Africans and convince them to act in their "best interest."[104]

More troubling than Sikundar's conventional mythic-moral tale or Allende's romantic magical-realist novel for young adults, is Jane Cutler's radical revision of history in *The Song of the Molimo* (1998), a woodenly written novelization of the months Ota Benga spent at the St. Louis World's Fair. Again, the book is well-meaning, but plays fast and loose with the facts of Ota Benga's life and death and uses him as a counterweight to racist early anthropological thinking. Here, Ota Benga functions as the moral compass for twelve-year-old Harry Jones, whose ignorant assumptions about pygmies—informed by newspaper articles, senior anthropologists, and the crowds attending the exhibits—gradually shift, given the example of the intelligent, sensitive, and generous African. Ota Benga teaches Harry about enslavement and laments that both he and the performing animals at the Fair are slaves. When visiting the Fair disguised as an African American boy, Ota Benga is horrified by the exhibit of a fake plantation complete with "slaves" entertaining audiences with soft-shoe antics, yet he also feels at home with them. Eventually, Ota Benga disappears into St. Louis, and it is suggested that he will be absorbed into the African-American community. By rewriting Ota Benga's life as a happy story of African assimilation into American culture, his last act of defiance or of despair—who can know what drove him to suicide?—is denied and erased.

Both revision and erasure trade upon the ideology of

"othering" that creates the problem of hierarchies, First World/ Third World, North/South, white/black, and big/small in the first place. Revision offers its own dangers: when we try to make the past acceptable, when we "convert" without looking back from colonialist thinking to the shared benefits and yes, even burdens, of the postcolonial world (postcoloniality is a privilege not universally enjoyed) we run the danger of erasing history. If we evacuate "pygmy" of all meaning, then we occlude the racist history that has created the idea and discourse of the pygmy, and erase the life and death of Ota Benga. Once books such as Hugh Lofting's are seen as representing an evolutionary "dead end" and thus are doomed to fall out of print or to revision, contested content and its consequences can be lost. And it's the conflict that must remain. This is the space inhabited by *The Last Giants*. Place's cautionary morality tale, while trading in part on the idea of the Noble Savage, also revives the nineteenth-century colonial explorer with his top hat—a marker of civilized excess given its impracticality in the jungle—and brings the story of his conquests to the conclusion denied or ignored by the similarly top-hatted Doctor Dolittle and Willy Wonka.

While valuable and necessary for educational reasons, morality tales such as Place's are tragic and, perhaps, less enter-taining than the popular adventures of the traveling Doctor or inventive Willy Wonka. Humorlessness (by this I don't mean an absence of jokes, but reliance on didacticism and a sense of what is "good for you" as a guiding principle) often concludes, regard-less of merit or prizes won, with avoidance by young readers. I would like to consider another children's book of the late twentieth century that attempts to bridge the gap between *Doctor Dolittle* and *The Last Giants*, a book that similarly confronts colonialism by way of using the miniaturized, racialized other as a metonym for nature, harmony, and the past: *The Indian in the Cupboard* (1980) by Lynne Reid Banks, the first in a series of very popular books for young readers.

Omri, Banks's pre-teen protagonist, receives two seemingly unrelated birthday gifts—the prosaic miniature plastic figurine given by his best friend and a curious battered metal cabinet presented by his brother—that in combination ultimately create the fantastic adventure that follows. The gift of an ancient key from his mother completes the raw material needed for the magic to work. Omri assembles the three items and joins them by means of a birthday wish: "Now he closed his eyes and unwished the test pass and wished instead that this little twisty key would turn Gillon's present into a secret cupboard."[105] The cupboard does indeed become a place of secrets—and transformation—as plastic becomes real once the cupboard door is closed and locked. By means of this magic, Omri unwittingly brings to life his tiny plastic figurine. The living being this twentieth-century London child has summoned from the past is an eighteenth-century Iroquois Indian named Little Bear.[106] The differences between Omri and the Indian are profound and include size, age, historical time, region, language, culture, and race. Questions about the ethical treatment of the tiny that were raised in *Mistress Masham's Repose* come to the forefront of this novel as well; yet, I argue, Banks fails to negotiate successfully the dilemmas raised by the tensions between the big white boy and tiny Indian, past and present, master and slave.

Just as in colonial children's books from the early twentieth century, such as *Bomba the Jungle Boy and the Cannibals, or Winning Against Native Dangers* (1932),[107] or even *The Forest of the Pygmies* in which the western child is made more "superior," more "white" in contrast with native pygmies, Omri's potential to become a sensitive man (and good father) is realized through his nurturing interaction with the miniature's "otherness." By entertaining and fascinating the white boys Little Bear is placed both in the role of "pygmy"—or miniature racialized other—as well as simultaneously offered as a symbol of resistance to previously dominant theories of racial superiority and Manifest Destiny that resulted in colonial expansion, and the displacement and deaths of native peoples (in Africa and America). Even the conventional and hackneyed vision of the Noble Savage— promoted in the 1995 American film version of *The Indian in the*

Cupboard and gestured at in the novel, similarly reduces the native character to "other." The role of the Noble Savage in children's literature tends to educate the white child in the ways of nature, conservation, and ecology.[108] This postcolonial schizophrenia, or desire both to validate and, at times, worship the cultural and racial other *and* sustain the primacy of values "claimed" by whiteness—civility, order, authority, among others— fails to be resolved in the course of the novel and ultimately results in a misrepresentation and flattening of the miniature characters into racial and gender stereotypes.

Banks's popular *Indian in the Cupboard* series is part of the tradition of books in which toy characters are real or become real.[109] Yet, the Indian and Cowboy—Little Bear and Boone—the two primary miniatures from *Indian in the Cupboard*, do not have toy natures; their perspective does not originate from the miracle of animation since they were alive in another time and dimension, and their location within the plastic figure analogues is an accident of representation that the magic key and cupboard effect. Omri, no less than Boone and Little Bear, sees the world anew through his experience with people of radically different size. Omri's relationship with these miniature men transforms him.

Like the Lilliputian Schoolmaster and the toy soldiers from Pauline Clarke's *Return of the Twelves* (1962; originally published in the UK as *The Twelve and the Genii*), both Little Bear and Boone are men, not boys. When Little Bear is first brought to Omri's room, he is fierce, brave and ready to fight his enormous adversary. He soon begins to boss Omri around, using his authority as an adult, refusing to perform for Omri and vigorously resisting being touched or being made into a pet. The cowboy Boone, although his crybaby ways play him against type, similarly prepares to do violence in order to protect himself. Little Bear rejects the helplessness that accompanies being tiny in a big world when he insists that his size is the correct one and that it's his surroundings (including Omri) that are exaggerated. He shouts to Omri, early on, " 'I not small! You, big!' "[110] Yet the violence that has been done to the past—Little Bear and Boone (as well as other characters such as Tommy and Matron) are plucked from their individual times and inserted into the far future—transforms the present for both man and child. As the narrative progresses, the roles of man and boy are essentially reversed so that each tiny man becomes more childlike (this is especially notable in the case of Little Bear who, unlike Boone, displayed no childish qualities at first), and more akin to the toy he is not. Thus they are increasingly "pygmyfied." To the men, Omri is a giant of a boy and yet he becomes man-like as their relationship grows and he begins to treat "his" living toys as if they were children, even as he acknowledges that he does not own them. The ethics of big and small advanced in *Mistress Masham's Repose* fails to resonate in Banks's novel. Omri's perspective—as "large" and as "white"—begins to take precedence, a position that is familiar in many well-intentioned multicultural books and forms the starting point for postcolonial cautionary tales such as Place's *The Last Giants*.

In "Reading Children's Literature Multiculturally" Dan Hade argues that many examples of multicultural children's literature use non-western or non-white cultures as *signs* to create meaning for white America. Thus, in the example of Susan Jeffers's 1991 picture book *Brother Eagle, Sister Sky* (a speech attributed to Chief Seattle), the book essentially sends a message to European Americans about environmental responsibility. According to Hade, "This, in effect, turns Native American subjectivity into white American objectivity."[111] When Little Bear's demands appear to Omri to get out of hand, he thinks, "While giving Little Bear every respect as a person, he was not about to be turned into his slave. He began to wonder if giving him those weapons, let alone letting him make himself into a chief, was such a good idea."[112] In Clarke's *The Return of the Twelves*, by contrast, eight-year-old Max never interferes with the maneuvers and desires of the living toy soldiers that had once been owned by the four Brontë children, although he does struggle to protect them: "[Max] had quite early realized that part of their life depended on their being left to do things by themselves and not being interfered with. He could oversee and suggest, but not dictate."[113] At first meeting the soldiers, his sister Jane wants to cuddle and coddle the tiny twelve, but she is stopped by Max: " 'Jane, don't treat him like a toy or a baby animal, will you?' warned Max. He felt that this would be wrong and insulting. 'He's a small, alive person,' he explained, 'and full of years and wisdom. He says so.' "[114] Max acknowledges the authority of the miniature men and refuses to give in to the delicious desire to manhandle and manipulate the miniature, a desire first indulged by Glumdalclitch in *Gulliver's Travels* and exhibited in much of children's literature ever since.

Ultimately, the Iroquois Indian and cowboy become increasingly toylike as a means to highlight Omri's growth. His dramatic maturation is not physical, of course, but emotional.[115] As a corollary to Omri's development, the miniature men are infantilized. For example, after Little Bear shoots Boone in an argument begun in the aftermath of watching a television Western together—another degree of "miniaturization" and thus distortion of the history of the conflict between white man and Native American—Omri takes the position of patriarchal authority, relegating the murderous intention of each tiny man to the significance of a schoolyard fight: "Omri's voice was steely, a voice Mr. Johnson [his headmaster] himself might have envied—it commanded obedience."[116] Later, sorry for his actions and overwhelmed by guilt, Little Bear acts like a spoiled child by stomping on his chief's headdress and destroying it.[117]

To complete the transformation of small man into child and large boy (from the perspective of the cowboy and Indian) into man, in one of the last scenes of the novel, Omri functions as a parent and creates a family by forcing the previously antagonistic men to become "blood brothers."[118] The three tiny figures, for Omri has kept his promise and "brought [Little Bear's] woman to life," now at peace, spend one bucolic night in a domestic grouping around the campfire: "Bright Stars was now crouched by the fire, tending it, singing softly. One of the horses whinnied.

Boone seemed to have dropped off to sleep, leaning on Little Bear's shoulder."[119] This "doll-play" heightens the reversal that has taken place in the power balance between the miniature and the large, between child and adult, white and native.[120]

Yet another aspect of miniaturization or "pygmyfication" that we have seen at work in earlier colonialist children's books and one that is also in play in Banks's novel is the "miniaturization" of the cultures of the Native American and Texan. At first, the plastic Indian has no meaning—no narratable qualities—without its antagonistic complement, the cowboy.[121] What *The Indian in the Cupboard* ultimately presents, in fact, is the history that children are given (via television and film, among other venues) that turns cultures and people into stereotypes. Omri and Patrick (and the readers) learn that "their" men are real and not characters designed to play roles in their or anyone else's drama; they are complex, flawed, sensitive, and talented individuals—which is all to the good. Similarly, but less helpfully, Banks also "miniaturizes" the cultures from which Boone and Little Bear hail, thereby performing her own miniaturizing transformation within the narrative. In his discussion of eighteenth-century portrait miniatures, Steven J. Gores reminds us of an important condition of most miniaturizing projects: nuances are lost in the translation of something large into something small, portable, condensed: ". . . although one may tend to forget that maps are miniaturizations, they are, in fact, exemplary of how the miniature in general claims to convert something that is inherently too large and complex for the comprehension or control of the individual eye into something that is easily mastered."[122] Much as she has clearly tried to avoid it (in terms of the short history of the French and Indian war, Little Bear's costume,[123] the longhouse, and some of the customs of the Iroquois), Banks's fantasy, akin to Cutler's over-determined reimagining of Ota Benga's life, also distorts history as well as proportion in this otherwise enormously appealing version of a time-slip fantasy.[124]

Although the book won a number of awards and was positively reviewed in both Britain and America, it is not universally liked. A number of teachers, critics, and librarians (some Native American, some not) are opposed to the use of the book in the classroom and, in the words of one educator, feel "aghast [at the] progress that *The Indian in the Cupboard* has made toward status as a *classic*."[125] Many complaints stem from the stereotypical portrayal of Little Bear as the "savage Indian" who grunts "Tontoese."[126] While I am very sympathetic to these views—and share them in most cases—I believe that some of the criticism of Banks's novel misses the mark. For example, Rhonda Taylor cavils at the depiction of Little Bear as "*the wild Indian*"[127] because he stabs Omri in an attempt to keep his hand away, has "fierce black eyes," and mimes chopping off the head of a fish, among other gestures. To be sure, Little Bear does all of these things – it's actually highly reasonable for him to try to protect himself. He is also a warrior who had recently been fighting against the French. Although his bragging about scalping thirty Frenchmen is not an attractive quality, his actions are not unwarranted given the circumstances. In sum, these descriptions of Little Bear do not stereotype him as a savage so much as reveal his positive (especially in comparison with Boone) characteristics of bravery, strength, and honor.[128]

Interestingly, I have not read any commentary that protests the portrayal of the other miniaturized man, the cowboy. Boone is a caricature of the Texan, a historical figure who has much to apologize for, clearly, and who is not protected by any group identity. The unfair aggressor, we now believe, who helped to "settle" the West by exterminating the buffalo, warring with Mexico, and working the cattle ranches that fenced off Native lands, the Texan could have been the strong, silent type. However, in Banks's fantasy he is a cowardly, fragile soul with a drinking problem. Boone could be no one's hero and so he is just another version of a stereotype, here inverted to make the cowboy a comic figure.[129] The problems with Little Bear's characterization are more complex. The fact that Little Bear speaks English can be relatively reasonably explained by the fact that the English and the Iroquois tribes fought together against the French and

Algonquin Indians (the arch-enemies of the Iroquois before white men arrived).[130] However, Little Bear would most likely not have referred to himself as "Iroquois," but perhaps by his tribe (Onondaga, Oneida, Seneca, Cayuga, Mohawk, or Tuscarora), or, in his own language, as one of the "Haudenosaunee" (People of the Longhouse). Perhaps most significantly, Bright Stars, Little Bear's new wife, would have played a more significant role if Banks's representation of Native life were to be accurate.[131]

The matrilineal organization of the Iroquois is one of its most distinguishing characteristics. The "double-miniaturization" of the one female character in the novel (besides Omri's mother), the Native woman, is therefore most surprising. Bright Stars (she is, at least, given a name—but one that relates to her beauty) has no personality other than her role as conventional helpmeet, cook, and nurse. She is distilled down to the color of her dress, her inarticulate (to Omri) attractiveness, and her function as Little Bear's sexual and life partner. Taylor comments that "[t]he book manages to perpetuate stereotypical images of Native women as property useful for their labor, while simultaneously reviving portrayals of Indian women as either beautiful *princesses* who collaborated with Whites (like the mythologized Pocahontas), or as ugly because they were not White."[132] In Iroquois culture, women are the clan mothers. They select the council members and have the ability to countermand men's decisions. When a man marries, he relocates to his wife's longhouse. Identity comes from the mother. Women owned all of the property. Although through their experiences with the tiny men Omri and Patrick learn lessons about what makes someone "real" and the ethical responsibilities each person has to another, Bright Stars is left out of this equation. When Omri decides to send everyone back to his own time and place, Bright Stars will return with Little Bear to his time. Little Bear, for a reason not explained in the text, functions as an anchor, as the keeper of the only past that registers. Thus, Little Bear, like the top-hatted and "civilized" Doctor Dolittle, appears to own Time. It is as if Bright Stars, unlike the two men, did *not* exist anywhere before Little

Bear had chosen her; we never learn of her time or background. She is miniaturized almost out of existence.

The Indian in the Cupboard exploits the power of exaggeration—by way of magic and the miniature—to highlight the importance of friendship and the healing that can occur once enemies have "played" together. In the novel, Omri and Patrick, Boone and Little Bear stage an elaborate, real-life game of Cowboys and Indians in which the seemingly inevitable ending has been transformed from violence and bloodshed to peace and brotherhood. Little Bear and Boone are transported from different pasts, from different locations, to a dominant present in which their histories have become miniaturized and diminished, just as their bodies have been reduced. Their presence as individuals mitigates those reductive images for the boys in the book and for the readers, while at the same time, Banks indulges other miniaturizing impulses. When Omri shuts the door of the cupboard with the tiny figures inside and then turns the key for the last time, Little Bear, Boone, Bright Stars and the two horses are sent back to the "unknown regions of time, space—proportion."[133] This return to an unknowable past armed with the lessons of a thoroughly contained present (Little Bear and Boone rarely leave their corner in Omri's bedroom) perfectly enacts the nostalgic journey identified by Susan Stewart as a hallmark of the miniature: "the transcendence presented by the miniature is spatial transcendence, a transcendence which erases the productive possibilities of understanding through time. Its locus is thereby the nostalgic. . . . Hence the miniature is often a material allusion to a text which is no longer available to us, or which, because of its fictiveness, never *was* available to us except through a second-order fictive world."[134] Thus "authenticity" and fantasy collide in The Indian in the Cupboard. Morris's comments about the film version of The Indian in the Cupboard (and the Disney Pocahontas film) are apt here: "Both Pocahontas and the warrior from Indian in the Cupboard represent the ethnic body as a combination of fantasy playground and locus of cultural anxiety; reworking them into more 'suitable' shapes both reinforces bourgeois social, racial, and gender forms and relieves the tension that comes from the continued disturbing accusatory presence of the Native American as the cultural imagination."[135] Yet the story of the racialized miniature in children's literature does not have to end with the containment and domestification—pygmyfication—of the racial other. As I discuss below, narratives of resistance and subversion can upend the typical hierarchies of size and race.

The Pygmy Strikes Back

Both the racist ideologies and misuse of the pygmy figure I have identified in colonialist fiction such as *Charlie and the Chocolate Factory, The Story of Doctor Dolittle, Forest of the Pygmies,* and *Song of the Molimo,* among other works, and the postcolonial schizophrenia I have sketched in *The Indian in the Cupboard* are confronted, and perhaps defeated, in *The Man* (1992), an unusual book by the British author/illustrator, Raymond Briggs. *The Man* is illustrated in Briggs's signature style—paneled drawings and speech bubbles—modeled on the comic strip. A true inheritor of White's *Mistress Masham's Repose,* the book features a racialized miniature and participates in the tradition of adaptations and revisions of *Gulliver's Travels.* The racial element is much more subtle in *The Man* than in Halliburton's tales, *The Last Giants, Doctor Dolittle* or *Charlie and the Chocolate Factory,* though it exists and forms a significant aspect of the text. The tiny figure, called, simply, "Man," is drawn and speaks as a kind of Celtic figure, a northerner with lower-class tastes than those of the boy, John, whose house he commandeers. Though Celtic people—Scots Highlanders and the Irish—and the English, of course, are all "white," the divisions and distrust between these cultures can be profound and inflected by ideologies of race and class.[136] While Man vehemently denies that he is a "foreigner," his costume—an adapted striped sock with red rubber-band belt that creates a kind of plaid kilt—red hair, bushy moustache and taste for Guinness beer all type him as "Celtic" and his tiny size, "nut-brown" skin and heavy musculature as an other. Man could also be a Pict—a member of that mysterious ancient race of people formerly of the British Isles. Yet, discovering Man's origins, labeling him, is a zero-sum game and one that Man himself takes pains to reject as racist objectification.

The complicated psychological conflict between the sentient, tiny, brown character and the large-scale white figure in the position of the grown-up (whether adult or child) is graphically and poignantly demonstrated in *The Man*.[137] When a tiny, naked, hairy and bossy man appears and awakens John by hitting him in the head with cough drops, John thinks that he is dreaming. Later, when trying to figure out the riddle of "the man's" existence, John hits upon a likely identity for Man: he must be a Borrower. The man is not aware of Borrowers and is highly insulted by the comparison: " 'How dare you suggest I live under the floorboards! You are prejudiced, aren't you? Just because I am smaller than you, you think I must live in small, dirty places— like a rat!' "[138] John also tries out other identities on Man—gnome, fairy, or extra-terrestrial—but Man rejects them all with venom: " 'I'm me! Just shut up! It's insulting to be asked what I am all the time. It implies that I'm not human.' " Man vehemently refuses the "missing link" labeling so common in colonial discourse, as well as the infantilizing labels of fairy or gnome.

Man, although not a child, needs some assistance in order to survive in the world of giants, just as Little Bear and Boone do. Man both enjoys bossing John around and being served while at the same time he is frustrated and angry at his own limitations and marginal status: " 'Why is it other people get all the gravy? When is *my* turn coming? . . . When will I have a nice big car? When will I own a whopping great house like this?' " John, too, both grumbles at all of the work and danger involved in hosting Man (such as repeatedly getting in trouble with his parents over the chaos Man causes), as well as delighting in having him around as a companion, a best mate, and a challenge. Over the four days of their acquaintance, John and Man engage in numerous serious philosophical arguments that highlight the ongoing struggles between big and small, adult and child, wealthy and under-privileged, able-bodied and differently abled, normal and abnormal, human and non, white and "colored," love and hate. What Briggs has done is to use size difference to strip away the sentimentality and nostalgia that attends much of adult responses to childhood and the adult perception of the child's point of view—as White and Clarke do in *Mistress Masham's Repose* and *The Return of the Twelves*, and Banks attempts in *The Indian in the Cupboard*. Where Briggs goes beyond these authors is in allowing the pygmy miniature to speak most eloquently and without "colonial" interpretation, mediation, or patronage from an adult or a child in the position of the (white) authorial adult. He also directly confronts the performing dwarf stereotype and avoids the moralizing or apologia of awkward revisions of children's classics such as the Doctor Dolittle books or Place's *The Last Giants*. *The Man* is both raw and unflinching. When John expresses that he likes to watch Man eat, Man explodes in a rage: " 'I'm not on stage! I'm not an actor! This is me! This is MY LIFE! I don't want you turning it into a PERFORMANCE! . . . I am ME!' "[139] Man refuses to perform as a whiteface minstrel. John is hurt and responds: " 'I like that! I've been like a mother to you. I've cooked for you! Bathed you! Clothed you! Cleaned up your babyish messes!' " The two combatants then get to the heart of their struggle and it is, not surprisingly, about size. Man accuses John of enjoying Man's tinyness, of playing with him like he was a toy, of erasing his humanity and turning him into a novelty whose charm has worn off. (Man perceptively states, " 'You are like all children with their pets. The novelty soon wears off. They don't really like *animals*. They like NOVELTIES.' ") John shoots back that Man "exploits" his smallness and uses it to manipulate people and that Man is not the "dear, sweet, helpless little chappie" he pretends to be, but, rather, is "bossy, messy, selfish and smelly . . . !" The argument escalates until John threatens to call Social Services to take Man away and Man threatens to burn the house down. The childlike Man and the man-like Boy are at loggerheads, trapped in mutual affection, need, and distrust. The typical "colonial" relationship is inverted here as the pygmy character invades the place of the white "master." While Man's infantile behavior is also part of the regressive fantasy of the pygmy, Man's character is always complicated. He likes being who he is and resists John's attempt to "civilize" him; he both admits his desire for human touch and companionship and refuses to become a pet.

Although she does not discuss Briggs's *The Man* or *Mistress Masham's Repose* in her book *When Toys Come Alive*, Lois Kuznets's comments about responsibility and privilege in narratives about miniatures seem apt here. Kuznets finds Banks's *The Indian in the Cupboard* and Clarke's *The Return of the Twelves*, two novels about miniature men and large boys, to have failed to consider the position that the boys will hold as they grow up: "Born to a class of powerful patriarchs, [Omri and Max] may, however, have many future opportunities to display toward 'others' less fortunate than themselves the behavior they practice in dealing with their vulnerable toy combatants. Perhaps fortunately for boys like these, they can take for granted the benevolence of their system. . . . Here the protagonists are not encouraged to examine these underlying assumptions or how such constructs govern their own behavior toward the less powerful 'others.'"[140] The same criticism cannot be leveled again *The Man* or *Mistress Masham's Repose*. In the latter, the heiress Maria, oppressed both due to her age and, it seems clear, for her supposed girlish weakness, uses her eventual wealth in a sustaining rather than conquering manner.[141] Man and John, by honestly revealing their negative feelings, have begun to breach the wide divide that separates big and small. Man wants to be seen for who he is ("I am ME," he repeats continually). This is the cry that both adults—and Man is an adult—*and* children make (Man is also "childlike" in his need for attention, affection, and assistance.) When John discovers that Man has left in the night, he is silent and holds Man's abandoned tiny makeshift clothing to his cheek, bereft.

Man has refused to perform for John in any minstrel or pygmyfied way; he rejects all the dwarf labels and conventions of tinyness in children's books—fairy, Borrower, etc. While he is dependent upon John for some of his bodily needs, he is not helpless and does not need a champion, a master, or a father.[142] In the figure of Man (even his name suggests the division between his adult status and John's boyishness), those issues of race, gender, class, and *size* that are at the heart of stereotyping, combine: he is tiny, racialized, working-class and conventionally male (relishing sport and typically masculine pursuits, unlike the gentle and artsy John). As Jan Nederveen Pieterse concludes, social inequality is the glue that binds the attitudes of racism, classism, and sexism together: "What racism, classism, sexism all have in common is social inequality: the key to all the social relations discussed above is the pathos of hierarchy. While common denominator is power—the power that arises from a hierarchical situation and the power required to maintain that situation—it is also a matter of the anxiety that comes with power and privilege. Existing differences and inequalities are magnified for fear they will diminish."[143] This insight about exaggerating otherness and growing it in order to ward off the perceived danger in the reduction, or shrinking, of differences—collapsing us and them—is both metonymic of the tensions under discussion in this chapter and between big and small more generally, and can be usefully applied to the idea of the pygmy as I have traced it in nineteenth- and twentieth-century children's books.

In the tradition of *Mistress Masham's Repose* and concomitant with *The Last Giants*, Briggs's *The Man* (published the same year) refutes the discourse of conversion—"to be respected, loved, valued, you must be more like me"—we have found so pervasive and popular in works for children such as Halliburton's *The Complete Book of Marvels* and *The Story of Doctor Dolittle*. Yet *The Man* is highly unusual. What does *The Man* represent that *The Indian in the Cupboard*, *Song of the Molimo*, and other pygmy narratives and adaptations of *Gulliver's Travels* fail to do? Like Omri and Little Bear, Man and John grow close after they have "played" together; yet their conversations, give-and-take, and even arguments demonstrate their equality and, most importantly, their position as individuals. Though Man and John would seem to be generic (given Man's name and mysterious origin, and his reference to John as "boy"—a reversal of the usual master/slave relationship in which all black men are "boys"), in fact he is unique. John cannot "discover" Man's race and then name it or declare ownership of it, or gain commercially from it by describing, photographing, and publishing it. Like the Lilliputians residing at Mistress Masham's Repose, Man is a *secret*—not to himself, but to others. Thus he subverts the conventional discourses of primitivism, childishness, or incompleteness and he cannot be stereotyped as a remnant of a mythic past and thus captured as a folktale dwarf, fairy, gnome, monkey, noble savage, or Lilliputian. Since Man cannot be possessed and his history cannot be told, he cannot be "authenticated" by others. His history is his own.

Unlike Ota Benga. Cutler's revision of Ota Benga's life in *Song of the Molimo* illustrates our conflicted relationship with the figure of the pygmy. Even when the pygmy is not conceived of as a minstrel entertainer performing primitivism, his story too often remains a tale of conversion, and his symbolic function is confined to marking difference—not only of lack (in size, mental capacity, Christian faith, or humanity)—but also of excess. Unlike the colonial explorer or children's adventure story writer whose cultural capital was never in doubt, the racialized miniature is made to carry an over-abundance of cultural debt. Overlaid with postcolonial guilt, pre-colonial nostalgia, and myths of phylogenetic or individual history, the diminutive pygmy emerges from such collective fantasies as *our* cultural gigantic.

PART II

BIG BODIES

INTRODUCTION
The Monstrous Giant

In this cultural history of big and small bodies I attempt to demonstrate how our affective engagement with extraordinary bodies leads us to insights and knowledge about the world and ourselves. As such, this book considers difference in bodily size and the meanings we attach to exaggeration and excess or to diminution and distillation. The quality, nature, and dimension of the bodies toward which we sometimes yearn and from which we sometimes recoil can take many forms: littleness is typically feminine, appealing, and inviting; the gigantic is often perceived as masculine, threatening, or disgusting. Interesting additional tensions can arise when these categories are inverted and the miniature is masculine—as we have seen in the first chapters of this book—or the giant is female. I would like to turn now from considerations of the small to focus on examinations of the big. This introduction to the second part of my discussion of size, scale, extraordinary bodies and the imagination will look at the close relationship between giganticism and monstrousness in particular, setting the stage for an in-depth consideration of two examples of gendered "giants": the giant mechanical man (robot) and the obese girl.

What is a monster and what is his relationship to great size?[1] Monsters are unnatural, often grotesque, hybrids. We recognize the monster as both familiar *and* other. They are typically over-sized and animalistic, even if they appear in human-like form. Monsters stand in for much more than their unusual bodies and appetites: they are portents, harbingers, symbols of wickedness. David Gilmore's definition of monsters includes giganticism: "transcending normal limits and domains, the monster-figure appears to be invincible or unstoppable; embodied as a giant beast, it becomes a perfect metaphor not only for the limitless power of evil, but also for dissolving of [*sic*] the boundaries that separate us from chaos."[2] In addition, enormity—as well as littleness—can imply an affront or challenge to God's power.[3] There are also key connections between the monster and the child: according to Gilmore, "monsters are children's alter egos, their inner selves."[4] Thinking about monsters often brings children to mind. Marina Warner notes astutely that "the monsters of popular dread, with their unbridled appetite, insatiable tyranny, unappeasable desire for gratification, are just like . . . babies, big babies, as big as babies are when they explode into a life and change it."[5] Childhood itself links the giant-as-monster and the child. That is, whether Frankenstein's creation, a Golem, or an enormous robot, the created monster is linked to the child through *lack*: like his miniature brethren the homunculus, created giants do not experience childhood and they do not grow. Frankenstein's monster felt this difference keenly. His awareness leads him both to bitterness and a crisis of identity as he laments, " 'From my earliest remembrance I had been as I then was in height and proportion. I had never yet seen a being resembling me, or who claimed any intercourse with me. What was I?' "[6] The big monster and small child are not always posi-tively linked, as we find in books for young readers such as Dahl's *The BFG* or even Patrick Ness's psychologically complex *A Monster Calls* (2012). For example, while Frankenstein's monster hopes that William, Victor Frankenstein's young brother, will not harbor the same attitudes as adults—" 'Suddenly, as I gazed on [William], an idea seized me, that this little crea-ture was unprejudiced, and had lived too short a time to have imbibed a horror of deformity' "—these hopes are dashed and tragic consequences ensue.[7]

Small children create and fear monsters, to be sure, and through their interactions with large adults, they also encounter "giants" in everyday life. Psychiatrist Percy Cohen writes about how children experience scale differential psychically: ". . . all children have experienced adults as more powerful, more prestigious, and more experienced than they are; all children have also experienced adults as higher than they are and have come to recognize or, at least, to suppose that greater height has much to do with greater advantage."[8] While speaking for children in this way is problematic, I agree that size difference is part of the universal experience of, at least, early childhood, and that adults, as both large and powerful, may also be monstrous.

Just as I have attempted through close readings of various figurations of the dwarf and pygmy, examinations of cultural forms such as folktales, festivals, court masques, and paintings help to historicize the monstrous giant. By the mid-nineteenth century, like the disproportionate dwarf or the exotic pygmy, the bodily difference giganticism performed indicated "freakishness" to onlookers. Rosemarie Garland Thomson describes how the monster, or *lusus naturae* of the medieval and early modern period—a concept discussed in chapter one and chapter four— became the "freak": "As divine design disengages from the natural world in the human mind, the word 'freak' emerges to express capricious variegation or sudden, erratic change. . . . By the seventeenth century, 'freak' broadens to mean whimsy or fancy. Not until 1847 does the word become synonymous with human corporeal anomaly."[9] Once again, Susan Stewart provides a useful summary of the problems of bodily difference: "the physiological freak represents the problems of the boundary between self and other (Siamese twins), between male and female (the hermaphrodite), between the body and the world outside the body (the *monstré par exces*), and between the animal and the human (feral and wild men)."[10] The freak show was an attempt to bridge those boundaries, to draw these "others" near

for close inspection by the "normal." Mainstays of the nineteenth-century freak show, an institution with roots in early
modern fairs and tavern exhibits, the giant and dwarf piqued the
interest of the curious, paying public. Indeed, the two anatomical anomalies were often paired in displays, entertainments and
at court. For example, the giant William Evans, porter to King
Charles I, succeeding—and exceeding in height by two inches—
his predecessor Walter Parsons, was once "partnered" with
Jeffrey Hudson in a dance between the acts of a court masque. In
The Worthies of England (1662), Thomas Fuller notes William
Evans's extreme physical awkwardness as well as his unusual
stature. Certainly, the imbalance of Evans's performance would
have been heightened by the visual "joke" created by the difference between his size and that of the tiny and nimble Jeffrey
Hudson, drawn out of Evans's pocket "first to the wonder, then
to the laughter of the beholders."[11] For his part, P. T. Barnum
continued this kind of exploitation of difference when he united
on the stage Tom Thumb and the giants in his employ.

Evans's extreme height and lack of grace are typed as comical.
More often, however, the giant is marked in the literary and
cultural imagination as dangerously powerful, a magnet for the
resentments of his target, the weaker small. Tales of ancient
races of giants populated early literature and mythology: along
with the Titans, Rabelais's Gargantua and Pantagruel, and Swift's
Brobdingnagians, Homer's reviled Cyclops Polyphemus, son of
Poseidon, features among the most famous literary giants. At
first, his ruthlessness and raw power overwhelm the helpless
men in Ulysses's party, and he chooses victims to eat at will. Yet,
ultimately, in the struggle between the hero Ulysses—bearer of
culture—and the lawless, godless gigantic Cyclops, one of a
people who ignorantly fail to plant and reap (*Odyssey*, Book 9),
the clever miniature and his men escape and humiliate the giant
by taking advantage of his witlessness and desire for drink.

Thus, while the miniature's body is precious and precocious,
admirable in its completeness and tiny perfection, the giant's
body is both fascinating and fearsome. As Burke reminds us, tiny

bodies are often endearing and beautiful, while enormous beings are rarely considered so appealing: "A great beautiful thing, is a manner of expression scarcely ever used; but that of a great ugly thing is very common."[12] The stereotype of the Giant found in literature from epics to folklore and popular culture holds that with great size comes brute strength but little intellectual muscle. Like Homer's Polyphemus, most giants are stupid and easily outwitted by their smaller, more intelligent, adversaries. In an early edition of "Jack the Giant Killer," through clever sleights and illusions, Jack outsmarts even the two-headed Welsh giant whose modus operandi is "private and secret malice."[13] The conventional trope of the intelligence of the tiny and the dullness of the huge is presented somewhat unusually in Rodman Philbrick's young adult novel *Freak the Mighty* (1993).[14] In this novel, the undersized, genius kid (suffering from a rare genetic disease) and the oversized, learning disabled kid team up—literally, as Maxwell carries Freak on his shoulders—to become one effective gigantic nine-foot-tall unit called "Freak the Mighty." This "excess" is typed positively: the two boys' strengths complement each other and their friendship helps each "freak" to belong to someone other than family members.[15]

In a positive take on the big female, the Giant sometimes functions as a metaphor for Mother Nature in search of balance. Ted Hughes's *The Iron Woman* (1993) comes to life out of the marsh mud to wreak havoc as revenge for factory pollution of the ecosystem, but with the help of the Iron Man and two children, remains to teach humans (in particular, men) a lesson about mess and cleaning up. Similarly, in Melvin Burgess's *The Earth Giant* (1995) for young readers, the 13-foot tall silent earth giant who had slept for thousands of years in her "earth cradle" under an ancient oak tree must return to the soil to heal after her wounding by adults who fear her. Ultimately, she is reunited with her people, outer-space giants, whose planet nears Earth every five thousand years. Once again, it takes a child to understand the giant-figure and to save her.[16] Generally, however, the Giant is viewed as overproduction, as exceeding balance.

Miniaturization, by contrast provides useful condensation, an economy of size (in the Disney film *Mulan*, the tiny dragon Mu-Shu boasts that he is "travel-sized for your convenience"). The gigantic is not so easily moved, contained, or able to escape notice.

Just as our imaginings of fairies, leprechauns, brownies, pixies and other races of little people have been expressed through folktales, ancient stories, and their retellings, giant beings populate these same folk genres. Akin to the Cottingley fairy photographs in England that "proved" the existence of tiny people, evidence of giants may also be found. An American example is the "Cardiff Giant," a successful nineteenth-century hoax that convinced crowds of curious onlookers that a gigantic race of prehistoric people once walked in what would become New York State.[17] Monster movies of the 1930s and '40s, such as *King Kong* and *Frankenstein*, exploited white America's anxieties over racial purity and the fear of the enormous other. And B-movies of the '50s highlighted the discontents of oversized beasts such as Godzilla and his progeny who menaced entire cities of tiny nameless, faceless people. The obsession with sightings of the Sasquatch—a giant ape-like man/monster commonly known as "Bigfoot"—to this day continue to be chronicled in newspaper and magazine articles and websites.

Fears about the giant's capacity for violence can never be completely allayed—even in children's literature in which the domestication of the giant often provides an important aspect of the story, as I will discuss below. In many children's books that include gigantic characters, a central problem is how to satisfy the creature's hunger. From Clifford the Big Red Dog to Norbert the Norwegian Ridgeback (Hagrid the gamekeeper's dragon in the first Harry Potter book), unrelenting appetite in the large is a vexed issue for the small.[18] Many giants like to eat children in particular. Ogres and ogresses in popular folktales such as "Puss in Boots" and "The Sleeping Beauty" desire children as food above all other dishes. In George MacDonald's story "The Giant's Heart" (1863), a boy and a girl find themselves in Giantland and attempt to cure the giant, whose heart resides outside of his body, of his appetite for child flesh.[19] The children steal the heart in an effort to persuade the giant to eschew children as food. Although promising never to eat children again, the giant betrays his oath and attempts to grab the children while his heart is being returned. The boy kills the giant in order to save himself and his sister.

As the traditional tale "The Giant's Heart" demonstrates, given their great size and strength it is often difficult for the small to trust giants. In C. S. Lewis's fantasy *The Lion, the Witch and the Wardrobe* (1950), the "giant" is a carnivorous animal. When Susan Pevensey inquires whether or not Aslan, "the great Lion," is safe, Mr. Beaver retorts: " 'Course he isn't safe.' But he's good. He's the King, I tell you.' "[20] Even after his reformation, the giant in Oscar Wilde's sentimental fable about the selfish giant immediately falls back into anger when his favorite child friend appears with injuries to his feet and hands: " 'Who hath dared to wound thee?' cried the Giant; 'tell me, that I may take my big sword and slay him.' "[21] In both Lewis and Wilde, the "ur-giant," God—whether in the form of God's terrifying love (via Aslan), or anger on God's behalf—embodies the threat of violence or danger. In a movement perhaps related to the awe and fear that accompany great physical power, the ancient history of the giants reveals a fall from deity to demonized figure.[22] The legend of the Golem, a giant formed from clay for the purpose of protecting the Jewish people, tells the story of another giant in whose figure God and humanity collide.[23] The fear of being eaten by the large runs deep in myth and legend, as well as in children's books that draw upon these traditions.

In the folktale world and in American popular culture, the figure of the giant typically disrupts social order. Stewart comments that ". . . the miniature represents a mental world of proportion, control, and balance[;] the gigantic presents a physical world of disorder and disproportion."[24] This disorder extends to the disruption of hierarchies of gender, class, or nation, chaos that must be mediated and contained in order to restore "balance" and proportion. For example, when the enraged wealthy housewife, Nancy Archer, in the camp film classic *Attack of the Fifty-Foot Woman* (1958, dir. Nathan Juran), grows to 50 feet tall and stalks her cad of a husband, she creates chaos in a patriarchal world. Her inversion of the "natural" order must be righted—in this case, by her death and that of her philandering and murderous husband.[25]

Because the gigantic can appear to be fixed, immovable, and to embody collective fears, the giant is often transformed into a gentle and domesticated figure in children's literature and popular media. Friendly giants from children's books, such as Arnold Lobel's *Giant John* (1964) or Roald Dahl's *The BFG* ("big friendly giant"), turn out not to be giants after all, but children. The BFG, for example is childlike both in size (in relation to the other giants) and in disposition (relishing food, physical humor, and affection). The true giants are rapacious people-eaters, as the BFG's description of the typical giant's appetite makes clear: " 'Giants is all cannybully and murderful! . . . Out there us has the famous Bonecrunching Giant! Bonecrunching Giant crunches up two wopsey whiffling human beans for supper every night! Noise is earbursting! Noise of crunching bones goes crackety-crack for miles around!' "[26] When the child Sophie's wakefulness during the "witching hour" first enables her to see the BFG, she immediately describes the figure whose "head was higher than the upstairs windows of the houses"[27] as a "giant," but his child-loving nature and victimization by the other giants sets him apart. With Sophie's help and assistance from the Queen of England, the BFG deflates these cruel and ferocious enemies of childhood by caging them like wild animals displayed in the zoo and transforming them into captive dependents. The Brad Bird animated film *The Iron Giant*, set in the 1950s (based on Ted Hughes's *The Iron Man: A Story in Five Nights* [1968]—a book I discuss in detail in chapter five), depicts the giant as huge and lovable innocent who rejects the definition placed upon him by ignorant adults obsessed by the Red Scare: that he is a Soviet weapon sent to destroy America. The

Iron Giant's plaintive line, " 'I not a gun' " is one of the most poignant in this fine film.[28] Since the face identifies a creature as human/human-like, and therefore determines our identification with, or difference from, the figure, the delineation of the giant's face is crucial to ascertaining the "correct" meaning of the gigantic in any given context.[29] The Iron Giant's great hinged jaw creates a smile. Significantly, the first time the boy Hogarth sees him, framed against the tall trees, the giant tilts his head inquisitively, sending a clear signal that he is gentle and childlike.

Although functioning within the general parameters of disorder and disproportion set forth above, male and female giants typically operate in distinct ways in the popular imagination, in artistic forms, and in children's books. Two "giants" of the late twentieth and twenty-first centuries—the obese female and the male machine—figure prominently in children's and young adult fiction as well as in popular culture writ large: one such character of great power and strength "saves the world," while the other both wrecks domestic havoc and sustains great personal loss. The male machine solves problems in conjunction with his "boy" or master; the obese female *is* a problem.[30] In chapter five I examine the giant robot's mechanical body as a symbol of scientific utopianism relied upon in mass entertainments in the form of inter-war world's fairs and in boy culture as one way to communicate the fantasy of the "future perfect." In chapter six I consider visions from two different artistic vantage points that problematize the paradigm of the disruptive obese or excessive female body: the tall tale and the contemporary fine art photograph. Using the techniques of humorous exaggeration within a fantastic framework, the tall tale recuperates the gigantic female body in obvious and straightforward ways; in photographs of an obese child, by contrast, both social class and aesthetics inform a complicated artistic articulation of the girl's "excessive" body in a fat-phobic world.

The obese female represents one especially revealing form of the monstrous, gigantic female body. By "revealing" I mean that by interrogating our responses to big size and the female gender, cultural biases and prejudices about the obese female, the obese girl, are thrown into high relief. I am sensitive to the fact that while "obesity" has a medical definition—according to the CDC, an obese child or teen has a BMI at or above the 95th percentile for youth of the same age and sex—it has been defined culturally, as well. Thinking about the female giant offers us one way to understand how the obese are constructed and treated. The animating figure of this chapter is a young woman named Barbara, the subject of photographer Andrea Modica's work between 1986 and 1995. Modica took a series of black and white photographs of a family of fourteen children living in an impoverished area in upstate New York and published some of them in her book *Treadwell*. Modica first began photographing Barbara and her family when Barbara was a young girl. Her final images of Barbara were taken when she was twenty-two years old and dying from complications due to diabetes. As my analysis will, I hope, make clear, I find Modica's work with Barbara to be both complex and moving; her extraordinary body and spirit enliven each photograph.

While Burke's maxim that "it is impossible to suppose a giant the object of love"[31] obtains in many cultural contexts—including traditional folktales, monster movies, and myth—other giant narratives subvert this teleology and resist the "giant as monster" paradigm. As the following chapters demonstrate, we may imagine the obese girl and giant robot as giants of both fear and familiarity, imagination and reality, self and other.

Chapter 5

GIGANTIC MECHANICAL BOY SCOUTS

Our perceptions of size—and our reactions to those objects and persons "out" of scale—are inextricably linked to the proportions of the typical adult body. This rather obvious observation underpins pervasive ideas about the meanings and constructions of both big and small: the giant-as-monster as well as the Tom Thumb trope, the idea of the pygmy and dwarf discourse. This fact also reminds us of two important aspects of the giant in particular: first, the giant appears to be "greater" than the ordinary human; and second, the giant presents a challenge for the ordinary human to overcome. For their part, small figures, as previous chapters have acknowledged, are also burdened with cultural valuations indexed to their atypically small size in relation to a fully grown adult. And if we consider the child body, it is certainly the case that our understanding of the child as dependent, vulnerable, and innocent is informed, in part, by his/her cute appearance: small stature, physical features such as button noses, chubby hands and feet and short limbs.[1] While many of the small bodies and historical characters I have discussed thus far are cultural constructions as much as they are biological beings (with the exception of the discursive elements of the Tom Thumb, dwarf and pygmy figures), as I turn to discuss the giant figure, I step away from the body constructed outside of, or even in spite of, the biological and natural to consider instead the mechanical body.

Providing the impetus for this shift from the biological to the mechanical is the notion of perfectibility. As a metonym for the human body, the mechanical body can be built as a *better* body: one that reflects back to us what we value in the human physique and what we fantasize the human body might become. These are bodies informed, but not hampered, by the limitations of the bodies we inherit. That is, although our bodies may be altered through excessive weight loss or gain, plastic surgery, amputation or even gender reassignment, we must largely accept the vulnerabilities and the contours of the body we inhabit and that takes shape after birth. Since the mechanical body does not truly live, it cannot die. Grappling with these utopian and fantastic aspects of the built body underlies, I believe, much of the fascination the mechanical body holds in our literary as well as our scientific imagination.

The determination of industrialists, scientists, and engineers to create and then capture the strength and power of the machine to do "man's" work and solve "man's" problems (what they conceived as problems in labor, costs, efficiency, productivity, profits) fueled the Industrial Revolution and ultimately found an outlet in dreaming about the mechanical man. How does size affect the meanings attached to the mechanical body? By building the mechanical body to an exaggerated size, the contrastive ordinary human body comes into focus. The gigantic mechanical body, in fact, sharpens our articulations of what it means to be human. And there is a gender component to consider, too, as most mechanical bodies are typed as male. Men are meant to create and work with machines, thus most mechanical bodies are fashioned in man's image and extend masculine power and privilege.

Thus far I have been sketching general cultural beliefs about the gigantic that the giant mechanical body symbolizes. In the chapter that follows I will locate these ideas more precisely by focusing especially on the inter-war years and mid-twentieth century and particularly on mass entertainment (world's fairs) and popular culture (children's books and toys) as expressions of cultural values in an era of great instability. Boy culture, in particular, transmitted via character education organizations and serial publications of the early to mid-twentieth century in both England and America informs and is informed by mechanical age fantasies of progress and perfectibility. In this chapter I will argue that the gigantic mechanical body—the robot—helped to construct an ideal masculinity for the modern age and helped to articulate fantasies of scientific utopianism. One site of particular interest to me in making this argument is the 1933–1934 Chicago Century of Progress exposition in which both scientists and captains of industry chose the robot as an avatar of the concept of futurist progress. The mechanical super-man, the giant robot, conquers the weaknesses of the biological in order to transcend the frailties of human nature and the corruptible body as well as to point the way toward mechanical and industrial dominance. The combination of a super-sized and invincible mechanical body with an ideal masculinity, in both the robot and his human mastermind—typically a boy—creates the context for the powerful idea of great size embodying the fantasy of the "future perfect." In this context I engage the concept of the "future perfect" on two levels: one, as the refinement and perfection of the body itself that the giant robot represents through its competence, strength, and incorruptibility; and two, as the vision of a future world in which science/technology and human beings/culture—represented by the robot-and-his-boy—are engaged in a mutually beneficial relationship.[2] As these ideas suggest, the future perfect is always utopian.[3]

The Industrial Revolution as a Problem of Scale

Telling the mid-century story of giant male machines—robots—and their transformation from monster to hero and marker of human progress actually requires a step backward in time. The

Industrial Revolution of the late eighteenth and early nineteenth century, with its power looms, factory system, and steam power set the stage for the machine age to emerge, in which the combative relationship between humans and machines was renegotiated. Through their labor, children, prized both for their size and their easy exploitation, played a key role in the mining and textile industries of the early nineteenth century, in particular. Children as young as four years old could be "employed" (the youngest children generally worked without pay and no child was paid even the same insufficient rate as an adult worker) as cogs in the great manufacturing machines of the Industrial Revolution. Some of the most iconic photographic imagery of the Industrial Revolution features small children juxtaposed with big machines, highlighting the differences in size and substance between the two: flesh and metal. In the images of small children and big machines, the child's body reads as pliable and vulnerable in contrast to the unyielding and dangerous machinery that threatens to engulf it. Thus, the Industrial Revolution created, for some, a problem of scale that cried out for action.

Various people heeded this cry, of course. The contrast between big and small, hard and soft, machine and human, and the very real damage done to children, encouraged the formation of nineteenth-century child labor reform movements aimed at reducing the number of hours children could work. Philanthropists, politicians, religious leaders, and poets focused on the body of the child laborer in making their persuasive cases against child labor practices. The child workers' bodies of interest were described as "blackened" in the case of the boy sweeps or climbing boys, or stunted in the case of the factory child or infant collier, or diseased or disfigured by the demands and dangers of punishing hours, corrosive chemicals, airborne fibers, and/or moving, crushing machinery. Although it proved challenging to pass legislation to reduce child labor, it was easy to argue that poor children were harmed as a result of its lack of regulation. The trick was getting powerful people first to care about this harm and then to challenge the interests of mill, mine, and factory owners or to accommodate the political goals of competing movements such as those working against the Corn Laws. Describing the child's body as vulnerable and weak and his mind as impressionable and unformed was a particularly convincing way not only to talk about the tragedies of unregulated child labor but also to reference a related idea: a new understanding of childhood. The "new childhood" posited an ideal childhood in which the child's nature and needs were understood to be distinct from that of the adult. Roughly speaking, the child needed play and the adult needed work.[4] The newly vulnerable child—whether of privilege or privation—incited greater scrutiny than before; thus, the Industrial Revolution provided one important context for renewed interest in children and childhood.

As Hugh Cunningham reminds us, the child's body in the Industrial Revolution would not have become a catalyst for change over the many years that laws governing child labor were debated and enacted in England (and later, in America) without the widespread acceptance of this compelling new story of childhood that resolved the "crisis" the Industrial Revolution had wrought.[5] In the pre-industrial age poor children certainly labored, but their work was closely connected to the home: children worked for their parents when young and later, perhaps, would be placed out as servants in another home. Cunningham notes, "It was a hard life, but it was endurable, for it was sanctioned by custom and contained within the bounds of family and community."[6] The children and grandchildren of pre-industrial parents, however, would become "victims" of the factory system, separated from the domestic economy of their own homes and communities. This break between traditional child labor and domestic spaces and the transition of child labor from the home to industrial and public locations—factories, mills, mines, and the street—enabled the new story of childhood to percolate and permeate the social consciences of many. The writing and speeches of MP Lord Ashley, the 7th Earl of Shaftesbury; Robert Owen; Sir Robert Peel; William Wilberforce and other reformers helped to construct a narrative of the moral responsibility owed to laboring children and the social instability that could ensue if the needs of children were not met.[7]

Early on, the new story of the children of the poor was promoted by the conservative philanthropist and Sunday School founder and educator Mrs. Trimmer, whose multivolume *The Oeconomy of Charity* (1787) was influential in the success of the eighteenth-century Sunday School movement. Trimmer paints a vivid picture of the suffering factory child by comparing his pallid complexion and arrested physical development to the rosy and lively youth he could be if differently located: "I cannot indeed think of little children, who work in Manufactories, without the utmost commiseration. It is impossible, surely, to view those countenances, in which, according to their time of life, the roses of health should bloom, pale and sodden—those limbs which should be straight, robust and active, stunted in their growth, or distorted by sitting in one continued posture . . . ."[8]

Some decades later, as demands for the regulation of child labor grew, Shaftesbury, in his 1840 article "Infant Labour" for the *Quarterly Review*, passionately described the devastating consequences that long, punishing hours wrought upon pauper youth. Along the way he also described the unnaturally small size and weak limbs of the child worker in terms of the resulting "pygmification" of the child's strength:

Emerging from these lairs of filth and disorder [unhealthy tenements], the young workers, 'rising early, and late taking rest,' go forth that they may toil through fifteen, sixteen, nay, seventeen relentless hours, in sinks and abysses, oftentimes more offensive and pernicious than the holes they have quitted. Enfeebled in health, and exasperated in spirit, having neither that repose which is restorative to the body, nor that precious medicine which alone can tranquillise the soul, they are forced to live and die as though it were the interest of the state to make them pigmies in strength, and heathens in religion . . . .[9]

According to reformers such as Trimmer and Shaftesbury, it is the very *childhood* of the laboring child, which has both physical and psychological markers, that is sacrificed to the callousness and greed of industry.

Figurative language describing child workers as pathetic victims helpless before devouring monster machines did much to expose the plight of the late eighteenth-century and nineteenth-century poor laboring child. Similarly, in early twentieth-century America, the work of the influential American documentary photographer Lewis Hine made visual the problem of scale between the child body and the machine. These powerful portraits of child workers, like the colorful speeches and writings of English politicians, Evangelicals, and philanthropists before them, assisted American Progressive-era reformers in making a persuasive case against child labor. In 1907, Hine was hired by the National Child Labor Committee (NCLC, founded in 1904) to investigate and document industrial child labor practices. According to Vicki Goldberg, the NCLC was the first American organization to use photography "consistently and extensively" as a method of instigating social change.[10] From 1908 to 1924, Hine traveled the country preparing reports and taking photographs for the NCLC. As a persuasive and easily reproducible form of "testimony" (Hine's word), photography enabled Hine to call attention to the wrongs of industrial child labor. Over his ten-year association with the NCLC, Hine took upward of 5,000 photographs. Kate Sampsell-Willmann, in *Lewis Hine as Social Critic*, contends that through his photographs "Hine advocated; he agitated; he indicted. But because his medium contained a high degree of verisimilitude and his methodology looked 'objective' as a social science survey, his visual product was more effective than words."[11]

Certainly, Hine's photographs are well-known social documents and have taken on iconic status in the story of American child labor reform. As such, they offer a clear look at the tension between child and machine. Some of this tension is due to scale. Given industrialists' and capitalists' increasing secrecy around child labor opposition to its practices grew, Hine was not welcome inside many factories, mines, or mills and thus many of his child subjects were posed outside of the factory. Hine preferred to photograph within buildings, however. To gain entrance into a mill, he often had to assume a different identity—as a fire inspector, postcard vendor or bible salesman. A clever disguise he sometimes used was to pose as an industrial photographer documenting the machinery used in the mill, etc. In this case, he would ask for a child to be included in the image he was taking in order to establish a sense of scale; he used his knowledge of the height of his jacket buttons to measure the children he photographed, often including their heights in his captions.

By juxtaposing big and small, child and machine, the photographs argue that children do not belong in factories. For example, in a 1910 photograph of eight-year-old "Leo" in the Elk Cotton Mills of Fayetteville, Tennessee, the boy stands in the middle ground of the photograph pressed against the bobbin machine that stretches along behind him and fades into the diffuse light seen through the far-off windows of the factory (see Plate 26). The foreground features the same machine, emphasizing the repetition of the bobbins both forward and backward in space. The tow-headed boy stares directly at the camera, his pant legs rolled and his feet bare. One hand is tucked behind his leg and the other splayed against the end of the machine. Unlike the four adults also pictured for whom the bobbins are waist-high, the machine rises well over Leo's head. Indeed, Hine underscores the importance of Leo's size in the caption to the photo: "Leo, 48 inches high, 8 years old. Picks up bobbins at 15 cents a day in Elk Cotton Mills." The boy's small stature is accentuated not only through contrast with the much taller adults, but also by the cinched waist of his too-large pants, and his small hands and thin legs. But it is the seeming endlessness of the bobbin machine, the piston-like character of the bobbins and the towering height of the machine taking up nearly all the space in the huge mill room that creates an unnatural setting for a child. In her essay on Hine and child labor

Goldberg makes a similar point about childhood and scale: "the sharp perspectives racing to the center of the frame make the mills seem even longer than they are and the children even smaller; at times the machinery seems to be advancing on us."[12] In Hine's photographs we find child bodies that "should" be playing outdoors but instead are held captive in the rigid and harsh environment of the factory and its machines.

Sometimes Hine included brief quotations from his subjects in his captions. On Leo's photograph Hine transcribed the following: " 'No, I don't help me sister or mother, just myself.' " This anecdote—which reveals the child's self-interest and agency as a worker—appears to challenge the notion of the vulnerable child laborer exploited by the factory system. For Leo, work is part of a childhood he constructs. Yet while Leo's admission that he works for himself certainly complicates the perhaps sentimental view of child-as-victim, it also does little to change the nature of the argument demonstrated in the photograph itself, which presents a clear contrast between child and machine.[13] In fact, for adults, Leo's jaded view may actually underscore his loss of "natural" childishness and innocence.

We find a similar theme in another Hine portrait of a child mill worker. *Rhodes Mfg. Co., Lincolnton, N.C., Spinner* was taken in November 1908 and features a ten-year-old girl staring out of a factory window (see Plate 27). The girl wears a simple cotton dress and apron, her hair pulled back in a plait. By looking out the window, she turns away from the long line of bobbins that stretch behind her. The massive machine, close behind her back, seems to threaten to push her slight figure through the window. In contrast to the solid machinery behind her, the light of the sun comes through and illuminates her youthful face. Hine further captions the photograph, "A moments [*sic*] glimpse of the outer world. Said she was 10 years old. Been working over a year." Interestingly, the figure of the girl is in focus in the photo's middle ground while the foreground and background— the factory walls and the machine itself—are largely out of focus. Thus, the girl's stillness is emphasized, like a breath-hold, a "moments glimpse." In his caption Hine provides a backstory: a story about the child worker in constant motion. If this girl's job is like Leo's—picking up bobbins—her perpetual movement is likely to be repetitive, perhaps even machine-like, and thus the opposite of the ideal of childishness. Unlike Leo, this girl is alone in the photograph. She contemplates not the photographer before her, but something outside of the factory. We cannot know if she yearns to be outside, though it seems likely given the nature of mill work, the long hours and the poor working conditions. Hine's caption certainly assumes that this is her desire. The photograph proposes that there is no vista in the girl's "inner world," the world of her daily life in the mill: the enormous machine and its demands will dominate and fill the frame of what the child can see and do once she turns around and begins nearly endless work. At that moment of turning away, so the photograph suggests, sunshine will no longer be available to light her face or to anoint her with childhood.

With the help of Hine and other reformers, the narrative of the innocent, playful child and fleeting, vulnerable childhood took hold as a foundational myth of modern Anglo-American culture in the nineteenth and especially the early twentieth centuries.[14] The myth—tied to "truth" by way of photographic "evidence"—held that the child was formed for play and the machine for work. It seemed that the child and the machine were destined to remain forever at odds. Perhaps they remain so today. And yet, if we remove children from the equation of human and machine and look beyond the factory, a different picture comes into focus. The steam age, for example, also gave us images of the cooperation between man and machine. Innovations in locomotion—in particular, steam engines for trains and steam-ships—required strong men to feed the firebox. Without the participation of man in making the engines run and regulating the heat and pressure, the machine was useless. By shrinking the world and bringing people and their goods where they needed to go more quickly and thus more cheaply, the invention of steam transportation excited both industry and the masses. With laboring children out of the picture of steam locomotion, the union of man and machine in steam-powered ships and trains was generally viewed as progress (though industrial boiler accidents caused many workmen's deaths and injuries) promising future industrial and engineering greatness for western societies employing these universally accepted technologies.

But we can't discount childhood altogether in the renegotiated relationship between human and machine. The notion of progress aided by science and engineering—and the fantasy of the future perfect—are ideologies ripe for childhood's participation, given the universal belief that it is the next generation that will primarily promote and profit by new technologies. Boys were particularly targeted as the natural enthusiasts of the machine age. For character and citizenship organizations such as Robert Baden-Powell's Boy Scouts, the machine's abilities and qualities—including precision, strength, and tirelessness—encouraged admiration in and even emulation by scouts. In fact, by performing its job well and assisting humanity in its endeavors, the machine might be considered to exhibit traits of an ideal masculinity for the twentieth century, one that the Boy Scout organization (of Britain and later the U.S.) sought to inspire in its members. A good example of such encouragement may be found in *Young Knights of the Empire: Their Code and Further Scout Yarns* (1917) a follow-up publication to Baden-Powell's popular *Scouting for Boys* (1908) and *Yarns for Boy Scouts* (1909). Baden-Powell describes the engine room of the great steamship R. M. S. *Orsova* in terms that explicitly link the mighty machine with the manly boy:

And it is indeed an impressive sight to stand below these great monsters of steel and watch them faithfully and untiringly pounding at their work, all in order, and exactly in agreement with each other, taking no notice of night or day, of storm or calm, but slinging along at all times, doing their duty with an energetic goodwill which makes them seem almost human—almost like gigantic Boy Scouts![15]

Baden-Powell's admiration for the giant anthropomorphized pistons' efforts relies upon a kind of epistemology of both scientific utopianism and size: dutiful and loyal machines help (British) mankind, their selfless devotion enhanced by their giganticism.

The strong men required to make these engines work are also credited in Baden-Powell's autobiographical "yarn" about the trip he and his wife took on the *Orsova*: "Then we go into the stokehold among the mighty boilers. Here are powerful, grimy men at work getting coal out of the coal bunkers, and shovelling it into the furnaces. It sounds easy to shovel coal on to a fire, but it takes a lot of practice to get the knack of stoking a fire properly and a lot of strength and skill to throw great shovelfuls quickly and well into the right part of the furnace."[16]

In *Young Knights of the Empire*, the *Orsova*'s engines, her stokers, and Baden-Powell's audience—the Boy Scouts themselves—are described as sharing similar strengths in discipline, endurance, and resilience. For Baden-Powell, there is little to differentiate the "faithful" machine from the cheerful Boy Scout, or the skillful stoker: all are expected to fulfill their duties for the glory of the Empire. Similarly, the attributes that the machine, the boy, and grimy stoker "embody" are, according to Baden-Powell, particularly manly. His ideal of the "young knight of the Empire" harks back, certainly, to the myths of a chivalrous age and the "gallant fellow[s] who were always ready to defend weaker people when they were being bullied; [they were] brave and honourable, and ready to risk [their lives] in doing [their] duty according to the code or law of Chivalry."[17] This evocation of the knights of the past is not simply nostalgic: Baden-Powell uses the legendary knights not only to underscore the Scout's code, but also to link the old ways with the promise of the future greatness to come as the British Empire is defended: "Well, nowadays there are thousands of boys all over the British Empire carrying out the same idea [as the honor code of the knights], and making themselves into fine, reliable men, ready to take the place of those who have gone away to fight and who have fallen at the Front."[18] Baden-Powell appealed to a triumphalist interpretation of Britain's history—shared by popular boys' periodicals—in which the boys of today could carry on the successful adventures of the past into the future. They could do this, however, only if they subscribed to the physical fitness and character-building exercises outlined by scouting.[19]

While a machine may be patriotic only in metaphorical terms, unlike the Boy Scout, whose patriotism is a key element in his character, the machine may be used as a tool of the Empire and work in service of the Empire's goals, just as the Scout is meant to do. In the case of the giant pleasure steamship the *Orsova*, the advent of World War I altered her function: during the war she served as a troopship ferrying Australian soldiers to various fields of battle. Baden-Powell's tale of giant mechanical boy scouts and the skilled men who make them work unites the ingenuity of the big machine/man dyad with the triumph of Empire, and, by association, ensures the boy's place in it.

"Science Finds, Industry Applies, Man Conforms"

Behind big machines lie big ideas. And animating these ideas were the desires to reduce human labor, solve agricultural, industrial, transportation, and communication problems, increase efficiency and profits as well as to entertain. Innovations in science and technology lay claim to many of the machines built to answer these desires, machines that were showcased in expositions and world's fairs from the mid-nineteenth century forward. Among other purposes such as bringing the world "home" via the exhibition of native peoples from around the globe, as I discussed in the previous chapter, world's fairs also advertised and celebrated the host nation's progress in research, development, and design. Indeed, the world's fair was a stage upon which new inventions with far-reaching social implications were launched: for example, the Colt revolver (London, 1851), telephone (Philadelphia, 1876), motion picture (Paris, 1900) and the ice cream cone (St. Louis, 1904). World's fairs of

the late nineteenth and early twentieth centuries were nationalistic, commercial, and cultural ventures, undertaken to assuage
social anxieties and economic worries, as well as to make money
for their shareholders. For example, the 1933–1934 Chicago
World's Fair, a century-of-progress exposition, celebrated
Chicago's centennial while at the same time it promoted both
business interests and spectacle. The fair's motto—"science finds,
industry applies, man conforms"—made perfectly evident its
focus on elevating industry's status to that of science. And man?
Man "conforms" to the dictates of both.

The century-of-progress international exposition took place
in 1933 and 1934, the mid-point of what would become known
as "the Great Depression" and after FDR's morale-boosting land-
slide victory in 1932. The exposition was years in the making,
however, and its planning necessarily had begun long before
opening day. In fact, the fair was conceived and organized during
the worst of the Depression when unemployment rose precipi-
tously, banks failed and desperate Americans struck, marched,
and rioted. Who could have thought that an expensive World's
Fair was a good idea while so many Americans were hungry and
suffering? The answer: a think tank of prominent scientists,
industrialists, engineers, philanthropists, and politicians.

According to Robert W. Rydell, the foremost authority on
American world's fairs, fueled by a common belief that uniting
science and business could help to relieve the economic crisis
that threatened America's global reputation and what was
perceived to be the American way of life, scientists and industrialists together settled on a world's fair as a way to educate the
average American about the importance of technology and
corporate values to a successful American future:

> There was more to the fan dance of science than met the eye.
> It was part of the persistent effort by American scientists
> after World War 1 to popularize science, mold a 'true'
> American culture with scientific values, and affirm the
> hegemony of the corporate state. These efforts continued

through the 1920s and intensified in the 1930s as scientists, confronted by a 'revolt against science,' joined corporate backers of the fairs in trying to pin popular hopes for national recovery on the positive results expected from the fusion of science and business.[20]

Did the 1933–1934 Century of Progress Exposition succeed in meeting the goals—both lofty and capitalistic—set by its corporate sponsors, as well as by President Roosevelt and the prominent scientists who became involved in an entertainment venture that might seem far from the abstraction of pure science or directed purpose of applied science? Rydell argues yes:

Attended by some one hundred million visitors, [Depression-era world's fairs] left in their wake a vision of the United States emerging from the Great Depression as a consumer-driven, corporation-driven nation-state powered forward by science and technology and governed by a federal system made newly attentive by the circumstances of the 1930s to the welfare of its citizens. The fairs of the 1930s sustained and remade the American nation at a time of crisis second only to the Civil War.[21]

How the fair responded to America's economic woes with an ideological argument promoting technology and business and the important role that size played in this argument through the mechanical giant—the robot—provides a compelling story of an ambitious inter-war American identity project. First, however, a keynote had to be struck; that task was fulfilled by the Science Advisory Committee (SAC). The SAC, constituted in 1929 to advise the exposition's organizers, suggested the fair's overall philosophy of "scientific idealism." The SAC and its subcommittees, formed from members of Woodrow Wilson's World-War-I-era National Research Council (NRC) keen to support the idea of an exposition focused on scientific and industrial development, along with other "salesman-scientists," met regularly over a four-month period in the years 1929–1930 and produced multiple reports with advice about designing the fair's exhibits as well as implementing its theme.[22] The term "scientific idealism" was coined by Michael Pupin (an electrical engineer at Columbia University and a member of the SAC). "Scientific idealism" provided purpose and direction to the many moving parts of the colossal event, including the content of many of the exhibits as well as the fair's industrial design and corporate sponsorships.[23] Fairgoers were to be provided with an entertaining, but clear, vision of what "progress" meant in the context of a "century of progress." According to the SAC, scientific idealism would be expressed through "the 'deification' of science displayed in a 'Temple of Pure Science' where 'thoughtful' visitors receive a 'quiet unconscious schooling,' learning that 'science is at the root of most of the material things and many of the social things which make up modern life.' "[24]

The site of the greatest concentration of exhibits designed to produce this educational effect could be found in the "Temple of Science." Although renamed the "Hall of Science," the original appellation linking worship with science was perhaps more insightful and reflective of the fair's celebratory anticipation of future progress led by science and industry. Through its inclusion in exhibits, sculpture, and even entertainments, the figure of the robot was both a key player and an important symbol that assisted the scientist with the promotion of these goals: "Specific exhibits—including robots, working auto assembly lines, and the rocket-shaped cars of the Sky Ride—added weight to the message that science was modern man's salvation and that the scientist-engineer was priest, if not savior."[25] The robot figure was featured in artistic articulations of the fair's philosophy, as well. Located in the rotunda of the Hall of Science, an enormous U-shaped structure well situated within the spacious grounds in order to attract the most visitors, fair-goers were greeted by the imposing fountain *Science Advancing Mankind* (see Plate 28).[26] Here, the central figure of the science "god" is not a scientist or engineer, or human at all: he is a gigantic robot.

"Science" is depicted as a massive robot leaning over two nearly naked human figures—a man and a woman—urging them forward, toward the future, by placing its huge hands at their backs. *Science Advancing Mankind* was sculpted by Louise Lentz Woodruff as a series of pools. The large central pool is dominated by the sculpture of the robot and humans. Eight lower pools, each one representing a different scientific discipline, circle the central pool. The fact that "science" is shown to be a man-machine and out of scale with human figures underscores significant twin beliefs: that robotics best typify the future perfect aspirations of scientific design and practical use, and that great size indicates power and performance. Interestingly, in "Science Advancing Mankind," the gigantic robot guides rather than serves mankind. Knowledge, contained within "science," is the province of the robot, rather than man or woman. The latter figures walk forward tentatively, holding their hands out in front of them in a gesture suggesting caution or even blindness. Indeed, as proclaimed in the pamphlet illustrating the most significant sculptures to be found at the fair, the sculpted robot "is by no means an automaton bent on destruction. On the contrary, it is depicted as an onward-going force whose hands are placed at the backs of the male and female figures, urging them on to greater endeavors."[27] The caption to a close-up of "Science Advancing Mankind" from the same publication goes even further in glorifying the enormous man-machine: "The great robot-like figure typifies the exactitude, force, and onward movement of science, with its powerful hands at the backs of the figures of a man and woman, representing mankind."[28]

The Depression-era world's fairs settled upon the giant robot as one powerful and compelling symbol of scientific utopianism, keeping the ideas of industrial, capitalistic progress as well as cultural progress alive in one figure. The robot's hybrid nature as a kind of man-machine helps to maintain the symbol's relevance in different venues, from the stage of the world's fairs, as we have seen, to literature: drama, science fiction, and children's books, as I will discuss below. As Igor Aleksander and Piers Burnett suggest in their historical overview and explanation of the mechanics of robotics from its beginnings to the late twentieth century, "the robot's status, somewhere in an uneasy limbo between man and machine, makes it the ideal dramatic device for exploring the relationship between the two. The robot can conveniently stand for the whole of machine-kind which twentieth century man has interestingly come to see as a potential threat, or even successor, to mankind."[29] Certainly, the fear of the annihilation or oppression of the human by the machine is belied in "Science Advancing Mankind." That benevolent yet patriarchal gigantic robot is a far cry from the race of robots in Czech playwright Karel Čapek's *Rossum's Universal Robots* or *R.U.R.* (1921) from which the word "robot" was first popularized.[30] Written in the aftermath of a world war in which chemicals and machines were used to wreak havoc and kill people in new ways, Čapek's play anticipates the threat Aleksander and Burnett acknowledge as enduring throughout the twentieth century.[31] In *R.U.R,* robots revolt against their human masters and ultimately destroy the human race. Rather than avoid the troubling idea that robots could replace humans or were the enemies of humankind, as Čapek's play suggested, some exhibits at the 1933–1934 Century of Progress Exposition embraced the close connection between man-as-machine and the machine-man, or robot. For example, in the chemistry exhibit, every half-hour a 10-foot-tall robot delivered a speech and demonstration on food and digestion in the Robot Theater. A short film was projected from behind onto the robot's white shirt front, illustrating various digestive processes, while the robot narrated them. In the medical arena, the six-foot-tall "Transparent Man," a kind of man-machine built to make the inner "mechanics" of the human body visible, visitors "saw themselves exposed before a powerful deity—the modern god of science."[32] In this exhibit, according to Rydell, humans find awe-inspiring science within machines much like themselves, built to elicit faith from the American people: faith and trust in the intellectual prowess of

American scientists and engineers and faith in the "American way of life," which was capitalism, optimism, and progress. Much of the power of this god of science, as depicted by the ubiquitous presence of gigantic robots at the fair, was indebted to size, as well as to certain notions of ideal masculinity. That is, the robot figure is never simply about the mechanics or the science that has created it; the robot always calls to mind and grapples with his double—the man. Thus, robots, especially giant ones, tell us as much about ordinary man as they do about ingenious machine.

"Science Once Saved Your Life; What Have You Got Against It?": The Giant Robot in Mid-Century Children's Literature and Material Culture

While science and engineering may help to construct a man's world, science is also a boy's game. Although it is beyond the scope of this chapter to discuss Anglo-American science education in the inter-war or post-World-War-II era generally, I turn now to another educational method for "building the world of tomorrow," as it was expressed in children's material culture. I'm thinking of the popular constructional toy Meccano, its "guild" (boys' club) and the accompanying *Meccano Magazine*.[33]

The 1930s were Meccano's "golden age" as it soared into the future with airplane and motor car constructor sets and chemistry and electrical experiment sets adding innovation to the more typical engineering outfits.

According to Frank Hornby, the Liverpool businessman who invented Meccano (as well as Hornby trains sets and Dinky model vehicles), the original Meccano construction set was not really a toy, but " 'engineering in 'miniature.' "[34] Promotional materials for the Meccano brand of toys suggested that success in learning the principles of mechanics and using them to build industrial models from manufactured kits was linked to success in life. Indeed, the Meccano philosophy resembled that of Baden-Powell's Boy Scouts, with a businessman's twist.[35] The

charismatic and paternalistic Hornby, ever interested in his
Meccano boys and factory workers, as well as in maintaining
worldwide dominance in construction sets, believed his
Meccano outfits would assist boys in developing manly spirits
characterized by ambition, precision, wholesomeness, and initiative. Hornby's advertising campaigns made this point clearly
and often. For example, a 1919 pamphlet promoting the products directly related playing with Meccano to the creation of "a
nation of supermen" in future leaders as well as workers.[36]

The *Meccano Magazine* began publication in 1916. The
magazine grew quickly from a free, four-page publication to a
monthly publication of twelve pages in 1922. The magazine
eventually developed into a full-length quality boys' serial with a
variety of features and reached its circulation peak of 70,000
subscribers in 1930.[37] Translated into numerous languages so as
to reach a larger audience, the magazine contained factual information on engineering, construction, and railway sets as well as
introducing new products, information about the worldwide
distribution of Meccano and the different cultures into which it
had spread. The general goal of the magazine was education and
self-improvement.[38]

The Meccano Guild, for which the *Meccano Magazine* was
the official organ, was instituted in 1919 and first headed up by
Hornby. Its purpose, according to the instructional booklet *How
To Run a Meccano Club* (1949), was to support the many happy
boys worldwide who desired to share their hobby with like-
minded boys: "The really happy boys throughout the world are
those who have a hobby in which they take an enthusiastic
interest; and the happiest of all are Meccano boys, for theirs is
the greatest of all hobbies." *How to Run a Meccano Club* adds that
the Meccano hobby is tied not only to model-building and
sharing, but also to discussions of "all kinds of plans and schemes
for the future."[39] Brown notes that ". . . Hornby set the moral tone
and selected the term 'Guild' precisely because it reflected
notions of comradeship and the unselfish mutuality characteristic, so he believed, of the old medieval guilds."[40] Thus, the

Meccano Guild, like the Boy Scouts, alludes both to an idealized past and to the belief in future progress. By 1932, membership in the Meccano Guild had grown to over 100,000 boys worldwide.[41] *How to Run a Meccano Club* provides a shorthand glimpse into the boyhood world of Meccano: according to the official General Club Rules, membership of a club was open to any boy who possessed a Meccano Outfit or Hornby Train Set. Clubs were meant to meet monthly, prepare reports for Headquarters, and to arrange seasonal programs for members—many of which (such as rambling and cycling, attending lectures, and holding public exhibitions) were not limited to building models individually or in groups. The content of these programs and activities demonstrate the kind of boy a Meccano boy should be: lively, competitive, sports-minded, social and, above all, inventive: "Meccano encourages boys to invent, and in the world of invention the best qualities of an individual—initiative, keen thought, patience, and perseverance—are brought into play."[42]

This last sentence is a rather crucial one as the word "play" does double-duty within the "world of invention": that is, in the "world of invention" (understood to be mechanics, engineering, industry, construction, or science more generally), the sterling qualities of invention are brought into being and acknowledged (into "play") and the important connection between boys' play and creativity is stressed. Inventiveness is an attribute of the boy scientist who dominates, rather than is dominated by, the machines he builds. These machines might be bridges, block cranes, model trains or, yes, robots.

What makes the robot—or, more precisely, the boy-and-his-giant-robot—a particularly apt avatar of the kind of ideal masculinity and scientific utopianism born of the post-Industrial Revolution age, geared up in the Depression-era inter-war years and promoted in post-war (that is, 1950s and 1960s) Anglo-American middle-class culture? Building on the wholesomeness and usefulness of engineering games such as Meccano, in children's literature the boy-and-his-robot bring into play a powerful dyad that answers or sublimates the

anxieties about the relationship between man and machine that
at times erupted within machine-era culture. In performing this
feat, the stories of boy and his machine must be retold as heroic
tales. These tales are informed by the ideologies of progress and
the future perfect that I have sketched in this chapter. Typically,
in children's popular culture the giant robot is cast as a friend or
a slave. The burdens of giganticism, like the promise of scientific
utopianism, are largely accepted on faith, that most *un*scientific
of beliefs.

In the opening to this chapter I mentioned two key elements
of the successful giant/human relationship: first, that the giant
appears to be greater than his human counterpart (thus causing
anxiety) and second, that the human must meet and overcome
the challenges that the first item suggests (thus ensuring
heroism). Two other core beliefs about the robot within the
context of scientific utopianism may be restated here as well:
robots function as appropriate symbols of future perfect aspirations and great size suggests power and performance. We shall
see how in mid-century children's literature the contrast and/or
collaboration between giant robot and his boy genius creator
or companion brings together notions of heroic masculinity,
progress, and scientific utopianism (or its inversion). In *Tom
Swift and His Giant Robot* (1954), one of the books in the Tom
Swift Jr. Adventures series by Victor Appleton II, the patriotic,
persistent, and polite young inventor creates gigantic robots to
assist humankind in entering the nuclear age (see Plate 29).[43] In
designing and testing his robots, the model boy relies upon
science, logic, and unexamined notions of nationalism and
progress. He thus exhibits the qualities of both a Meccano Boy
and a Boy Scout. Over the course of the novel (part of the
formula of the Tom Swift books generally), Tom Swift Jr. brings
criminals to justice and innovations in technology and
engineering to light. The latter is first for the betterment of Swift
Enterprises (the company started by his father, the original boy
inventor, Tom Swift), but Tom's inventions—and the giant robots
are no exceptions to this—are also always meant to maintain

American leadership in industry and national defense. The popular Tom Swift Jr. books are an obvious repository of the ideologies of the future perfect and scientific utopianism exhibited at the Depression-era world's fairs and in the Meccano empire. And they are anticipated by Baden-Powell's heroic boys' tales, too, as we recall the story of the *Orsova*'s pistons as "giant mechanical boy scouts."

Tom's giant robots are designed to take the place of human workers in the nuclear power plant—called "atomic energy plant"—his father is building in the American West.[44] Their jobs would be to repair and maintain the plant in areas where the high concentration of radiation would be fatal to men. These giant robots are still in the testing phase and Tom's problems with controlling them arise with frequency, adding tension to the plot. The eight-foot-tall robots are depicted in a stereo-typical manner, resembling the barrel-chested, large-jointed Tin Man from *The Wizard of Oz*, and sport pincers as hands, bulbs for eyes and long antennas.

While the giant robots are humanoid in appearance and plot elements underscore the nearly human behavior of Tom's inven-tion, thus mitigating the difference between man and robot, these machines are designed to fulfill industrial functions that man cannot do, rather than to replace him in industry. The giant robots are powerful—and even heroic—but at their control resides the boy genius, Tom Swift. In this way, the novel both elevates science and subordinates the man-machine to human creativity and ingenuity.[45]

Tom's most impressive robots are the giants "Ator" and "Sermek"—the former is named for the union of "atom" and "robot" and the latter honors "the field of servomechanics."[46] Before Tom can reasonably trust the work of his robots he must test them repeatedly. The robots' final test is "by fire" in which Ator will simulate replacing "neutron-soaking rods" within an enormous blast furnace. Emphasizing Ator's human-like quali-ties, the narrator asks, "Would Ator 'live' or 'die'?"[47] Ator's work within the furnace is described, once again, in terms that call to mind the brave and chivalrous knights of old: "Ator strode back and forth inside the furnace, looking like a giant knight in armor. Jets of chemical fire deluged his Tomasite-protected body, but not once did he waver or display a defect."[48] Ator's triumph is Tom's and vice versa. And yet, in the penultimate climax to the novel, the giant Ator appears to turn disloyal as "*the giant robot seemed to have developed a mind of his own!*" as he advances on Mr. Swift and "seized him between his massive hands."[49] Tom's only recourse to save his father was to instigate a fight between Sermek—controlled, of course, by Tom—and Ator, remotely powered, it is eventually revealed, by the mad scientist antagonist to Swift Enterprises and the atomic energy plant.

The giant robot Sermek is certainly strong, but it is Tom's superior knowledge of science that allows Sermek/Tom to win the day: "A clanging din filled the air as each giant fought for a hold on the other's vulnerable head mechanism. A contest of strategy, not strength, was exactly what Tom wanted. Now he could use scientific tactics based on his knowledge of the robot's structural operations."[50] And Ator's previous disloyalty is forgotten when he is called into action to find and destroy the plutonium-rich slug the mad scientist had hidden within the Uranium-238 which threatens to blow up the thermopile of the atomic energy plant and thus demolish it (killing everyone inside). This plutonium-rich slug is described as a "miniature atom bomb."[51] Certainly, in 1954, the year of *Tom Swift and His Giant Robot's* publication, any description of an atom bomb would not be undertaken lightly. The dangers and destruction of the atom bomb that saved the United States and the free world by ending World War II, so many believed in the 1950s (and some still believe), were very fresh. In the scientific utopianism of *Tom Swift and His Giant Robot*, atomic energy, nuclear energy, is good science, "moral" science, when in the "right" hands—in this case, the capable, steady hands of the boy-and-his-robot. The novel concludes when representatives of the American government and military assemble to watch and applaud the opening of the Citadel, Swift Enterprises' atomic energy plant:

"In impressive speeches, the government officials lauded the Swifts and pointed out the tremendous advances in medicine, industry, and national defense which the products of the [thermo]pile would make possible."[52]

Tom Swift novels not only showcase futuristic inventions and underscore the potential for feats of engineering and science to help humankind or to solve problems, they are also formula fiction: each novel contains a mystery to be solved enhanced by a new Tom Swift invention. But there is no mystery to the central hero of each number in the series: it is invention itself, located in the boy genius and the fruits of his keen mind—here, the giant robot. Typically, Tom Swift and his friends foil plots to steal their technology for nefarious use. In *Tom Swift and His Giant Robot*, a mad scientist whose mind has broken down "from sheer mental exhaustion during his intensive research work"[53] and a gang of professional thieves nearly succeed in killing Tom and his friends in their quest to steal information about robotics and to stop the completion of the atomic energy plant. As Tom, his father, and their employees puzzle about who could be behind the bombings of the plant, Tom suggests the possibility that it could be " 'some crank who is opposed to atomic progress and wants us all back in the Stone Age.' "[54] This thought may be directly traced back to the ideas behind the century-of-progress exposition we see articulated in the fountain *Science Advancing Mankind*. Anyone not supporting "atomic progress" must be a "crank" and unworthy of the kind of model masculinity presented in the Tom Swift books. At one point, Tom challenges a cornered criminal who owed his life and mobility to the metal surgical pins inserted into his spine, " 'Come on, Pins. Open up! Science once saved your life. What have you got against it?' "[55] While Tom is polite, dutiful, loyal, generous, and humble—old-fashioned values—he is also a brave, bold, risk-taker who upholds the scientific method as a kind of religion and tirelessly pursues new scientific knowledge. His giant robots can do what man cannot, and as strong, selfless, and tireless workers they reflect back— just as the *Orsova*'s engines suggested to Baden-Powell—the values of an ideal masculinity for the modern machine age: "Tom explained sadly that the now-radioactive robot must never leave the concrete-shielded pile. He would remain forever in the plant which he helped to save."[56]

By the mid-1960s, the "morning" (if not exactly the dawn) of the computer age, the simple robot could be domesticated and, indeed, may be found in the comic children's tale. Heroic robots, some giant, some miniature, play key roles in the fantasy novel *Andy Buckram's Tin Men* (1966) by Carol Ryrie Brink, a well-respected children's author best known for her award-winning book *Caddie Woodlawn* (1935). Young Andy Buckram, a reader of *The Boy's Popular Mechanics Magazine* and regularly described as "inventive," builds four robots to help him with his chores around his family's farm. Andy's robots perform useful tasks such as bailing the rowboat, carrying water and doing sums. His junkyard-owning neighbor, from whom Andy gets many of the parts for his robots, praises Andy for his prescience in creating the tin men: " 'Well, it's a mechanical age,' Grandpa Clayton said. 'Soon everything will be done for us by tin men, I expect. You are very smart, my boy, to be in on the ground floor, so to speak.' "[57] After the robots are electrified and animated by a terrific lightning storm and threatening events ensue such as a flood and bear attack, each performs a heroic deed that results in saving Andy's life and that of his friend as well as his toddler cousin. Yet, as he is the robots' master, Andy's commands are obeyed absolutely and literally. After telling the largest robot, Supercan, who rows the boat, to "stop a minute" at the town dock, the children are saved from the flood and reunited with their parents. Precisely after one minute, however, the robots row off to an unknown future. While Andy mourns the loss of his creations, he immediately resolves to build new robots. For Andy and Tom Swift, Jr., inventiveness and the ability to keep a cool head in a catastrophe allows for nearly limitless potential in the boyhood landscape of the scientific future perfect.

Scientifically minded works such as The Tom Swift Jr. books in general, and *Tom Swift and His Giant Robot* in particular, inform essentially comic robot novels like *Andy Buckram's Tin Men*, and illustrate how scientific utopianism and the idea of the future perfect was packaged and presented within middle-class boy culture through the heroic figure of the boy-and-his-robot. I will conclude this chapter with a close examination of another mid-century boy-and-his-robot tale about size responsive to many of the same ideas emergent throughout the Industrial Revolution, inter-war period and machine age—capitalist, industrialist, nationalist, and militarist ideals. The story I have in mind, however, Ted Hughes's modern fable, *The Iron Giant* (1968), challenges and inverts scientific utopianism by imagining a new version of the relationship between man and giant man-machine.

In Ted Hughes's fable *The Iron Giant* (originally published as *The Iron Man* in 1968), the main character, an enormous sentient machine, must consume metal in order to survive. Resembling a man in his desires for survival, the Iron Giant functions as a kind of biological/mechanical hybrid. His size and appearance produce a striking contrast to the natural world around him: "[The Iron Giant] really was a monster. This was the first time most of them had had a good look at him. His chest was as big as a cattle truck. His arms were like cranes, and he was getting rust, probably from eating all the old barbed wire."[58] Remarkably, after being dismembered into a set of machine parts from his fall off the cliff, the Iron Giant reconstructs himself. This unusual skill knits together biological and industrial processes.[59] Once reconstituted, the Iron Giant resumes his quest to feed his insatiable hunger for metal. However, his diet conflicts with the needs of the rural community as he eats the trucks and tractors and barbed wire that help to make land arable, thus interfering with the farmers' livelihoods. A compromise must be reached and, not surprisingly, a child finds the way.

After the farming community, led by the boy, Hogarth, makes its peace with the Iron Giant by setting him up to consume their metal waste (becoming a kind of super-efficient recycling plant), it would appear that the giant machine has been transformed from a marginalized, fearsome technology into a simple tool.[60] However, the tale does not end with the Iron Giant relegated to the simple role of eliminating human-created industrial trash. Another gigantic antagonist arrives that threatens to destroy the entire planet—this one the size of Australia: the space-bat-angel-dragon.

The global community's first response to the space-bat-angel-dragon is to declare war on it: "Rockets, projectiles of all sorts, missiles and bombs, shells and flame throwers–everything was tried. The smoke of the explosions drifted out over the Pacific like a black, crawling continent. The noise of the battle shook the world almost as much as the landing of the dragon had done, and for much longer."[61] And yet, "human weapons had no effect on it."[62] Where weaponry or group action fail to work— as many traditional tales and American films alike tell us—an individual might succeed. In the face of the supernatural agent's power and anger, the world required a new champion, not a new weapon. And so the male machine becomes the hero, combating the alien space creature and winning by virtue of his superior cleverness and ability to withstand heat. His unnaturalness stands as his badge of honor and the clearest indication that he remains untouched by the violent and selfish aspects of human nature. Indeed, we learn that the human world has brought destruction upon itself. The space-bat-angel-dragon confesses that his interest in coming to earth and eating it up was inspired by the earth's noise of conflict and aggression, overheard in space: " 'It just came over me, listening to the battling shouts and the war cries of the earth—I got excited, I wanted to join in.' "[63]

In the scenes of the seemingly unequal contest between enormous dragon and giant metal man, we are reminded of the folktale world in which clever boys can best huge ogres. Once machine beats animal (even a supernatural one), the hierarchy of the human, the natural and biological over machinery and technology seems upended. The Iron Giant, a kind of self-animated robot, fulfills the anxieties of countless science-fiction stories of antagonistic and vengeful robots and makes the exhausted, burned, and defeated creature his slave. He attempts to find some use value in the enormous creature, some role for him to play. He learns that the space-bat-angel-dragon has no practical purpose at all: his beautiful, harmonious singing gives pleasure, but has no apparent function. The Iron Giant decides that listening to the space-bat-angel-dragon's music will give the humans, in fact, just what they need to heal their discontents—a fantasy of the healing power of the gentle giant that Place, in *The Last Giants* (discussed in the previous chapter) also suggests. And so the former opponents go back to their respective homes: the scrapyard and outer space. In space, the space-bat-angel (no longer called dragon) flies each night making his beautiful music. The effect of this harmonious music on the people of the earth is wondrous: "The strange, soft, eerie space-music began to alter all the people of the world. They stopped making weapons. The countries began to think how they could live pleasantly alongside each other, rather than how to get rid of each other. All they wanted to do was to have peace to enjoy this strange, wild, blissful music from the giant singer in space."[64] Here is a different form of scientific utopianism, a new view of the future perfect in which human and non-human interactions are not valued primarily for their capitalist or industrialist value. The mysterious Iron Giant, in the tradition of non-human characters inspiring others to act with more humanity (Swift's Houyhnhnms, Charlotte from *Charlotte's Web*, Lt. Commander Data from *Star Trek: The Next Generation*, E.T.), is "more than human" not only in terms of size and strength, but also in sensibility and sensitivity.

Ultimately, however, this utopian vision of the benevolent robot of great size and superhuman power—science advancing mankind and helping it, so to speak, become "better" than it could be on its own—pervasive in the 1933–1934 World-of-Progress Exposition and subsequently reappearing in children's fantasy and popular entertainment, may be played out. Harking back to the Industrial Revolution's "problem of scale" in the relationship between human and machine, the Digital Revolution brings its own conflicts related to size and to humanity's future in an age of increasingly smart machines. Just as the Luddites feared (with good reason) that the advent and proliferation of the power loom would cost them jobs, the increasing use of robots and machines to do the work formerly reserved for people—from building cars, to sorting mail, to checking out retail customers, to handling customer service inquiries, to performing as virtual bank tellers, etc.—appears to promise a future of labor imbalance and unemployment. As Kevin Drum notes rather dramatically, "During the Industrial Revolution, machines were limited to performing physical tasks. The Digital Revolution is different because computers can perform cognitive tasks too, and that means machines will eventually be able to run themselves. When that happens, they won't just put individuals out of work temporarily. Entire classes of workers will be out of work permanently."[65] Could the new future perfect be a world *without* labor rather than the simplified world of reduced labor and increased consumerism that the Depression-era world-of-progress fairs promised? Or a world in which giant machines are not "like" Boy Scouts, but replace Boy Scouts? Perhaps. Drum believes that the robot revolution will eventually bring about "a robotic paradise of leisure and contemplation" but he also emphasizes the difficulties that will present themselves along the way and acknowledges that some (those, of course, with capital) will more easily participate in this utopic scenario than others.[66] I'm less sanguine about this future than is Drum, certainly, but my main point has to do with how significantly the idea of the future perfect, as defined by the relationship between science/technology and humanity can shift, even in a few decades, and how ideas about the meaning attached to size may wobble as well. For many, consumerism and industrialization kill rather than coddle. The future perfect looks different in an age of increasingly sophisticated artificial intelligence, globalization, dramatic climate change, the ever-widening gulf between the haves and have-nots, and nanotechnology in which the greatest power attaches to the tiny rather than the large.

Whether relating to the body itself or to the "body scientific," the future perfect is a search for stability: the giant robot body never forgets, never tires, never dies. The future scientifically and industrially perfected world promised by the world-of-progress expositions never betrays humanity by war, or economic depression or genocide. Alluring and elusive, like most fantasies, I suppose, the quest for the future perfect must fail given that as humans we are "programmed" to be curious, to adapt, to learn, and to communicate. That is, the future perfect promises only that the fulfillment, the completion, of our actions is always in the future. Mid-century children's culture, however—literature, games, organizations, and entertainments—provided a creative space for the expression of this kind of fantasy through the giant robot and through the union between smart boys and smart machines. And it continues today in *Robot City Adventures*, a series of graphic novels for pre-teens by Paul Collicutt (2009—) about a future world in which enormous robots and humans live in harmony. The first novel in the series, *City in Peril!*, features the heroic Curtis, a gigantic sentient coastguard robot that cleans up a devastating oil leak, saves the city and protects marine life. Ultimately, Curtis works to ensure peaceful relations between the different species. A man reading the *Robot City Herald* newspaper article about Curtis says about him, "What a hero. He's still out there [in the sea] leading the cleanup and negotiating with the sea creatures.'"[67] Collicutt imagines a future perfect world in which human and giant robot are equal partners in improving life on earth. Similarly, some forty years earlier, in Hughes's tale the robot's power and the masculine prerogatives of science, machinery, and domination give way before organic and natural artistry, suggesting a new harmonic utopia for the world in which science and masculinity combine in a way that does not promote industrial and capitalist values over humanitarian/ecological ones. Future perfect, indeed.

Where else outside of children's books might we find a competing version of a future perfect world successfully conceptualized and communicated through a giant body? While, as this chapter discusses, the masculine giant robot has functioned as an avatar of industrial, technological, martial, and commercial "progress," another giant being—conceived, by contrast, as female—represents a different kind of progress: one that is an emotional, powerfully feminine ideal. To find this giant we may look no further than New York Harbor and the iconic "Statue of Liberty Enlightening the World," given by France to the United States in 1886. Once again, size and scale make arguments about how we understand our relationship to others. Lady Liberty's great height, 93 meters from the pedestal foundation to the tip of her torch, symbolizes many things, among them the significance of her message to humankind, the uniqueness of France's gift to America and the vastness of the effort required to fund and build the statue. Culturally constructed and mutable, the meanings attached to Miss Liberty have changed over time from a statement on democracy and freedom intended by abolitionist Édouard de Laboulaye, the statue's prime mover, to a more particular focus on welcoming immigrants, as the 1883 Emma Lazarus poem imagines. Yet, in every case, the hope of a "future perfect" that Lady Liberty in all of her majesty represents is driven by faith in the human virtues of *caritas* and *humilitas*. Lazarus's poem, "The New Colossus," engraved on a bronze plaque and mounted inside the statue in 1903, explicitly contrasts the monumentality of the "mighty woman with a torch" with that of the Colossus of Rhodes, and celebrates the welcoming, light-bearing American "Mother of Exiles" over the martial "brazen giant of Greek fame."

Certainly, there are other enormous statues that symbolize noble ideals and abstract notions; the ancient Giant Buddha of Leshan and Christ the Redeemer come to mind immediately. Lady Liberty is different insofar as she functions within a political and worldly sphere. The Statue of Liberty stands for America and literally stands tall for the American ideals of "world-wide welcome," in Lazarus's words, and the right to live free of oppression. In the aftermath of an historic election in which a captain of industry (one way to describe Donald J. Trump) repeatedly vows he will build a wall to separate the United States from Mexico, delivers executive orders targeting travelers from some majority Muslim nations, and flirts with the idea of a registry for American Muslims and Syrian refugees, we need the giant matriarch more than ever as a secular figure of faith in humanity in this life and on this earth.

Although it remains to be seen at the time of writing the degree to which the "feminine" qualities of succor and hospitality—and I acknowledge both the useful as well as the reductive nature of typing them as such—may be downgraded or dismissed in "Trump's America," it is my deep desire, along with so many others, that we retrain our focus on the giant statue's guiding light and the deep darkness it dispels. A giant anthropomorphized lighthouse, Lady Liberty has offered safe harbor to millions over the decades. But for all of her size and strength and symbolic power, she remains a figurehead. Let us see her anew, rescue her from becoming a footnote in American history, and re-dedicate Liberty for all.

Chapter 6

THE OBESE GIRL

As I discussed in the previous chapter about male robots, we expect our giants to be masculine. Of course, as the example of the Statue of Liberty demonstrates, giants are not necessarily men, or even male, but since great size suggests masculine qualities—power, strength, aggression, and dominance—the link between the giant and masculinity seems especially strong. Indeed, according to *Of Giants* by Jeffrey Jerome Cohen, ". . . the giant is encountered in the performance of a masculinity as necessary as it is obscene."[1] The fact that the masculine giant meets expectations, as it were, offers a kind of reassurance, even if the giant is frightening or disturbing. Yet, the same cannot be said about most female giants. A disconnect exists between the tenets of femininity and the features of giganticism. The female giant, when we find her at all, is overlaid with the characteristics of power and strength in addition to great size. She thus functions mostly outside of conventional femininity which tends toward softness, fragility, compassion, and delicacy. In addition, the female giant may well display a ferocious maternal instinct or a rapacious sexuality. Whether a big mother or a big lover, the female giant is likely to be very, very scary indeed.

Given that these scary female giants threaten disorder and confusion at every turn, they—along with some of the other figures discussed in preceding chapters such as homunculi, dwarfs, and pygmies—may be typed as "monsters," beings that, to borrow David Skal's useful phrasing, function as "supreme paradoxes, dreamlike constructions that attempt to reconcile the irreconcilable."[2] The female giant, like other monsters, is a boundary-crosser, uniting male and female, human and extra-human, familiar and strange.

In this chapter I am interested in exploring the fears, anxieties, taboos, and powers that attach to the figure of the female giant. How does the clash between femininity and giganticism play out in children's literature, gender ideologies, and culture—both high and popular—more generally? In particular, this chapter discusses how the female giant has been typed as monstrous or grotesque, and links this trope specifically to the obese female. In defining the "monstrous" Asa Simon Mittman asserts, "above all, the monstrous is that which . . . calls into question our (their, anyone's) epistemological worldview, highlights its fragmentary and inadequate nature, and thereby asks us . . . to acknowledge the failures of our systems of categorization."[3] In this chapter I argue that the obese female represents one such failure of categorization—the obese female body as monstrous—which reveals our inability to reconcile femininity with giganticism. Ultimately, reading the obese female body requires reading ourselves. That is, by interrogating our responses to big size and the female gender, we throw cultural biases and prejudices about the obese female into high relief. Indeed, Sander Gilman asserts, "the study of obesity in its cultural and social contexts provides a wide range of inter-locking questions about the cultural construction of the body."[4] This chapter will raise and attempt to answer some of these questions as they relate to gender and giganticism, in particular.

Using the term "obese" to describe fat individuals in life and in literature itself suggests one bias: the label "obese" (defined medically as a BMI over 30), imposes, according to Abigail C. Saguy in *What's Wrong with Fat?*, a "medical frame" implying that "fat bodies are pathological."[5] Thinking about the female giant offers us one way to understand how the obese are constructed and treated. As we have seen with the figure of the pygmy, race and class add to the complexity and otherness of the female giant.

Although not as prevalent as miniatures, female giants populate literary genres ranging from the tall tale to the contemporary YA novel. We may read an interesting and even radical history of the female giant through both genres. Recent picture books have recast the tall tale to feature female protagonists and have reimagined the typically misogynistic genre as female empowering. We may also discern in recent YA literature attempts to rewrite the "tragedy" of the obese girl, a figure who is easily found in earlier books for youth as a sidekick to the main character.[6] However, even this secondary role seemed to disappear for the fat girl as she became invisible in late twentieth-century books for teens, not considered worthy of a story at all. The chapter will also consider examples of real-life obese girls who have become objects of fascination, resulting in media-documented lives. When the very big female body is interpreted not as, or not only as, too much, but also as too little, then the giant's bulk becomes ever more threatening, ever more strange, to those of ordinary size. As Kathleen LeBesco and Jana Evans Braziel note, in psychological discourses fat is often coded as symptomatic of both excess and lack: "Fat equals reckless excess, prodigality, indulgence, lack of restraint, violation of order and space, transgression of boundary."[7] How might the woman giant or the obese girl ever transcend the taboos that great size represents for the female in western culture?

Gender and the Giant in the Tall Tale and Youth Literature

Akin to the traditions of fable and legend, American tall tales are typically stories of men of great deeds and great size told with comic exaggeration. Some male figures in the American tall tale tradition include Paul Bunyan, the giant lumberjack and owner of Babe, the Blue Ox; African-American John Henry,

noted for his superhuman steel-driving strength; and Pecos
Bill, the towering, rough-riding cowboy.[8] Although tall tale literature appears in other cultures, the literary tall tale, which
flourished in America from approximately 1831 until 1860, is
particularly well suited to the large land mass that was becoming
America in the nineteenth century and to those who colonized
it.[9] As Carol S. Brown explains, "From almost the beginning, the
incomprehensible vastness of the continent, the extraordinary
fertility of the land, and the variety of natural peculiarities
inspired a humor of extravagance and exaggeration, while the
American's need to affirm the value of a culture in many ways
independent of European refinements, constraints, and mores
engendered a humor that was clubby, exclusive. The vast difference among America's geographic sections, too, gave impetus to
comic exaggeration."[10]

While blatant misogyny characterizes aspects of this comic
exaggeration, a few stories feature the exploits of strong women.[11]
Annie Christmas, for example, the gigantic, New Orleans river-
woman, was

> two hundred and fifty pounds, stood six-foot-eight bare-
> footed, wore the largest and most beautifully curled
> mustache along the entire river, and was more powerful than
> any riverman who ever lived. Annie Christmas could carry
> three barrels of flour at once, one balanced on her head and
> one under each arm. When the river got high one spring and
> was about to flood the country above New Orleans, Annie
> Christmas prevented the disaster by throwing up a new and
> higher levee all by herself in one day . . . .[12]

In some versions of the folk ballad of the larger-than-life
African-American hero John Henry, his wife Polly Ann drives
steel "just like a man."

In contemporary reimagined tall tales for children that
feature female characters, the gigantic female body is recast as a
metaphor for fortitude, pluck, cleverness, and care-taking.[13]

Anne Isaacs and Paul O. Zelinsky's *Swamp Angel* (1994) and its sequel *Dust Devil* (2010) add to the tall tale tradition in just this way. Both picture books revise the typical plot by featuring the achievements of a frontier woman. By employing the humorous techniques of the tall tale, *Swamp Angel* and *Dust Devil* comment on gender biases found in that genre of American literature, and recuperate the gigantic female body as positive. Certainly, white men were not the only people struggling on the American plains or in the West, and *Swamp Angel* and *Dust Devil* highlight both the gender-bending and the traditional women's crafts in which Angelica Longrider, the title character, participates. In her first book, the gigantic Angelica, "second to none in buckskin bravery," harnesses rain clouds to put out a flaming cabin, catches a river in her apron to divert it from a settlement, and plucks a wagon train out of Dejection Swamp to save the settlers attempting to cross.

At the same time, she cooks and knits and wears homespun dresses. Trouble comes to the Tennessee wilderness in the form of an enormous black bear, Thundering Tarnation, who terrorizes the settlers. Angelica enters the competition to fight the bear and win his enormous pelt. Some of the male daredevils scoff at her desire to join in: " 'Hey Angel! Shouldn't you be home, mending a quilt?' " but she retorts, "Says she, 'Quiltin' is men's work!' 'Well, how about baking a pie, Angel?' 'I aim to,' says she. 'A bear pie.' Their hoots and taunts didn't stop Swamp Angel from signing up and setting out to find that bear." After the men are all defeated, Angel finds the bear and fights it for three days, lassoing it with a tornado, drinking up an entire lake, and creating the Great Smoky Mountains along the way. When the bear is finally vanquished after Swamp Angel snores down "one last tree," the entire settlement has a party to eat the bear and dance. Swamp Angel decides to move to Montana where there would be room for her bear pelt and creates the Shortgrass Prairie by laying it at the front of her cabin door.[14] The Swamp Angel's enormous bare feet—no dainty toes here—sturdy legs, and wide, wide smile placed against the dramatic setting of the looming Tennessee hills, tall forests, and expansive sky focus attention on her appropriateness for the setting of "open" America, land of opportunity for the risk-taker. Angelica Longrider is part of the exaggeration that is Nature itself. In each spread of the picture book, Swamp Angel's great size and strength are celebrated as honorable and appropriate, not to be feared or hidden, but enjoyed. The text and award-winning illustrations—*Swamp Angel* was named a Caldecott Honor Book—are filled with references to early nineteenth-century backwoods American life. Each full-page illustration is painted on the smooth and varnished hardwoods of the Tennessee forests. A bald eagle, America's national symbol since 1782, appears on every page. In both picture books, giant woman and giant nature/nation coalesce to create a seamless, comic narrative of origin and adventure informed by a flexible gender ideology that combines traditional female tropes—angel, domestic worker—with male-order plots about feats of skill and conquest.

In the contemporary landscape, we may locate triumphant narratives of skill, competition, nation, and size beyond the female tall tale within the worlds of sports. There we find both "miniatures" and "giants." The tiny gymnasts steal the limelight every four years at the Summer Olympic Games as they dazzle spectators by reaching new heights in athletic technique, event difficulty and daring while wearing dramatic makeup and sparkly costumes. These athletes are prized for their small size and childlike bodies (many of the top gymnasts are actually youth in their teens). Overwhelmingly, however, the sports arena is the realm of the giant and many of today's American female heroes are very tall athletes such as the Williams sisters (tennis) and Kerri Walsh Jennings (beach volleyball), each of whom has dominated her sport for years. The successes and power of these "giants" may help to transform the aspirational woman's body from small to "big."[15]

As *Swamp Angel* and many other examples from literature, popular culture and even the sporting world attest, issues of gender, identity, and sexuality are as important in theorizing the gigantic as they are in understanding the functions of the miniature. As I suggest in the opening to this chapter, although there are exceptions, most gigantic figures in literature and popular culture are male. The miniature, too, is often male (although troped as female), which may have to do with the adventuring spirit that informs many characters whose size is exaggerated—whether large or small. In chapter four I discussed the "double miniaturization" that occurs in Lynne Reid Banks's *The Indian in the Cupboard*: the presence of Bright Stars, the Native American female miniature, defies the book's internal logic as she has no history and is seemingly conjured solely in her capacity as Little Bear's wife and sexual partner. For those adults reading children's literature in which miniatures abound, it is certainly more comforting to find that miniatures are generally sexless, prepubescent—like dolls with effaced sexual anatomy. Miniatures often function as analogues of children in children's books, and ignoring the discomfiting fact of childhood sexuality is commonplace in this literature. It may feel similarly uncomfortable to confront the issue of the sexuality of the gigantic. In contemporary YA literature, the cultural constructions of fat and femininity are thrown into high relief when we compare obese male and female characters and their characterizations.

To return to the giant: the large body of the giant points ineluctably to the issue of appetite, one aspect of which is sexual appetite. Both cannibalism and various forms of sexual expression—in many contexts children's sexuality and certainly sexual predation by adults against children—are considered taboo. Part of the fear of the gigantic is the fear of being eaten by a large, overpowering other. The fear of being consumed can be conquered by defeating the unlawful eater. However, the revulsion at the giant taboo eater—and the suggestion of a sexual lust that accompanies it—is not always so simply negotiated. As Carolyn Daniel argues in *Voracious Children*, her book about children and eating in children's literature, "One of the most fundamental cultural messages that children have to learn concerns how to eat correctly, that is, to put it simply, what to eat and what not to eat or who eats whom."[16]

Giant taboo eaters abound in children's and young adult books. The "giant" is often an overweight child or teen, and the character's excessive appetite is generally emotional (leading to physical hunger), rather than sexual. In realistic children's books, unlawful eating for girls and boys tends to be overeating. Robert Lipsyte's *One Fat Summer* (1977), set in 1952, introduces the insecure and emotionally fragile fourteen-year-old, 200-pound, Bobby Marks, who gains self-confidence and a mature perspective on human nature after spending the summer doing lawn work for an abusive and cheap employer. As Bobby interacts with others around him who espouse competing notions of manhood, he learns that "being a man" is more than taking risks off the high dive, or physical domination. He begins to see the sadness and fear behind others' actions—even those who hurt and humiliate him. Bobby loses weight and is proud of himself for the achievement. In response to a request for fair wages for his efforts, Bobby's formerly intimidating employer tells him that he should pay *him* instead: " 'I've watched you change from a miserable fat boy into a fairly presentable young man. On my lawn. On my time.' " Bobby replies, " 'You didn't do it, Dr. Kahn. I did it.' "[17] Bobby's new voice emerges organically with his altered physique.[18] *One Fat Summer* has withstood the test of time, remaining in print, and, although out of date in some ways (in these days of body-building and steroid use among teens, 200 pounds does not necessarily signal obesity), the book skillfully negotiates both identity and body image issues by focusing on masculinity.

While *One Fat Summer* is a YA novel about physical transformation informing identity work, typically in children's pop culture, especially that which is aimed at boy readers and viewers, fat is not necessarily a problem to be solved or an "issue" in the text, film, or television episode. In any group of child characters (whether in books or in visual media), there is often a "fat kid," generally not the protagonist, who is part of the gang. In YA books, solving a different problem—low self-esteem, a dysfunctional family—"cures" the teen (or child) of being overweight, or the overweight character "balances" the needs of other characters by offering contrast. In Kimberly Willis Holt's *When Zachary Beaver Came to Town* (1999) set in Texas during the Vietnam War era, an obese boy—who "performs" as a side-show exhibit freak—is the foil against which Toby, the thirteen-year-old first-person narrator, comes to terms with his mother's departure and the death of his closest friend's brother in Vietnam. Toby describes Zachary as "the size of a two-man pup tent. His short black hair tops his huge moon face like a snug cap that's two sizes too small. His skin is pale as buttermilk, and his hazel eyes are practically lost in his puffy cheeks."[19] As this objectifying description anticipates, Zachary Beaver never actually becomes a fully developed character in the novel (though he begins to make friends with a few of the boys in town). His primary literary function is to provide a distracting project for Toby, the implementation of which helps Toby to begin to grow up: ensconced in a trailer and abandoned in Antler, Texas, the orphaned obese boy is seemingly trapped, but Toby and his friend Cal concoct a plan to extricate him. After a complicated set of moves, Zachary Beaver is transported to a local lake and then baptized.

Toby's reactions to Zachary overshadow the character himself, whose feelings and motivations are rarely described: "Zachary smiles, and I wonder if he's feeling different. Because standing out here waist deep in Gossimer Lake, next to my best friend [Cal], I'm feeling different—light and good and maybe even holy."[20] Zachary merely smiles enigmatically in response to the baptism he does not request. His physical "imprisonment" in his fat body contrasts with Toby's "entrapment" in despair and abandonment; "releasing" the gigantic, heavy, Zachary (en)lightens Toby. Something momentous needs to happen to Toby to propel him forward emotionally. Zachary's giant body serves as that large something.

The gigantic body often appears inscrutable, "blank" and in need of an overlay of external interpretation, a label. Toby's relief and release is directly related to his wordless relationship to

Zachary's giganticism. Another example of the giant as *tabula rasa* may be found in Brad Bird's animated film version of Ted Hughes's *The Iron Giant* (1999), mentioned earlier in this study. The seemingly unknowable and threatening Iron Giant is called a "gun" and then designated a national security threat by the American government that seeks to destroy it. In *When Zachary Beaver Came to Town*, the obese boy's body is reconfigured from sideshow curiosity to feel-good exercise for characters who use him as "growth" potential in their own searches for clarity and understanding.

If self-labeled or accepted by a wider community, however, the obese male body, in particular, can become the focus of positive activity and strength. Ignored by his New York City junior high school classmates, musical prodigy Junior Brown, in Virginia Hamilton's *The Planet of Junior Brown* (1971), falls through the cracks: "With his talent, Junior should have been given all the care he needed. But so fat, so awful to look at."[21] When out in the world, the 300-pound Junior Brown worries that everyone "shrinks" from him and he becomes more and more alienated, lonely and defined by his fears.[22] Surrounded by people who fail to see the person behind the talent or the fat, Junior becomes so insular and his fantasies so real that his sanity is threatened. Yet, his "label" is changed through his acceptance by a group of homeless boys whose interdependence creates a new home, a new "planet of Junior Brown."

Also set in New York, a more recent contemporary YA American novel than *The Planet of Junior Brown*, K. L. Going's *Fat Kid Rules the World* (2003), similarly confronts the fears of exposure and ridicule that the overweight male teen faces. *Fat Kid* features a seventeen-year-old obese boy, Troy Billings. Through music and a challenging friendship with a Kurt-Cobain-like figure, Troy's powerful feelings of despair and self-hatred are transformed—with difficulty and humiliation along the way—into attitudes of defiance and joy. As the book opens, 296-pound Troy seriously contemplates committing suicide by jumping in front of a commuter train, but he worries that his death, too, would be considered a joke: "Like it or not, there's something funny about fat people. Something unpredictable. Like when I put on my jacket and everyone in the hallway stifles laughter. . . . I don't get angry. I just think, *What was funny about that? Did my butt jiggle? Did I make the bench creak so that it sounded like a fart?*"[23] By the book's conclusion, Troy reclaims the self-applied label of "Fat Kid" and uses it proudly. He hasn't lost any weight but he gains a voice as a grunge, punk-rock drummer: "I slide in behind the drum set and let my huge ass sprawl over the chair. I'm the poster boy for obese drummers and I *know* I look funny. I lift my arms high above my head and hold them there, flesh dangling, waiting for Curt's signal. . . . Then my arms are crashing down and for the first time, live and in public, the drumsticks snap against the skins."[24] After sizing Troy up, Curt announces to his rocker friends that the overweight teen has "mass appeal," positively reassessing Troy's physical stature as both influential and desirable.[25]

Musical skill and sensitivity is often offered as a kind of counterweight to obesity in YA novels whether the protagonist is male or female. Indeed, many novels seem to suggest, if you are going to be morbidly obese, you'd better also be prodigiously talented. *Butter* by Erin Jade Lange (2012) shares many qualities with *Fat Kid Rules the World* and other novels featuring obese males: scenes of humiliation, a flirtation with suicide, musical talent and deep self-hatred. Butter, nicknamed for a stick of butter he was forced to eat, weighs 423 pounds and binge-eats. Nearly anonymous at school, Butter's engaging personality and musical abilities emerge only in hiding: he charms a beautiful classmate, Anna, through internet chatting (never revealing himself) and plays the saxophone in his room. Anna, an alphagirl, falls in love with Butter online and Butter rashly agrees to meet her on New Year's Eve. Butter's desperation at what he believes will be the inevitable result of this meeting, coupled with his despair and loneliness, lead him to hatch a plan that will solve his problems: suicide by overeating. Butter's website, butterslastmeal.com, is an instant hit and he becomes a celebrity with the popular kids.

Somewhat problematically, the novel becomes a "how-to" manual for bad choices likely to cause serious harm. Butter is a type 2 diabetic and insulin-dependent. After weeks of his new-found popularity, the night of his suicide arrives and after Anna discovers to her horror that her internet boyfriend is Butter and that he had been lying to her, Butter feels he can't back down from his pledge to commit suicide. He begins by overdosing on insulin and then binge-eats enormous quantities of food, including strawberries; the last act he knows will cause a severe allergic reaction. On a live feed, the high schoolers watch him overeat and fall into a diabetic coma. Anna calls the police and he is rescued and admitted to the hospital's intensive care unit and later psychiatric ward. Although Butter's "friends" all disappear, Anna remains. She visits him in the hospital and seems willing to get to know him. Along the way, Butter's dread had been so great as the night of his suicide approached that once hospitalized he finds he has lost 50 pounds without feeling hungry.

What may we observe from these novels featuring male protagonists? For one thing, obese characters are getting larger and larger, and becoming a "normal" weight is not a goal by the novels' conclusions. And what are we to take from these novels? One message seems to be that self-acceptance breeds choices. Butter felt he had no choice but to kill himself, but after his suicide attempt and stunning realization—"when it came down to making a decision between life and death, it was my own mistakes that had pushed me over the edge. . . . In the end, I was my own biggest disappointment"—choices multiplied.[26] Butter's parents are willing to move to another state to enable him to finish high school at an institution for the obese; his music teacher has gotten him an interview with a musician at Juilliard who could recommend him for an audition. Friendship and community can come for Junior Brown, Troy, and Butter only when they share themselves with others. In these YA novels featuring "giant" male characters, the obese male body is allowed to take up space, to be embraced as comedic, as unique and talented.

By contrast, shame and disgust typically characterize the literary gigantic female body. The cultural anxieties that attend the gigantic female's excessive body and appetite are expressed especially pointedly in literature for girls. Although, as I have outlined above, the gigantic is the repository of collective anxieties writ large, there is a particular concern that attends the "gigantic" female.[27] Gigantic females with unnatural appetites perform a specific cultural disorder. The rapacious folktale mother-figure threatens familial organization by attempting to remove the younger generation. By committing acts of infanticide, real-life mothers, such as Susan Smith and Andrea Yates, are sensationalized as "giants" of monstrosity. We can include the Fat Woman in this sisterhood of abhorred giants, although her "crime" is contained to her own body. Or is it? Mary Russo comments that, "as a certain kind of bodily enactment, the Fat Woman has been an important figure of spectacularized womanhood in the West since the nineteenth century."[28] Like other unusual bodies determined by size and shape, the obese female is always a spectacle and seemingly always public.

The fat female remains open for interpretation and degradation not only because she is highly visible, but also because she is easily constructed as deviant. Nita Mary McKinley explains this construction by unpacking how "ideal weight" (the first American ideal weight charts were published in 1942 and 1943, for men and women, respectively) became identified as "normal weight." Thus, McKinley argues, "Rather than being normally distributed as other attributes, such as height, 'normal weight' *is* 'ideal weight.' Those whose weights vary even slightly from ideal are deviant."[29] In failing to participate in the economy of (male) desire, the exaggerated and excessive female body exists outside of this system of exchange and receives little but loathing and disgust from the community: twenty-first-century western culture is female-fat-phobic. Amy Erdman Farrell argues in *Fat Shame: Stigma and the Fat Body in American Culture*, that "fatness continues to be such a powerful, easily understood marker of the 'fallen body' that it can be drawn as effortlessly to portray the upward and downward mobility of a large cast of characters."[30]

Although the social as well as personal problems that accompany obesity–often metaphorized as monstrosity—are present in fiction featuring boys (as I discuss above), they have emerged as especially popular topics in YA fiction specifically targeted for a female audience. In these texts, obese females, I argue, function as "monsters of prohibition," to use Jeffrey Jerome Cohen's phrase. The "monster of prohibition," Cohen contends, "exists to demarcate the bonds that hold together that system of relations we call culture, to call horrid attention to the borders that cannot—*must* not—be crossed."[31] It is because the overweight female functions as such a feared monster that she appears in twentieth- and twenty-first-century young adult literature either as a destabilizing figure or as one who is self-consciously rehabilitated—rather like the previously marginalized or invisible "ethnic kid" whose stories are now told with greater frequency in children's and young adult books.[32]

Akin to *Fat Kid* and *Butter, The Earth, My Butt, and Other Big Round Things* (2003) by Carolyn Mackler uses comedy and an engaging first-person narrative voice, that of 15-year old Virginia Shreves (another New Yorker) to explore the anxieties of an overweight teen trapped in a "perfect" family. Virginia's insecurities are compounded by the competence and attractiveness of her family members: she has a skinny older sister in the Peace Corps, a handsome, smart, and popular older brother at Columbia, and athletic, accomplished, and wealthy parents. Virginia's weight is a nagging problem that overshadows, at first, the personal and social troubles that the outwardly happy and well-adjusted family only seem not to have. Virginia is devastated to learn that her beloved brother date-raped a college classmate and that her parents are primarily concerned with avoiding scandal rather than with acknowledging the criminal nature of their son's abusive behavior. Ultimately, Virginia's solution to her low self-esteem, alienation, and confusion is self-expression through body piercing, hair dyeing and wearing stylish shape-revealing clothes. By developing her body's strength and agility via kick-boxing classes, she begins to formulate a healthy body image (she had flirted with disordered eating when trying to lose weight). These responses are very twenty-first-century, teen magazine do-as-I-say-not-as-I-look solutions. Yet, to be fat remains a problem for girls in teen fiction. Fat can be rehabilitated, however, as one more "non-traditional" and thus empowering choice if it is coupled with self-expression such as wearing body art, performing rock music or, in *My Earth*, writing a zine that fosters not only communication but also social interaction among the outcast kids who create it. In this way, *My Earth* participates in "fat acceptance," a cultural movement similar to the anti-discrimination movements that focus on race, age, gender, and sexuality.[33] Fat acceptance, many argue, is a civil right.[34]

The overall starting premise of the fiction I have been discussing is that it is not acceptable for teenagers to be fat—though, in life, many of them are. And even when this premise is challenged and the youth protagonists practice self-acceptance by the novels' conclusions, this acceptance is achieved in spite of being fat. In her overview of late twentieth- and early twenty-first-century YA novels about obesity (many of them discussed here), Catherine S. Quick comments that fat acceptance must be viewed within the overall context that "Thin is still represented as the absolute ideal for body image, and the fat person, although willing to accept fat as integral to identity, undoubtedly prefers thin."[35] Much of the fear and hatred of the fat female body expressed in YA fiction comes from self-loathing (a quality seen in novels focused on male protagonists, too, but perhaps not to the same degree. While Butter, for example, attempts suicide out of desperation informed by his fear of rejection, he has the self-confidence to initiate and sustain an intimate relationship with a desirable girl).

What might change the narrative of helplessness in the face of fat? One road, as discussed, is fat acceptance. Another is bariatric surgery, a medical intervention for morbid obesity not widely available for minor patients, yet growing in popularity.[36] While there are few studies currently that track bariatric surgery for teens, a 2007 report indicated that from 2000 to 2003, operations rose to about 800, a tripling from three years prior.[37] As fiction inevitably follows social reality, it is not surprising to find that bariatric surgery is now a topic in YA literature confronting the "social problem" of obesity. Donna Cooner's *Skinny* reimagines the Cinderella tale through the life of her fictional main character, obese fifteen-year-old Ever Davies. She has thin and beautiful stepsisters (although the younger stepsister, Briella, is perhaps misunderstood); enjoys a "transformation" into popularity and prettiness via her weight loss after surgery and the makeover she receives at the hands of a popular girl; attends the "ball" (a high school dance); and "Rat," an intelligent and loyal friend, falls in love with her. Most importantly, Ever gains the self-confidence to try out for the school musical—she has a stupendous singing voice—earns the lead in "Cinderella" and learns that her Prince Charming had loved her even when she weighed 302 pounds. However, Ever isn't able to sing or to see the humanity and vulnerability of others or even to recognize the lovable qualities of her "Rat" until she loses more than 100 pounds. It's difficult not to read the book as equating lost weight with emotional gains.

It's also difficult not to see bariatric surgery for youth as an extreme measure that owes as much to fat hatred as it does to concerns for health and wellness given that the recipient's digestive tract is changed forever and that there are other means by which significant weight loss may be achieved, namely lifestyle changes. Is there a danger that bariatic surgery may become a kind of plastic surgery marketed to ever younger patients? Might *Skinny* present one form of marketing? The accuracy of such marketing is one area in which *Skinny* slips a bit, perhaps for obvious reasons having to do with pacing. Teens undergoing bariatric surgery must take part in intensive counseling over many months. However, in the novel, Ever attends one quick meeting with a doctor in which her father gives permission for

the surgery and one group counseling session and dietary education session before the operation is scheduled a mere few weeks
later. While Ever's steady and dramatic weight loss is tracked by
a chart indicating her weight, exercise, and "playlist" (how she's
feeling) week by week, her transformation and the many
wonderful consequences her weight loss brings seem to happen
quickly. In the novel's acknowledgments, Donna Cooner relates
her own positive experience with gastric bypass surgery, but
admits that "it wasn't a magic wand."[38] And yet, in the novel,
weight loss due to the operation works a kind of magic on Ever's
life. By the novel's end, although Ever is still overweight, she has
lost 117 pounds, beaten back the negative voice inside her head
(the "Skinny" of the title) and achieved everything she has ever
wanted—a happier family life, a boyfriend, friends and community, self-confidence and an audience eager to hear her sing.

Cherie Bennett's *Life in the Fat Lane* (1998) similarly obsesses
about numbers on the scale and features a teen with musical
talents and problems with her weight—but with an interesting
twist. Although the book was published some years ago, the
creative way Bennett approaches identity and body size keeps
the novel current. The book opens at chapter 118: sixteen-year-
old Lara Ardeche's weight. Each chapter is titled as a number:
Lara's weight as it climbs over a year's time from her perfect
homecoming queen 118 pounds to a high of 218 (also called
"the end" although the book has not concluded at that point).
Lara's "journey" through obesity instigates painful moments of
self-knowledge and recognition that are consistently related to
her struggles with weight gain.[39] The novel confronts the
fetishization of "ideal weight" in the context of female coming-
of-age fiction.

Lest we think that this weight fixation is the sole province of
teen fiction, recall Helen Fielding's hugely successful novel for
adults, *Bridget Jones's Diary* (1996), a relatively early example of
the genre now known as "chick lit." The obsessed and shallow
American high school characters have nothing on the frantic
singletons of Fielding's 1990s-era London who, as the character

Bridget Jones exemplifies, organize their lives and emotional states around the number on the bathroom scale. Bennett's chapters, which begin by recording Lara's weight—her most important feature—resemble Bridget's style of diary entry that catalogue her drinks intake, calories consumed, cigarettes smoked, and up-to-the-minute weight. Fielding's work is certainly comic, but the extreme popularity of the book demonstrates that its concerns also resonate with many women past the teen years. Bridget frets: "Sometimes I wonder what I would be like if left to revert to nature—with a full beard and handlebar moustache on each shin, Dennis [sic] Healey eyebrows, face a graveyard of dead skin cells, spots erupting, long curly fingernails like Struwwelpeter . . . flabby body flobbering around. Ugh. Ugh. Is it any wonder girls have no confidence?"[40] The horror that Lara feels as her weight balloons is starkly communicated through ever-increasing numbers and without the Fieldingesque humor that might mitigate the seriousness of her distress. In *Fat: A Fate Worse Than Death?* Ruth Raymond Thone quotes a survey of American women that asked what one thing they would change in their lives if able, and more than half responded that they wanted to lose weight. Girls, aged 11 to 17, given a choice of three wishes, overwhelmingly chose losing weight as their first wish.[41] Weight obsession is a feminist issue. McKinley argues that "working to achieve and maintain ideal weight keeps women focused on their bodies and reinforces the construction of women as primarily bodies. At the same time, while women's attention is focused inward, they presumably will not be focused on challenging external constraints to their lives."[42]

Life in the Fat Lane takes a hard look at the gendered social disease of fat-phobia and relates obesity—quite explicitly—with monstrosity. While Lara is still beauty-queen thin, she aids the hapless Patty Asher—"by far the fattest girl in our class"[43]—in drying her prom dress; at the same time, she also thinks to herself, "Although she had beautiful long brown hair, her brown eyes, which might have been pretty, were sunken under twin cushions of fat. . . . Her shoulders, which weren't all that broad, blossomed into a huge bosom. Below that, her waist exploded into an inner tube of fat, which sat on top of an even huger role of flesh."[44] And yet, as Lara continues, inexplicably, to put on pounds, the tables are turned and she thinks of herself as looking like a monster and begins to feel like one, as well: "With every pound I gained, I was filled with an ever growing, impotent rage. Some monster was swelling up inside me, making me get fatter and fatter. I had to force myself to be nice, sweet, good Lara, when actually I felt like this ugly, angry, hideous monster-Lara."[45] In her sleep she has nightmares that she has become a Godzilla-like, giant creature frightening everyone she meets: "I had turned into a huge, hideous monster, and people were running from me, screaming in fear."[46] The folklore characters of giant and miniature are brought out and compared, with preference given to the small: the girls in her new high school cruelly call Lara "Jolly Green Giant" when she first wears her gymsuit on the basketball court.[47] And a young child in an actual 20/20 television segment quoted in the novel laments, " 'I wish I could shrink, . . . I would rather be Thumbelina.' "[48] In fact Lara *does* transform into the stock, fairy-tale giant who is ugly both on the outside and on the inside. She "falls" from beauty into ugliness, from composure to rage, from "niceness" to bitchiness, and from self-censure to brutal honesty—all as a result of her mysterious gain of 100 pounds.

This exaggerated, unrelenting weight gain—finally explained by a (fictitious) rare metabolic disease called Axell-Crowne (a kind of pseudo, adult-onset Prader-Willi Syndrome[49])— spotlights Lara's character, her family members, and society at large. Along the way of exploring the issues of fat, self-esteem, and beauty, the book—rather like *The Earth, My Butt and Other Big Round Things*—explodes the myth of the "perfect" teen and the perfect family: the father loses interest in his wife, expects his children to be flawless in all ways, and conducts a long-standing affair; the mother is a pathetic former beauty queen who smothers her husband emotionally, smokes to stay thin, begins to abuse drugs and alcohol, considers sharing her husband with his mistress in order to stay married to him, and sees her daughter's medical and emotional problems as issues of self-control and finding the right diet; the brother rejects the phoniness of the rest of his family yet cannot accept the changes in his sister's appearance from thin to fat.

On her "journey of fat," Lara learns first-hand about self-loathing, the cruelty of thin America, and the erasure that occurs when you don't fit into conventional ideas of beauty (Lara thinks to herself, "It was the ultimate irony—I had become both huge and invisible").[50] She also learns to scrutinize her own past failings and to make friends who do not judge her on her appearance. Although she is pageant-trained ("Beauty queens are friendly, controlled, sweet, and soft-spoken at all times"[51]—perhaps *as a result* of her pageant training and poor parenting—until she is fat herself, Lara does not recognize that her responses to other girls who do not share her gift of outward beauty are patronizing, shallow, and ultimately belittling. This realization of her own responsibility to others—and a dawning sense that her previous life was flawed—lead Lara to accept the fact that she is not perfect but is going to be "okay" even if she is unable to return to her previous weight. The last image of the book is Lara rolling over in bed—bedsprings creaking under her weight—with "a happy-sad-cool-hot-classical-jazz–angry–peaceful–thin–girl–fat–girl smile on [her] lips."[52]

The novel does not try to resolve the social fat-phobia that informs Lara's self-hatred, the disapproval she receives from adults, and the incessant insults and teasing she suffers from peers. As Lara says with resignation, " 'If you ask a thin girl with no talent or brains if she'd rather be her or you, she'll pick her. Skinny girls who chain-smoke four packs of cigarettes a day would rather get lung cancer than get fat. Being fat is the worst thing in the world. Everyone knows it. So no matter what you say, the world wins. And [fat girls] lose.' "[53] It would have been highly unrealistic for Bennett to have included some kind of social readjustment to obesity at the novel's conclusion; the reality of the fear and hatred of the gigantic female body retains its cultural power within—and without—the text.[54]

Visual and News Media Narratives of the Giant Girl

There is almost nothing in fiction that real life can't top for tragedy, comedy, coincidence, or sheer weirdness. A living Lara Ardeche exists in the person of young Anamarie Martinez-Regino of Albuquerque, New Mexico.[55] Born in 1998 weighing just under seven pounds, the infant girl immediately started growing at a highly unusual rate. By the time she was eight months old she weighed 38 pounds. Alarmed, her mother, Adela Martinez-Regino, began to take her from one doctor to another in an attempt to understand why her daughter continued to gain weight and grow so rapidly. When Anamarie was two, her father, Miguel Regino, left his job in order to replace Adela's mother as Anamarie's babysitter during the day while Adela worked. Adela could no longer carry the over-70-pound child (unable to walk because her bones and muscles could not support her weight). Although Anamarie was put on a variety of increasingly calorie-restrictive diets (at one point at age three she was allowed only 500 calories a day), she continued to gain more weight and to grow taller while her social skills and motor skills were somewhat delayed. Mutual suspicion and distrust between Anamarie's desperate and worried family and the professionals who sought to help her ensued. The medical community could not diagnose a condition for Anamarie nor could they control her weight while she lived at home. She was hospitalized and put on a liquid diet. There, she finally began to lose a few pounds, which precipitated a crisis: convinced that Anamarie's parents could not or would not care for her properly, and that her life was in danger, the New Mexico Children, Youth, and Families Department, in collusion with doctors, social workers, and nutritionists, recommended that Anamarie be placed in foster care. To her parents' horror, Anamarie was taken away, screaming. After a media firestorm (mostly negative against the state and supportive of the Martinez-Regino family) and two and a half months in foster care (where Anamarie lost about ten pounds), physical custody was restored to Anamarie's parents while the state retained legal custody. Finally, in early 2001, as Anamarie continued to lose weight, the charges of abuse against Mr. Regino and Mrs. Martinez-Regino were dropped and they regained legal custody of their child.

A number of parties have watched this situation with interest over the years—including the media, childhood obesity experts, size acceptance organizations and academics. Any attempt at understanding what happened to this family and why, however, is complicated by three contributing factors: Anamarie remains a medical mystery, she is a child (now a teen), and she is a member of an ethnic minority. Anamarie's saga is ongoing. She remains morbidly obese and very tall for her age: at her eighth birthday she weighed 210 pounds and was 5 foot 2 inches in height. She is both a medical anomaly and a poster child in the war on fat—but her obese body's meaning varies according to which side of the war you're on: from a medical standpoint, Anamarie appears to be a time bomb waiting to explode into diabetes and heart disease; for fat-phobics she represents disturbing excess, gluttony, and misery; for nutritionists her size results from bad food choices; for fat-acceptance advocates Anamarie is a victim of prejudice and an over-zealous state machine; for parents and children's rights advocates, she is a symbol of vulnerability and perhaps racism. Of course, this list is simplistic: healthcare professionals, social workers, parents, or advocates do not speak in one voice. In every case, however, adults are speaking *for* Anamarie: as a child, she has little choice in treatment options and cannot control the ways in which her size and treatment are debated in the court of public opinion. She might wish, for example, that *Good Morning America* would lose interest in her (or perhaps that her mother would lose interest in *Good Morning America*).[56] At the same time, Anamarie's youth "protects" her from the judgments that will surely come her way as she grows up. As Anamarie is a child, her body is not entirely her own. As a child, "it's not her "fault" that she's fat. In considering this case, fat-acceptance advocates argue that fear and prejudice encouraged the creation of monsters. That is, the state turned Anamarie into the puppet-monster of other monsters—her overweight parents.[57] At one point, Adela Martinez-Regino was accused of having Munchausen syndrome by proxy, a psychological disorder that causes a family member to intentionally harm a child in order to gain attention (these charges were later dropped). The Martinez-Regino family and its advocates believe that they have been the victims of prejudice: that their child would not have been removed from the family if they had been middle-class and white. Misunderstandings—perhaps willful—between the state and the family were continually exacerbated by perceived issues of ethnic and national identity: Mr. Regino is a native speaker of Spanish, but Mrs. Martinez-Regino is a second-generation American whose first language is English. Although she preferred to hear her daughter's treatment options in English, some members of the healthcare profession insisted upon speaking to her in Spanish. The affidavit accusing the parents of abuse concluded that "the family does not fully understand the threat to their daughter's safety and welfare due to language or cultural barriers."[58] Mexican-American cuisine is commonly perceived as high in fat and calories—as unhealthy. "Here were so many veiled comments which added up to 'You know those Mexican people, all they eat is fried junk, of course they're slipping her food,'" argued Troy Prichard, the family's attorney, as reported in Lisa Belkin's 2001 *New York Times Magazine* feature story about Anamarie. Another perceived prejudice, a particularly class-based one, relates to size itself. Not Anamarie's size—*everyone else's size*: everyone they dealt with, according to Mrs. Martinez-Regino, was skinny and thus not likely to understand them.[59]

The threat of the removal of obese children from their homes has not been confined to the story of Anamarie, nor has it receded. In an opinion piece that ran in the esteemed *Journal of the American Medical Association* (JAMA) in 2011, Dr. David Ludwig, a childhood obesity expert from Harvard University, wrote with Lindsey Martagh, a lawyer and researcher also from

Harvard, that " ' In severe instances of childhood obesity, removal from the home may be justifiable, from a legal standpoint, because of imminent health risks and the parents' chronic failure to address medical problems.' "[60]

Though there is little comedy to be found in the Anamarie Martinez-Regino case, if presented iconically, or ironically, the obese child can function within the visual joke of the enormous baby, the phenomenon in which the physically small child, although made enormous and thus threatening by some fantastic means, retains his/her innocence and youthful preoccupations. In the 1992 Disney film *Honey, I Blew Up the Kid*, a two-year-old is mistakenly zapped by his father's size-altering machine. Every time he approaches electricity he grows bigger, ultimately becoming over 100 feet tall. Las Vegas is this child's playground, but he needs his mother (who chooses to grow enormous herself) to protect him—no matter his height—because he remains in the position of the small (i.e., dependent and needy). This visual joke makes the enormous responsibility and degree of effort required in caring for infants and young children *literal* and yokes the helplessness of the small with the great "destruction" they can wreak upon the family. In "Father's Day," William Joyce's cover art for the June 12, 2000 issue of the *New Yorker*, a gigantic toddler picks up his father's desk in one hand, scattering papers, and clutches his tiny, hapless parent (who had clearly been working at the desk, dressed in business attire and holding the phone) in another. His mother offers up his Father's Day gift from the boy, a tie with the message "I ♥ Dad." If he so chooses, the gigantic child can interrupt the father and reorder his priorities to reflect the child's desires. Given Y2K anxiety coupled with the anticipation a new millennium elicted, Carter Goodrich's cover art, also for the *New Yorker* (October 18 and 25, 1999) imagining a gargantuan Baby New Year (wearing his year 2000 sash and diaper) as rampaging robot trampling the New York skyline, seems a comic and iconographically perfect way to visualize the big and small world I've been describing throughout this book.

A certain tongue-in-cheek humor characterizes these visual jokes about the monstrous child body tyrannizing the people and things around him. Yet, when is a picture of the big child, the fat child, something other than funny or poignant? When is the obese girl's body used as a measure of montrosity? To answer these questions with a specific example, I would like to return to the rarefied world of Baroque Spanish court painting and consider the Juan Carreño de Miranda portraits of five- or six-year-old Eugenia Martínez Vallejo, nicknamed "La Monstrua." In 1680, at the request of King Charles II, Carreño painted a pair of portraits of the obese girl who had been brought to court because of her anomalous size (see Plates 30 and 31).[61]

Carreño, although his talents were overshadowed by the greatness of Velázquez before him, was a skilled court painter held in high regard. Once appointed to the rank of royal painter by the queen in 1669 and to the higher rank of court painter in 1671, his primary subjects shifted to the royal family, although, as in the case of Eugenia Martínez Vallejo, he also painted non-royals at his patron's request.[62] The "monstrua" portraits, like the Velázquez and van Dyck paintings of dwarfs and "buffoons," take disproportion or disability to be a subject matter worthy of record. The reasons for this are many, and I have discussed some of them in previous chapters: the dwarf body and its "low" position may highlight the exalted nature and position of the aristocratic body; may contextualize ideologies of savagery, incompleteness, childhood or witless innocence indexed to size; may provide visual evidence of patronage, power, and privilege of big over small. In the case of the Carreño portraits, however, the subject is not littleness, but obesity and an over-abundance of size. The girl is typed as a monster because she is too big.

In fact, Eugenia, whether dressed or nude, is seemingly neither girl nor child. While this is obviously the case in the painting in which she alludes to Bacchus, the Roman god of wine, even in *vestida* Eugenia's size removes her from girlhood. While holding pieces of fruit in each hand—an apple and perhaps a pear—as is conventional in portraits of children,

Eugenia's massive presence, filling the frame, speaks of something other than childhood. Her story is "corpulence" even while clothed in a beautiful dress. Depicted wearing a sumptuous brocade gown overlaid with gold pattern and embellished by large sleeves and bows at the shoulder, bright reds and golds fill the frame of the painting. Yet Eugenia is not dressed in the fashion of the times and femininity seems to fight with her balloon-like body. Eugenia's waist cannot be cinched; her farthingale cannot emphasize width in contrast to a slender center point of the female body as we see in other Golden Age portraits of women and girls, including those depicted in *Las Meninas*.[63] Eugenia's overblouse is buttoned only at the top so as to allow for her protruding abdomen. The contrast between the child's dark eyes, hair, accessories, brows and background of the painting with the brilliant reds of the dress is most striking. Taken together, her low and dramatic eyebrows, and down-turned cupid's bow mouth suggest a scowl. This expression draws the viewer, wonderingly, to her face. What is she thinking? What has her life been like?

Plenty of commentators have responded to the portraits of Eugenia—not for their artistry, but as illustrations of disease.[64] For example, in his popular retelling of the story of the human genome, Matt Ridley uses Eugenia's portrait to illustrate the genetic disorder Prader-Willi syndrome. In a rather offhand manner, Ridley rattles off the symptoms he sees in Eugenia from her portrait and diagnoses her as both "wrong" and defective: "There is indeed clearly something wrong with her: she is obese, enormous for her age, has tiny hands and feet and strange-shaped eyes and mouth. She was probably exhibited as a freak at a circus. With hindsight, it is plain that she shows all the classic signs of a rare inherited disease called Prader-Willi syndrome . . . ."[65] But—not so fast. It does not appear to this viewer that Eugenia's eyes and mouth are "strange-shaped" or that she displays all of the physical symptoms of Prader-Willi (which include undeveloped genitals. Eugenia's genitals are not shown in either portrait). In any event, this diagnosis through art—although a kind of hobby—leaves something to be desired in terms of accuracy and objectivity. Another example of discovering what you're looking for in what you're looking at may be found in the collaboration between Alan E. H. Emery and Marcia L. H. Emery in their book *Mother and Child Care in Art*. The third in a trilogy on the topic of medicine and art, the work focuses on obstetrics and pediatrics. *Mother and Child Care in Art* is organized in rough chronology of the depicted events, so beginning with fertility and pregnancy and ending up with artistic renderings of contemporary medical discoveries or problems—in this case, genetics and obesity.

Once again, Eugenia's portrait is contemplated (oddly, the painting has been reversed in reproduction). The Emerys choose Eugenia *desnuda* as the basis for their diagnosis of Prader-Willi Syndrome. But Prader-Willi is not the main concern of the brief essay that accompanies the plate; rather, the Emerys are interested in highlighting the prevalence of obesity in children that is due not to genetics—that is, obesity that is not the child's "fault," presumably—but to obesity that results from poor eating habits and behavioral choices: "Whatever the nature of this little girl's affliction, she is certainly obese. But genetic causes of obesity are rare, and the majority of cases result from an inappropriate diet and lack of physical activity—both factors stemming from lifestyle and behavioural changes in recent years."[66]

What follows from such exploitations of the giant girl's body—from being labeled as "monster" to being contained by the diagnosis of a particular disorder, to cautionary tale?[67] The actual obese child carries the burdens and expectations of *both* big and small: the child's large body functions in opposition to her youth (her "smallness"). Anamarie and Eugenia were such children; Barbara was another. As I note in the introduction to Part Two of this study, between 1986 and 1995, photographer Andrea Modica took black and white photographs of Barbara's family of fourteen children living in a low-income, rural area in upstate New York. Barbara, the family's seven-year-old daughter, became one of Modica's favorite models; many of the images they made together over the years appear in Modica's book, *Treadwell* (an actual place, population 200, but not the setting for most of the photographs). Barbara's obesity and her young age make her an unusual photographer's subject; in many images, age and size seem locked in conflict. Photographs in which Barbara is depicted wearing the masks of childhood— such as face paint and bunny ears—highlight the tension between Barbara's childishness and her heavy body anchoring the tilting composition of the image. In other photographs, Barbara's unconventional beauty and vibrant personality glow. Yet each of Barbara's photographs may serve to discomfit the viewer who looks for the lightness, the quickness, we treasure in the child because it is so different from the weighted cares of adulthood. Even if this construction of childhood is little more than a fantasy, do we mourn its absence in the narrative we presume to read through Barbara's body?[68]

Barbara's obesity, like Anamarie's, is marked by her social class and rural context. In image after image, the rooms devoid of decoration, the worn and dirty furnishings, littered unkempt yard, mark Barbara and her family as poor and perhaps in need of care. In one image, a cherubic little girl wearing a filmy party dress and crouched on a mattress that appears to be in a state of decomposition, smiles and points a handgun directly at the camera. Images of children in poverty, illness, loneliness, or despair—as in photographs of Darfur, Afghanistan, post-Katrina New Orleans—give rise to the desire to relieve their suffering. Certainly, given the assumed relationship between photography and the "truth" (in particular in the case of quasi-journalistic visual evidence of human deprivation), wide distribution of photographs of homeless, injured, and hungry children helps to advertise their plight and encourage relief efforts. Without knowing anything about Barbara's family or her life other than what is reflected in the photographs, the viewer might supply the "missing" details along stereotypical lines: chronic under-employment, limited education, lack of medical care, bad diet, failure to family-plan, overcrowding. It's easy to generalize and to patronize. The viewer of Modica's images might even want to remove Barbara from her home, to help her, to fix her obesity and somehow relieve her poverty. But wait: we've heard that story before. Informed by the connected consciousnesses of size and class, these sympathetic responses to girlhood obesity—one girl a medical anomaly and the other the subject of a series of aesthetically pleasing fine art photographs—surely run the risk of reducing each individual to a type, a conundrum—even as they seek to empathize and perhaps to protect. Yet, unlike the YA novel that packages size as a problem to be solved or constructs obese protagonists as "monsters of prohibition," Modica's photographs record Barbara freed from most master narratives— except those, I would argue, about social class. She is not a character or a case study; she is representative of no one but herself—yet at the same time she reflects our fears about poverty, dirt and "monstrous" underclass children.

The fears of obesity are not entirely groundless. Barbara's weight contributed to her death at age 22 from complications of diabetes. Barbara's fate, of course, could become Anamarie's, and the desire to avoid such a tragedy fueled much of the strong-arm tactics that the Martinez-Regino family faced. Modica could not prevent Barbara's death through her photography. But she was a witness to the passing of her friend and muse, taking new pictures with the same 8" x 10" camera she had used in earlier portraits. Their collaboration continued through Barbara's last year when she was mostly bed-ridden. The result was the emotionally moving collection entitled *Barbara* (2004).

Modica's final portraits of Barbara demonstrate a transformation of the "giant" from flesh to spirit. Although Barbara's childlikeness is interrogated in many of the photos, her groundedness and solidity ultimately become essence and light. In life, Barbara was larger and heavier than ever when she died. Yet Modica's images make a different argument: not "fat acceptance," but an argument about aestheticized form. Viewing this argument is a special privilege afforded to the viewer. I feel honored to witness Barbara's living-in-dying moments, her last journey.

At the same time, I am a bit troubled by my attraction to the *Barbara* photographs—not because she is dying and this is sad, or seems too private, but because as I interrogate my response, something about big and small in conflict becomes clear to me, something that answers a prior discomfort about the absence of lightness and quickness in Barbara's childhood photos: the tender, "out of focus" photographs of the dying young woman are reassuring and attractive, in part, because within them Barbara becomes "small." That is, she appears almost fetal, embryonic. In these images her big head and dark, exaggerated eye sockets, her head or torso seemingly floating in space, remind us of fetal imagery, the sonogram photograph beloved by parents and grandparents and often exploited politically, as I argue in chapter one, by ascribing an identity of innocence and vulnerability to the fetus. In looking at Barbara we lose our sense of scale, that profound and compelling instinct that organizes the world and to which we cling. That scale determining normal/ abnormal, big/small typed Barbara, throughout her life, as gigantic. Perhaps we appreciate Barbara most when we don't know exactly how we are seeing her. She could be under a microscope or viewed through a telescope. In dying she is "disembodied," after all. No longer labeled "obese," Barbara fades to a ghostly presence and we let her go.

In the beginning of this chapter I ask whether the female giant or the obese girl may surmount or transcend the disorder, the seemingly irreconcilable duality of excess and lack, femininity and enormity, their bodies announce to a fat-phobic and size-obsessed world. I think that the answer is certainly "yes" in the fictional realm, but in the real world the answer is "maybe." Here's a real-world example from a 2011 and 2012 well-meaning anti-obesity campaign sponsored by Strong4Life and Children's Healthcare of America that highlights the disparity between big size and childhood: the advertisement, which was displayed in Georgia on billboards and television, featured obese girls and the tagline "It's hard to be a little girl if you're not."[69] I'm dodging, perhaps, but obesity, especially when read inflected by gender and in this era of reality television programming in which becoming "the biggest loser" is both an ideal and an insult, is a category of difference unloved by most and very difficult to talk about in terms other than the moral or the defensive. If obesity can be translated from gluttony to genetic disorder and accepted as a disease, if all women become fat and the "other" becomes thin (an increasing likelihood, in America, at least), or if large can somehow communicate the emotions that attach to small—tenderness, protectiveness, wonder—then "La Monstrua," for example, might be unburdened from the label of monster and restored to her given name Eugenia and to the positions of childhood.

The monstrous body, Cohen maintains, is "pure culture."[70] By disordering scale, the giant challenges our cultural myths about Nature, Art, relationships, human ability and ingenuity, appearance and conduct (in taboos related to the body such as sexuality, appetite). Fables and legends of heroism and derring-do rely upon the giant as either champion or enemy; as such, in these formative narratives, we ask the giant to save us, or we destroy the giant and save ourselves. In the example of Ted Hughes's contemporary fable, discussed in chapter five, the two giant figures, representing technology and the arts, alter the course of global disorder and violence, replacing chaos with peace. Angelica Longrider, as a force of Nature, defies gender expectations and successfully, if comically, triumphs over her large adversaries and changes the natural world by creating new landscapes and topographical features. Anamarie Regino's story, which validates neither nature nor nurture in the attempt to assign "blame" for her size, challenges cultural norms delimiting happiness and normality and forces us to examine the prejudices that intrude even as we want to "help" the obese girl by defeating her obese body. In the case of Barbara, our relationship to her body is mediated by the camera and Modica's affection and thus asks for a different emotional response than a sensationalized girl's story told through print and television media. In the photographs of Barbara's body we see and interpret the space she occupies as she grows up, as her body continues to enlarge. And in her dying images, we feel the loss that her absent presence demands.

As Cohen trenchantly observes in his comment about the monstrous body as "pure culture," the monster/giant is a constructed being. While appearing supremely other, the monster/giant actually evolves from within our own fears and ambitions and cannot exist outside the margins of our expansive imaginations and desires. And while the giant's mysterious origins defy understanding—in life as in literature—we focus not on their pre-existence (as we do with the miniature), but on their gross physicality, their "thereness." The bigger and more frightening the giant (or, by contrast, the bigger and more docile) the better for enabling comfort and self-satisfaction once the balance the giant upsets is restored and the giant contained. We are indeed defined by our giants, giants created from the inter-play between sites of fear and imagination: the guts and the brain.

AFTERWORD
The Human Measure

And what was King Kong ever going to do
With Fay Wray, or Jessica Lange,
But climb, climb, climb, and get shot down?
No wonder Gulliver's amiably chatting
With that six-inch woman in his palm.
Desire's huge, there's really nowhere to put it
in our small world that it will stay put:
might as well just talk.
Rage also, and fear, and elation
are windswept summits, your poor mind
half the time an F6 tornado
that could drive a blade of grass through armor plate.
But a lit match inches from your eyes?
Unwavering. Out there,
in the world we call Real, is calm.
When you stalk down Broadway, fifty feet tall
and building like a thunderhead, your clothes
tattering and whirled away like leaves,
you can nonchalant it, you can be at peace:
it's only in movies that anyone notices.

—"Big Scenes," James Richardson © 2016[1]

This book brings our attention to a category of difference—size—that informs our everyday thoughts and actions. While there is no end to interesting art objects, products, buildings, and exhibits that use scale to create powerful effects and experiences—discussions of which might have formed the core of this study—my focus has been on big and small bodies in life, literature, and art. Unlike gender (which attaches only to animal life) or race (which attaches, albeit uneasily, only to human animals), things as well as people may be big or small. Yet it is through the body that the ideologies of size speak most eloquently. Children, for example, are small people and one of the arguments of this book is that we cannot understand the adult/child relationship without an awareness of how the child's small size affects that relationship. It might be easier or more comfortable to continue to ignore what size means culturally, aesthetically, and politically, yet I believe to do so constitutes a missed opportunity to understand how size difference, as well as those categories we now see with greater clarity—race, gender, and class—has impacted human history and culture. Indeed, the time has come to evaluate and analyze how size works both with and against these categories, as similar markers of difference but unique in their cultural effects. The idea that size forms essential aspects of human identity and culture is not new; in fact, the very pervasiveness of valuations and consequences of size difference make it difficult to see and thus interrogate. Throughout this book I have discussed a number of different exceptional bodies from dwarfs and pygmies to giants and robots, from embryos and thumblings to tall-tale heroes and monsters. They are the creatures of the world around us as well as the stuff of fiction. By encouraging us to look with care at extraordinary bodies and the cultures that created them, painted and photographed them, caressed and manipulated them, dominated and destroyed them, I am also encouraging the discomfort that comes along with recognizing difference and being responsible to it. I am not arguing for an erasure of difference—that would be a pointless and ahistorical argument—but that we should "think what we are doing" as Hannah Arendt urged in *The Human Condition.*[2]

The aim of this afterword is not to rehearse the book's arguments or to suggest additional examples of big and small bodies to contemplate. Rather, my goal here is to introduce the idea of the "human measure," a related way to think about big and small bodies that expands upon the book's main points about power, identity, otherness, awe. We are not straying far from the body at all—indeed, as itself the instrument of measuring, the human measure cannot function outside of the body. The human measure provides one way to talk about scale, an important concept in the book. But it also provides a method of discussing big and small thinking that goes beyond our knee-jerk method of evaluating the world around us—bigger than a man? Smaller than a woman?—or our fears and anxieties over otherness in individuals. The human measure may begin by giving information about size and scale, yet pictorial examples of the human measure (and it only works visually) tell us much more than that, and these are often the things we most need to hear. Let me explain.

We have always been addicted to the human measure. From antiquity, length measurement was inspired by the idealized human form and defined locally and independently. Though the digits, knuckles, cubits (forearm), strides or spans (distance between outstretched arms) may have been imprecise, body-centered measurement was both coherent and essential. As Robert Tavernor suggests in his cultural history of measuring standards, "nothing is more readily accessible in everyday experience than the human body and its constituent parts, and—once—nothing was more meaningful."[3] Even as we have separated the human measure from its divine symbolism or turned away from the king's body as a ruler in more than one sense of the word, we are reminded of the body every time we measure the length of nearly anything in "feet." "Hands" are still used to indicate the distance from the ground to a horse's wither. Tavernor relates the amusing and unusual story of the "smoot," a unit of measurement derived precisely from one man's body. The task, as MIT's Lambda Chi Alpha fraternity of 1958 created it, was to measure the Harvard Bridge, the longest bridge crossing the Charles River. The means by which this feat was accomplished was via one Oliver R. Smoot, an MIT freshman, and the shortest pledge. Smoot was required to lie down over and over again as chalk marks delineated each Smoot. As it happens, the Harvard Bridge measures 364.4 Smoots, plus or minus an ear.[4]

In addition to providing a standard mensural system, the human measure is used any time we want the body to function as an indicator of relative size. We know, we think, how big the body is, or how small, and thus the body provides a practical rough estimate for the size of things in relation to it. Plus, our inflated egos compare everything to "us," and why should size be any different? Certainly there are limitations to the human measure: we are bound by the ability of the eye to see something in its entirety in order for the human measure to perform acts of scale. Or, if a camera or other device coupled with great height provided by a plane or tall building or any number of means of gaining distance, allows for teeny tiny humans to be seen against an immense backdrop such as a mountain or a mass demonstration, the visual field and scale remain bound by the image's frame. Indeed, the human measure is not much help in understanding the diameter of a star or the length of a river. But no matter these caveats or any competitor to the primacy of the human measure, the human body remains, as Devin Fore notes, "the most intuitive and expressive of measure."[5] The human measure is a tool the use of which provides a certain smug comfort and confidence. As the soul's host and God's image, Nature's beautiful child and the mind's machine, the human body is both our ruler and our obsession.

The human measure assisted the nineteenth-century French archeological photographer Maxime Du Camp in his demonstration of the vastness of the Egyptian temples formed out of rock on the west bank of the Nile at Abu Simbel on Egypt's southern borderland.

Certainly Du Camp was not the first or only photographer to use the human scale for documentary or other purposes, but this well-known image provides a good example of how the human measure may be used not only practically or aesthetically but also ideologically (or politically). Over the course of the nineteenth century, France had established itself as a leader in Egyptology as well as in the new technologies and developing sciences of archeology and photography. The image under consideration was taken during Du Camp's government-sponsored 1849–1851 trip to Egypt and the Near East with Gustave Flaubert. The scholarly and scientific goals of the Du Camp and Flaubert expedition were in keeping with the mission to extend France's dominance in these fields within a culturally rich and politically interesting part of the world.[6]

The first European in modern times to arrive at the partially buried temple at Abu Simbel was the Swiss explorer J.L. Burckhardt in 1813. Four years later the Italian explorer and archeologist Giovanni Battista Belzoni, whose methods today might be called "plunder," visited the rock temple and organized its clearing of hardened sand and excavation. Thus, when Du Camp arrived with Flaubert, the imposing temple (actually two temples) dedicated to the sun gods Amon-Re and Re-Horakhte (or Ra-Horakty, Ptah, and the deified Ramses II) was a newly discovered wonder of the world to interested Europeans and antiquities hunters. It is certainly easy to understand why photographs of any aspect of the Great Temples' principal façade graced by four enormous seated figures of Ramses II would themselves be counted as trophies by those lucky enough to see them. Images of the inscrutable seated colossi (some 69 feet tall and among the tallest in Egypt) would certainly fascinate enthusiasts who had little hope of ever traveling to Egypt themselves. Du Camp, with Flaubert, and a crew of Egyptians, arrived at Abu Simbel in 1850. Du Camp prepared to take a number of photographs, the best-known of which is reproduced here (see Plate 32).[7]

Variations in the color of the rock highlight the lips, chin, and right ear of the dramatic and regal head which, in the photograph, appears to be rising out of shifting sand, though Ramses's headdress nearly fades into the façade behind it. The most interesting aspect of the photograph is the juxtaposition of man with rock: sitting atop a monumental stone head is a bearded human figure, wearing a head covering, whose face is deeply shadowed. In order to show the statue's immense size to viewers who would never see the temples otherwise, Du Camp had an Egyptian servant enter the frame and provide a body that would immediately be perceived as small once it was put into contrast with the big head. In the gray-scale of the photograph's palette, the colors of the man's clothing reflect the colors of the rock. There's perhaps more to the story of this photograph's composition: Du Camp allegedly coerced the servant to be still once on the statue's head by telling him that unless he remained motionless, the camera, which he claimed was also a gun, would shoot.[8]

This photograph is about the "human measure" in more ways than simply using it as a scaling device, although this is the most obvious use. Indeed, the Du Camp photograph of the temple at Abu Simbel and the servant on top of Ramses II's head tells us much more about the culture that produced it—the admiring, exploring, claiming, plundering, commercializing, collecting Europeans—than about ancient or nineteenth-century Egypt, a relationship that I have referred to elsewhere in the book as violating the "eth(n)ics of size." In other words, in their archeological expeditions that used native knowledge as well as creating a market for the labor that assisted the expeditions, colonialist maps, antiquities removal, and documentary photographs (relatively) small nations could master big ones by providing interpretations of ancient civilizations, religions, and human origins as well as by "preserving" their artifacts elsewhere. In discussing what she calls the "art and science of antiquity" expressed through nineteenth-century archeological photography, Claire L. Lyons argues that Du Camp's work and others assisted imperialist thinking: "Behind the spectacle of remote, emblematic, and picturesque places stood implicit assumptions about the future progress and destiny of nations."[9]

I am not arguing that nineteenth-century archeological expeditions funded by Lord Elgin or the British Museum and imple-
mented by agents such as Henry Salt and John Turtle Wood, for
example, did not on a purely scientific level perform a valuable
service to world heritage by shipping off pieces of Near Eastern
and Mediterranean treasures to museums, treasures that were in
danger of permanent loss by destruction or by being hidden
(those sold to individuals are another story). At the very least,
arguments may be offered on both sides of the preservation/
plunder and legally purchased/repatriation debate. The argument from science is one aspect of this debate. However, there is
no such thing as "pure science" that exists apart from people.
And wherever we find people we find greed, avarice, and self-
interest. Not a new argument, but one I have discussed in my
focus on size difference, is that all forms of science are cultural
and ideological, too. Ideas about religion, progress, social class,
identity, gender, race, and nation—and size—will always intrude
and attempt to appropriate or infiltrate scientific endeavors
whether those endeavors are hESC research, anthropological
racial profiling, limb lengthening or bariatric surgery, nanotechnology, atom smashing, space travel, or AI and robotics.

Thinking about the clashes between the scientific and political imaginary, one example of which I discuss in terms of the
various appropriations of the notion of the miniature man,
returns us to Du Camp's photograph and the human measure.

Looking at the photograph as an example of the human
measure, and contemplating the figure on top of the ancient
head and the story that is told about its composition, reminded
me of other ways we use the human body as an instrument of
measurement—as a measurement of the "depth" of humanity
itself. And by "humanity" I mean the degree to which our
behavior matches the morals, manners, and codes of civility and
conduct that form the bedrock of all human society regardless
of religious belief or doctrine. We use our bodies to express our
humanity—or its lack—toward each other by performing acts of
politeness, assistance, consideration, patience, and sacrifice. It

can be challenging to perform acts of physical humanity (known as the "corporal acts of mercy" in Catholicism) over the divide of difference if otherness scares us. Differences in age, nation, gender, race, physical or mental ability do not change what is expected but can affect what is accomplished or even offered. How does big and small thinking, the human measure, affect what we owe and what we offer the other?

The shadowed face of the Egyptian servant is not the only shadow I see when I study Du Camp's oft-published image. For me, this nineteenth-century photograph is haunted by an image from my own time. The sense of haunting was present from the first moment I began looking carefully at the Du Camp photograph. I did not need to have that other image in front of me as it is burned into my visual memory (and that of the world, I expect.) Shape and color are powerful and meaningful elements of any visual image and they often alert the eye first when examining a picture or even glancing at one. Before I knew the exact date of Du Camp's photograph or the location of the temple or the circumstances surrounding its composition, I recognized a shape and a dark center to the image, an ominous dark center where a man's face should be.

For me, the dark shadows covering the servant's head and the shape and placement of that shadow erasing his face and identity, evoke the infamous photographs of the hooded prisoners of Abu Ghraib (the notorious detention center located just outside of Baghdad), in particular, the image of the man standing on a box with arms outstretched and connected to wires.[10] This photograph has become a kind of shorthand image representing the abuse *in toto*. But shape and color are not the only elements that create in me a feeling of connection between Abu Simbel and Abu Ghraib. In every photograph there is an absent presence—the photographer—and a purpose (at least one) for taking the photograph. In the case of the Du Camp photograph, the photographer is on a mission to record the wondrous architectural and sculptural remains of ancient civilizations of the Near East and Egypt. The reason for publishing the photograph and others he took on the trip with Flaubert was to advance "science," French dominance in the fields of Egyptology and archeology, and his own career. These are professional, personal, and documentary reasons. The explanation for the Abu Ghraib torture photograph is murkier given that the photograph is illicit, though some might argue similarly state-sponsored (an American soldier on an American-led mission took the image). Although the torture photograph was not meant to be published, the image from Abu Ghraib was a trophy of sorts, as was the Du Camp photograph at Abu Simbel. Where is the human measure in the photograph of the prisoner at Abu Ghraib?

Let me be clear: by no means am I equating the Du Camp photograph with the torture photograph. My argument is decidedly not that Du Camp's image has the same purpose or is in the same moral register as those from Abu Ghraib. Yet I am arguing that a correspondence may be found between the infamous torture photograph, released in 2004, of a hooded man cloaked in a large fringed blanket, arms spread and wires attached, standing on top of a small case and this dramatic archeological photograph from the mid-nineteenth century documenting the glory and downfall of an ancient civilization through the sheer size of its monuments and their cultural impermanence. This "echo" between photographs is suggested not only by the eerily similar shape and cocked head of the hood and face in shadow, but also by the documentary impulse accompanied by drumbeats that sound behind both images. In the case of Du Camp, the impetus for the drumbeat is national pride, scientific inquiry, artistic technique and colonialist and patronizing ideologies of saving a country from itself. That's what I hear, anyway, from the position of an outsider, more than a century and a half later. What I hear—although, again, everyone will hear something different—in the Abu Ghraib photograph, is the keening of 9/11 overlaid with the shredding of human rights and the shattering of cherished beliefs.

The human measure can be used aggressively to dominate. This is part of big and small thinking. In the Du Camp image the human measure—the man by which the photograph's humanity is "measured"—is outside of the frame. That is, Du Camp himself, and his culture, his tools and techniques, and his status all combine to create the ruler, making a scale against which both ancient and contemporary Egypt are measured. So, too, in the Abu Ghraib photograph. It is again the photographer (man or woman) and anyone else outside of the frame who watched or participated in acts of humiliation and torture, whose human measure is revealed.

When we forget the "humane" part, as we often do, the human measure can be dangerous and violent. The human measure, as this book reminds us, is also the measure that tells us how to respond to bodies out of scale with our own. In our confrontations with exceptional bodies, from dwarfs, pygmies, children and embryos, to giants, the obese, monsters, and mechanical men, we first size up the body in front of us using our own bodies as rulers and then decide what they mean. In the poem "Big Scenes" by James Richardson, used as the epigraph to this Afterword, a few of our favorite characters appear in their glory: King Kong, Gulliver and a Lilliputian, the 50 Foot Woman. They're all here, bringing their intensity, love and despair, both victors and victims, into view.

These iconic figures positioned closely with their contrastive counterparts make it easy to see how big and small work both aesthetically and metaphorically to put scale and size at the center of arguments about civil society, gender, politics, race, art, and science. It's the human measure that's most important in the poem and in this book, too. This is a book that explores the ways in which big and small have been made to explain the mysteries of life, to create categories of beautiful and monstrous, us and them. This historicized analysis of big and small bodies acting within diverse cultural spheres, including children's culture, reveals at various moments my particular political positions on contemporary issues. As I hope that this book has shown, aided by a fulcrum of desire, big and small move the world.

NOTES

Introduction: People Big and People Small

1. Andrew Solomon, *Far From the Tree: Parents, Children, and the Search for Identity* (New York: Scribner, 2012), 4.
2. Quoted in the 1967 Michael Foot introduction to *Gulliver's Travels* by Jonathan Swift. Penguin. Rpt. 1984, 13.
3. Darwin was not the only scientist to be working on the "species question." In 1858, an unpublished paper on his theory of natural selection by the English naturalist Alfred Russel Wallace was read, along with two unpublished papers by Charles Darwin, to a special meeting of the Linnean Society.
4. Felicity Nussbaum, *The Limits of the Human: Fictions of Anomaly, Race, and Gender in the Long Eighteenth Century* (Cambridge: Cambridge University Press, 2003), 41–42.
5. Edmund Burke, *A Philosophical Enquiry into the Origin of our Ideas of the Sublime and Beautiful*, ed. J. T. Boulton (London: Routledge and Kegan Paul and New York: Columbia University Press, 1958), 72.
6. E. B. White, *Stuart Little*. 1945 (New York: Harper and Row, 1973), 92.
7. Lori Merish, "Cuteness and Commodity Aesthetics: Tom Thumb and Shirley Temple," *Freakery: Cultural Spectacles of the Extraordinary Body*, ed. Rosemarie Garland Thomson (New York: New York University Press, 1996), 188.
8. Solomon, *Far From the Tree*, 128.
9. *The Various*, for example, in Steve Augarde's children's fantasy of the same name (2003), describes an interdependent community of tribes of little people, tree-dwellers (Ickri), land-dwellers (Naiad and Wisp) and underground-dwellers (Tinklers and Troggles). The history of community of miniatures is further explored in the second volume and third volumes, *Celandine* (2005) and *Winter Wood* (2008), respectively.
10. Mary W. Shelley, *Frankenstein: or, The Modern Prometheus*. 1818 (London: Henry Colburn and Richard Bentley, 1831), 103.
11. Jeffrey Jerome Cohen, ed. *Monster Theory: Reading Culture* (Minneapolis: University of Minnesota Press, 1996), 7.
12. Director Peter Jackson's *King Kong* (2005) is a remake of the 1933 film original. Elliot Goldenthal's opera (with Julie Taymor) *Grendel* opened at the Lincoln Center Festival in New York City in July 2006.
13. Cohen, *Monster Theory*, vii.

14. David J. Skal, *Speaking of Monsters: A Teratological Anthology*, eds. Caroline Joan S. Picart and John Edgar Browning (New York: Palgrave Macmillan, 2012), xii.

15. Suzanne Anker and Dorothy Nelkin, *The Molecular Gaze: Art in the Genetic Age* (Cold Spring Harbor, NY: Cold Spring Harbor Laboratory Press, 2004), 185. Inspired, in part, by Anker and Nelkin, and by the work of literary and cultural critics Jack Zipes and Marina Warner, the Frist Center for the Visual Arts (Nashville, TN) organized a major exhibit, *Fairy Tales, Monsters, and the Genetic Imagination* (February 24–May 28, 2012). See the exhibit catalogue edited by Mark W. Scala (with essays by Anker, Warner and Zipes), published by Vanderbilt University Press, 2012.

16. Anker and Nelkin, *The Molecular Gaze*, 76.

Part I Introduction: The Little Man

1. Edmund Burke, *A Philosophical Enquiry into the Origin of our Idea of the Sublime and Beautiful*, ed. J. T. Boulton (London: Routledge and Kegan Paul and New York: Columbia University Press, 1958), 157.

2. John Earle, *Microcosmographie, or a Peece of the World Discovered* (London: Printed by W. S. for Ed. Blount, 1628): B.

3. Ibid., B2–B3.

4. See Susan Stewart, *On Longing: Narratives of the Miniature, the Gigantic, the Souvenir, the Collection* (Durham, NC and London: Duke University Press, 1993).

5. Patricia Pace, "The Body-in-Writing: Miniatures in Mary Norton's *Borrowers*." *Text and Performance Quarterly*. 11, no. 4 (October 1991), 280. Jerry Griswold makes a similar point in *Feeling Like a Kid: Childhood and Children's Literature*: "The powerlessness of the young and the vulnerability of the small explain the aroma of timidity and agoraphobia that hovers over Norton's presentation of this tiny world. The marginalized Borrowers are essentially voyeurs in a realm of giants, echoing the situation of children in the company of adults" (62).

6. Carolyn Steedman, *Strange Dislocations: Childhood and the Idea of Human Interiority, 1780–1930.* (Cambridge, MA: Harvard University Press, 1995), 15.

7. Ibid., 9. See also Susan Hancock's thoughtful Jungian analysis of "miniature literature" in *The Child That Haunts Us: Symbols and Images in Fairytale and Miniature Literature* (London and New York: Routledge, 2009).

8. Pace, "The Body-in-Writing," 279.

9. Steedman, *Strange Dislocations*, 20.

10. John Mack, *The Art of Small Things* (London: The British Museum Press, 2007), 44.

11. To name just two examples of this activity in American public schools: in the southern Pennsylvania town of Dover, the school board mandated that, beginning in January 2005, high schoolers must be introduced to "intelligent design" (ID) theory. This decision was controversial and prompted two school board members to resign. In December 2004, a set of parents with the ACLU and Americans United for the Separation of Church and State, sued the school board in federal court. On December 20, 2005, Judge John E. Jones III ruled that the Dover, PA district policy was unconstitutional, violating the establishment clause of the Constitution. While the Supreme Court outlawed the teaching of creationism in public schools in 1987 and the Dover decision represents a loss for the young-earth creationists, ID continues to be a hot button political and pedagogical issue in some states, as the 2016 Republican Party platform makes clear. See also "Anti-evolution Teachings Gain Foothold in U.S. Schools: Evangelicals see Flaws in Darwinism" by Anna Badkhan, which summarizes in detail recent actions in the teaching of evolution. (Anna Badkhan, *San Francisco Chronicle*, November 30, 2004.) In May 2005 hearings on Kansas public schools' teaching about the origins of life were held in Topeka. Those critiquing biological evolution argued that it "postulates an unpredictable and unguided natural process that has no discernable [*sic*] direction or goal." (Quoted in "The Terms of the Debate in Kansas" by Jodi Wilgoren, *The New York Times*, May 15, 2005, 16.)

This attitude against Darwinism is illuminated by the following statistic: 46% of adults who responded to a 2012 Gallup poll of approximately 1,000 participants agreed with the statement that " 'God created human beings pretty much in their present form at one time within the last 10,000 years.' " See Frank Newport, "In US, 46% Hold Creationist View of Human Origins." June 1, 2012. http://www.gallup.com/poll/155003/hold-creationist-view-human-origins.aspx. Accessed November 3, 2016.

12. 2016 Republican Party Platform, 33.
13. Marina Warner, "Fee fie fo fum: The Child in the Jaws of the Story" in *Cannibalism and the Colonial World*, eds. Francis Barker, Peter Hulme, and Margaret Iverson (Cambridge: Cambridge University Press, 1998), 176.
14. According to the Little People of America website, there are over 200 diagnosed types of dwarfism. Achondroplasia, the most common form, accounting for approximately 70% of all cases of dwarfism, occurs in one in 26,000 to one in 40,000 births. The gene for achondroplasia was discovered in 1994. See the LPA website for additional information about dwarfism: http://www.lpaonline.org/
15. See Betty Adelson's comprehensive *The Lives of Dwarfs*, for a discussion of medical aspects of dwarfism and its "treatment," controversial procedures such as limb-lengthening, genetic developments and institutional problems in the medical system (*The Lives of the Dwarfs: Their Journey from Public Curiosity Toward Social Liberation*. New Brunswick: Rutgers University Press, 2005, 122–135).
16. Solomon, *Far From the Tree*, 145.
17. Tiffanie and Rennie Dyball, *Dwarf: A Memoir* (New York: Plume [Penguin Group USA], 2012), 89.
18. DiDonato, *Dwarf*, 113.
19. Ibid., 245–246.
20. Yi-Fu Tuan, *Dominance and Affection: The Making of Pets* (New Haven and London: Yale University Press, 1984), 153. Tuan notes that the earliest recorded information about a court dwarf dates from 5th Dynasty Egypt (*c*. 2500 BC), 154.
21. Solomon, *Far from the Tree*, 118.
22. Oscar Wilde, "The Birthday of the Infanta." Illus. by Pamela Bianco (New York: Macmillan Company, 1929). This story first appeared in the collection *A House of Pomegranates* (London: James R. Osgood McIlvaine and Company, 1891).
23. Stewart, *On Longing*, 54.
24. Kairn A. Klieman, *"The Pygmies Were Our Compass": Bantu and Batwa in the History of West Central Africa, Early Times to c. 1900 C.E.* (Portsmouth, NH: Heinemann, 2003), 3.
25. Ibid..
26. See James A. Clifton for a discussion of the term "invented Indian:" "The Indian Story: A Cultural Fiction," in *The Invented Indian: Cultural Fictions and Governmental Policies*. ed. James A. Clifford (New Brunswick, NJ: Transaction Publishers, 1994), 29–47. Clifton writes, "The aim of producers of the Indian narrative is not simply to inform or enlighten, but also to persuade—within the permissible confines of the narrative's structure. And above all else, the task of persuasion is greatly eased by sticking to a well-trodden path, one whose twists and turns are well known to audiences. Hence versions of the Indian story are mostly pieced together from borrowed hand-me-downs, with enough ruffles and flourishes sewn on to suggest innovativeness" (42). In addition, as film critic Gary Morris notes, Native Americans have joined other ethnic minorities as objects of miniaturization. In a discussion of the film version of Lynne Reid Banks's *The Indian in the Cupboard* (a text I will discuss in detail below), Morris comments, "Views of (particularly male) ethnic minorities as miniaturized dependents are nothing new: sitcom watchers will recall shows like *Webster* and *Different Strokes*, which featured midget blacks living as dependents of large, well-fed, wealthy whites." Gary Morris, "The Incredible Shrinking . . . and Expanding Ethnic Minority, or The Racist in the Cupboard." Issue 15. *Bright Lights Film Journal Online* Issue 15. (November 1995). http://brightlightsfilm.com/15/racist.php#.UxdSafRdVCw

27. The species has been named Flores Man (*Homo floresiensis*). Isolated environments such as remote islands can produce examples in animal species of dwarfism and gigantism such as miniature elephants and large lizards (the Komodo dragon is one example). Both tiny elephants and enormous lizards were found at the same site as the Flores hominins. See "Human Evolution Writ Small" by Marta Mirazón Lahr and Robert Foley *(Nature* Vol. 431 [28 October 2004]: 1043–1044), and "A new small-bodied Hominin from the Late Pleistocene of Flores, Indonesia" by P. Brown, T. Sutikna, M. J. Morwood, R. P. Soejono, Jatmiko, E. Wayhu Saptomo, and Rokus Awe Due(*Nature* Vol. 431 [28 October 2004]: 1055–1061). The interpretation of this discovery is not uncontroversial, however. A fierce debate has arisen around the claims that the skeletons represent a new human species. Other high-level scientists have argued that the bones belong to a pygmy version of *Homo sapiens*. See the report "Bones of Contention" by John Vidal (*Guardian Weekly*). The debate is not likely to be settled anytime soon. Arguments are advanced in the popular scientific press (*Smithsonian Magazine*, for example, in the article "Were 'Hobbits' Human?" by Guy Gugliotta (first published in *Smithsonian Magazine* [July 2008] and reprinted online: http://www.smithsonianmag. com/history-archaeology/migration-hobbits.html) as well as in books such as *A New Human: The Startling Discovery and Strange Story of the "Hobbits" of Flores, Indonesia* (Mike Morwood and Penny Van Oosterzee. Smithsonian Books/ HarperCollins, 2007).

28. The conclusion of the abstract to the Brown, et. al. article states, "The combination of primitive and derived features assigns this hominin to a new species, *Homo floresiensis*. The most likely explanation for its existence on Flores is long-term isolation, with subsequent endemic dwarfing, of an ancestral *H. erectus* population. Importantly, *H. floresiensis* shows that the genus Homo is morphologically more varied and flexible in its adaptive responses than previously thought." Brown, et al., "A New small-bodied hominin" (1055).

29. Hancock, *The Child That Haunts Us*, 24.

30. Charlotte Yonge, *The History of the Life and Death of the Good Knight Sir Thomas Thumb* (Edinburgh: Thomas Constable and Co., 1855), 46.

Chapter 1: In the Beginning was Tom Thumb

1. Michael Patrick Hearn, preface to *The History of Tom Thumbe*. 1621 (New York: Garland, 1977, vii–xxiii), xv.

2. For a thumbnail sketch of the history of Tom Thumb tales, see "Early Print Versions of Tom Thumb" from the Oryx Multicultural Folktale Series (ed. Margaret Read MacDonald, *Tom Thumb*. The Oryx Multicultural Folktale Series, Phoenix, Arizona: Oryx Press, 1993). See also Curt Bühler, ed., *The History of Tom Thumb* (Evanston, IL: Northwestern University Press for the Renaissance English Text Society, 1965); Iona and Peter Opie's *The Classic Fairy Tales* (London: Oxford University Press, 1974); see Michael Patrick Hearn's preface (vii–xxiii); and Weiss, "Three Hundred Years of Tom Thumb," (157–166) in *The History of Tom Thumbe* (1621). *Classics of Children's Literature, 1621–1932*. Selected by Alison Lurie and Justin G. Schiller (New York and London: Garland Publishing, 1977).

3. In a 1787 "defense" of the microscope, George Adams reassures readers that scientific inquiry aided by the microscope follows God's plan for human knowledge: "It is true, the instrument discovers to us as it were a new creation, new series of animals, new forests of vegetables; but he who gave being to these, gave us an understanding capable of inventing means to assist our organs in the discovery of their hidden beauties." George Adams, *Essays on the Microscope; containing a Practical Description of the Most Improved Microscopes* (London: 1787), 1.

4. Reading Kerckring's image, Eve Keller argues, "Taken together, the figures are seemingly embued [*sic*] not only with structural completeness but also with some sense of personhood." See "Embryonic Individuals: The Rhetoric of Seventeenth-Century

Embryology and the Construction of Early-Modern Identity." *Eighteenth-Century Studies* 33.3 (2000): 321–348, 323.

5. See Eve Keller's book, *Generating Bodies and Gendered Selves: The Rhetoric of Reproduction in Early Modern England* (Seattle and London: University of Washington Press, 2007) for an extended investigation into the science of embryology as it informed the construction of early modern identity. For a very readable distillation of early debates over the "facts of life" see Jill Lepore, *The Mansion of Happiness: A History of Life and Death* (New York: Alfred A. Knopf, 2012), 5–22.

6. Early modern scientists and scholars used the term "generation" rather than "reproduction" although both terms reflect theories about the ability of organisms to recreate themselves. I will use the terms essentially interchangeably in this chapter. See Keller's *Generating Bodies*, 148 and 191, n. 1 for a further clarification of early modern uses of these two terms.

7. Quoted in Iona and Peter Opie, *The Classic Fairy Tales* (London: Oxford University Press, 1974), 34.

8. Following the Tom Thumb figure's duality down a different path, Susan Hancock argues, ". . . Tom Thumb could also conceivably be regarded as a conjoint ego, hero and trickster image within a text that metaphorically represents the journey of such a figure into the unconscious." *The Child That Haunts Us: Symbols and Images in Fairytale and Miniature Literature*. London: Routledge (2009), 35.

9. Patricia Pace, "The Body-in-Writing: Miniatures in Mary Norton's *Borrowers*." *Text and Performance Quarterly* 11.4 (October 1991): 279–290, 284. Stewart comments that the fairy world is generally depicted as female—"a world of ornament and detail" (*On Longing*, 112). Hans Christian Andersen's *Thumbelina* (1835), of course, represents female thumbling characters. In his literary fairy tale, Andersen adapts the story into a conventional romance, maintaining only the wish for a child and extra-uterine birth from the traditional tales.

10. "Le petit Poucet," in *Perrault's Fairy Tales*. 1697(New York: Dover Publications 1969), 115.

11. From the 1630 chapbook, titled in full: "Tom Thumbe, His Life and Death: Wherein is declared many Maruailous [*sic*] Acts of Manhood, full of wonder, and strange merriments: Which little Knight liued [*sic*] in King Arthurs time, and famous in the Court of Great Brittaine."

12. Jonathan Swift. *Gulliver's Travels*. 1726 (Penguin, 1967), 163.

13. Stewart, *On Longing*, 44.

14. *An Account of the Life, Personal Appearance, Character, and Manners, of Charles S. Stratton, the American Dwarf, known as General Tom Thumb, 12 Years Old, Twenty-Five Inches in Height, and Weighing Fifteen Pounds* (London: Printed by J. Mitchell and Company, 1844), 12–13.

15. "Sketch of the Life, Personal Appearance, Character, and Manners of Charles S. Stratton, the Man in Miniature, Known as General Tom Thumb, and His Wife, Lavinia Warren Stratton; Including the History of Their Courtship and Marriage, With Some Account of Remarkable Dwarfs, Giants, & Other Human Phenomena, of Ancient and Modern Times, and Songs Given at Their Public Levees" (New York: Press of Wynkoop & Hallenbeck): paragraph 119, Disability History Museum, http://www.disabilitymuseum.org/lib/stills/2077.htm Accessed May 19, 2010.

16. In addition to explaining natural history and connecting it to codes of conduct, the character of Tom Thumb can be used promoting literacy to child readers. In the chapbook school reader *The New Tom Thumb; or, Reading Made Quite Easy* (1850), the figure of Tom Thumb dressed as Cupid introduces children to the power of reading. After learning the alphabet and vowel sounds, children advance to reading short pieces consisting of words of two or three letters and go from there to reading more challenging sentences. In each example, the text consists of a moral lesson outlining a child's duty and the consequences of failure to perform that duty. Lesson 5, for example, reads: "Rod is for him that is bad./Sin is the way to the pit./Try to do as you are bid./Use not the way of bad men." *The New Tom Thumb; or, Reading Made Quite Easy* (Newcastle: T. Simpson and Sons, 1850), n.p.

17. See the first chapter of Swift's *Gulliver's Travels*.

18. For a discussion of the idea of the *lusus naturae*, see Paula Findlen, "Jokes of Nature and Jokes of Knowledge: The Playfulness of Scientific Discourse in Early Modern Europe," *SRen* 43 (1990): 292–331.

19. Swift, *Gulliver's Travels*, 142. The work we call *Gulliver's Travels* was first published anonymously in 1726, although many of Swift's friends knew the identity of the author. The poet and translator Alexander Pope wrote a set of humorous verses about the different voyages for Swift, who liked them so well that they were included in early editions. The King of Brobdingnag's poem, "The Words of the King of Brobdingnag, as he held Captain Gulliver between his Finger and Thumb for the Inspection of the Sages and Learned Men of the Court" (xiv–xv) recalls the scene of the learned sages and suggests the homunculus theory of sperm: ". . . The microscope explains,/That the Blood, circling, flows in human Veins;/See, in the Tube he pants, and sprawling lies,/Stretches his little Hands, and rolls his Eyes!" *Travels into Several Remote Nations of the World. In Four Parts*. By Captain Lemuel Gulliver (London: printed for P. Turnbull, 1766 [2 vols]), xiv. In Brobdingnag we learn that Gulliver's name is "Grildrig" (given to him by the nine-year-old girl who serves as his nurse), which means "manikin" (or homunculus). Interestingly, the giant may also gesture toward the same anxiety over origins. Frankenstein's eight-foot-tall monster complains bitterly to Walton that he is unjustly execrated ". . . as an abortion, to be spurned at, and kicked, and trampled on" (Mary Shelley, *Frankenstein: Or, The Modern Prometheus*. 1818. London: Henry Colburn and Richard Bentley, 1831, 200).

20. And, as Michael Patrick Hearn notes about this scene, Gulliver's birth resembles Tom Thumb's origin in that both Tom and Gulliver are given gifts of gold rings by the court: "It seems impossible not to conclude after reading these two stories that Jonathan Swift must have had something of the history of Tom Thumb, King Arthur's dwarf, in mind when he penned the voyages of Lemuel Gulliver." Michael Patrick Hearn, preface to the Garland edition of *The History of Tom Thumbe* (1621), xviii–xix.

21. And yet, the actual fetus—or infant—with its big head and shortened limbs resembles the proportions of a dwarf more than an average-sized adult man or woman.

22. The homunculus as motif can also be traced in literature. For example, in the second part of Goethe's *Faust* (published posthumously as a five-act verse drama in 1832), a homunculus plays an important role in the play. Interestingly, a hundred years earlier, in 1730, Paracelsus is briefly invoked in Fielding's *Tom Thumb* (II.vi. l. 4). See *Tom Thumb and The Tragedy of Tragedies*, ed. L. J. Morrissey. (Berkeley: University of California Press, 1970), 33.

23. Paracelsus later discussed the creation of the homunculi in other works such as his "Treatise of Nymphes, Sylphes, Salamanders and other beings," *The Ovary of Eve: Egg and Sperm and Preformation*. (Chicago and London: University of Chicago Press, 1997), 221, note 25.

24. The phrase "venter equines" is also translated as "horse's womb." In either case, the technical alchemical term generally refers to hot, decaying excrement used as a heat source. Yet Paracelsus also used this term to mean any source of low, incubating heat. See William Newman's "The Homunculus and His Forebears: Wonders of Art and Nature" in *Natural Particulars: Nature and the Disciplines in Renaissance Europe*, eds Anthony Grafton and Nancy Siraisi (Cambridge, MA: MIT Press, 1999): 321–345, 327, and 332.

25. Quoted in Pinto-Correia, *The Ovary of Eve*, 222.

26. For example, for Henry More, Paracelsus was the " 'great boaster' " whose " 'uncouth and supine inventions' " found their greatest expression in the belief that men could be created artificially (quoted in Newman, "Homunculus and His Forebears," 336). Margaret Cavendish, too, condemns alchemy and the belief that the artificial is superior to the natural (see Newman, "Homunculus and His Forebears," 337). Pinto-Correia comments that the term "homunculus" was "a nest of malignant connotations" connecting the little man with the desire to play God in the artificial creation of life, to dabble in black magic and evildoing" (Pinto-Correia, *Ovary of Eve*, 214–215).

27. In the second book in the Harry Potter series by J. K. Rowling, *The Chamber of Secrets* (New York: Scholastic, 1998), the Hogwarts students learn to work with the human/plant mandrakes.

28. Other examples of homunculi creation include the following: the Scottish doctor William Maxwell, in his 1679 *De Medicina Magnetica*, held that the "salt of human blood," properly prepared, could create a tiny man in a test tube. In the eighteenth century, Dr. David Christianus of the University of Giessen (in Germany) revealed another method for creating the homunculus; this procedure involved a black hen's egg, human sperm and a thirty-day incubation period commencing with the March lunar cycle. At the end of the cycle, a miniature man would break free of the egg and become its creator's guardian. See Pinto-Correia, *Ovary of Eve*, 222–223.

29. Quoted in Pinto-Correia, *Ovary of Eve*, 222.

30. As "the final expression of man's power over nature," Newman argues, Paracelsus's homunculus "is not merely an artificial marvel in itself but a key to further marvels." See Newman, "The Homunculus and His Forebears," 329.

31. In his *A History of Embryology*, Joseph Needham conjectures that Aristotle dissected a human embryo (2nd ed., New York: Arno Press, 1975), 38–39. The practices of anatomization of human cadavers throughout Europe went through cycles of legalization and prohibition—tending toward the latter—from the Classical period until the eighteenth century, when in England, for example, limited dissections were allowed by law.

32. Laurence Sterne, *The Life and Opinions of Tristram Shandy, Gentleman*. 1759 (Mineola, NY: Dover Publications, 2007, Vol. 1, Chapter 2), 2. Sterne's comic homunculus may be traced, centuries later, in Ian McEwan's *Nutshell*, narrated by a highly intelligent fetus (McEwan, *Nutshell*, New York: Nan A.Talese/Doubleday, 2016).

33. Ibid.

34. Ibid.

35. There's another level of relationship between the homunculus and *Tristram Shandy*: the novel's unusual form—in particular, the convoluted and twisted narrative that seems unable to complete itself—is reminiscent of the spermists' theory of the homunculus in which each sperm cell contains the miniature man (or woman, though this fact is rarely discussed in the literature) that has the potential to grow within a woman's uterus and become a fetus. Yet this theory led to its own undoing since each little man contains the seeds—spermatozoa—of another generation of men who contain the seeds for yet another generation; the endless regress led to the collapse of the theory through this *reductio ad absurdum*.

36. Reprinted in *The Metrical History of Tom Thumb the Little*, as issued early in the eighteenth century, in three parts. Ed. J.O. Halliwell(London: Printed for the editor, 1860), 71.

37. At the Little Theatre in the Haymarket, the drama ran for nearly forty nights in a row: from Friday April 24, 1730 until Monday, June, 22. See *Tom Thumb and The Tragedy of Tragedies*, ed. L. J. Morrissey (Berkeley: University of California Press, 1970), 3.

38. The play has enjoyed enduring popularity: it was produced throughout the eighteenth and nineteenth centuries in Britain and America and adapted numerous times, including a ballad opera by Eliza Haywood and William Hatchett in 1733, among other adaptations. Beatrix Potter used the names of some of the characters (Huncamunca and Tom Thumb) in her *Tale of Two Bad Mice* (1904). See Morrissey, *Tom Thumb*, 8–9. In the published version of the revised playtext, the parodies and political satire were sharpened and literary satire introduced through the introduction of the pedantic scholar, H. Scriblerus Secundus, whose commentary and annotations offered readers "learned" scholarship. As Albert J. Rivero notes, ". . . the published version of *The Tragedy of Tragedies* treated its readers to a mock scholarly feast of a scope and wit surpassed in previous eighteenth-century literature only by

A Tale of a Tub (1704) and *The Dunciad Variorum* (1729) . . . ." Albert J. Rivero, *The Plays of Henry Fielding: A Critical Study of His Dramatic Career* (Charlottesville: University of Virginia Press, 1989), 74.

39. Rivero, *Plays of Henry Fielding*, 61.

40. In *Tom Thumb*, the King urges Tom to marry Huncamunca and impregnate her, to which he readily assents: KING: "And if I guess aright, *Tom Thumb* this Night/Shall give a Being to a new *Tom Thumb*." TOM THUMB: "It shall be my Endeavour so to do" (Act 2, Scene 8, ll. 13–15). In response to Tom's comment that his love has made him "lose himself," Huncamunca delivers this double entendre: " 'Forbid it, all the Stars; for you're so small,/That were you lost, you'd find your self no more./So the unhappy Sempstress, once, they say,/ Her needle in a Pottle, lost, of Hay./ In vain she look'd, and look'd, and made her Moan;/ For ah! the Needle was for ever gone" (Act 2, Scene 8, ll. 20–25). In *The Tragedy of Tragedies*, the competition between the queen of the giants and Huncamunca takes the form of a catfight made of words: Glumdalca insults Huncamunca, asserting that Tom, who has once worn her "easy Chains," will never choose Huncamunca over her, and the princess answers, "Well may your Chains be easy, since if Fame/ Says true, they have been try'd on twenty Husbands./ The Glove or Boot, so many times pull'd on,/ May well sit easy on the Hand or Foot" (Act. 2, Scene 7, ll. 11–13).

41. *Tragedy of Tragedies*, Act I, Scene 1, l. 21. The verses in *Tom Thumbe, His Life and Death: Wherein is declared many Maruailous Acts of Manhood, full of wonder, and strange merriments: Which little Knight liued in King Arthurs time, and famous in the Court of Great Brittaine* (1630), describe the thumbling as "No blood nor bones in him should be."

42. *Tragedy of Tragedies*, Act 2, Scene 10, ll. 15–16.

43. William Steig, *The Toy Brother* (New York: Michael di Capua Books, HarperCollins Publishers, 1996).

44. Albertus Magnus (?–1280) was canonized in 1931. Interestingly, young Victor Frankenstein eagerly reads both Paracelsus and Albertus Magnus as he seeks to understand "the secrets of nature" and the "elixir of life" (*Frankenstein, or the Modern Prometheus*, 1831 ed., 26 and 27). In his monster, Frankenstein, of course, creates a giant homunculus. Although his university professors scoff at these early masters, Victor's desire to return to his "ancient studies" with renewed vigor, informed by every branch of natural philosophy and "unfold to the world the deepest mysteries of creation" is fired anew at the University of Ingolstadt (34). The YA novel *Clay* (2005) by David Almond is a retelling of the Frankenstein story in which two boys make and animate a massive clay homunculus with tragic consequences.

45. Steig, *The Toy Brother*, unpaged.

46. In this iteration of the Tom Thumb trope, the little man is the means by which brothers become friends. Their discord is assuaged once the older brother is forced to assume a different—smaller, inferior—position and perspective, and the care-taking and games-playing and loyal qualities of the younger take center stage. Yorick becomes a kind of baby—a toy, perhaps even a second phallus—for his little brother to play with and manipulate: "Running the show was so gratifying that Charles found himself wishing Yorick would fit in his pocket forever." Ibid.

47. Simon Mawer, *Mendel's Dwarf* (New York: Penguin Books, 1998).

48. Katherine Dunn, *Geek Love*. 1983 (New York: Warner Books, 1989), 20.

49. See "What's Happened to Thalidomide Babies?" *BBC News Magazine*. November 2, 2011. http://www.bbc.co.uk/news/magazine-15536544?print=true. Accessed October 22, 2012.

50. See "Thalidomide Apology Insulting, Campaigners Say." *BBC News Health*. September 1, 2012. http://www.bbc.co.uk/news/health-19448046?print=true. Accessed October 22, 2012.

51. Although the drug had not been approved for the US market, some American women did obtain prescriptions for it. Sherri Chessen was among those women, and her story, while fascinating in any context, is particularly apt here in the discussion

of the politicization of the fetus and embryo. In 1962, Ms Chessen had obtained thalidomide from her husband, who had been given a prescription for the drug as a sleep aid while on a business trip in London. The Phoenix mother of four took the drug early in her pregnancy for morning sickness and then learned about the potential consequences for the fetus. Although abortions were illegal in the United States, the well-connected could often find a doctor and hospital to provide them. Chessen's scheduled procedure was canceled once her identity became known: she had given an interview to a Phoenix newspaper, hoping to assist other women and warn them away from thalidomide. Although the interview was given anonymously, Chessen's story was made public and she was put on the cover of *Life* magazine. She obtained an abortion in Sweden (her fetus was found to have no arms or legs) and she lost her job as a television host on Phoenix's *Romper Room*. See Linda Greenhouse, "A Never-Ending Story." NY Times.com. September 5, 2012. http://opinionator.blogs.nytimes.com/2012/09/05/a-never-ending-story/. Accessed October 22, 2012.

52. Other seventeenth-century European scientists and philosophers whose work helped to create new knowledge about reproductive biology, theories of generation, and embryology include the Dutch physician Reinier De Graaf (1641–1673), the Italian physician Marcello Malpighi (1628–1694), and French philosopher Nicolas Malebranche (1638–1715).

53. Quoted in Keller, "Embryonic Individuals," 321. See Fig. 2 within Kerckring's drawing.

54. The idea of preformation, Jane M. Oppenheimer explains, endured as long as it did in part because of its deep roots in ancient philosophy (*Essays in the History of Embryology and Biology* (Cambridge, MA and London: MIT Press, 1967), 129–130. Shirley A. Roe adds, "Preexistence avoided the atheistic and materialistic implications of development by epigenesis, while also accounting for the source of animal organization. Embryos develop into the proper organisms because all of their parts were created at one time and arranged in the proper fashion by God" (*Matter, Life, and Generation: Eighteenth-Century Embryology and the Haller–Wolff Debate.* Cambridge: Cambridge University Press, 1981), 8.

55. Harvey's "egge," as Oppenheimer describes it, is a "metaphysical egg" (*Essays in The History of Embryology and Biology,* 128). In his 1653 *Anatomical Exercitations, Concerning the Generation of Human Creatures,* Harvey described the wondrous ovum as not only "compounded of both [sexes]" but also ". . . a being neither absolutely impowered with life, nor absolutely without it. It is a Midway or Passage between the Parents and the Children; between those that were, and those that are to come . . ." (quoted in Oppenheimer, *Essays in The History of Embryology,* 128).

56. Quoted in Pinto-Correia, *Ovary of Eve,* 70.

57. Thomas Laqueur, *Making Sex: Body and Gender From the Greeks to Freud* (Cambridge, MA: Harvard University Press, 1990), 173. Laqueur continues, "Social sex thus projected downward into biological sex at the level of the microscopic generative products themselves. Very quickly the egg came to be seen as a merely passive nest or trough where the boy or girl person, compressed in each animalcule, was fattened up before birth" (171–172).

58. Pinto-Correia's book as a whole, and Chapter 6 in particular, takes pains to distinguish the homunculus myth from the facts—that the term "homunculus" was not used by the spermists themselves, but was adopted to help explain spermism much later.

59. Newman, "The Homunculus and His Forebears," 328.

60. *The Wonders of the Microscope; or, An Explanation of the Wisdom of the Creator in Objects Comparatively Minute: adapted to the Understanding of Young Persons.* 1808. (London: printed for William Darnton, 1823), 26. I am not arguing that one finds complementarity between God and the microscope only in nineteenth-century children's texts. Many of the seventeenth-century scientists who used the microscope as the basis for their discoveries in anatomy and reproductive biology were deeply

religious. John Mack argues that for many, early microscopic technology was conso-
nant with God's intentions that his tiniest creations be known. In fact, the microscope helped to revive knowledge lost in the Fall: "Micro-technologies, as they were
developing in Europe in the 1600s, seemed to offer the opportunity to restore this
lost world—not just a lost innocence but a diminished understanding" (*Art of Small
Things*. London: The British Museum Press, 2007), 37.

61. *Wonders of the Microscope*, 115. In *The Invisible World: Early Modern Philosophy and
the Invention of the Microscope* (Princeton: Princeton University Press, 1995),
Catherine Wilson offers a different interpretation of how the microscope changed
our relationship with Divine mysteries, suggesting that the invention of the microscope, rather than reinforcing God's intentions, actually flirted with disproportion.
She writes, "And Locke was troubled by disproportion. If our interests had really
depended on a knowledge of the microworld, a benevolent God would not have put
it out of our reach; this thought was shared by the other great empiricist and occasional microscope-skeptic, George Berkeley" (244).

62. Wilson, *The Invisible World*, 25.

63. Quoted in Wilson, ibid.

64. Mrs. Barwell's *The Novel Adventures of Tom Thumb the Great, Showing How He
Visited the Insect World and Learned Much Wisdom* (1838), begins conventionally (in
didactic stories that marry fancy with reason) with a dialogue between a rational
mother and her children asking for a story. After confirming that her children do not
actually believe in little people or giants, she relates a "true" story about Tom Thumb
that features him as a conduit of wisdom between nature and humanity by returning
him to the animal world (which, Mrs. Barwell notes, similarly operates by way of
"instinct"). The book is organized into seven conversations in which various physical principles are demonstrated and a moral advanced. The infamous scene in
which Tom is swallowed by a cow becomes a lesson about rumination, multiple
stomachs and other animals that digest food in this manner. Each time Tom visits an
animal or insect he learns valuable life lessons as well as the science of the natural
world. Mrs. Barwell, *The Novel Adventures of Tom Thumb the Great, Showing How He
Visited the Insect World, and Learned Much Wisdom* (London: Chapman and Hall,
1838).

65. Ibid., 98–99.

66. Charlotte Yonge, *The History of the Life and Death of the Good Knight Sir Thomas
Thumb* (Edinburgh: Thomas Constable and Co, 1855).

67. One aspect of the text's didacticism can be found in the inclusion of the scholarly
apparatus: an introduction outlining the history of the thumbling tale to date, and a
50-page fairy lore appendix. Yonge comments, "Fielding's burlesque only added the
evils of the literature of his age to the dull poverty of the old story, and thus the field
appeared to be open to an endeavour to weave the traditional mishaps of the pigmy-
knight into a tale that might be free from the former offences against good taste."
(Ibid., iii.)

68. Yonge, *History of the Life and Death*, 9–10.

69. Ibid., 23.

70. Ibid., 35.

71. Ibid., 50.

72. Ibid., 87.

73. Ibid., 90.

74. In *Fetal Positions: Individualism, Science, Visuality* (Stanford: Stanford University
Press, 1997), Karen Newman traces the history of embryology and visual science that
has helped to create the autonomous fetal subject as a powerful marker of individualism and pawn in political and gendered power struggles. She concludes her
thoughtful, extended essay by remarking, "the right's insistent inscription of fetus as
'baby' and feminist demands to restore the woman's body to obstetrical representations *both* display a profound humanist nostalgia for the realist image; at the same
time, they perhaps seek to allay a profound anxiety about what constitutes 'life' and

the 'individual' in the postmodern scientific environment of the cyborg" (113). This state of affairs surrounding the contemporary embryo would likely disgust historians of science such as Joseph Needham who, in his comprehensive 1959 history of embryology, concludes rather triumphantly (if naïvely), "the expulsion of ethics from biology and embryology forms another excellent example of [pseudo-problems solved]. That good and bad, noble and ignoble, beautiful and ugly, honourable and dishonourable, are not terms with biological meaning, is a proposition which it has taken many centuries for biologists to realize" (*A History of Embryology*, 1959. 2nd ed. (New York: Arno Press, 1975), 235.

75. Lauren Berlant, *The Queen of America Goes to Washington City: Essays on Sex and Citizenship* (Durham, NC and London: Duke University Press, 1997), 123. This dissociation of fetus from mother has a long history that predates fetal photography by three centuries. See Eve Keller's discussion of illustrations from seventeenth-century midwifery manuals in *Generating Bodies,* 134–138. Referencing issues of size and power, Berlant argues that the fetus displaces the mother as the ideal citizen: ". . . the pregnant woman becomes the child to the fetus, becoming more minor and less politically represented than the fetus, which in turn is made more *national*, more central to seeing the privileges of law, paternity, and other less institutional family strategies of contemporary American culture" (85). See Berlant's chapter three, "America, 'Fat', the Fetus" (83–144) for a fascinating analysis of fetal personhood in twentieth-century America. See also Rosalind Pollack Petcheski, "Fetal Images: The Power of Visual Culture in the Politics of Reproduction." *Feminist Studies* 13.2 (Summer 1987): 263–292; and Carole Stabile, "Shooting the Mother: Fetal Photography and the Politics of Disappearance." *Camera Obscura* 28.1 (Fall 1992): 178–205. Lennart Nilsson, the Swedish medical photographer, is perhaps the best known fetal photographer. His 1965 cover article for *Life*, "The Drama of Life Before Birth," made the issue an immediate best-seller, as was the book *A Child Is Born*, published the same year (5th ed. 2009). In her history of ideas about life and death, *The Mansion of Happiness*, Jill Lepore notes that *A Child is Born* remains the best-selling illustrated book ever published (Lepore, *The Mansion of Happiness*, 6). Nilsson's work afforded the average person clear glimpses of fetal life and *in utero* human development.

76. Clara Lejeune, "The Story of Tom Thumb." *Human Life Review* 28.1/2 (Winter/ Spring 2002): 78–86, 79. The biography was first published in France as *La Vie est un bonheur: Jérôme Lejeune, mon père* (1997) and then published in English as *Life is a Blessing: A Biography of Jérôme Lejeune* (San Francisco: Ignatius Press, 2000).

77. Lejeune, "Story of Tom Thumb," 84.

78. See Ada Calhoun, "Mommy Had to Go Away For a While." *New York Times Magazine.* April 29, 2012, 31–36, 44. An amicus brief to the Court of Criminal Appeals of Alabama was filed on Kimbrough's behalf by 23 Alabama and national organizations with expertise in maternal, fetal, and infant health and addiction. In the view of the "amici," the social interest in protecting the health of women and children is not served by allowing chemical endangerment laws to be expanded to include pregnant women with addictions who choose to take their pregnancies to term. Examples of negative social consequences of Kimbrough's conviction include additional terminations of pregnancies by women afraid of prosecution, a disincentive to seek any prenatal health care, and a disincentive to seek addiction treatment while pregnant. The amicus brief summary of the argument states "The prosecution and conviction of Amanda Kimbrough violates the plain language and intent of Alabama's chemical endangerment statute, is unsupported by scientific research, is contrary to the consensus judgment of medical practitioners and their professional organizations, and undermines individual and public health. This Court should refuse prosecutorial invitation to judicially expand the chemical endangerment law and should instead overturn Kimbrough's conviction" (3). Kimbrough's case went to the Supreme Court of Alabama, which concurred with her conviction in the chemical endangerment of a child. Amanda Helaine Borden Kimbrough vs. The State of Alabama (the

Circuit Court of Franklin County, Alabama. CR-09-0485. 9 July 2010: i–iv, 1–36. See Ed Pilkington, "Alone in Alabama: Dispatches From an Inmate Jailed for her Son's Stillbirth." *The Guardian*. October 7, 2015. https://www.theguardian.com/us-news/2015/oct/07/alabama-chemical-endangerment-pregnancy-amanda-kimbrough. See also Imani Gandy, "Roe v. Wade and Fetal Personhood: Juridical Persons and Not Natural Persons, And Why It Matters." *Rewire*. January 3, 2013. https://rewire.news/article/2013/01/03/fetal-personhood-laws-juridical-persons-are-not-natural-persons-and-why-it-matter/

79. http://www.personhoodusa.com/. A similar argument about the rights of the embryo—though one attempted through biology—is advanced by Robert P. George and Christopher Tollefsen in *Embryo: A Defense of Human Life* (New York: Doubleday, 2008).

80. See "Aftershocks: The Impact of Clinic Violence on Abortion Services" by Mireille Jacobson and Heather Royer. Users.nber.org/~JacobsenRoyer6.2.10.pdf

81. Calhoun, "Mommy Had to Go Away For a While," 33. The 2016 Republican Party platform also opposed embryonic stem cell research and federal funding for hESC research (14). See Sandhya Somashekhar, "Ohio Governor Vetoes 'Heartbeat Bill' but Signs Another Abortion Restriction Into Law." *The Washington Post*. December 13, 2016. https://www.washingtonpost.com/news/post-nation/wp/2016/12/13/ohio-governor-vetoes-heartbeat-bill-but-signs-into-law-another-abortion-restriction/?utm_term=.dc56b849a129

82. Republican Party Platform 2016, 13.

83. Berlant, *Queen of America*, 93.

84. John R. Gillis, "Birth of the Virtual Child: Origins of Our Contradictory Images of Children" in *Childhood and Its Discontents*, eds Joseph Dunn and James Kelly (Dublin: Liffey Press, 2002): 31–50, p. 44.

    In an epilogue to *Generating Bodies*, Keller discusses the rhetoric of U.S. Senate bill "The Unborn Child Pain Awareness Act of 2005" (S. 51) in which the section on Definitions defines an "unborn child" as "a member of the species homo sapiens at any stage of development, who is carried in the womb" (sec. 2901) (Keller, "Unborn Child," 188). Keller comments, "The implicit claim here is not simply that 'life' begins at conception, but that childhood does. Like Kerckring over three hundred years ago, this bill grants not just life, but *childhood* to an embryo" (188). This bill never became law. It was proposed again in 2007 (S. 356; H. R. 3442) but did not pass at that time either.

85. The purpose behind the gathering, besides highlighting the Snowflakes program was to protest H. R. 4682, the Stem Cell Research Enhancement Act of 2004 which would have turned back Bush's policy restricting federal funding for research on embryonic stem cell lines created before August 2001. The bill never became law. See Lynn Harris, "Clump of Cells or 'Microscopic Americans?' " *Salon*, February 5, 2005. http://www.salon.com/life/feature/2005/02/05/embryos (accessed June 24, 2009). See also Nina J. Easton, "Stem Cell Vote May Challenge President," *Boston Globe*, May 24, 2005. boston.com (accessed May 24, 2005).

86. The terminology used to describe human embryonic stem cell research, and embryo donation is often slippery and reflects the differing desires and designs of the groups involved. Fertility clinics, for example, now use the term "embryos" for test-tube zygotes (fertilized eggs) that have never been embedded in a woman's uterus. "Adoption" focuses on the child that may eventually evolve if implanted, not on the reality that fertilized eggs are a group of cells that cannot grow without a uterus. See Harris, "Clump of Cells or 'Microscopic Americans'?" See also Margaret Wertheim's useful discussion of the science and emotion of hESC research in her online article "Life Begins at 'Want a Cigarette?' " *Alternet*, June 23, 2005. http://www.alternet.org/story/22261 (accessed June 23, 2005).

87. See the website for the Nightlight Christian Adoptions Agency, http://www.nightlight.org. Other agencies that facilitate embryo adoption include the National Embryo Donation Center in Tennessee and Embryos Alive in Ohio.

88. Overwhelmingly, however, the excess embryos created for infertility treatments are not donated, and many couples at first attracted by the idea of donation ultimately choose to store their embryos. One can easily understand the reluctance to donate embryos—the decision is akin to putting up for adoption one's biological child and full genetic sibling to one's other children. Many parents are uncomfortable with this idea. A 2003 survey conducted by the American Society for Reproductive Medicine revealed that of approximately 400,000 frozen embryos (at that time), 2% were donated to other couples and 3% were given to research (Belluck, 5). The ethical and emotional complexities of the issue—for example, many frozen embryos are created from donated eggs and thus the original donor might have some say in their re-donation to a different couple—is often ignored by organizations such as Nightlight Christian Adoptions. See Pam Belluck, "It's Not So Easy to Adopt an Embryo." *The New York Times*. Week in Review. Sunday, June 12, 2005, 5. See also "Souls on Ice: America's Human Embryo Glut and the Unbearable Lightness of Almost Being," *Mother Jones*. July/August 2006. http://www.motherjones.com/politics/2006/07/souls-ice-americas-embryo-glut-and-wasted-promise-stem-cell-research (accessed June 24, 2009) and "Enter the Wild West of the Embryo Adoption Industry" by Daniela Hernandez. Fusion. June 6, 2015. http://fusion.net/story/145489/enter-the-wild-west-of-the-embryo-adoption-industry/.

89. The fact that best-selling author Jodi Picoult centers the plot of her novel *Sing You Home* (2011) on the ethics of embryo adoption supplies some evidence of the topicality of the issue in popular culture.

90. Named for Rep. Jay Dickey (R-Ark.) and Representative Roger Wicker (R.-Miss.), the amendment, buried within the 465–page appropriations bill, explicitly forbade federal funding for "research in which a human embryo or embryos are destroyed, discarded, or knowingly subjected to risk of injury or death" (Omnibus Appropriations Act, 2009, Sec. 509(a), 280). For well over a decade, this long-standing rider effectively relegated all hESC research to the private sector, thus delaying crucial research and restricting funding. Of course, given the outcome of the 2016 presidential election, the future of hESC research is once again unclear.

91. In August 2010, Judge Royce C. Lamberth, of the Federal District Court for the District of Columbia ruled that federal funding for hESC research violated the tenets of the Dickey–Wicker ban on the use of public money for hESC research in which human embryos would be destroyed. This ruling stunned the scientific community and threatened the research conducted by many National Institute of Health (NIH)-funded grants, projects, and labs. After an appeal by the NIH to the D.C. Circuit court in which a three-judge panel first stayed the injunction and then a second three-judge panel vacated the preliminary injunction, Lamberth could feel which way that the wind was blowing and he reluctantly granted summary judgment in favor of the government. In August 2012, this summary judgment ruling was upheld by yet another three-judge panel of the D.C. Circuit, this time unanimously. Barack Obama's re-election in 2012 supplied some relief to scientists and organizations engaged in hESC research; however, the situation has become so politically hot and volatile that no researcher may feel confident that politics will not intervene in further work with human embryos.

92. Lisa Mundy's article profiles a number of couples who have used IVF treatments and who agonize over what to do with their surplus embryos. Mundy cites a 2005 study of 58 couples who had embryos in storage that found that 72% could not decide what to do with them—implant them, continue to store them, donate them, or thaw them. This issue is not going to go away: Mundy noted at the time of the publication of her article that half a million frozen embryos were in storage facilities in the United States and this number grows by year. http://www.motherjones.com/politics/2006/07/souls-ice-americas-embryo-glut-and-wasted-promise-stem-cell-research. Accessed June 24, 2009.

93. The first phrase is Steven Ertelt's, LifeNews.com's editor, in his article "Capitol Hill Children's Event Places Spotlight on Human Embryo Adoptions." LifeNews.com.

September 23, 2004. In the same article, then Senator Rick Santorum (R-PA) is quoted as saying that the embryo adoption program " 'take[s] these little children and give[s] them the potential to live the rest of their lives as the gifts from God that they are.' " The "microscopic Americans" phrase is by Deroy Murdock ("The Adoption Option." *National Review* online. August 27, 2001. Accessed June 24, 2009). Note that in all of these instances the embryos are figured as tiny children—as homunculi, essentially.

94. See Peter J. Bowler's *Monkey Trials and Gorilla Sermons: Evolution and Christianity from Darwin to Intelligent Design* (Cambridge and London: Harvard University Press, 2007) for a history of the controversies and debates over Darwinism (and science more generally) within the religious and scientific communities. The purpose of this history, Bowler makes clear in his introduction, is to "show that such a rigidly polarized model of the relationship [between creationism and evolutionism] benefits only those who want us to believe that no compromise is possible" (3).

95. Simon Mawer, *Mendel's Dwarf* (New York: Penguin Books, 1998), 133.

96. Mack, *Art of Small Things*, 208.

97. Also known as "the God Particle," the Higgs boson is a subatomic building block of matter. The Higgs boson was first theorized in 1964 by British physicist Peter Higgs as part of the Standard Model of quantum physics. The announcement by CERN, the European Institute for Nuclear Research that the particle had been discovered experimentally helps scientists to understand how mass is added to matter (the Higgs boson's role) and thus how the universe works.

98. Jay Curlin, "The Evidence of Things Not Seen." *The New Yorker*. 30 July 2012, 77. Reprinted with the permission of the author.

Chapter 2: The Dwarf in High and Popular Culture

1. "Dwarf planet" is not the smallest classification for objects orbiting the sun: "small solar system bodies" are smaller than dwarf planets. See the IAU website at www.iau. org for more information.

2. John Felton, Buckingham's killer, miscalculated the treatment he would receive after the assassination and announced that he was responsible for stabbing Buckingham in a Portsmouth public house. Felton was hanged at Tyburn in November 1628, three months after the murder; his body was returned to Portsmouth and hung in chains for viewing.

3. Erika Tietze-Conrat comments that this bakery method of introducing the court dwarf was popular in Russia: ". . . it is still done in Russia in the 18th century, where two such pies were sent on one occasion, from which a male and female dwarf were conjured up, who danced a minuet together" (*Dwarfs and Jesters in Art*. New York: Phaidon, 1957, 80). Indeed, the Russian courts were also known for their dwarf members.

4. Evidence of Hudson's standing in the queen's household may be found in records of Henrietta Maria's household expenses. She spent lavishly on clothing for Hudson and another dwarf, "Little Sara." In addition to his suits (including a suit of armor), there were bills for boots, shoes, linen, cloaks, hats, gloves, and embroidered handkerchiefs. He had a special bed made for him and cases for his looking-glass and combs. See Caroline Hibbard, " 'By Our Direction and For Our Use:' The Queen's Patronage of Artists and Artisans seen through her Household Accounts" in *Henrietta Maria: Piety, Politics and Patronage*. ed. Erin Griffey (Burlington, VT and Aldershot, England: Ashgate: 115–137), 131–133.

5. One notable exception to Hudson's calm life was the terrifying but brief period of time in 1630 in which the young dwarf was captured by Dunkirk pirates along with other members of Henrietta Maria's household—including the French midwife and nurse the queen had sent for in her second pregnancy. Her first child, a son baptized Charles, had been born prematurely and died after a few hours of life. William D'Avenant pokes fun at the event of Hudson's capture, adding fantasy elements such

as a fight between Hudson and a turkey, in his mock-heroic poem *Jeffereidos, Or The Captivitie of Jeffery* (1630), a publication that became very popular. Among other appellations, Hudson is called a "walking Thumbe" in the poem, linking Hudson to his folktale forebear, Tom Thumb (*Jeffereidos*, 38).

6. See Nick Page, *Lord Minimus: The Extraordinary Life of Britain's Smallest Man* (London: HarperCollins Publishers, 2001).

7. E.H. Gombrich, *The Story of Art* (1950. London: Phaidon Press, 2006), 309.

8. Graham Parry, *The Golden Age Restor'd: The Culture of the Stuart Court, 1603–42* (Manchester: Manchester University Press, 1981), 224.

9. Karen Hearn, "Van Dyck in Britain" in *Van Dyck & Britain*. (London: Tate Publishing [2009]: 11–13), 13. Oliver Millar makes a similar point about these paintings in *Van Dyck in England* (London: National Portrait Gallery, 1982), 21.

10. See Robin Blake, *Anthony Van Dyck: A Life* (Chicago: Ivan R. Dee, 1999), 267.

11. Gudrun Raatschen credits this early van Dyck portrait of Charles I as the first official royal family portrait since Henry VIII, arguing that its enormous size (3.02 x 2.55 meters) as well as its subject impressed all who viewed it ("Merely Ornamental? Van Dyck's Portraits of Henrietta Maria," in Griffey, ed. *Henrietta Maria: Piety, Politics and Patronage*: 139–163, 154).

12. Raatschen makes a compelling argument that the orange tree references Henrietta Maria's mother, Marie de' Medici, as oranges were emblems of the Medici family ("Merely Ornamental?" 160). See also Sharpe on the orange tree ("Van Dyck, The Royal Image and the Caroline Court: in *Van Dyck & Britain*: 14–23, 20); In his biography of van Dyck, Blake suggests that the orange tree symbolizes the queen's love of gardens as well as her fertility: "In the summer of 1633 she was in the middle of her third successful pregnancy (Prince James was born in October) and the orange tree, capable of fruiting and flowering simultaneously, refers to the co-existence in one person of beauty and fecundity" (*Anthony Van Dyck: A Life*, 270). See also James Knowles, " 'Can Ye Not Tell a Man from a Marmoset?' Apes and Others on the Early Modern Stage" in *Renaissance Beasts: Of Animals, Humans, and Other Wonderful Creatures*, ed. Erica Fudge (Urbana and Chicago: University of Illinois Press, 2004: 138–163, 157–58) and Arthur Wheelock, "The Queen, The Dwarf and the Court: Van Dyck and the Ideals of the English Monarchy" in *Van Dyck 1599–1999: Conjectures and Refutations*, ed. Hans Vlieghe (Turnhout, Belgium: Brepols Publisher, 2001: 151–166).

13. The intended recipient for the portrait is not known, but a workshop copy was given to Thomas Wentworth in October 1633. See Raatschen, "Merely Ornamental?" 158.

14. Before van Dyck was on the scene at court, in 1628 Henrietta Maria had commissioned Daniel Mytens for three portraits of herself with Hudson; these portraits were meant as gifts. None has survived. See Wheelock, "The Queen, the Dwarf, and the Court," 161.

15. Bindman comments on the presence of Africans in the Caroline court: "[I]n early seventeenth-century England, the masque and the courtly culture behind it became increasingly politicized as the court came under threat from those opposed to the divine right of kings. At the same time, black chattel slaves, used as domestic servants and as horse grooms, became more of a familiar presence, initially in families closely associated with the court" ("The Black Presence in British Art: Sixteenth and Seventeenth Centuries" in *The Image of the Black in Western Art, Vol. III: From the "Age of Discovery" to the "Age of Abolition," Part 1: Artists of the Renaissance and Baroque*. eds David Bindman and Henry Louis Gates, Jr. Cambridge, MA: Belknap Press, 2010: 235–270, 249).

16. See Bindman, "Black Presence in British Art," 249. On Henrietta Maria's love for the exotic, see Wheelock, "The Queen, the Dwarf, and the Court," 161.

17. See Paul Kaplan, "Italy, 1490–1700" in *The Image of the Black in Western Art, Vol. III: From the "Age of Discovery" to the "Age of Abolition,"* 93–190, 180.

18. Knowles, " 'Can Ye Not Tell a Man from a Marmoset?' ", 139.

19. Blake explicitly calls *Queen Henrietta Maria and Jeffrey Hudson* a reinterpretation of *Elena Grimaldi*, but reads the former work as displaying a "warmer, more relaxed figure who enjoys her garden and pets and is solicitous towards the servant" (268). Wheelock similarly notes the compositional congruences between *Queen Henrietta Maria with Jeffrey Hudson* and *Elena Grimaldi* (*Anthony Van Dyck: A Life*, 161).

20. Apes (generally played by actors) and dwarfs were common figures in the Caroline masque tradition. Knowles writes, ". . . in the later Caroline masques in particular, apes belong with the hybrid, liminal, and fantastical forms that proliferated in the antimasques, especially dwarves and, less frequently, giants. The presence of these liminal creatures suggests that the Caroline masque synthesized not only the emblematic and mythic traditions about apes but also the newer geographic and scientific discourses that cross-fertilized in early modern writing" (" 'Can Ye Not Tell a Man from a Marmoset?' ", 146).

21. Page reads this painting as focused solely on Hudson's status as pet and the love shared (though unequally) between Hudson and the queen: "[Jeffrey] may be sumptuously clothed, he may be skilled at hunting, he may have all the accoutrements of a courtier, but he still has no will of his own, just a canine-like devotion, like an anxious dog, waiting for his mistress to issue a command or throw a stick" (*Lord Minimus*, 95). Raatschen argues that, in comparison with *Charles I and Henrietta Maria Departing for the Chase*, Hudson in van Dyck's portrait "gains prominence and appears as an agile and attentive little companion to the queen" ("Merely Ornamental?" 159). While I do not disagree, the image of Hudson is much more complex than this comment suggests.

22. Interestingly, a late twentieth-century restoration of *Queen Henrietta Maria and Jeffrey Hudson* (owned by the National Gallery of Art in Washington, DC) revealed areas of pentimenti (earlier images or strokes painted over) in the masterpiece: the figure of the dwarf was more separated from the queen and larger. See Wheelock, "The Queen, the Dwarf and the Court," 151–156.

23. Knowles, " 'Can Ye Not Tell a Man from a Marmoset' "? 159.

24. Page, *Lord Minimus*, 99–102.

25. Ibid., 103.

26. Ibid., 106.

27. Ibid. Robert Heath included a derivative poem about Jeffrey Hudson in his *Clarastella; Together with Poems occasional, Elegie, Epigrams, Satyrs* (1650). This poem extends the textual metaphors found in *The New Yeare's Gift*: ". . . You may write man, in th'abstract so you are,/Though printed in a smaller character./ The pocket volume hath as much within't/ As the broad folio in a larger print/ . . ." (Qtd. in Page, *Lord Minimus*, 198).

28. Page, while noting the *memento mori* aspect of parts of *The New Yeare's Gift* and anticipating my argument about Hudson's emblematic function, finds the seriousness of such "moral symbolism to "strike a false note" (*Lord Minimus*, 105) in the work as a whole, which is primarily dedicated to joking about Hudson's size and expressing fondness for the merriment Hudson provided the court. Page concludes his biography, however, by crediting Hudson's symbolic nature as "determination and courage and, above all, the greatness of the human spirit" (*Lord Minimus*, 233).

29. See Rosalie L. Colie, *The Resources of Kind: Genre-Theory in the Renaissance*, ed. Barbara K. Lewalski (Berkeley: University of California Press, 1973), 36.

30. Discussing the emblematists Laurence Haecht (*Mikrokosmos* 1579) and Henry Peacham (*Minerva Britanna* 1612), Judith Dundas comments on the early modern emblematists' reliance on the myths of the past and the need to turn them to Christian account in order for their works to be "morally useful" ("Unriddling the Antique: Peacham's Emblematic Art" in *Deviceful Settings: The English Renaissance Emblem and its Contexts*, eds Michael Bath and Daniel Russell (New York: AMS Press, 1999: 55–81, 79).

31. Charles Moseley, *A Century of Emblems: An Introductory Anthology* (Aldershot, England and Brookfield, VT: Scolar Press, 1989), 2.

32. The translation is Moseley's (*A Century of Emblems*, 43).
33. The translation "What lies above us is none of our business" is from the searchable and comprehensive collection of French versions of Alciato as well as French emblem books. "French Emblems at Glasgow" (http://www.emblems.arts.gla.ac.uk/french/index.php).
34. Moseley, *A Century of Emblems*, 44.
35. Ibid. Emblem characters, or icons, were reused frequently—and often for different purposes—in emblem books of the same era as well as over time. Prometheus, for example, while on some level a figure symbolizing pride for Alciato, was also employed to call to mind the most potent Christian symbol of all: Christ on the cross. The picture of Prometheus found in Henry Peacham's *Minerva Britanna* (1612), for example, reveals Prometheus hanging from a cross, a clear reference to Christ. See Judith Dundas, "Unriddling the Antique," 76–79.
36. Moseley, *A Century of Emblems*, 10.
37. Elizabeth See Watson, *Achille Bocchi and the Emblem Book as Symbolic Form* (Cambridge: Cambridge University Press, 1993), 117.
38. Colie, *Resources of Kind*, 37.
39. In a poem prefacing Heywood's play *Apology for Actors* (1612), John Taylor understands drama to be a kind of miniature form necessarily both verbal and visual—the very elements that make an emblem an emblem: "A Play's a briefe Epitome of time,/ Where man may see his virtue or his crime/Layd open, either to their vices shame,/ Or to their virtues memorable fame." (Qtd. in the introduction to Virginia Mason Vaughan, et. al., eds, *Speaking Pictures: The Visual/Verbal Nexus of Dramatic Performance* Madison and Teaneck, NJ: Fairleigh Dickinson University Press [2010]: 11–22, 13).
40. Qtd. in Knowles, " 'Can Ye Not tell a Man from a Marmoset?' " 158; *The New Yeare's Gift* (London 1636, F5r).
41. Crouch, a London bookseller, wrote and published a number of historical texts aimed at "the people" rather than elites. Robert Mayer writes, "In seventeenth-century London 'the people' were what Burke calls 'ordinary Londoners'—individuals who did not attend grammar school or the university, had no Latin, were not at the court or in one of the great professions, did not attend the private theater or buy many books" ("Nathaniel Crouch, Bookseller and Historian: Popular Historiography and Cultural Power in Late Seventeenth England." *Eighteenth Century Studies* 27.3 [Spring 1994]: 391–419, 395). The audience for his works very likely included young readers, a demographic Crouch was eager to please. In statements "to the reader" found in each work he typically discussed or described other works by "R. B."—or Richard Burton (his pseudonym). In one such note to the reader Crouch maintained that his historical works had "occasioned many (especially young people) to lay aside those vain and idle Songs and Romances wherewith they were formerly Conversant and to divert their vacant hours with reading the real Transactions, Revolutions and Accidents that are recorded by Authors on the greatest Veracity" (qtd. in Mayer, 398).
42. The canonical order of Alciato's emblems was established in 1548 when the poems were organized thematically. Emblem LVIII may be found under "Vitia" (vices) and "Stultitia" (stupidity).
43. Geffrey Whitney, *A Choice of Emblems: for the moste parte gathered out of Sundrie Writers, Englished and Moralized* (Leyden:1586), 16.
44. Ibid. "Sotte" is an obsolete word meaning fool or stupid person.
45. Later editions are titled *Choice Emblems, Divine and Moral, Antient and Modern, or, Delights for the Ingenious . . . .*
46. Mayer makes this point about Crouch's works of history ("Nathaniel Crouch," 402).
47. Jane Farnsworth comments on this aspect of Wither's book of emblems: "[Withers] also suggests that the lottery (a fortune-telling game with two wheels, two movable pointers and emblem lots, found at the end of the *Collection*) will also be enjoyed by children and makes it clear that he considers it to be a proper pastime for 'a vertuous Court' " (" 'An *Equall*, and a *Mutuall Flame*': George Wither's *A Collection*

of *Emblemes* 1635 and Caroline Court Culture" in *Deviceful Settings: The English Renaissance Emblem and Its Contexts*: 83–96, 89).

48. R.B. [Nathaniel Crouch] *Delights for the Ingenious* (London, 1684), 207. This work is tiny and surviving copies are very fragile. It is rare to find the paper pointer still attached to the volvelle.

49. Crouch, *Choice Emblems . . . or, Delights for the Ingenious* (1732 ed.), 31.

50. Ibid. Emphasis in the original.

51. Ibid., 31–32.

52. Emblem 17 (66–69) and Emblem 44 (174–177), respectively, in the 1732 edition of R. B.'s *Delights for the Ingenious*, titled *Choice Emblems, Divine and Moral* (London: printed for Edmund Parker, 1732).

53. John Huddleston Wynne, *Choice Emblems, Natural, Historical, Fabulous, Moral, and Divine, for the Improvement and Pastime of Youth* (London, George Riley, 1772), 110.

54. Ibid. Emphasis in the original.

55. Ibid., 223.

56. Richard Pigot, Introduction to *Moral Emblems with aphorisms, adages and proverbs, of all ages and nations, from Jacob Cats and Robert Farlie by John Leighton*. Trans. and edited by Richard Pigot (London: Longman, Green, Longman and Roberts, 1860), xii.

57. Ibid., 125.

58. Ibid., 126.

59. Ibid.

60. Watson, *Achille Bocchi and the Emblem Book*, 116.

61. It is important to note that Bunyan's original work did not include illustrations. However, the many eighteenth-century editions of his work tend to be illustrated— "profusely," in Warren Wooden's opinion—and "mutilated": "dropping Bunyan's poetical preface, chopping up the poems (deleting especially verses not directly moral in intent), and even changing the title, to *Divine Emblems, or Temporal Things Spiritualized*." (*Children's Literature of the English Renaissance*, Lexington, KY: University of Kentucky Press, 1986, 139).

62. John Bunyan, *A Book for Boys and Girls or, County Rimes for Children* (1686. London, 1868), n.p.

63. Isabella Clara Eugenia (1566–1633), a member of the House of Hapsburg (which filled the monarchies around Europe), married her cousin Archduke Albert of Austria. The two ruled jointly over the Spanish Netherlands.

64. Fernando Checa makes this point in referring to Velázquez's portrait titled *Antonia de Ipeñarrieta y Galdós and her Son Luis* (1631–32) in *Velázquez: The Complete Paintings*. Trans. Donald Pistolesi. (London: Thames and Hudson, 2008), 117.

65. Svetlana Alpers, *The Vexations of Art: Velázquez and Others* (New Haven and London: Yale University Press, 2005), 153.

66. Ibid., 121.

67. Interestingly, the grounds of the Buen Retiro palace—which have mostly fallen into ruin after centuries of neglect and destruction—ultimately became the setting for the Museo Nacional del Prado which holds the greatest collection of Velázquez paintings and serves as one of the most famous public art museums in the world.

68. This difficult dressage movement is typical in Velázquez's equestrian portraits in which the martial authority of the horseman is meant to be emphasized. See, for example, *Philip IV on Horseback* (c. 1628–34/35), *The Count-Duke of Olivares on Horseback* (c. 1634), *Prince Baltasar Carlos on Horseback* (1635) and *Philip III on Horseback* (c. 1628–34/35).

I disagree with Checa regarding the position of the horse in *Philip IV on Horseback*. In his catalogue of Velázquez's paintings Checa describes the horse in "courbette position" (*Velázquez*, 136) yet the courbette is a jumping air in which the horse must rear back very far in order to gather his legs under him before hopping forward. The king's horse is not in the proper position for the courbette and the uneven ground makes it unlikely a courbette could be attempted. (Checa makes a similar remark about the dressage air in *The Count-Duke of Olivares on Horseback, Velázquez*, 149). The pesade or levade, by contrast, are balancing airs easier for the horse to execute although still very difficult positions that require great strength in the horse and skill in the rider. In the pesade the horse rears, with control, about 45 degrees off the ground and in the levade, a more difficult position, the horse's forelegs are about 30–35 degrees off the ground.

69. Checa writes, "The painting's symbolic meaning is clear: the appearance of the king and queen alludes to dynastic continuity: the education of the prince is represented through his control over the horse, which evokes his capacity for both self-mastery and mastery of his political subjects, with the inevitable Olivares, the court factotum, and Juan Mateos as mediators" (*Velázquez*, 30).

70. Sebastián de Morra is typically associated with this painting—see Checa, *Velázquez*, 129 in his discussion of Velázquez's *The Buffoon Sebastián de Morra* (c. 1643–49)—but this attribution in *Prince Baltasar Carlos at the Riding School* complicates the dating of the latter painting. According to Checa, Morra was in Flanders serving the Cardinal-Infante Ferdinand of Austria until 1641. He did not enter the prince's service until 1643; the approximate date Checa gives to *Prince Baltasar Carlos in the Riding School* is 1639–40. While a date of 1642 has been suggested for this painting (qtd. in Checa, *Velázquez*, 151) by Barbeito, this is still one year before the dwarf entered the prince's household. While it is possible that Morra was a member of the Spanish court in 1642 and not assigned to the crown prince, 1642 or 1643 would age the prince to 12 or 13. The painting itself suggests a younger child; about ten years old seems correct. By 1642 Olivares's power was in deep decline; he would be dismissed in 1643. It is unclear if Olivares would be given such prominence in this painting about the education of the future monarch as late as 1642. Thus, the identity of the dwarf in the painting, although he resembles Morra, may never be accurately ascertained.

71. Alpers notes how Velázquez uses far and near within his canvases for various effects, commenting, "It is better not to describe it as far and near. It is rather the juxtaposition of the large and the small" (*Vexations of Art*, 138). She also refers to the interesting power imbalance suggested in small monarchs and large servants or others of little status in *Prince Baltasar Carlos in the Riding School* as well as *The Spinners* and *Las Meninas* (*Vexations of Art*, 177–78).

72. Alpers, *Vexations of Art*, 178; Checa, *Velázquez*, 151.

73. Philip married his niece, Mariana of Austria, in 1649. She had been Baltasar Carlos's fiancée and was only twelve years old at the time of Baltasar Carlos's death in 1646. Mariana gave birth to a number of children, including boys, but they died young. Finally, a new direct male heir was delivered when Mariana gave birth to the future Charles (Carlos) II in 1661, just a few years before Philip IV's death. The unfortunate Charles—who was plagued by physical and mental disabilities likely due to the centuries of inbreeding that preceded his birth—would be the last Hapsburg ruler.

74. Checa, *Velázquez*, 114.

75. Checa notes a concession to the prince's age in the hat which replaces the table upon which the male sitter typically rests his hand (*Velázquez*, 29).

76. Erika Langmuir asserts that the figure is male—"himself an unbreeched child, though older than his companion" (*Imagining Childhood*. New Haven and London: Yale University Press [2006], 195). While the figure's hairstyle appears masculine, the standing collar and beaded necklace would not be typical fashion for a boy. Also, Langmuir repeats the supposition advanced in a 1990 Madrid exhibit of Velázquez's works that the identity of the dwarf is Francisco de Lezcano (254 n. 33). However, according to Checa, Lezcano's service with Baltasar Carlos has been documented between 1634 and 1648 (he died in 1649) (*Velázquez*, 165). If he was the prince's dwarf in 1632 (the date of *Prince Baltasar Carlos With a Dwarf*) and unbreeched himself, he would have been about five years old in 1632. His solo portrait by Velázquez, *Francisco de Lezcano, 'El niño de Vallecas'* (1634–36), strongly suggests a youth older than 7–9 years. In addition, he was considered to be a "cretin" and

"mentally retarded" (Checa, *Velázquez*, 165) and it is doubtful that a dwarf with mental challenges would be paired in a serious official portrait such as this one. Thus, given these facts, it is unlikely that the dwarf depicted in *Prince Baltasar Carlos with a Dwarf* is Lezcano or male.

77. See Checa, *Velázquez*, 114 and the Museum of Fine Arts web collection site for this painting (http://www.mfa.org/collections/object/don-baltasar-carlos-with-a-dwarf–31124), for example. Tietze-Conrat concurs that the rattle and apple symbolize precious objects, but she interprets the dwarf to be performing the role of the jester: "He is playing at being a king—like Danga who danced a God. The fact that he could do it unpunished and even in the presence of the heir to the throne proves that the idea of the parallel between king and fool has unconsciously been retained" (*Dwarfs and Jesters in Art*, 25). This reading of the painting ignores the context of dynastic succession which was so important in the Spanish child portraits of the seventeenth century and makes little sense within that context.

78. An exception to this rule may be found in the unusual *An Interior with King Charles I, Queen Henrietta Maria, Jeffery [sic] Hudson, William Herbert, 3rd Earl of Pembroke and his brother Philip Herbert, later 4th Earl of Pembroke* (c. 1630–1635) by Hendrick van Steenwijck the younger. In this painting the tiny figure of the dwarf is nearly centered in a vast palace interior (a lively dog is in the actual foreground center) and the aristocrats are clustered near or under an entrance to the room at the right of the painting.

79. The art historian and Velázquez expert José López-Rey discerns the difference between the dwarf and royal child to be emphasized by way of Velázquez's "handling of pigment." He continues, "It is mainly this contrast that makes the child-dwarf appear as a foil to the majesty embodied in the figure of the child-prince" (*Velázquez's Work and World*, 63).

80. Checa, *Velázquez*, 51.

81. On the last point, see López-Rey (*Velázquez's Work and World*, 138–139). Gombrich indulges in a little fantasy, imagining that the king and queen were bored with their sitting and asked to have their little daughter brought in to them. The fond parents, his fantasy continues, comment that the Infanta is worthy of a painting: "The words spoken by a monarch are always treated as a command and so we may owe this masterpiece to a passing wish which only Velázquez was able to turn into reality" (*Story of Art*, 312). By contrast, Jerry Griswold posits that *Las Meninas* represents a disparaging view of childhood given its play with scale: "Velázquez seems to be saying, all the attention paid this doted-upon and foregrounded five-year-old is incommensurate and out of scale: children *are* small, *ergo* insignificant. Equally revealing is the inclusion, on the right, of Maribarbola, the child's female dwarf . . . by which Velázquez presents again a sense of disproportion, a "stunted" adult, and something out of scale" (*Feeling Like a Kid: Childhood and Children's Literature*. Baltimore: Johns Hopkins University Press [2006], 70).

82. López-Rey, *Velázquez's Work and World*, 139.

83. Langmuir, *Imagining Childhood*, 200. Tietze-Conrat finds in nearly every dwarf portrait a certain antagonism between big and small: "The normal grown-up ridicules the abnormal one, secure in the knowledge that he is big and the other one is not" (*Dwarfs and Jesters in Art*, 26). While there is much to agree with in this assessment particularly in terms of the performing dwarf figure of popular culture—and the dwarf within portraiture is indeed framed, in part, by performance—this kind of reductive reading fails to consider the complexities of the dwarf figure in portraiture, especially of the Baroque era.

84. Laura Bass, *The Drama of the Portrait: Theater and Visual Culture in Early Modern Spain* (University Park, PA: Pennsylvania State University Press, 2008), 108.

85. Alpers, *Vexations in Art*, 188.

86. Karen Pinkus, *Picturing Silence: Emblem, Language, Counter-Reformation Materiality* (Ann Arbor: University of Michigan Press, 1997), 162.

87. Interestingly, the painting, and the life of Margarita Theresa, inspired playwright

Lynn Nottage to write *Las Meninas* (2002) about the romance between the princess (the wife of Louis XIV) and the African dwarf Nabo Sensugali who was sent to France to join her household. The play is based on actual events and represents the hidden history of both the monarchy and dwarf servants in royal courts. The affair also offers a delightful play of opposites: big and small, black and white, high status and low and the equalizing, if fleeting, effects of love.

Chapter 3: Staging the Dwarf

1. López-Rey, *Velázquez' Work and World*, 92.
2. Michael M. Chemers, *Staging Stigma: A Critical Examination of the American Freak Show* (New York: Palgrave Macmillan, 2008), 15. Additional useful studies and social histories of the freak show and its incursion into literature and other cultural sites include Robin Blyn, *The Freak-Garde: Extraordinary Bodies and Revolutionary Art in America* (Minneapolis: University of Minnesota Press, 2013), Robert Bogdan, *Freak Show: Presenting Human Oddities for Amusement and Profit* (Chicago and London: Chicago University Press, 1988), Lillian Craton, *The Victorian Freak Show: The Significance of Disability and Physical Differences in 19th-Century Fiction* (Amherst, NY: Cambria Press, 2009), and Leslie Fiedler, *Freaks* (New York: Simon and Schuster, 1978).
3. The term "normate" was coined by Rosemarie Garland Thomson (*Extraordinary Bodies: Figuring Physical Disability in American Culture and Literature*. New York: Columbia University Press [1997], 8.
4. Ferris, introduction to *Staging Stigma*, 5.
5. This tradition may have begun with P. T. Barnum and General Tom Thumb as the showman and his most famous employee were often dressed similarly when in public. Chemers, "Jumpin' Tom Thumb," 17.
6. Bogdan, *Freak Show*, 97.
7. Kotar and Gessler, *Rise of the American Circus*, 153.
8. Frederick Drimmer, *Very Special People: The Struggles, Loves, and Triumphs of Human Oddities* (New York: Amjon Publishers, 1973), 351. Zip, the stage name of William Henry Johnson, was a diminutive African American man whose career in freak shows spanned over sixty years. He was popular at Barnum's American Museum as well as other museums, circuses, and Coney Island until his death in 1926. See Bogdan, 134–142. Johnson was promoted as the "What Is It?" as well as "The Monkey Man" and "The Missing Link" and also by his stage name "Zip" (from 1870 or so), a reference to "Zip Coon," a minstrel show character (Bogdan, 137).
9. The American Museum was a New York City landmark for over twenty years (1841–1865). When the original building burned to the ground on July 13, 1865, Barnum started again at a new location. Unfortunately, just three years later, this building, too, was destroyed in a fire. After these losses, Barnum turned his attention to developing his circus.
10. Craton, *Victorian Freak Show*, 28.
11. Bogdan, *Freak Show*, 268.
12. Neil Harris, *Humbug: The Art of P. T. Barnum* (Boston and Toronto: Little Brown and Co., 1973), 56.
13. Charlie's mother was to receive an additional four dollars per week plus board. Charlie would also receive an additional fifty dollars one month before his contract expired, but if the child fell sick for more than a week, he would not receive his pay. See Harris, *Humbug: The Art of P. T. Barnum*, 50.
14. Quoted in Alice Curtis Desmond, *Barnum Presents General Tom Thumb* (New York: Macmillan Company, 1954), 19. Charles Stratton was born on January 4, 1838, but Barnum added six years to his age in order to convince the public that the child was a true dwarf and not simply a very small boy. Stratton would eventually grow to a height of three feet, four inches. For a full-length biography of Stratton, and his relationship to P. T. Barnum in particular, see Eric D. Lehman, *Becoming Tom Thumb: Charles Stratton, P. T. Barnum, and the Dawn of American Celebrity* (Middletown, CT:

Wesleyan University Press, 2013). See Bogdan for a concise and accurate overview of Stratton's career and marriage (148–161).

15. See Desmond, *Barnum Presents General Tom Thumb*, 55–56. See Thomson for a brilliant articulation of the meaning of the nineteenth-century American freak show (55–80): "In an era of social transformation and economic reorganization, the nineteenth-century freak show was a cultural ritual that dramatized the era's physical and social hierarchy by spotlighting bodily stigmata that could be choreographed as an absolute contrast to 'normal' American embodiment and authenticated as corporeal truth" (*Extraordinary Bodies*, 63).

16. In fact, I would argue that General Tom Thumb never functioned in the mode of "freak" at all. Thomson argues that in giving those with extraordinary bodies stage names such as "King" or "Queen" or "General," the "freak" is invested with an "ironic celebrity": "Freak shows thus conflated kings and fools in a tawdry, satiric extravaganza that inverted the old ceremonial spectacle of royal pomp and power by ritually displaying a person stigmatized by bodily particularity, silenced by the pitchman's imposed narrative, and managed by the showman" (*Extraordinary Bodies*, 67). While there were certainly elements of stigma and control (by Barnum) in Charles Stratton's early career, in particular, his worldwide celebrity was not ironic but real. In addition, Thomson argues that dwarfs and men and women displayed for their lack of limbs provoke the audience to "determine the precise parameters of human wholeness and the limits of free agency" (59). I would suggest that the "wholeness" of Stratton, given Barnum's persona for Stratton—dandified, gentlemanly, and clever—was never in question.

17. Lehman, *Becoming Tom Thumb*, ix.

18. Phineas T. Barnum, *The Life of P. T. Barnum, Written By Himself*. 1855 (Urbana and Chicago: University of Illinois Press, 2000), 261.

19. Ibid.

20. The play opened at the Lyceum in London on March 16, 1846 as a vehicle for the Strattons' international debut and was staged in New York productions into the 1850s. See Michael Chemers's history of Stratton's involvement in the play in "On the Boards in Brobdignag [*sic*]: Performing Tom Thumb." *New England Theatre Journal* 12.1 (2001): 79–104. See also S. L. Kotar and J. E. Gessler, *The Rise of the American Circus, 1716–1899* (Jefferson, NC and London: McFarland and Co., 2011), 152–153.

21. Stratton's wife's memoirs, published after his death, comment upon his loss of childhood given that his life was given over to performing when he had just turned five years old: " 'He had, as he said, no childhood, and as he developed into manhood the sense of this loss made him particularly tender of children . . . He was taught to take wine at dinner when only five, to smoke at seven and 'chew' at nine' " (qtd. in Chemers, *Staging Stigma*, 52).

22. "The Original and Celebrated General Tom Thumb, the World-Renowned American Man in Miniature." 1860. Http://shnm.gmu.edu/lostmuseum/lm/212/. Accessed November 16, 2012.

23. In the pamphlet "Sketch of the Life, Personal Appearance, Character and Manner of Charles S. Stratton, The Man in Miniature, Known as General Tom Thumb, And His Wife, Lavinia Warren Stratton," Warren's "natural qualities" are emphasized: "We look at her, and we know that her diminished stature does not arise from compression or mutilation, but from natural causes alone, and we are led to exclaim, 'How rare and remarkable the phenomena' " (1874 ed., 8). This 24-page pamphlet was originally published in 1856 (before Warren married Stratton). It was expanded and subsequently re-published in 1868 (44 pages by Wykoop and Hallenbeck) and again in 1874 (46 pages by Samuel Booth).

24. Harris, *Humbug: The Art of P. T. Barnum*, 49.

25. Stewart, *On Longing*, 123.

26. Lori Merish connects cute child performers with the performing dwarf of the nineteenth century ". . . part of the pleasure of watching precocious child and 'little person' perform[ances] derived from how they unsettled, in a contained but dramatic fashion, the conventional boundary between child and adult." ("Cuteness and

Commodity Aesthetics: Tom Thumb and Shirley Temple" in *Freakery: Cultural Spectacles of the Extraordinary Body*. Ed. Rosemarie Garland Thomson [New York and London: New York University Press, 1996: 185–206], 190). Lillian Craton offers an interesting reading of littleness in Dickens that links the performing dwarf with the suffering child character (Craton, *The Victorian Freak Show*, 41–85).

27. See the 1848 advertisement for the American Museum Lecture Room performances of Stratton archived at the Lost Museum website: http://chnm.gmu.edu/lostmuseum/lm/211/. Accessed November 16, 2012. Interestingly and ironically, the same advertisement promotes "the famous GIANT OR MAMMOTH BABY, who, though only 16 months old, weighs 90 pounds!"

28. Notably, until the Civil War era, African Americans were generally barred from entering the American Museum. On an irregular basis, "respectable colored persons" were admitted to the museum before the 1860s. An advertisement for the American Museum in the *New York Tribune* for February 27, 1849 concluded with a "note to persons of color" indicating that this "class of people" would be admitted, "by the grace of the Manager, on March 1 from 8a.m to 1p.m. Archived at the Barnum Museum Archive. Http://www.lostmuseum.cuny.edu/archives/museumimage5.htm. Accessed November 16, 2012.

29. Qtd in Desmond, *Barnum Presents General Tom Thumb*, 122.

30. Qtd ibid., 78.

31. Merish, "Cuteness and Commodity Aesthetics," 188.

32. In her study of the aesthetic category of the "cute" (among others), Sianne Ngai argues that we acknowledge its inherent power dynamic: ". . . 'cute' designates not just the site of a static power differential but also the site of a surprisingly complex power struggle" (*Our Aesthetic Categories: Zany, Cute, Interesting* [Cambridge, MA and London: Harvard University Press, 2012], 11).

33. Chemers, "Jumpin' Tom Thumb," 16. See also Chemers, "On the Boards in Brobdignag [*sic*]", in which he argues that Stratton's appeal is based in part on his "admittedly pedophiliac reflective sexuality" (92). While I am not entirely sure what this means—the audience employs a pedophiliac-inflected gaze when admiring the body of the tiny man (who was, at least in the first bloom of his popularity, a boy)?—certainly Stratton's masculinity in miniature is exploited as entertainment. That is, one aspect of his act was to kiss attractive female members of the audience, an action that a full-grown man could not do, but a child-like man or boy *could* do within the bounds of propriety. Does this make Tom Thumb "hypermasculine and hypererotic" as Chemers claims? (Ibid.). I think not.

34. Lavinia Warren's full name was Mercy Lavinia Warren Bump; she changed it to the more musical Lavinia Warren as a stage name, but after her marriage was known as "Mrs. General Tom Thumb." Although after Stratton's death she married "Count Magri," Lavinia tended to refer to herself as "the former Mrs. General Tom Thumb." A fictional autobiography of Warren by Melanie Benjamin, based in part on her autobiography, was published in 2011: *The Autobiography of Mrs. Tom Thumb* (New York: Delacorte Press, 2011). Warren's autobiographical sketch was published in the *New York Tribune Sunday Magazine* in 1906.

35. Qtd. in *Sketch of the Life . . .*, 9. The *New York Commercial Advertiser* similarly noted, at her debut, "her bust would be a study for a sculptor, and the symmetry of her form is such that, were she of the average size, she would be one of the most handsome of women. She is now—but in a miniature form." Qtd. in *Sketch of the Life*, 10.

36. Disability Museum website, para. 117. Barnum's exploitation of the marriage of two dwarfs was not the first such event in history. Two of the dwarfs in the court of Charles I, Anne Shepherd and Richard Gibson, were married in 1633 to some fanfare. The king gave the bride away and the marriage was celebrated with a poem by Edmund Waller entitled "Of the Marriage of the Dwarfs." The second line reads, "Nature did this match contrive." (*The Poems of Edmund Waller*, Vol. 1. Ed. G. Thorn Drury. 1686. London: A. H. Bullen and New York: Charles Scribner's Sons, 1901, 92.) In 1710 Peter the Great of Russia planned the wedding of his niece alongside that of two of his royal dwarfs. See Adelson, *The Lives of Dwarfs*, 17.

37. *Sketch of the Life* . . ., 8.
38. Qtd. in Marlis Schweitzer, "Barnum's Last Laugh? General Tom Thumb's Wedding Cake in the Library of Congress." *Performing Arts Resources* 28. 1 (2011), 119.
39. See Schweitzer, "Barnum's Last Laugh?" 119.
40. "Marriage a la Barnum." *Brooklyn Eagle*, January 26, 1863. http://chnm.gmu.edu/lostmuseum/lm/210. Accessed November 16, 2012.
41. *Sketch of the Life* . . ., 18–21.
42. Rachel Poliquin, "The Visual Erotics of Mini-Marriages." *The Believer*. November/December 2007. Http://believermag.com/issues/200711/?read=article_poliquin. Accessed June 22, 2012.
43. Harris notes, "Much of the notoriety the marriage attracted was founded on sexual curiosity, and Barnum was blamed for encouraging a rather crude level of speculation" (*Humbug: The Art of P. T. Barnum*, 163).
44. The commercial success of the wedding between Stratton and Warren spurred other dwarf weddings as spectacles. See Bogdan, *Freak Show*, 208–210.
45. For a key discussion of the history and cultural significance of Tom Thumb weddings see Susan Stewart, *On Longing*, 119–124. See also Michelle V. Agins, "Tom Thumb Weddings: Only for the Very Young." *New York Times*, June 16, 1991, 34. See also Melanie Benjamin, "America's Royal Wedding: Gender and Mrs Tom Thumb." *Huffington Post* April 19, 2011. Accessed November 30, 2012.
46. Stewart, *On Longing*, 121.
47. Ibid., 119.
48. In fact, in her later years, after General Tom Thumb's death and her marriage to Count Magri, Lavinia Warren was exhibited at Dreamland in Coney Island.
49. Adelson, *The Lives of Dwarfs*, 32. Emphasis in the original.
50. Harris, *Humbug*, 49. Though writing about "freaks" in the freak show (where General Tom Thumb, I would argue, is not really at home), Thomson seconds this notion about the identification that may occur between performer and audience—although adding a conflicting emotion, as well: "Freaks were celebrities as well as spectacles, their popularity suggesting that audiences simultaneously identified with and were repulsed by the performers" (*Extraordinary Bodies*, 66).
51. Adelson, *Lives of Dwarfs*, 229. See especially 229–232 for her discussion of children's books.
52. Craton makes this point about Dickens's juxtaposition of the child and dwarf: "Dickens's images of unusual littleness, for instance, demonstrate the close ties between ideal and radically different bodies. The idealized child shares space with the grotesque performing dwarf, and the two extremes of littleness often merge in Dickens's fiction" (*Victorian Freak Show*, 208).
53. Wilde, "The Birthday of the Infanta," 14.
54. Ibid. Adelson critiques the story as accepting the notion that the dwarf body must be viewed as grotesque: "In spite of his attempt to impart social criticism, Wilde offers a message carrying an implicit acceptance of traditional standards of beauty, a message that precludes any chance that his dwarf character can transcend stereotype" (*Lives of the Dwarfs*, 208).
55. Wilde, "The Birthday of the Infanta," 20.
56. Ibid.
57. Ibid.
58. Adelson relates that in an interview with Oprah Winfrey about *Stones from a River*, Hegi explained that she chose a dwarf to tell her story about Nazi-era Germany because "Trudi's angle of vision was ideal because as a little person she understood what it was like to be *other*: because people tended to separate themselves from her, she could more easily stand back and acknowledge what was happening to the Jews of Germany" (*Lives of the Dwarfs*, 223).
59. Lisa Graff, *The Thing About Georgie*. (New York: Harper Trophy, 2006), 90.
60. This is not a merely a rhetorical question as dwarf books for children routinely are set in performance spaces. Holly Goldberg Sloan's middle grade novel *Short* features

both a very small-statured child and a wise dwarf woman. They meet as actors in a semiprofessional production of *The Wizard of Oz* in which they have both been cast as Munchkins (New York: Dial Books, 2017).

61. Hegi, *Trudi and Pia*, n.p.
62. Ibid.
63. Ibid.
64. Ibid.
65. Ibid.
66. M. E. Kerr, *Little Little* (New York: Harper Collins, 1981), 5.
67. Ibid., 222.
68. Ibid., 127.
69. Marsh based the character of the dwarf Lia on what she could discern about the figure in the Frans Pourbus portrait of Isabella Clara Eugenia and her dwarf (discussed in chapter two). She also indicates in her Author's Note that she changed the dates of some historical events. For example, Infanta Isabella Clara Eugenia does not assume the throne of the Spanish Netherlands until 1599; in the novel, she is already on the throne when Jepp enters the court in 1597.
70. Katherine Marsh, *Jepp, Who Defied the Stars* (New York: Hyperion, 2012), 233.
71. Ibid., 368.
72. Ibid., 369.
73. See Marsh, *Jepp Who Defied the Stars*, 370–371. She writes, "This seventeenth-century painter, who depicted the court of Philip IV of Spain, captured a dignity and directness of gaze in his dwarf subjects that made them seem more alive than almost anyone else around them" (370–371).
74. The family owns a pumpkin farm outside of Portland, Oregon. A spin-off series was launched in 2012 called *Wedding Farm*. In this series, the popular tourist destination becomes a wedding venue.
75. Henry Nasiff, aka Hank the Angry Drunken Dwarf, was a frequent guest on *The Howard Stern Show* until his death in 2001. In his segments, Hank was interviewed while (seemingly) drunk and questioned about his sexual exploits and bigoted opinions. See Adelson, 405 n.89. The dwarf Chuy Bravo (the stage name for Jesus Melgoza) is a regular on the late-night talk show *Chelsea Lately* (E! Network, 2007–2014). He provides one-liner commentary and video segments for the show. The actor Peter Dinklage, in his many film and television roles, is an exception to the tragicomic dwarf mode.
76. See the profile of Gervais in " 'If I Have Offended Anyone, and I'm Sure I Have, I Don't Apologize,' " by Dave Itzkoff. *New York Times Magazine* January 15, 2012, 24, 26–27, 54. The show ran in the UK for one season between 2011–2013.
77. Craton, *Victorian Freak Show*, 54.

Chapter 4: Lilliputians in Blackface

1. Guy Burrows. *The Land of the Pigmies* (New York and Boston: Thomas Y. Crowell and Co., 1898), 172.
2. Edward Tyson, *The Anatomy of a Pygmy* (1699. 2nd ed. London: T. O. Osborne, 1751), n.p.
   In 1870, a Russian scientist and explorer, George Schweinfurth, located Akka (or Aka) Pygmies within the Ituri Forest and claimed, contrary to popular belief, that they were neither monkeys nor mythological beings. Henry Morton Stanley's popular *In Darkest Africa* (1890) reached a wider audience and his description of pygmies intrigued the Victorian reading public as well as scientific communities (physical anthropologists, craniologists, and ethnologists). See Carole G. Silver, *Strange and Secret Peoples: Fairies and Victorian Consciousness* (New York and Oxford: Oxford University Press, 1999), 129–134, and Peter McAllister, *Pygmonia: In Search of the Secret Land of the Pygmies* (St. Lucia, Queensland: University of Queensland Press, 2010), 39–40. For a fascinating biography of Patrick Tracy Lowell

Putnam, an early/mid-twentieth century amateur anthropologist and perhaps exploiter of African pygmies, see *The King of the World in the Land of the Pygmies* by Joan Mark (Lincoln and London: University of Nebraska Press, 1995).

3. Bertram C. A. Windle, ed. Introduction. *A Philological Essay Concerning the Pygmies of the Ancients* by Edward Tyson (London: David Nutt, 1894: ix–civ), liii.

4. Ashis Nandy, *Traditions, Tyranny and Utopias: Essays in the Politics of Awareness* (Delhi: Oxford University Press, 1987), 57.

5. Silver, *Strange and Secret Peoples*, 133.

6. Burrows. *The Land of the Pigmies*, 172.

7. William Edgar Geil, *A Yankee in Pigmy Land* (London: Hodder and Stoughton, 1905), 204. Geil's travelogue, like so many of the missionary, travel, and natural history books of the period, is painfully racist in many ways. Geil's patronizing, nationalistic, dismissive, and inaccurate pseudo-scientific discourse sums up the pygmy people as a "race." For Geil, the pygmies' small size is a marker of relative intelligence when compared with other Africans: "This diminutive man of the sylvan shades is of a far higher order of intelligence than the blacks of superior physique beside whose villages he encamps. He will become the Jap of the forest. It is to be remembered that of the yellow races the Japanese, the most aggressive and Yankee-like, are the smallest" (279).

8. Geil, *Yankee in Pigmy Land*, 206.

9. Another example can be found in Rev. Donald A. Fairley's *Hunting Pygmy Hunters*. In this short work Fairley describes establishing with his wife and family the Gabon Pygmy Church in western Africa in the 1930s, and refers to their camp as "Pygmyland." See also A. B. Lloyd, *In Dwarf Land and Cannibal Country. A Record of Travel and Discovery in Central Africa* (London: T. Fisher Unwin, 1899).

Uniting folklore with Darwin's theory of natural selection, Captain Burrows believes that the remnants of fairy folk can be discerned in African pygmies: "... I have no doubt that at one time [mannikins (*sic*) as German mountain dwarfs and Irish Leprechauns] flourished on the face of the earth in the flesh, being ultimately killed off to allow the survival of the fittest; consequently it was of the highest interest to find some of them in their primitive and aboriginal state" (173–174).

Even a twenty-first-century book about global pygmy peoples, Peter McAllister's *Pygmonia: In Search of the Secret Land of the Pygmies*, as the title makes clear, seems unable or unwilling to avoid making the same gesture uniting myth and fantasy with travelogue when discussing pygmies. The book is informative on many levels—especially in detailing genetic analyses of pygmy peoples—yet frustrating in the dearth of scholarly notes and attribution of sources.

10. Ruth B. Fisher, *On the Border of Pigmy-Land* (3rd ed. London: Marshall Brothers, 1905), v.

11. Fisher, *On the Border of Pigmy-Land*, 161.

12. Paul S. Landau, "Empires of the Visual: Photography and Colonial Administration in Africa" in *Images and Empires: Visuality in Colonial and Postcolonial Africa*. Eds. Paul S. Landau and Deborah D. Kaspin (Berkeley: University of California Press, 2002), 145.

13. Qtd. in Meena Khorana, Introduction, *Africa in Literature for Children and Young Adults: An Annotated Bibliography of English-Language Books* (Westport, CT: Greenwood Press, 1994), xix.

14. Charles Dickens, "The Noble Savage," *Household Words*. Vol. 8 no. 168 (Saturday, June 11, 1853): 337–339. The western idea of the comely and honorable native was first advanced by Michel de Montaigne in his 1580 essay "On Cannibals"—about the Tupinambá people of Brazil (first translated into English in 1603). The idea was later adopted and adapted by J. J. Rousseau in his *Discourse on Inequality* (1755) into the ideal of the Noble Savage.

15. Laura M. Stevens, *The Poor Indians: British Missionaries, Native Americans, and Colonial Sensibility* (Philadelphia: University of Pennsylvania Press, 2004), 19.

16. Geil, *A Yankee in Pigmy Land*, 222.

17. Ibid., 283.

18. The title of Chapter 18 of Geil's book, 265–283.
19. Jan Nederveen Pieterse, *White on Black: Images of Africa and Blacks in Western Popular Culture* (New Haven and London: Yale University Press, 1992), 64.
20. For example, in *David Livingstone* (London and Edinburgh: Oliphants, Ltd [1953]), the second chapter opens with a description of the ease of traveling to South Africa from England: "A fast train would take you to Southampton, a big steamer would carry you over the sea to Cape Town, and another train would take you right over the veldt to the heart of the Dark Continent, or by plane in a few hours" (13). See Patrick Brantlinger,"Victorians and Africans: The Genealogy of the Myth of the Dark Continent." *Critical Inquiry* 12 (Autumn 1985): 166–203.
21. Anonymous, *David Livingstone*, 14.
22. Ibid., 37.
23. This children's book, which promotes a religious message of tolerance (but also supports conversion), also negatively commented upon white racism: "Some white people look down on black men and women because of the colour of their skin; but Livingstone loved the negroes of Africa, and he really gave his life to them. He knew God made both white and black people, and that God does not care what colour people's skins may be, so long as their hearts are clean and their lives good" (15).
24. Although short-statured, the Bushmen (a term, such as "pygmy," that is inexact, but still in use today to describe nomadic hunter-gatherer people of southern Africa) of the Kalahari Desert are not pygmies. "Pygmies" are similarly nomadic and live particularly in the Congo valley and include the Akkas of the upper Nile River valley, the Batwas of the Congo River bend and the Mbuti of the Ituri forest. In children's literature such as *David Livingstone* and Lesley Beake's *Song of Be* (1993), pygmies and Bushmen function similarly as exotic racialized miniatures.
    In her chapter on racialized miniatures, "Little Goblin Men: On Dwarfs and Pygmies, Racial Myths and Mythic Races," from her book *Strange and Secret Peoples* (117–147), Carole G. Silver focuses on the menacing aspects of the mythologies of pygmies as dwarfish quasi-supernatural beings, citing the many examples of grotesque goblin men in late Victorian art and literature. Some of these examples include Aubrey Beardsley's illustrations, the Ape-Man in H. G. Wells's *The Island of Dr. Moreau* (1895), Arthur Conan Doyle's *The Sign of Four* (1890) and John Buchan's short stories (from *The Watcher By the Threshold*, 1902). See especially Silver, 137–147.
25. Other venues on the circuit of late nineteenth-century Aboriginal shows included the Crystal Palace in London (after it had been moved from Hyde Park to Sydenham Hill), Folies Bergère in Paris, the Panoptikum in Berlin, and "Arcadia" in St. Petersburg, among other locations. See Roslyn Poignant, *Professional Savages: Captive Lives and Western Spectacle* (New Haven and London: Yale University Press, 2004). See also the lavishly illustrated *Reinventing Africa: Museums, Material Culture and Popular Imagination in Late Victorian and Edwardian England* by Annie E. Coombes (New Haven and London: Yale University Press, 1994), especially chapters four and five (63–108).
    In 1868, after Barnum's American Museum burned down (for the second time), the entrepreneur teamed up with W. C. Coup who, in 1872, assisted Barnum in transforming the museum into a traveling show, the Great Travelling World's Fair. See Poignant, *Professional Savages*, 80.
26. Ibid., 7.
27. Coombes, *Reinventing Africa*, 85.
28. Poignant, *Professional Savages*, 7.
29. Barnum's letter reads, in part, "My aim is to *exhibit* to the American public, not only *human beings of different races*, but also where practicable, those who possess extraordinary peculiarities such as giants, dwarfs, singular disfigurements of the person, dexterity in the use of weapons, dancing, singing, juggling, unusual feats of strength or agility, etc." (Qtd. in Poignant, *Professional Savages*, 58. Emphasis in

Barnum's original.) Pygmies from South Africa were displayed at the Royal Aquarium in Westminster, Central London in 1884. See Poignant, *Professional Savages*, 124.

30. After the success of Prince Albert's Great Exhibition of 1851, world's fairs— international expositions of science, culture, and industry—were launched every few years throughout the second half of the nineteenth century through the twentieth century. The first Centennial World's Fair was held in America in Philadelphia in 1876 on the 100th anniversary of America's independence. I return to the connections between world's fairs and size difference in chapter five's discussion of giant robots and the "future perfect."

31. See Phillips Verner Bradford and Harvey Blume's *Ota: The Pygmy in the Zoo* for a succinct synopsis of the St. Louis World's Fair (New York: St. Martin's Press, 1992), 1–16. See also Pamela Newkirk's *Spectacle: The Astonishing Life of Ota Benga* (New York: HarperCollins, 2015).

32. Coombes argues that anthropology, while a struggling academic discipline, was gaining recognition in the "leisure industry" of late Victorian and Edwardian England (*Reinventing Africa*, 107). Exhibitions—even those sponsored by august bodies such as the Royal Geographical Society—were assisted in their popularity not only by anthropology's rising profile, but also by their association with colonial adventure stories. Coombes comments that no matter the desires of such institutions (which might well have sought greater separation between their serious "scientific" goals and the romantic colonial novel), "Significantly . . . the racialisation perpetuated through such events was not immutable" (107). Joan Mark defines early iterations of American anthropology as "a child of colonial empires of the nineteenth century and of western expansion in the United States" (xiv).

33. Bradford and Blume, *Ota: The Pygmy in the Zoo*, 5.

34. Conventional wisdom, informed by Verner's writings about his adventures, held that pygmies were cannibals. Ota Benga, in particular, "had the reputation of being a man eater" (quoted in Bradford and Blume from a *St. Louis Post-Dispatch* article dated September 4, 1904, 255). Visitors who wanted to see Ota Benga's pointed teeth were required to pay an additional 5 cents.

35. *Ota Benga: A Pygmy in America*. Short documentary film (17 minutes) written and directed by Alfeu França (2002).

36. Bradford and Blume, *Ota: The Pygmy in the Zoo*, 174. In his chapter on Ota Benga in *Pygmonia* (2010), McAllister offers a different view of Ota Benga's time at the zoo. McAllister suggests that it was Ota Benga's love for a chimp Verner sold to the zoo and the resident orang-utan that caused him to spend his days in the Monkey House. The exhibit sign authorized by the zoo director, Dr. William Hornaday, McAllister explains, was created because "in Hornaday's eyes it seemed that Ota Benga had effectively turned himself into an exhibit" through his apparent delight in stirring up the crowd and residing with the apes (195). McAllister insists that Ota Benga did not sleep in the Monkey House but in "an entirely respectable bed in an entirely respectable apartment" (196). Frustratingly, McAllister offers very few sources as support for his version of Ota Benga's story (Bradford and Blume do not appear in the bibliography, for example). In any event, attributing Ota Benga's role at the zoo to a desire to be exhibited or the appeal to notions of "respectability"—even if vaguely tongue in cheek—provide a clear view of McAllister's perspective on the African man.

37. Bradford and Blume, *Ota: The Pygmy in the Zoo*, 179.

38. It is beyond the boundaries of this chapter to discuss in any detail the 1925 "Scopes Monkey Trial" held in Dayton, Tennessee, yet it is worth noting that during both Ota Benga's brief incarceration at the Bronx Zoo and the twelve-day trial—the first ever to be broadcast live on national radio—theories of evolution (however imprecisely argued) were debated in the public sphere, as they continue to be today.

39. Burrows, *The Land of the Pigmies*, 182.

40. The useful and apt term "anthropological reductionism" is that of Terence Rodgers in "Empires of the Imagination: Rider Haggard, Popular Fiction and Africa" in

Writing and Africa, eds. Mpalive-Hangson Msiska and Paul Hyland (London and New York: Longman, 1997), 114.

41. As reported in *Ota Benga: A Pygmy in America*.
42. Qtd. in Bradford and Blume, *Ota: The Pygmy in the Zoo*, 183.
43. A poem published on September 19, 1906 in *The Times* is indicative of both the protests against the actions of the Zoo, as well as the confusion over Ota Benga's potential status as "missing link": "From his native land of darkness,/To the country of the free,/In the interest of science,/And of broad humanity,/Brought we a little Ota Benga,/Dwarfed, benighted, without guile,/Scarcely more than apes or monkey,/Yet a man the while!" (qtd. in Bradford and Blume, *Ota: The Pygmy in the Zoo*, 186). Other missives to the *Times* took the opposite view: "I saw the pigmy on exhibition, and must frankly state that the storm of indignation which some well-meaning clergymen are trying to raise around it is absurd. The unprejudiced observer cannot possibly get the impression that there is in the exhibition any element implying the slightest reflection upon human nature or the colored race" (from a September 13, 1906 letter, qtd in Bradford and Blume, 265). Bradford and Blume's appendix reveals a fascinating series of documents relating to Ota Benga's life and times.
44. McAllister suggests that Ota Benga was exiled to Long Island after he was found in a compromising position with one of the young female orphans. As suggested above, without any sources to back up this claim, it is difficult to establish its validity.
45. Bradford and Blume, *Ota: The Pygmy in the Zoo*, xix.
46. Tambo, the North Queensland Aboriginal whose tragic history Roslyn Poignant traces, was similarly manipulated, along with his fellow troupe members, into performing a particular conception of race-as-entertainment: ". . . in American popular culture, in books and performances, the Black American character Sambo/Tambo represented the non-threatening savage, childish and comical, slave and servant, and a natural entertainer" (*Professional Savages*, 25).
47. Lofting was born in England but became a United States citizen after the First World War.

    Examples of boys' adventure novels set in Africa include Ballantyne's *The Gorilla Hunters: A Tale of the Wilds of Africa* (1861), G. A. Henty's *The Young Colonists: A Story of the Zulu and Boer Wars* (1885), H. Rider Haggard's *She* (1887), and Edgar Rice Burroughs' *Tarzan of the Apes* (1912). See Donnarae MacCann, "Hugh Lofting" in *Writers for Children: Critical Studies of Major Authors since the Seventeenth Century*, ed. Jane M. Bingham (New York: Charles Scribner's Sons, 1988), for a discussion of the African connection in Lofting's Doctor Dolittle series (365–371).
48. David Steege, in "Doctor Dolittle and the Empire: Hugh Lofting's Response to British Colonialism," argues that in setting his tales in the earlier decades of the nineteenth century, Lofting was able to ignore "the imperial scramble for Africa that Britain participated in after 1876" as well as the "military, political, or economic realities of the British Empire in the Africa of his own day" (94).
49. Terence Rodgers argues that ". . . Haggard's African terrain, his specifically African 'empire of the imagination,' may be seen not just as complementary to, but as an integral component of the cultural apparatus of British imperialism and its mechanisms of propaganda, subordination and control at the *fin-de-siècle* and for some time beyond" ("Empires of the Imagination: Rider Haggard, Popular Fiction and Africa." In *Writing and Africa*. eds Mpalive-Hangson Msiska and Paul Hyland (London and New York: Longman, 1997: 103–121), 104.
50. Hugh Walpole, introduction to the Canadian edition of *The Story of Doctor Dolittle* (Toronto: McClelland and Stewart, 1923), viii.
51. MacCann, "Hugh Lofting" in *Writers for Children*, 365. See also Bob Dixon, *Catching Them Young 1: Sex, Race and Class in Children's Literature* (London: Pluto Press, 1977), 104–105, and its companion volume, *Catching Them Young 2: Political Ideas in Children's Fiction* (London: Pluto Press, 1977), 105–107.

In *African Images in Juvenile Literature*, Yulisa Amadu Maddy and Donnarae MacCann note, "In *The Story of Doctor Dolittle* and its sequels, the Doctor symbolizes the conservationist cause with his strategies to sabotage the fox hunts, bull fights, badly managed circuses, etc. His African characters are a blend of self-hate, irrationality, and cannibalistic violence" (Jefferson, NC: McFarland and Co., Inc., 1996), 54.

Lofting is not completely ignorant of the wages of colonialism on the African continent, however. The King of Jolliginki refuses to let Dolittle and the animals travel through his lands as another white man had pillaged the countryside years before: " 'Many years ago a white man came to these shores; and I was very kind to him. But after he had dug holes in the ground to get the gold, and killed all the elephants to get their ivory tusks, he went away secretly in his ship—without so much as saying "Thank you' " (*The Story of Doctor Dolittle*, 47–48).

52. The watch, for example, indicates that Doctor Dolittle "owns" Time by capturing it in a mechanical time-piece. The "primitive" monkeys (and Africans), this illustration seems to suggest, would have little use for such a device. The image recalls the story of *Curious George* (1940, by H. A. Rey and Margaret Rey) in which the Man in the Yellow Hat "rescues" the African monkey and names him "George."

53. See Bradford and Blume, *Ota: The Pygmy in the Zoo*, 188. In the conclusion to his 2002 documentary of Ota Benga's life, França notes that when he contacted the Bronx Zoo asking for permission to view the photographs of Ota Benga for a scholarly purpose—the making of the documentary—he was told that the pictures in the archives were "unavailable." Later attempts to gain access to the images were also unsuccessful.

54. Lofting, *The Story of Doctor Dolittle*, 101.

55. Ibid., 102.

56. Ibid., 103.

57. In *The Voyages of Doctor Dolittle*, when Bumpo arrives in Puddleby-on-the-Marsh from Oxford (where he had been sent by his father to get an education) he speaks in the malapropisms recognizable from minstrel entertainments and is dressed as a "Sambo" figure in frock coat and with a green umbrella. (MacCann makes this point in "Hugh Lofting," 367). His cannibalistic desires are made clear when he suggests salting and eating their stowaway (166). Ota Benga, we will recall, was branded a cannibal in order to increase the perception of his dangerousness in the minds of his viewers.

58. Lofting, *The Voyages of Doctor Dolittle*, 326.

59. David Steege, "Doctor Dolittle and Empire: Hugh Lofting's Response to British Colonialism." *The Presence of the Past in Children's Literature*. Ed. Ann Lawson Lucas (Westport, CT: Prager, 2003), 91–97, 96.

60. Two later volumes in the series are set in West Africa: *Doctor Dolittle's Post Office* (1923) and the posthumously published *Doctor Dolittle and the Secret Lake* (1948).

61. *Richard Halliburton's Complete Book of Marvels: The Occident* (1937) and *Richard Halliburton's Complete Book of Marvels: The Orient* (1938) were published together as *Richard Halliburton's Complete Book of Marvels* in 1941. Stephen Greenblatt introduces his book *Marvelous Possessions: The Wonder of the New World* (Chicago: University of Chicago Press, 1991) by recalling Halliburton's work as his favorite childhood reading (1–2).

62. Timbuktu was colonized by the French in the late nineteenth century.

63. Richard Halliburton, *The Famous Adventures of Richard Halliburton* (1932. Indianapolis: The Bobbs-Merrill Company, 1940), 22.

64. Ibid., 23.

65. Ibid., 25.

66. Ibid.

67. Ibid., 26.

68. Halliburton, *Richard Halliburton's Complete Book of Marvels* (Indianapolis, Indiana: Bobbs-Merrill, 1941), 68.

69. Ibid.
70. Ibid., 72.
71. Indeed, Bodger continues this thought and argues that the "clash of Might and Right" and the relationship between the large and the little, is not only the central theme of English books for children, but the through-line of all of English history" (Bodger, *How the Heather Looks: A Joyous Journey to the British Sources of Children's Books*. New York: Viking, 1965), 203. My thanks to Kim Reynolds for this reference.
72. Qtd. in Martin Kellman's *T. H. White and the Matter of Britain* (Lewiston/Queenston: Edwin Mellen Press, 1988), 182. A 1988 second edition of the book (reprinted in 2002) was published in Britain and introduced by the noted children's book author, Anne Fine. In her introduction, Fine calls White's book "her favourite children's novel" (5).
73. Kellman, *T. H. White and the Matter of Britain*, 177.
74. T. H. White, *Mistress Masham's Repose* (1947. 2nd. ed. 1988. Reprint G. P. Putnam's Sons and Jonathan Cape Children's Books, 2002), 21.
75. Ibid.
76. Qtd. in Sylvia Townsend Warner, *T. H. White: A Biography* (New York: Viking, 1967, 228). The novel was ultimately titled after the name of the island upon which the "repose," or pseudo-temple, was built for Mistress Masham, one of Maria's ancestors.
77. White, *Mistress Masham's Repose*, 21.
78. Ibid., 37–38. Interestingly, White was intrigued by the story of Jeffrey Hudson and wrote a life of the court dwarf in his unpublished book *Three Lives* (completed in 1929). The other figures in this study are Joanna Southcott and Admiral Byng. See Sylvia Warner, *T. H. White*, 49.
79. White, *Mistress Masham's Repose*, 54.
80. Ibid., 60.
81. Ibid., 61. The Boy, in Mary Norton's *The Borrowers* (1952), by contrast, receives no such cautionary advice and he spoils the miniature Borrowers with gifts and luxuries that distract them from their natural and balanced way of life. Ultimately, the Boy's excessive largesse causes their discovery and expulsion from the big house.
82. White, *Mistress Masham's Repose*, 63.
83. Ibid.
84. Ibid., 21.
85. Ibid., 87.
86. I'm thinking here particularly of Dahl's *The BFG* (1982), Heide's *The Shrinking of Treehorn* (1971) and Briggs's *The Man* (1992); I will discuss the last in some detail below.
87. The book won three major prizes in France in 1992: The Grand Prize for Children's Literature, the Totem Prize, and the Golden Circles Prize for Children's Literature.
88. François Place, *The Last Giants* (1992. Trans. William Rodarmor, 1993. London: Chrysalis Children's Books, 1999), 36.
89. Ibid., 38. The giant space creature in Ted Hughes's fable for children, *The Iron Giant* (1968), may have inspired Place. The space-bat-angel-dragon spends its time flying about space, singing the music of the spheres and spreading harmony. Although the creature is returned to its peaceful lifestyle only after losing a contest of strength and determination with the Iron Giant, readers learn that it was the example of the warmongering and discord of earth that had infected the celestial giant in the first place.
90. Another children's book about a child character who learns about the ethical treatment of others within a form of miniaturization is Selma Lagerlöf's *The Wonderful Adventure of Nils* (1906/1907). In *Nils* (published in two volumes in Swedish and typically in one volume in English translations), the hard-hearted and lazy Nils is transformed into a *tomte* (a kind of elf figure) by a tomte he has wronged. All of the animals he has tormented when a human turn against the tiny Nils and he escapes his parents' farm on the back of the domestic goose who seeks adventure. Nils, the goose and the flock of wild geese traverse all of Sweden. Nils (and the child readers) visits every region in Sweden and learns good manners, compassion for animals and respect for nature along the way.

91. Place, *The Last Giants*, 48.
92. For the critic Marina Warner, King Kong is a giant within the tradition of cannibalistic fairy tale ogres: "[The 1933 film *King Kong*] introduces Kong at the beginning as a giant of hugely exaggerated size, the ravenous monarch of a terrifying, distant, enclosed kingdom (Skull Island), who requires a tribute of young bodies, preferably female." Marina Warner, "Fee fi fo fum: The Child in the Jaws of the Story", in *Cannibalism and the Colonial World*, eds Francis Barker, Peter Hulme and Margaret Iverson (Cambridge: Cambridge University Press [1998]), 158–182, 167.
93. In this chapter I have by no means exhausted the bibliography of pygmy stories or pygmy characters in western children's literature and popular culture. Other examples include *Toro of the Little People* by Leo Walmsley (1925), Reba Paeff Mirsky's *Thirty-One Brothers and Sisters* (1952), Willard Price's *Elephant Adventure* (1964), the Ewoks in George Lucas's film *The Return of the Jedi* (1983), and Lesley Beake's *Song of Be* (1993). (Paul Landau mentions this connection between Ewoks and African pygmies in his essay "Empires of the Visual," 150). *Toro* is a somewhat unusual boys' adventure tale featuring pygmies from the Mountains of the Moon that subscribes to many of the conventions of the idea of the pygmy (they are described as "pixie-like," "devilish," and self-interested), but the hero is clever and brave and there are no white characters in the book at all and thus no comparisons are made between "civilized" whites and "savage" natives (although the book is entirely about warfare between different pygmy bands and other African peoples). *Elephant Adventure* credits the pygmies (also from the Mountains of the Moon) and the "Watussis" with courage, but relies upon hackneyed plot elements. Two white teenage boys on safari in Africa solve mysteries, uncover and defeat a band of Arab slave-traders and capture a rare white elephant; they get results that the pygmies and other indigenes cannot manage on their own because they are superstitious, gullible, and passive as contrasted with the boys' pluck, ingenuity, and keen intelligence. A note on the publication page informs readers that "the characters in this story are fictional. The descriptions of the habits of animals and customs of the people are factual." Many children's books, such as Reba Paeff Mirsky's *Thirty-One Brothers and Sisters*, create a hierarchy according to size; Mirsky contrasts the Zulu characters with the pygmies, describing the latter as animal-like: they "swarm like black ants" (156), "scamper" like monkeys (169) and are merry and playful (159). Beake's *Song of Be* is a first-person narrative of a teenage Bushman girl, Be, living in southwest Africa in the days prior to the establishment of an independent Namibia (formed in 1990). The book is a long suicide note for traditional Africa: the novel opens with the startling line, " 'I have just killed myself' " (3), as Be has stabbed her leg with a poison-tipped arrow and is waiting to die. Be's narrative, as she lies dying (so she believes) is the story of her life and the tragedies of southwestern postcolonial Africa. Maddy and MacCann comment that the Bushmen in Beake's novel "are like walking corpses, a people for whom place, time, wealth, security, and even life itself hold no purpose" (38). See Chapter 4 of *African Images in Juvenile Literature*, "Traditional African Cultures in Juvenile Novels: Dysfunctional or Evolutionary?" (27–44). They also contend that the hope expressed at the conclusion of the novel is misleading as it suggests that the Bushmen had lost their way and identity before Namibian independence in 1990. In fact, Maddy and MacCann argue, "the quaint description of contemporary Africans as hunter/gatherers says more about the critic than the West African" (41).
94. Qtd. in Bob Dixon, *Catching Them Young*, 112.
95. Roald Dahl, *Charlie and the Chocolate Factory* (1964. New York: Alfred A. Knopf, 1973), 83. Notably, Hamida Bosmajian calls this transformation turning the Oompa-Loompas into "little Tarzans." See "*Charlie and the Chocolate Factory* and Other Excremental Visions." *The Lion and the Unicorn* 9 (1985): 36–49, 46.
96. Christopher Lofting. Afterword. *The Story of Doctor Dolittle*. Centenary Edition (Delacorte Press, 1988), 152. Anne Collett, in " 'Sharing a 'Common Destiny': Censorship, Imperialism and the Stories of Doctor Dolittle" considers the alterations to the texts to be a "superficial censoring [that] may have no real effect or may even

prove counter-productive" (84), in part because the complexity and contradictory nature of Lofting's mockery of British values and imperialism resists easy categorization as simply racist (*New Literature Review* 33 [1997]: 81–93, 84).

97. Patricia and Fredrick McKissack, Foreword. *The Story of Doctor Dolittle*. Illustrated by Michael Hague (New York: William Morrow and Company, 1997), xi–xiv.
98. Anne Collett, "Sharing a Common Destiny," 81.
99. Qtd. in the appendix to Bradford and Blume, *Ota: The Pygmy in the Zoo*, 275.
100. Ibid., 276.
101. Leela Gandhi, *Postcolonial Theory: A Critical Introduction* (New York: Columbia University Press, 1998), 7–8.
102. Isabel Allende describes the Pygmies of equatorial Africa as "human figures as small as children . . . the tallest no more than four and a half feet tall. They had yellowish brown skin, nappy hair, wide-set eyes, short legs, long trunks and arms, and flattened noses." They are also described in animal terms: "feet pointed out like ducks" and "jabbering." *Forest of the Pygmies*. Trans. Margaret Sayers Peden. (New York: HarperCollins Publishers, 2005), 106, 109.
103. Ibid., 126.
104. For example, "Alexander stopped [the pygmies]. They couldn't go quite yet, he told them. He explained that they wouldn't be safe, even in the deepest heart of the jungle where no other human could survive. . . . They had to deliver the blow to slavery and to reestablish friendly relations they once had with the people of Ngoubé, which meant that they had to rob Mbembelé of his power and chase him and his soldiers from the region forever" (Allende, *Forest of the Pygmies*, 280).
105. Lynne Reid Banks, *The Indian in the Cupboard* (1980. New York: Avon Books, 1982), 5.
106. The book was originally published in the UK and the Indian's name was "Little Bull." Perhaps he was renamed for an American audience in order not to offend the sensibilities of white Americans for whom the Native American name "Bull" connotes embarrassing loss. Sitting Bull, the Sioux leader, defeated General George Armstrong Custer and the American army at the Battle of Little Bighorn in 1876.
107. Meena Khorana describes this series of thirteen books for boys as "reminiscent of Tarzan's adventures in West Africa" (*Africa in Literature for Children and Young Adults*, ed. Meena Khorana. Westport, CT: Greenwood Press, 1994), 190. The fourteen-year-old protagonist survives numerous exciting and dangerous situations "because of his superior intelligence, strength, and courage. Even though he is only fourteen, Bomba single-handedly gains leadership of an entire tribe of Pygmies and selflessly provides for them" (190).
108. In the film version of *The Indian in the Cupboard*, the setting is inexplicably transformed from London to New York City. There are two significant "Indian" characters in the film: Little Bear and Patrick, Omri's best friend, whose heritage is South Asian. Most significantly, in a dream-sequence (not found in the novel) that takes place just before Little Bear returns home, he and Omri meet in Little Bear's original setting—the forest—in their correct sizes. But not really: Little Bear's height is exaggerated—he is impossibly tall and elongated (both mimicking the primeval trees surrounding the two figures and emphasizing his lofty wisdom). Little Bear's wise speechifying reverses the emotional and ethical superiority that Omri exhibits in the novel and restores the "natural" hierarchy between man and boy, Noble Savage and culturally impoverished white.
109. Lois Kuznets discusses this plot device in her 1994 study *When Toys Come Alive: Narratives of Animation, Metamorphosis, and Development*. Other books in this tradition include Pauline Clarke's *The Return of the Twelves*, the Raggedy Ann and Andy series by Johnny Gruelle (beginning with *Raggedy Ann Stories*, 1918), *Hitty: Her First Hundred Years* (by Rachel Field, 1929), *The Memoirs of a London Doll* (by Mrs. Fairstar [Richard Horne], 1846), and Russell Hoban's *The Mouse and His Child* (1967), among many other examples.
110. Banks, *The Indian in the Cupboard*, 11. See also Roderick McGillis's discussion of a similar point in " 'And the Celt Knew the Indian': Knowingness, Postcolonialism,

Children's Literature" (*Voices of the Other: Children's Literature and the Postcolonial Context*. Ed. Roderick McGillis. New York: Garland Publishing [1999]: 223–235).

Summarizing Nancy Schmidt's position, Meena Khorana argues that the prevalence of folktales in available African children's literature does not necessarily achieve the aims of promoting African children's literature within world literature more generally, as "African folklore for Euro-American children is merely a vehicle for artist-authors to make drawings, while the folktales are generally stylized plot summaries" (Khorana, *Africa in Literature for Children and Young Adults*, xli).

111. Dan Hade, "Reading Children's Literature Multiculturally." (*Reflections of Change: Children's Literature Since 1945*, ed. Sandra Beckett (Westport, CT: Greenwood Press, 1997), 116–122, 118.

112. Banks, *The Indian in the Cupboard*, 59.

113. Pauline Clarke, *The Return of the Twelves* (1962. New York: Coward, McCann & Geoghegan, Inc., 1963), 222.

114. Ibid., 102.

115. J. J. Bone's (rather unfortunately titled) book, *Going Native* (1989), is a non-fiction account of a maturation process instigated by exposure to "miniatures" that reminds us of Omri's journey to young adulthood. As a romantic and ignorant nineteen-year-old, Bone left Pennsylvania to live with Mbuti pygmies for two years. His diary/memoir reveals so much immaturity, unconscious racism, naïveté and earnestness to learn about the world and himself that it almost feels unfair to quote him: "I had felt for too, too long inhibited by my culture and raped of my identity. White represented sterility and in blackness was the vitality and unrefinedness of black bread. I could not go on with my life until I had breathed, eaten, hunted, danced and slept with the pygmies. . . . I was intuitively certain that a dose of this was just what I needed. Then I could continue with my life" (New Hope, PA: The Pygmy Press 1989), xxii. Most significantly, as we have seen, a degree of this kind of exploitation of the pygmies for their small size, blackness, exoticism, and their presumed abilities to help the white youth become "more white" or to grow in maturity, pervades literature for children.

116. Banks, *The Indian in the Cupboard*, 151.

117. Ibid., 153. Kuznets also makes this point (*When Toys Come Alive*, 90–91).

118. As Little Bear pressures Omri to produce a wife for him, he tells Omri that in the Iroquois tradition, a man's mother will choose his wife: "But Little Bear mother not here. Omri be mother and find" (Banks, *The Indian in the Cupboard*, 83).

119. Ibid., 176–177.

120. Kuznets comments that "some of [*Indian's*] attraction obviously comes from the dangerous subversion of parental roles implicit in these role reversals—reversals already present in having adult soldiers at a child's command" (*When Toys Come Alive*, 91).

121. Omri is disappointed with Patrick's cast-off present of the plastic Indian because neither can think of how to play with him in his uniqueness: Omri comments, " 'I haven't got any cowboys either.' 'Nor have I' [Patrick responds]. 'That's why I couldn't play anything with him' " (Banks, *The Indian in the Cupboard*, 2).

122. Steven J. Gores, "The Miniature as Reduction and Talisman in Fielding's *Amelia*." *Studies in English Literature* 37 (1997): 573–593, 592, n.12. Certainly, any miniaturization, encapsulation, minimization of a culture or race, is necessarily problematic. See McGillis, " 'And the Celt Knew the Indian' " for a useful discussion of another recent award-winning "multicultural" children's book, Welwyn Wilton Katz's *False Face* (1987), that mishandles the presentation of Iroquois culture (227–233).

123. One exception to the accuracy of Little Bear's dress is the chief's headdress that Little Bear takes from the dead Indian. Iroquois men wore feathered hats that can be easily distinguished from the Plains Indian-style war bonnets such as the one Little Bear removes from the dead Indian.

124. As mentioned above, the book was adapted for the large screen in 1995 and found a ready audience of children and adults. Some critics feel that the movie, due to

casting decisions and research, repaired some of the damage caused by the book, while others reject the movie as well. For the former view, see Victoria E. Sanchez and Mary E. Stuckey ("Coming of Age as a Culture? Emancipatory and Hegemonic Readings of *The Indian in the Cupboard*." *Western Journal of Communications* 64. 1 [Winter 2000]: 78–91); for the latter view, see Rhonda Taylor ("*Indian in the Cupboard*: a case study in perspective." *Qualitative Studies in Education* 13.4 (2000): 371–384).

125. Taylor, "*Indian in the Cupboard*," 379.

126. See Taylor ("*Indian in the Cupboard*") and Jim Charles ("Out of the Cupboard and Into the Classroom: Children and the American Indian Literary Experience." *Children's Literature in Education* 27.3 [1996]: 167–179), for example. I am in complete agreement that the descriptions of Little Bear's speech—especially the overuse of "grunting" and "growling"—are unfortunate and serve to mark Little Bear as a "Hollywood" Indian. Certainly, these unselfconscious repetitions of dominant culture stereotypes are shelf-worn, and damaging to Natives as well as whites.

127. Taylor, "*Indian in the Cupboard*," 374.

128. Some of Taylor's discomfort seems to stem from the fact that Little Bear is a miniature person (again, Boone is ignored). Although I do not think that Little Bear's size in relation to Omri diminishes him as a person in any way (while it does necessarily make him dependent upon Omri for survival), Taylor implies that his tiny stature is a kind of demeaning insult: "How charming would the plot appear if the miniature character was African American, or a blonde, 17th-century woman?" ("*Indian in the Cupboard*," 381).

129. Kuznets argues that Little Bear is "more stereotyped" than is Boone (*When Toys Come Alive*, 91), yet I would counter that the depiction of Boone, although against the Hollywood image of the cowboy, is similarly reductive.

130. This war was called the French and Indian War (1754–1763) in North America, and the Seven Years War in England. For a brief introduction to the pivotal role the Iroquois played in shaping the political organization of the United States, see Bruce E. Johansen, *Shapers of the Great Debate on Native Americans: Land, Spirit, and Power* (Westport, CT: Greenwood Press, 2000), 25–51.
Banks rather anachronistically and sentimentally implies that the white man created the antagonism between the Iroquois and the Algonquin. This is untrue. The six tribes that made up the Iroquois federation had guns from the early 1600s on (received from Dutch traders) and they extended their territory (by suppressing their Indian enemies) beyond upstate New York to include most of the northeastern United States, as well as eastern Canada (See Robert E. Powless. "Iroquois Indians," Discovery Channel School. June 28, 2001. http://www.discoveryschool. com/homeworkhelp/worldbook/atozgeography/i/281880.html).

131. Interestingly, the folklore of the Iroquois nations is replete with stories of miniatures. See *The Deetkatoo: Native American stories About Little People*. Ed. John Bierhorst(New York: William Morrow and Co., 1998). My thanks to Ann Sullivan for providing this reference.

132. Taylor, "*Indian in the Cupboard*," 377.

133. Banks, *The Indian in the Cupboard*, 178.

134. Stewart, *On Longing*, 60.

135. Gary Morris, "The Incredible Shrinking . . . and Expanding Ethnic Minority, Or, the Racist in the Cupboard." *Bright Lights Film Online* 15 (November 1995). http://brightlightsfilm.com/15/racist.php#.UxdSafRdVCw.

136. As I discuss later in the chapter, Man rejects the discourse and behaviors of "whiteface minstrelsy" and refuses to perform for John or to be objectified. A nineteenth-century American entertainment derived from vaudeville and blackface minstrelsy, whiteface minstrelsy showcased the whiteface type—the caricatured Stage Irishman: "hirsute, muscular laborer, with cheek whiskers, a broad lip, a button nose, and prognathous jaws" (Byrne, "The Genesis of Whiteface," 139)—in order to associate the Irish immigrant with the figure of the "darkie." See

James P. Byrne, "The Genesis of Whiteface in Nineteenth-Century American Popular Culture." MELUS 29. ¾ (Fall–Winter 2004): 133–149. This description (except for the "prognathous jaws") appears to fit Man very well.

In the wake of the famines of the 1840s and debates over Home Rule later in the century, the Irish were simianized and compared with Africans in political cartoons, editorials, advertisements, and caricatures. This transformation of the Irish "Paddy" into a racialized and demonized figure has been well documented. (See, for example, L. Perry Curtis, Jr., *Apes and Angels: The Irishman in Victorian Caricature* (Newton Abbot: David and Charles, 1971); H. A. MacDougall, *Racial Myth in English History* (Montreal: Hannover, 1978); P. B. Rich, *Race and Empire in British Politics* (Cambridge: Cambridge University Press, 1986); Noel Ignatiev, *How the Irish Became White* (New York: Routledge, 1995). Man's racial background is unknown—and that is part of the point of the book—yet I believe that a Celtic, or even Pictish, origin is hinted at, as a Celtic background (Irish, in particular) was the basis for nineteenth-century racial- and class-based stereotypes held by many English: "The distinction between Celtic and Anglo-Saxon 'races' in the British Isles is one of long-standing, but from the mid-nineteenth century onward the British image of the Irish was recast in biological racial terms" (Jan Nederveen Pieterse, *White on Black: Images of Africa and Blacks in Western Popular Culture*. New Haven and London: Yale University Press, 1992), 213. The savage little Picts in John Buchan's "No-Man's-Land" (1902) are clearly racialized miniature figures and a form of Scots "pygmy"; they are described as "little and squat and dark; naked, apparently, but so rough with hair that it wore the appearance of a skin-covered being . . ." (qtd. in Silver, *Strange and Secret Peoples*, 145).

A personal example illustrates the racialized nature of both the Scots and English, at least according to one Scot: one day when working in London in the summer of 2001, I was interested and surprised when my chance breakfast companion, a middle-aged, middle-class Scotswoman who had come down to London for a theater holiday, disdainfully referred to the English as "the white invaders."

137. Most of the illustrations are from John's perspective, from "normal" human scale, looking down at Man. However, on Thursday (each section of the book is titled with the day of the week as people such as Man are not supposed to stay longer than three days with any large person), the illustrations are all from Man's perspective. The reader is graphically introduced to the difficulties and limitations of Man's existence as well as to his cleverness and ingenuity.

138. In fact, in *The Borrowers*, it is the Boy, not the thoroughly middle-class English Borrowers, who is racialized and exoticized. He is "Indian"—"brought up among mystery and magic and legend" (Norton, *The Borrowers*, 7). Homily, however, is once described in decidedly racial terms as a "washed-out golliwog" (ibid., 121).

139. Raymond Briggs, *The Man* (1992. London: Red Fox Books [Random House UK], 1994). *The Man* is unpaged. All quotations cited in the text are from this edition.

140. Kuznets, *When Toys Come Alive*, 94.

141. This identification with the young, or the small, may be read politically, as Susan Hancock notes about *Mistress Masham's Repose*: "[White's] novel] suggest[s] that in this immediate post-war era there is a crisis of belief in the power of adults from the 'real' world to respond ethically to the challenges of coexisting in the aftermath of the evils of what Hobsbawm terms an 'age of catastrophe' " (*The Child That Haunts Us: Symbols and Images in Fairy, Tale and Miniature Literature*. London and New York: Routledge [2009], 118).

142. Man's independence can be contrasted with another set of small people in a popular children's series: J. K. Rowling's enslaved house-elves of Hogwarts School, described in most detail in J. K. Rowling's "House-Elf Liberation Front" chapter of *Harry Potter and the Goblet of Fire* (2000). The smooth running of the Hogwarts and much of the wizardly world, we learn, is dependent on the largely unseen labor of the house elf system.

143. Pieterse, *White on Black*, 223.

Part II Introduction: The Monstrous Giant

1. Wes Williams opens his discussion of early modern monsters by asserting the connection between monstrosity and giganticism: "To call something 'monstrueux' in the mid-sixteenth century, is more often than not, to wonder at its enormous size" (*Monsters and their Meanings in Early Modern Culture: Mighty Magic*. Oxford: Oxford University Press, 2011), 1. Similarly, Marina Warner, in historicizing ogres and giants comments, "Size is of the essence, of course. . . ." (*No Go the Bogeyman: Scaring, Lulling, and Making Mock*. New York: Farrar, Straus and Giroux, 1998, 96.)

2. David D. Gilmore, *Monsters: Evil Beings, Mythical Beasts, and All Manner of Imaginary Terrors* (Philadelphia: University of Pennsylvania Press, 2003), 19.

3. Gilmore notes that in the Medieval Latin work *Liber Monstrorum* (written by many authors between the mid-ninth and early eleventh centuries CE), giganticism itself was evidence of evil: "Giganticism is itself regarded in the texts as a form of sinfulness: a challenge to the immensity of God, a double-sided metaphor implying hubris as well as power" (*Monsters*, 54).

4. Gilmore, *Monsters*, 175.

5. Warner, *No Go the Bogeyman*, 145.

6. Mary Shelley, *Frankenstein: Or, The Modern Prometheus* (1818. London: Henry Colburn and Richard Bentley, 1831), 124.

7. Ibid., 124. See Roald Dahl's *The BFG* (1982. Puffin Books, 1997) and Patrick Ness, *A Monster Calls* (Somerville, MA: Candlewick Press, 2011).

8. Quoted in Gilmore, *Monsters*, 175.

9. Rosemarie Garland Thomson, *Extraordinary Bodies: Figuring Physical Disability in American Culture and Literature* (New York: Columbia University Press, 1997), 4.

10. Susan Stewart, *On Longing*, 110.

11. Thomas Fuller, *The Worthies of England*. Ed. John Freeman (1662. London: George Allen and Unwin, 1952), 401.

12. Edmund Burke, *A Philosophical Enquiry in the Origin of our Ideas of the Sublime and Beautiful*, ed. J. T. Boulton (London: Routledge and Kegan Paul and New York: Columbia University Press, 1958), 113.

13. *History of Jack and the Giants*, facsimile page 14.

14. The novel was adapted for film in 1998, titled *The Mighty* and directed by Peter Chelsom.

15. Another children's novel that combines big with little to the benefit of both is Pamela Todd's *Pig and the Shrink* (New York: Delacorte Press, 1999). Tucker Harrison is a smaller-than-average seventh grader in search of a science fair project. He finds one in his classmate, obese Angelo Pighetti, called "Pig." Tucker's science fair project—enforcing and then tracking Pig's weight-loss efforts—is a failure, but the boys' friendship helps Tucker to learn "that people have a right to decide for themselves who they are and what they want to be" (181).

16. Ted Hughes, *The Iron Woman* (London: Faber and Faber, 1993); Melvin Burgess, *The Earth Giant*. (1995. New York: PaperStar, 1999).

17. The brain-child of George Hull of Binghamton, NY and H. B. Martin of Marshalltown, Iowa, the Cardiff Giant was carved in 1868 from a five-ton block of gypsum. The 10-foot-tall human figure was buried near Cardiff, NY and dug up in 1869 by well-diggers. The remains were touted as the petrified corpse of prehistoric man. After the Giant had achieved a great deal of notoriety, in the early 1900s Othniel C. Marsh of Yale University uncovered the hoax.

18. Hagrid is himself half-giant and the sad history of that disparaged race is one sub-theme in J. K. Rowling's fourth Harry Potter book, *Harry Potter and the Goblet of Fire* (2000).

19. MacDonald was inspired by a Norwegian folktale in writing "The Giant's Heart." He later incorporated the tale in his novel *Adela Cathcart* (1864).

20. C. S. Lewis, *The Lion, the Witch and the Wardrobe* (New York: Collier Books, 1950), 64.

21. Wilde, "The Selfish Giant." *Complete Shorter Fiction of Oscar Wilde*. Ed. Isobel Murray (Oxford: Oxford University Press, [1979]), 110–114, 114. Even kindly giants are dangerous. To mention just one example among many, Arnold Lobel's picture book *Giant John* (1964) features a sweet giant who loves to dance to his neighborhood fairies' magic music. John is also dutiful and he leaves his mother and his home in the enchanted forest to find a job because there are only two potato chips left in the cupboard. John easily makes friends with a royal family and its pet looking for a handyman about their castle. But the fairies find him, make him dance to their magic music, and John unwittingly destroys the castle and injures the dog. John repairs the castle, after a fashion, and the gently humorous story ends happily, but the threat inherent in his large size remains.

22. See H. J. Massingham, *Fee, Fi, Fo, Fum or The Giants in England* (London: Kegan, Paul, Trench, Trubner and Co., 1926).

23. A number of books for children about the golem have been published. See Amy Sonheim's, "Picture Books about the Golem: Acts of Creation Without and Within." *The Lion and the Unicorn* 27 (2003): 377–393. A notable addition to Golem literature is David Almond's *Clay* in which two boys create and bring to life an enormous man made out of earth and consecrated host and wine (London: Hodder Children's Books, 2005).

24. Stewart, *On Longing*, 74.

25. The film was remade into a 1993 television movie directed by Christopher Guest.

26. Dahl, *The BFG*, 25. The novel was adapted into a film in 2016 and directed by Steven Spielberg.

27. Ibid., 12.

28. The film version of *The Iron Giant*, in which the giant—who has a highly developed self-protection weaponry system—sacrifices himself to save Hogarth, his family, and all of New England, from the nuclear bomb, is highly reminiscent of Marge Piercy's 1991 novel for adults, *He, She, and It*. In this novel set in a post-nuclear-holocaust world, Yod, a cyborg who has been created as a protector of the remaining Jewish community, ultimately rejects his designation as a destructive force and willfully destroys himself, his creator and the laboratory that was his "birthplace." In his suicide "note"—a simulation of him speaking, viewed on a computer monitor—Yod informs his human lover, " 'I want there to be no more weapons like me. A weapon should not be conscious. A weapon should not have the capacity to suffer for what it does, to regret, to feel guilt. . . . I don't understand why anyone would want to be a soldier, a weapon, but at least people sometimes have a choice to obey or refuse. I have none' " (New York: Fawcett Crest, 1991, 415). See Lois Kuznet's acute discussion of *He, She, and It* in *When Toys Come Alive* (New Haven: Yale University Press, 1994), 197–203.

29. Many vegans have a saying, "Don't eat anything with a face," which encapsulates their ethical response to animals as food.

30. It may appear that by discussing boys and big robots alongside big girls and body image, I am reinforcing a gender binary that elevates the "perfected" male robot body over the "disfigured" obese female body. This is certainly not my intention: this study aims to analyze and understand the myths and realities that surround big bodies that are necessarily gendered. While certainly this seeming separation of the female from technology or the male from body politics is problematic, representations of the giant robot's and obese girl's extraordinary bodies can be historicized and analyzed, in my opinion, without perpetuating the gender binaries of the twentieth century—and present moment—we find when male and female, as well as big and small, are essentialized.

31. Burke, *The Sublime and Beautiful*, 157.

Chapter 5: Gigantic Mechanical Boy Scouts

1. As Sianne Ngai argues, ". . . the cute is an aesthetic of the small, the vulnerable, and the deformed . . ." (*Our Aesthetic Categories: Zany, Cute, Interesting*. Cambridge, MA and London: Harvard University Press, 2012), 97.

2. While my use of the "future perfect" is particularly tied to the figure of the robot, my discussion of the term has been informed and guided by the work of Robert Rydell in *World of Fairs: The Century-of-Progress Expositions* (Chicago and London: University of Chicago Press, 1993). For example, writing about both the Chicago and the New York fairs, Rydell comments, "The century-of-progress expositions were calculated responses to [the crises of the Great Depression and American disaffection] and presented Americans with blueprints for modernizing the United States— plans that, in the eyes of exposition organizers, would lead the nation out of the depression and place it on the road to future perfection" (213). An optimistic work that links the idea of the future perfect to science and technological advances—in this case in the digital age—is Steven Johnson's *Future Perfect: The Case for Progress in a Networked Age* (New York: Riverhead Hardcover, 2012).

3. In grammar, too, the future perfect simple is the tense in which actions will be completed at some future time, suggesting a faith in the possibility of completion.

4. The new story of childhood was linked to the ideal of play as much as it was to the problematic of work. Karen Sánchez-Eppler discusses play and work in terms of the relationship between depictions of working- and middle-class children of late nineteenth- and early twentieth-century America and argues that this relationship was not one-sided. That is, the poor child helped to formulate childhood's parameters for the middle-class child: "By the end of the century, play, and the worlds of the imagination, would become cultural markers for what was marvelous about childhood, and this culturally valuable play would be recognized as an attribute of middle-class affluence and leisure. Yet . . . it is through depictions of working-class children that these middle-class ideals are first and most forcefully articulated" (*Dependent States: The Child's Part in Nineteenth Century American Culture*, Chicago: University of Chicago Press, 2005), 154.

5. See Hugh Cunningham, *The Children of the Poor: Representations of Childhood Since the Seventeenth Century*. Oxford: Blackwell, (1991), 8–17.

6. Ibid., 8.

7. For an excellent overview of the wide variety of juvenile labor in the working classes and the debates surrounding child labor in the nineteenth century by politicians, journalists, industrialists, etc., see *The Victorian Town Child* by Pamela Horn (New York: New York University Press, 1997), especially 99–126 and Appendix 1, 211–212. See also the early, but comprehensive, critical history of the nineteenth-century Factory System and legislative response: R. W. Cooke-Taylor, *The Factory System and the Factory Acts* (London: Methuen and Co., 1894).

8. Qtd. in Cunningham, *Children of the Poor*, 67.

9. Anthony Ashley Cooper, "Infant Labour." *Quarterly Review* 67 (1840–41), December 1840: 171–81, 174.

10. Vicki Goldberg, *Lewis W. Hine: Children at Work* (Munich, London and New York: Prestel, 1999), 16.

11. Kate Sampsell-Willmann, *Lewis Hine as Social Critic* (Jackson: University Press of Mississippi, 2009), 77.

12. Goldberg, *Lewis W. Hine: Children at Work*, 17.

13. In reading the letters that newsboys and other street children assisted by the New York City Children's Aid Society wrote about their experiences, Sánchez-Eppler similarly recognizes the mediated nature of such sources. She argues that these expressions of children's voices both challenge and affirm the notions about childhood held by reformers and other adults: "The understandings of childhood work and play voiced by these children overlap with and diverge from the representations offered by philanthropists and novelists" (*Dependent States*, 167).

14. In addition to Cunningham, for an historical overview of the new story of childhood in Europe, see, for example, Colin Heywood, *A History of Childhood: Children and Childhood in the West from Medieval to Modern Times* (Polity Press, 2001). For a particularly American focus on the same topic, see Kriste Lindenmeyer, *A Right to Childhood: The U.S. Children's Bureau and Child Welfare, 1912–1946* (Champaign, IL:

University of Illinois Press, 1997); James Marten, *Childhood and Child Welfare in the Progressive Era: A Brief History with Documents* (Boston and New York: Bedford/St. Martin's, 2004); Steven Mintz, *Huck's Raft: A History of American Childhood* (Cambridge, MA: Belknap Press, 2004); and Viviana Zelizer, *Pricing the Priceless Child: The Changing Social Value of Children.* New York: Basic Books, 1985).

15. Robert Baden-Powell, *Young Knights of the Empire: Their Code and Further Scout Yarns* (Philadelphia: J. B. Lippincott Company, 1917), 163.
16. Baden-Powell, *Young Knights of the Empire*, 164.
17. Ibid., 13.
18. Ibid.
19. See Joseph Bristow, *Empire Boys: Adventures in a Man's World* (London: HarperCollins Academic, 1991). Bristow writes, "Scouting invited its members to live out a narrative in which the ideal protagonists were the trappers, hunters, and frontiersmen popularized in history textbooks and, more significantly, in the boys' weeklies that had been on the ascendant since the 1860s. In the popular representations of history to be found in these publications, the past unfolded as an adventure that began with the Crusades and led right up to the Victorians' exploits in all corners of the empire, including Baden-Powell's famous deeds in South Africa" (174).
20. Robert W. Rydell, *World of Fairs*, 93. Rydell's allusion to the "fan dance" is a reference to Sally Rand's very popular fan dance of the 1930s fairs.
21. Robert W. Rydell, "Making America (More) Modern: America's Depression-Era World's Fairs" in *Designing Tomorrow: America's World's Fairs of the 1930s*, eds. Robert W. Rydell and Laura Burd Schiavo (New Haven and London: Yale University Press, 2010:1–21), 1–2.
22. The term "salesman-scientists" is Rydell's. In *World of Fairs*, Rydell describes the link between the fairs and the NRC. The fair organizers turned to the NRC for assistance in planning due to its respected and long-standing position as "the primary agency for promoting cooperation among science, industry, and the military" (*World of Fairs*, 93). See chapter four, "The Empire of Science" in Rydell, *World of Fairs*, for an excellent overview of the history and importance of science to the 1930s world's fairs (92–114). See also John E. Findling, *Chicago's Great World's Fairs* (Manchester and New York: Manchester University Press, 1994).
23. Rydell explains further: "'The precise meaning of the cluster of ideas that formed the exposition's core science philosophy emerged in a letter Pupin sent to exposition trustees, in which he declared: 'American science and American industries welded to each other by scientific idealism are the most powerful arm of our national defense.' And national defense, in the aftermath of the stock market crash, meant shoring up public confidence in the future of the corporate state as much as protecting the state from external threat. Little wonder that scientists with corporate interests at heart took up the cause of the fair with the same zeal that exposition sponsors showed for science" (*World of Fairs*, 97).
24. Qtd. in John E. Findling, *Chicago's Great World's Fairs*, 93.
25. Rydell, *World of Fairs*, 99.
26. Designed by architect Paul Philippe Cret, the central theme exhibition hall became the most recognizable building of the 1933–34 Fair. The building was punctuated by a 53-meter-tall tower at the southwest corner. The likeness of the Hall of Science was reproduced on many different products sold at the fair, among them a version of the Brownie Special No. 2 camera which included a decorative front panel of the Hall of Science.
27. Jewett E. Ricker, ed. *Sculpture at a Century of Progress: Chicago, 1933, 1934* (Madison: University of Wisconsin, 1934).
28. Ricker, *Sculpture at a Century of Progress*, 8.
29. Igor Aleksander and Piers Burnett, *Reinventing Man: The Robot Becomes Reality* (London: Kogan Page, 1983), 10–11.
30. The word "robot," coined by the Czech playwright's painter brother Joseph but popularized in the play, is a combination of "robota" (drudgery or servitude, labor) and

"robotnik" (peasant or worker). The play premiered in Prague in 1921 and was first performed in New York in 1922 and translated into English in 1923.

31. See Harold B. Segal for this point, one that is taken up by many authors who consider the relationship between man and robot in literature (Segal, *Pinocchio's Progeny: Puppets, Marionettes, Automatons, and Robots in Modernist and Avant-Garde Drama.* Baltimore: Johns Hopkins University Press, 1995), 311. Lisa Zunshine's provocative book about how ideas from cognitive science can help us to interpret literary characters and to tease out our responses to fiction and functions in everyday life, takes up in some detail the cognitive underpinnings of the "Frankenstein complex." From Isaac Asimov, the fear of rebellious robots, Zunshine argues, has its roots in the story of Adam and Eve and remains a "perennially interesting" fictional motif (*Strange Concepts and the Stories They Make Possible: Cognition, Culture, Narrative* [Baltimore: Johns Hopkins University Press, 2008], 51–52). See part two of *Strange Concepts and the Stories They Make Possible*, 51–131.

Harry Bates's classic science fiction short story, "Farewell to the Master" (1940) offers a particularly subtle and interesting reading of the human/robot relationship in the context of "first contact" (between humans and aliens). In the story, the finesse and detail of the gigantic robot Gnut's enormous body fascinates humankind: "Hinged robots of crude manlike appearance were familiar enough, but never Earthling eyes lain on one like this. For Gnut had almost exactly the shape of a man—a giant, but a man—with greenish metal for man's covering flesh, and greenish metal for man's bulging muscles. Except for a loin cloth, he was nude. He stood like the powerful god of the machine of some undreamt-of scientific civilization and on his face a look of sullen, brooding thought" (Bates, "Farewell to the Master," 1940. Rpt. New Mexico: Sterling Publications, 2012), 2. The crux of the story's argument lies in its surprise ending when readers learn that it is Gnut and not the beautiful slain ambassador Klaatu—whom Gnut has been trying to reanimate from a recording of his voice—who is the mastermind behind their visit to Earth. The story concludes thus, " 'You misunderstand,' the mighty robot had said, '*I* am the master' " (62).

32. Rydell, *World of Fairs*, 103. The 1936 Texas Centennial Exposition took the issue of the relationship between man and machine head on. The Department of Labor constructed an exhibit in which a talking robot greeted visitors and informed them that while machines (for which he stood as a representative) had replaced people in some kinds of work, " '. . . I am and can be a real benefactor to mankind. In almost every case where I appeared in industry, I actually created more jobs and provided more employment for men and women. . . .' " (qtd. in Rydell, *World of Fairs*, 151).

The 1939 New York World's Fair only intensified the focus on a utopian future aided by science and industry. Popular pavilions included "Futurama," located inside the General Motors building. Electro, the seven-foot-tall giant robot, was produced by Westinghouse. The robot could perform twenty-six different movements and respond to spoken commands. The July 1939 issue of the *Meccano Magazine* introduced its readers to the features and some of the science that went into building Electro (called "Elektro" in the piece). It began, "After two years of life as a sheaf of blueprints and scattered pieces of metal in the laboratory of the Westinghouse Electric Company at Mansfield, Ohio, 'Elektro' is ready to go places and do things" ("A Robot that Walks, Talks and Smokes,") 342. See also Jasia Reichardt, *Robots: Fact, Fiction and Prediction* (London: Thames and Hudson, 1978), 74.

33. "Building the world of tomorrow" was the slogan of the 1939 New York World's Fair. For a detailed analysis of the role of the child within the culture of science, see Rebecca Onion's dissertation, "How Science Became Child's Play: Science and the Culture of American Childhood, 1900–1980" (2012). See Kenneth D. Brown, *Factory of Dreams: A History of Meccano Ltd, 1901–1979* (Lancaster: Crucible Books, 2007) for a comprehensive and lavishly illustrated history of Meccano. See also *Meccano* by Roger Marriott (Oxford, Shire Publications, 2012).

34. Qtd. in Brown, *Factory of Dreams*, 2.

35. Roger Marriott makes this point about the link between the "Meccano boy" and the Boy Scout, explicitly (22). The April 1923 editorial of the *Meccano Magazine* drew clear parallels for its boy readers between success in business and the Meccano project for boys: "Enjoyment, enthusiasm and keenness are the keywords to success in everything, but most of all in business" (reprinted in Joseph Manduca, *The Meccano Magazine, 1916–1981*. London: New Cavendish Books, 1987), 135.

36. Qtd. in Brown, *Factory of Dreams*, 52. Brown acknowledges Hornby's charitable interests in child welfare, as well (53).

37. See *The Meccano Magazine, 1916–1981*.

38. Brown, *Factory of Dreams*, 71–72.

39. "How To Run a Meccano Club" (Liverpool: Meccano Ltd., 1949), unpaged.

40. Brown, *Factory of Dreams*, 75.

41. Marriott, *Meccano*, 22.

42. "How To Run a Meccano Club," 6–7.

43. The purpose of these "spirited tales," as proclaimed on the Tom Swift books' dustjackets, was to "convey in a realistic way the wonderful advances in land and sea locomotion and to interest the boy of the present in the hope that he may be a factor in aiding the marvelous development that is coming in the future." The original Tom Swift books formed part of Edward Stratemeyer's Stratemeyer Syndicate of children's novels. The first series began in 1910 with *Tom Swift and His Motor Cycle* and ended in 1941. Most of these first books were written from outlines supplied to the Syndicate by Howard Garis under the pseudonym Victor Appleton. Garis was the author of the famous "Uncle Wiggily" series. The Tom Swift, Jr. series, written by "Victor Appleton II" (the pseudonym of Harriet S. Adams), ran from 1954 until 1971.

44. Victor Appleton II, *Tom Swift and His Giant Robot* (New York: Grosset and Dunlap, 1954), 2.

45. The robots behave erratically at times, as if controlled by their own desires rather than by their master's. After some modifications, Tom's robot "Herbert" sings and dances at a benefit performance for a local hospital. After watching Herbert perform, a strange man in evening dress approaches Tom and offers him one thousand dollars a month to rent Herbert for use in his magician's act, Tom coolly rebuffs the man, stating, " 'Herbert belongs to me and is not for rent. He's only an experimental model and could easily go berserk. I couldn't take the risk.' " Ibid., 68.

46. Ibid., 186. "Servomechanics," in the context of the mid-twentieth century, related to guidance or control systems and early computational systems.

47. Ibid., 186.

48. Ibid., 187.

49. Ibid., 193. Emphasis in the original.

50. Ibid., 195.

51. Ibid., 207.

52. Ibid., 211.

53. Ibid., 131.

54. Ibid., 121.

55. Ibid., 81.

56. Ibid., 211.

57. Carol Ryrie Brink, *Andy Buckram's Tin Men* (New York: Viking Press, 1966), 46.

58. Ted Hughes, *The Iron Giant*. (1968. New York: Alfred A. Knopf, [1999]), 38.

59. Hughes called this creation " 'a giant of the technological world' " (qtd. in Paul, "The Return of *The Iron Man*"), 220.

60. Paul notes that the recycling theme was twenty years ahead of its time. (Ibid., 219).

61. Hughes, *The Iron Giant*, 54–55.

62. Ibid., 56.

63. Ibid., 77.

64. Ibid., 79.

65. Kevin Drum, "Welcome, Robot Overlords. Please Don't Fire Us?" *Mother Jones*, May 13, 2013. http://www.motherjones.com/print/223026. Accessed May 14, 2013. Drum anticipates that middle-skill jobs will be the first to go—desk jobs that require repetitive tasks and little manual dexterity. But he also envisions a future in which driverless cars will replace taxi-drivers, bus-drivers, and truckers—a future that, in 2017 is nearly upon us—and when robots will diagnose illnesses better than doctors. For the latest thinking in economics, political theory, AI, and robotics, see Erik Brynjolfsson and Andrew McAfee's book, *The Second Machine Age: Work, Progress, and Prosperity in a Time of Brilliant Technologies* (New York: W.W. Norton, 2014) and Martin Ford, *Rise of the Robots: Technology and the Threat of a Jobless Future* (New York: Basic Books, 2015).
66. Ibid.
67. Paul Collicutt, *City in Peril!* (Somerville, MA: Templar Books 2009), unpaged.

Chapter 6: The Obese Girl

1. Jeffrey Jerome Cohen, *Of Giants: Sex, Monsters, and the Middle Ages* (Minneapolis and London: University of Minnesota Press, 1999), xii.
2. David Skal, "What We Talk About When We Talk About Monsters" in *Speaking of Monsters: A Teratological Anthology*, eds. Caroline Joan S. Picart and John Edgar Browning (New York: Palgrave Macmillan, 2012, xi–xiii), xiii.
3. Asa Simon Mittman, "The Impact of Monsters and Monster Studies" in *The Ashgate Research Companion to Monsters and the Monstrous*, eds. Asa Simon Mittman and Peter J. Dendle (Surrey, England and Burlington, VT: Ashgate Publishing, 2012, 1–14), 8.
4. Sander Gilman, "Defining Disability: The Case of Obesity." *PMLA* 120.2 (March 2005), 514–517, 516. See also his monograph charting the cultural history of the meanings attached to the obese body, *Obesity, The Biography* (Oxford: Oxford University Press, 2010).
   Susan Cohen and Christine Cosgrove's history of the use of hormones to treat "normally" tall or short children provides a pertinent and interesting side note to the cultural contexts of large and small bodies. Hormonal treatment for size "anomaly" has become big business, according to Cohen and Cosgrove. *See Normal At Any Cost? Tall Girls, Short Boys and the Medical Industry's Quest to Manipulate Height* (New York: Jeremy P. Tarcher/Penguin, 2009). Cohen and Cosgrove quote a 1942 *Parents* magazine article in which it was claimed, " 'tallness can be a real handicap for a girl' " (5). And shortness can be a benefit. While today, I think, many would shudder at the unnecessary, inappropriate and dangerous practice of subjecting children to growth hormones or to estrogen "therapy" to slow growth for cosmetic reasons alone, the situation looks different to some parents of severely disabled children. Growth-attenuation therapy has been prescribed for some non-ambulatory and severely cognitively and neurologically impaired children in order to keep their bodies small. The argument goes that smaller bodies make it easier for parents and caregivers to attend to a child's physical and emotional needs as he/she ages. The ethics of this practice are hotly debated. See "Small Comfort" by Genevieve Field. *New York Times Magazine.* March 27, 2016: 46–50, 53.
5. Abigail C. Saguy, *What's Wrong With Fat?* (Oxford: Oxford University Press, 2013), 5. Gilman discusses obesity in the context of disability, concluding, "Obesity as a disability is seen today as a fluke of the American experience rather than as a litmus test for the limits of what disability can and should be" ("Defining Disability," 517).
6. The necessary-but-marginal figure of the fat girl sidekick is confronted head-on in the YA novel *The Duff: Designated Ugly Fat Friend* by Kody Keplinger (New York: Poppy Books, 2010). The book was adapted as a film, *The DUFF*, and released in 2015 (directed by Ari Sandel). The film, however, largely dispenses with the issue of fat.
7. Introduction, *Bodies Out of Bounds: Fatness and Transgression* eds. Jane Evans Braziel and Kathleen LeBesco (Berkeley: University of California Press, 2001, 1–15), 3.

8. The tall tale was not originally a genre intended solely for children, as it has become, like the fairy tale, in the last hundred years or so. Daniel Hoffman, author of the definitive study of Paul Bunyan, disdains this last development: "The exploitation of [Paul Bunyan] in countless ads, tourist promotions, and vapid juvenilia at the least illustrates the sociology of popular culture, though perhaps no further analyses will be needed to show how the Paul Bunyan of the bunkhouse shrank into the bumcombe booby of fakelore, how the jests of grown men were reduced to kitsch for the kiddies" (*Paul Bunyan: Last of the Frontier Demigods*, 1952. Lincoln: University of Nebraska Press, 1982), xii. *The Bunyans*, a picture book by Audrey Wood and illustrated by David Shannon, is a good example of an extension of the Bunyan legend aimed at children. The story recounts how Paul and his wife, the gigantic pickax-wielding Carrie McIntie, and their two fine children shape the country's landscape by forming Niagara Falls and Bryce Canyons. It is not, however, "kitsch for kiddies" (New York: Blue Sky Press, 1996).

9. Carol S. Brown, *The Tall Tale in American Folklore and Literature* (Knoxville: University of Tennessee Press, 1987), 3.

10. Ibid., 2.

11. For example, Pecos Bill's bride has made it a condition of their marriage that she be able to ride his horse, Widow Maker, on their wedding day. Bill is not pleased about this request (though Sue is able to ride a whale-sized, bucking catfish, he doesn't believe she can handle his horse), but he allows it. Sue wears her brand-new springy bustle under her wedding dress and the nervous Widow Maker bucks her right off. She bounces into the sky so high that she nears the moon, comes down over the Rocky Mountains and then bounces over the moon. Pecos Bill could never figure out how to stop this endless rebounding, so Sue bounces still. See Carl Carmer, *The Hurricane's Children* (1937. New York: David McKay Company, 1965), 59–64.

12. Carmer. *The Hurricane's Children*, 103–104.

13. A similar effort to recuperate the giant female body may be found in the picture book *Stand Straight, Ella Kate* in which readers learn about the true-life story of a 8-foot-4-inch-tall woman, Ella Kate Ewing (1872–1913). The book describes how Ewing, who was exhibited in traveling shows, lived a fulfilling and heroic existence (Kate Klise and M. Sarah Klise, illustrator, *Stand Straight, Ella Kate: The True Story of a Real Giant*. New York: Dial Books, 2010).

14. Angelica's adventures in Montana are described in *Dust Devil* (Anne Isaacs and Paul. O. Zelinsky, illustrator. New York: Schwartz & Wade Books, 2010).

15. Racism and the commodity fetish attached to white blondes complicate this last point. Serena Williams, for example, has been criticized for her muscular body and, in 2015, earned less than Maria Sharapova, a lower-ranked player. See Claudia Rankine. "The Meaning of Serena Williams." August 25, 2015. www.nytimes.com/2015/08/30/magazine/the-meaning-of-serena-williams.html. Accessed December 12, 2016.

16. Carolyn Daniel, *Voracious Children: Who Eats Whom in Children's Literature*. (New York: Routledge, 2006), 4.

17. Robert Lipsyte, *One Fat Summer* (1977. New York: Harper Trophy, 1991), 230. Bobby's particular vulnerabilities as a fat person and the abuse heaped upon him are unflinchingly represented in Lipsyte's novel—to a degree that may seem startling today given the more conservative climate that affected U.S. young adult publishing in the 1980s and '90s. (The pendulum seems to be swinging the other way in the first decades of the twenty-first century). The 1970s, by contrast, were a time of great experimentation and exploration in young adult fiction. In 1970s-era novels by authors such as M. E. Kerr, Sandra Scoppetone, Judy Blume, and others, previously taboo subjects such as homosexuality, abuse, and sexual desire were explored with more freedom than in later decades. In particular, I am thinking of a scene in *One Fat Summer* in which Bobby is stripped, forced to bend over and threatened with sodomy by the thuggish tough who had previously had the job of mowing the Kahns' lawn: " 'If you move, just so much as move, I'm coming back with a sharp stick and guess where I'm going to put it' " (127).

A good example of a book for young adults that confronts previously ignored and misunderstood social problems—male anorexia nervosa and male rape—is Kathleen Jeffrie Johnson's *Target* (New York: Roaring Brook Press, 2003).

18. Daniel's view is that the obese child in children's literature performs didactic work, indicating for the child reader adult rules about appetite control and the necessity to transform the obese body into a more "suitable" body. This transformation, Daniel argues, is a necessary step "toward subjectivity and agency, which would otherwise be denied" (*Voracious Children*, 187). My view about the function of the obese child in children's literature is less doctrinaire, but I agree that physical transformation, for girls in particular, is a common trope and plot element in books for the young.

19. Kimberly Willis Holt, *When Zachary Beaver Came to Town* (New York: Henry Holt and Co., 1999), 12.

20. Ibid., 215.

21. Virginia Hamilton, *The Planet of Junior Brown* (1971. New York: Macmillan Publishing, 1991), 13.

22. Ibid., 33.

23. K. L. Going, *Fat Kid Rules the World* (New York: Puffin Books, 2003), 1.

24. Ibid., 182–183.

25. Ibid., 89.

26. Erin Jade Lange, *Butter* (New York: Bloomsbury, 2012), 278.

27. Kim Chernin comments that men are often threatened by the strong female, and that one response is a turn toward androgynous or childish female figures and against adult female bodies: " 'In this age of feminist assertion men are drawn to women of childish body and mind because there is something less disturbing about the vulnerability and helplessness of a small child and something truly disturbing about the body and mind of a mature woman." Qtd. in Ruth Raymond Thone, *Fat: A Fate Worse than Death? Women, Weight and Appearance* (New York and London: Haworth Press, 1997), 47.

28. Mary Russo, *The Female Grotesque: Risk, Excess and Modernity* (New York and London: Routledge, 1994), 24.

29. Nita Mary McKinley, "Ideal Weight/Ideal Women: Society Constructs the Female" in *Weighty Issues: Fatness and Thinness as Social Problems*, eds. Jeffery Sobal and Donna Maurer (New York: Aldine de Gruyter, 1999), 97–115, 100.

30. Amy Erdman Farrell, *Fat Shame: Stigma and the Fat Body in American Culture* (New York and London: New York University Press, 2011), 116.

31. Jeffrey Jerome Cohen, "Monster Culture (Seven Theses)" in *Monster Theory: Reading Culture*, ed. Jeffrey Jerome Cohen (Minneapolis: University of Minnesota Press, 1996), 3–25, 13.

32. Sometimes, as in *The Planet of Junior Brown*, but not that often, the kid is both fat and "ethnic." For example, see Lois-Ann Yamanaka's *Name Me Nobody* (1999) about an insecure Hawaiian teen of Japanese heritage who loses weight via diet pills and laxatives to please others and *Fat Hoochie Prom Queen* by Nico Medina (2008) about a sassy Puerto Rican girl who embraces her size, Lois-Ann Yamanaka. *Name Me Nobody* (New York: Hyperion, 1999) and Nico Medina, *Fat Hoochie Prom Queen* (New York: Simon Pulse, 2008).

33. The National Association to Advance Fat Acceptance (NAAFA), initiated in 1969, is the oldest American membership organization for people of large size. In a discussion of identity politics and the politics of representation, Elspeth Probyn describes the driving force behind pride movements such as fat acceptance: "One response on the part of those who fall outside the proper boundaries of representation has been to demand more accurate, more fulsome and more representative images: in short, more representation of the right sort. From the shadows of shame, the politics of pride has extended those efforts to unequivocally posit that there is nothing to be ashamed of if your body is gay, black, disabled, fat or old" (*Carnal Appetites: FoodSexIdentities*. London and New York: Routledge 2000), 125.

34. For example, see Saguy's *What's Wrong with Fat?* She discusses fat acceptance as a civil right throughout the book (14). See also Farrell, *Fat Shame*, 137–171.
    Fat Studies is an emergent field of cultural criticism. Other key works that help to define the academic field include Saguy's 2013 book as well as Farrell's 2011 *Fat Shame* and *The Fat Studies Reader* edited by Esther Rothblum and Sondra Solovay (New York and London: New York University Press, 2009) and the classic *Fat Is A Feminist Issue* by Susie Orbach (New York: Paddington Press, 1978).
35. Catherine S. Quick, " 'Meant to be Huge': Obesity and Body Image in Young Adult Novels." *ALAN Review* 35.2 (Winter 2008): 54–61, 55.
36. A YA novel that combines both bariatric surgery (taking the protagonist Libby— once called "America's Fattest Teen"—from 653 pounds to 351) and fat acceptance is Jennifer Niven's *Holding Up the Universe* (New York: Knopf, 2016).
37. See Laura Beil, "Surgery for Obese Children?" *The New York Times.* February 16, 2010, D5.
38. Donna Cooner, *Skinny* (New York: Scholastic, 2012), n.p.
39. Again it is worth noting how obesity is recast for teen girls of above average height (Ever is called 5 foot 6 inches and Lara somewhat taller) from weighing just over 200 pounds in the late 1990s to 300 pounds in 2012.
40. Helen Fielding, *Bridget Jones's Diary* (1996. Rpt. New York: Viking Penguin, 1998), 27.
41. Thone, *Fat: A Fate Worse Than Death?* 181.
42. McKinley, "Ideal Weight/Ideal Women," 107.
43. Cherie Bennet, *Life in the Fat Lane* (New York: Bantam, Doubleday Dell, 1998), 12. Most YA novels about fat girls include the fear that the protagonist will be thought a monster. In *Skinny*, for example, Ever Davies's inner voice tells her, " 'You're just a freak show. . . . They're just grateful for a little entertainment, Frankenstein' " (153).
44. Ibid., 32.
45. Ibid., 72.
46. Ibid., 117. Other monster movie references in the novel include films such as *Invasion of the Body Snatchers* in which innocent victims are taken over against their will by alien forces: "And then someone who was not me went back to the freezer and took out both frozen Snickers bars. . . . Whoever she was, she didn't even turn on her light to eat. She just sat there in the dark, like some fat, feral creature of the night, cracking the frozen chocolate off with her teeth, loving the sensation of rich, sweet, comforting chocolate in her mouth. . . . It wasn't me" (57). See also 80 and 88 for additional references to Lara's monster within.
    Even the original paperback book's cover is reminiscent of horror fiction: Lara is backlit against a "night" background, her mouth is opened in horror as she stares wide-eyed at the number on the scale, her face so excessively pale that she could be a zombie or a ghost.
47. Bennet, *Life in the Fat Lane*, 164. Qualitative and quantitative research from the US and the UK about the effects of bullying, identity formation, self-image, and stigmatization in adolescent girls due to weight that mirror the events of Bennett's novel, is a growing field of study. See, for a few examples, "Perceived Stigmatization among Overweight African-American and Caucasian Adolescent Girls" by Neumark-Sztainer et al. (1998) and "Issues of Self-Image among Overweight African-American and Caucasian Adolescent Girls: A Qualitative Study" (1999) also by Neumark-Sztainer et al., as well as "The Impact of Weight-related Victimization on Peer Relationships: The Female Adolescent Perspective" by Lucy J. Griffiths and Angie S. Page (2008), and "Adolescent Obesity, Overt and Relational Peer Victimization, and Romantic Relationships" by Michelle Je. Pearce et al. (2002).
48. Bennet, *Life in the Fat Lane*, 219.
49. Prader-Willi Syndrome (PWS) is a rare genetic disorder characterized by obesity in childhood, short stature, chronic hunger (hyperphagia), muscular weakness, and incomplete sexual development. Other symptoms include low IQ and learning disabilities. The syndrome was first identified by Swiss endocrinologists in the 1950s. See the Prader-Willi Syndrome Association (USA) website for more information:

http://www.pwsausa.org/. Their motto is "Still hungry for a cure." Articles about Prader-Willi syndrome and childhood in high visibility outlets such as the *New York Times Magazine* have brought attention to the rare genetic disorder. See "The Weight" by Kim Tingley (*New York Times Magazine*, January 25, 2015: 36–41, 48).

New research into obesity suggests that beyond behavior and genetics, certain intestinal microorganisms may make some subset of obese people fat. This theory is gaining ground and has stimulated the interest of the public. We are keenly interested in obesity research and finding answers to why so many people are obese—approximately 30% of American adults have a body-mass index over 30. A biological answer could change our responses to the obese, to ourselves. As Robin Marantz Henig comments in her article for the August 13, 2006 *New York Times Magazine*, "If microbes do turn out to be relevant, at least in some cases of obesity, it could change the way the public thinks about being fat. Along with the continuing research on the genetics of obesity, the study of other biological factors could help mitigate the negative stereotypes of fat people as slothful and gluttonous and somehow less virtuous than thin people" (30). "Fat Factors." (*New York Times Magazine*, August 13, 2006 (section 6): 28–33, 52–55, 57).

50. Bennet, *Life in the Fat Lane*, 159.
51. Ibid., 11.
52. Ibid., 260.
53. Ibid., 213.
54. Our response to obesity is not only socially troubling, it is also commercially successful. Jeffery Sobal reminds us that "the cultural focus on slimness in recent decades led to the development of a system of weight industries that developed vested social, economic, and political interests in portraying high levels of body weight as a social problem. These included the weight loss, medical, pharmaceutical, fitness, food, dieting, apparel, fashion, and insurance industries, all of which operated in the role of moral entrepreneurs who have vested interests in promoting slimness and rejecting fatness" ("The Size Acceptance Movement," 233).
55. Lisa Belkin's piece for the *New York Times Magazine* on July 8, 2001 brought the story of Anamarie and her family to a wide audience. Paul Campos's article for *spiked*, a London-based online magazine, among other publications, increased the audience for the story ("The Lock-up Diet." July 13, 2004. http://www.spiked-online.com/Articles/0000000CA5E7.htm)

    Campos, author of *The Obesity Myth: Why America's Obsession with Weight is Hazardous to Your Health* (2004), appears to have taken many of the details of Anamarie's story (including quotations) from Belkin's article.
56. The ABC morning show *Good Morning America* has reported on Anamarie over the years; the most recent interview took place in 2011. (See note 60.) In a May 24, 2005 segment, Dr. David Katz, an ABC medical contributor and director of Yale University Nutrition Center, first examined and evaluated the contents of the Martinez-Regino refrigerator, freezer, and pantry and then advised Adela Martinez-Regino on how best to feed Anamarie. See "Doctor Offers Advice to Severely Overweight Child" at http://abcnews.go.com/GMA.
57. In a 2002 editorial submitted to "Without Measure," a size-acceptance website, Adela Martinez-Regino writes, "We still don't know what Ana has. For us, yes, we want to know . . . so we have a reason for her being overweight, but also so we won't be blamed anymore." See http://www.size-acceptance.org/without_measure/wom_07_2002/. Tragically, both of Anamarie's parents died in 2011, a few months apart. The teen began to live with her maternal grandparents after her parents' deaths. See Astrid Galvan, "Teen Taken from Parents as Child Coping With Loss." *Albuquerque Journal*. October 14, 2011.
58. Qtd. in Belkin, "Watching Her Weight." *New York Times Magazine*. July 8, 2001: 30–33, 33.

    Adding to the argument that fat stigma is inflected by race and class, Farrell argues, "In today's terms, fat, if it had a color, would be black, and if it had a national origin, it would be illegal immigrant, non-U.S., and non-Western" (*Fat Shame*, 8).

59. Qtd. in Campos's online article, "The Lock-up Diet." Abigail C. Saguy notes the connection between fat and class in *What's Wrong With Fat?*: "Women's concerns about weight are as much or more about class as about health. Achieving and maintaining thinness is an important way in which the contemporary elite in rich nations, and especially elite women, signal their status" (13).

60. Qtd. in Dan Harris and Mikaela Conley, "Childhood Obesity: A Call for Parents to Lose Custody." The article also mentions Anamarie's story and quotes Anamarie who commented on Dr Ludwig's opinion: " 'It's not right what [Dr. Ludwig] is doing, because to get better you need to be with your family, instead of being surrounded by doctors.'" http://abcnews.go.com/Health/childhood-obesity-call-parents-lose-custody/story?id=14068280. Accessed June 6, 2014. The article was based on a *Good Morning America* segment on the JAMA opinion piece and a follow-up interview with Adela Martinez-Regino and Anamarie. See also "Should Parents Lose Custody of Their Extremely Obese Kids?" by Bonnie Rochman. *Time: Healthland.* http://healthland.time.com/2011/07/13/should-parents-lose-custody-of-their-very-obese-kids/ Accessed June 6, 2014. After citing a case in which a 555-pound teen was removed from the family home to live with an aunt and lost 200 pounds, Rochman concludes, "It seems there's got to be a better way than tearing kids from parents, but in truth, this extreme action might be in the best interests of everyone involved over the long-term."

61. A crude engraving, also published in 1680, of Eugenia's naked body illustrated brief details of the child's life, indicating that the "niña giganta" had been sent to the royal palace. Another example of the exhibition of an obese child was noted in Edward J. Wood's 1868 *Giants and Dwarfs*. He details a broadside that proclaimed the precise size of the teenaged Australian "Wonderful Dwarf Giantess": she weighed 13 stone 6 pounds while her height was a mere 35 inches. Miss Mary Jane Youngman could be seen at Saville House from 11a.m. to 11p.m. Twelve hours of display! The broadside proclaims the unique qualities of this obese child: "such truly magnificent female proportions were never before witnessed in England; or, indeed, the world" (*Giants and Dwarfs*, London: Richard Bentley, 1868), 432.

62. See Jonathan Brown, *Painting in Spain, 1500–1700* (New Haven and London: Yale University Press, 1998) for a useful short discussion of Carreño at court (238–239).

63. Even the stout dwarf Maribárbola, whose style of dress reflects her lower status as well as her physical body, has a waist.

64. A fascinating example to the contrary, in which Eugenia's portraits are considered to be significant and influential in terms of art history, may be found in the grand supposition art critic Karen Wilkin makes in linking the "monstrua" portraits with the work of Colombian artist Fernando Botero. Reviewing the 2006–2007 exhibit "Spanish Painting from El Greco to Picasso" held at the Solomon R. Guggenheim Museum in New York, Wilkin argues that the *desnuda* portrait of Eugenia, "a poignant image of an obese female child, ineffectively disguised as a classical deity, could be the source of all of the Colombian painter Fernando Botero's grotesque nudes . . ." ("Spain and Picasso." *The New Criterion.* January 2007: 48–52), 49.

65. Matt Ridley, *Genome: The Autobiography of a Species in 23 Chapters* (New York: HarperCollins, 1999), 206.

66. Alan E. H. Emery and Marcia L. H. Emery. *Mother and Child Care in Art* (London: Royal Society of Medicine Press, 2007), 132. See also "Pediatric Diseases in Juan Carreño de Miranda's Paintings" by Juan F. Martinez-Lage et al. *Child's Nervous System* 28 (2012): 181–184.

67. Elena Levy-Navarro complains about such callous treatment of Eugenia Martínez Vallejo, her portraits, and the issue of fat children in general in a letter to the editor of *PMLA* (Publication of the Modern Language Association). The January 2011 issue of *PMLA* featured Eugenia's clothed portrait as the cover image. However, the

issue did not engage in any critical discussion of the figure beyond her obesity. Levy-Navarro comments, "Because this stable, singularly modern meaning is attached to Eugenia [as obese], other pertinent questions are not considered, including what her lived experiences were like as a fat person known as 'La Monstrua'; how her fat body was seen as spectacular, even perhaps supernatural, as evidenced in the nude portrait of her in the guise of a Bacchus; and what some contemporary, alternative ways are in which her body can be understood by a human (Spanish) audience" (*PMLA* 126.3. 2011. Letter to the editor, 815).

68. Andrea Modica refused to grant permission to reproduce in this book any of her photographs of Barbara. They may be viewed on her website within the portfolios of both *Barbara* and *Treadwell*. See http://www.andreamodica.com/

69. Qtd. in Saguy, *What's Wrong With Fat?* 158.

70. Jeffrey Jerome Cohen, "Monster Culture (Seven Theses)," 4.

Afterword: The Human Measure

1. James Richardson, "Big Scenes" from *During*. Copyright © 2016 by James Richardson. Reprinted with the permission of The Permissions Company, Inc. on behalf of Copper Canyon Press, www.coppercanyonpress.org.

2. Hannah Arendt, *The Human Condition* (Chicago and London: University of Chicago Press, 1958), 5. In a way, her purpose represents an example of big and small thinking: "The purpose of the historical analysis . . . is to trace back modern world alienation, its twofold flight from the earth into the universe and from the world into the self, to its origins, in order to arrive at an understanding of the nature of society as it had developed and presented itself at the very moment when it was overcome by the advent of a new and yet unknown age" (6).

3. Robert Tavernor, *Smoot's Ear: The Measure of Humanity* (New Haven and London: Yale University Press, 2007), 7.

4. Smoot's story is retold in Tavernor's book. The Smoot is an enduring example of the human measure: even when the Harvard Bridge was rebuilt some three decades later, the Smoot lines were repainted and they continue to be carefully tended by Lambda Chi Alpha members biannually in order to keep the marks visible (xiv–xv).

5. Devin Fore, "The Entomic Age." *Grey Room* 33 (Fall 2008), 28.

6. Out of the 214 negatives Du Camp brought back to France, he chose 125 to publish in his book *Égypte, Nubie, Palestine et Syrie* (1852) in a small edition of 200 copies (Andrew Szegedy-Maszak, "Introduction." *Antiquity and Photography: Early Views of Ancient Mediterranean Sites*, eds. Clare L., Lyons, John K. Papadopoulos, Lindsey S. Stewart, and Andrew Szegedy-Maszak. (J. Paul Getty Museum, 2005, 2–18), 11.

7. For general information on the Great and Small Temples at Abu Simbel, see Richard H. Wilkinson, *The Complete Temples of Ancient Egypt* (New York: Thames and Hudson, 2000), 223–229.

8. *Antiquity and Photography*, 94.

9. Claire L. Lyons, "The Art and Science of Antiquity in Nineteenth-Century Photography" in *Antiquity and Photography*, 22–65, 25. Lyons continues in this vein, suggesting that "by materializing history as heritage, archeological photography was instrumental in formulating conceptions of cultural identity and nationhood. Photogenic fragments from classical and biblical lands painted a picture of the past that colored perceptions of ancient civilizations and their modern heirs in India, East Asia, Africa and Latin America" (65).

10. The abuses at Abu Ghraib took place in 2003. In April 2004 the photographs documenting torture, humiliation and abuse first became public. The bibliography of scholarship (both mainstream and specialized) on Abu Ghraib is very long. The following represents a few useful sources: Kari Andén-Papadopoulos, "The Abu Ghraib Torture Photographs: News Frames, Visual Culture, and the Power of Images." *Journalism* 9.1 (2008), 5–30; Mark Danner, *Torture and Truth: America, Abu*

Ghraib, and the War on Terror. (New York: New York Review Books, 2004); Seymour M. Hersh, *Chain of Command: The Road from 9/11 to Abu Ghraib* (New York: HarperCollins, 2004); George R. Mastroianni, "Looking Back: Understanding Abu Ghraib." *Parameters* 43.2 (Summer 2013), 53–65; Steven Strasser and Craig R. Whitney, *The Abu Ghraib Investigations: The Official Independent Panel and Pentagon Reports on the Shocking Prisoner Abuse in Iraq* (New York: Public Affairs, 2004).

BIBLIOGRAPHY

Adams, George. *Essays on the Microscope; containing a Practical Description of the Most Improved Microscopes.* London: Dillon and Keating, 1787.

Adelson, Betty. *The Lives of the Dwarfs: Their Journey from Public Curiosity Toward Social Liberation.* New Brunswick: Rutgers University Press, 2005.

Agins, Michelle V. "Tom Thumb Weddings: Only for the Very Young." *The New York Times.* June 16, 1991: 34.

Aleksander, Igor and Piers Burnett. *Reinventing Man: The Robot Becomes Reality.* London: Kogan Page, 1983.

Allende, Isabel. *Forest of the Pygmies.* Translated by Margaret Sayers Peden. New York: HarperCollins Publishers, 2005.

Almond, David. *Clay.* London: Hodder Children's Books, 2005.

Alpers, Svetlana. *The Vexations of Art: Velázquez and Others.* New Haven and London: Yale University Press, 2005.

An Account of the Life, Personal Appearance, Character, and Manners, of Charles S. Stratton, the American Dwarf, known as General Tom Thumb, 12 Years Old, Twenty-Five Inches Height, and Weighing Fifteen Pounds. London: Printed by J. Mitchell and Company, 1844.

Anker, Suzanne and Dorothy Nelkin. *The Molecular Gaze: Art in the Genetic Age.* Cold Spring Harbor, NY: Cold Spring Harbor Laboratory Press, 2004.

Appleton II, Victor. *Tom Swift and His Giant Robot.* New York: Grosset and Dunlap, 1954.

Augarde, Steve. *The Various.* Oxford: David Fickling Books, 2003.

———. *Celandine.* Oxford: David Fickling Books, 2005.

———. *Winter Wood.* Oxford: David Fickling Books, 2008.

Baden-Powell, Robert. *Young Knights of the Empire: Their Code and Further Scout Yarns.* Philadelphia: J. B. Lippincott Company, 1917.

Badkhan, Anna. "Anti-evolution Teachings Gain Foothold in U.S. Schools: Evangelicals see Flaws in Darwinism." *San Francisco Chronicle.* November 30, 2004.

Banks, Lynne Reid. *The Indian in the Cupboard.* 1980. New York: Avon Books, 1982.

Barbeito, J. "Velázquez: la realidad trascendida." *Academia* 80 (1995): 443–57.

Barnum, Phineas T. *The Life of P. T. Barnum: Written By Himself.* 1855. Urbana and Chicago: University of Illinois Press, 2000.

Barwell, Louisa Mary. *The Novel Adventures of Tom Thumb the Great, Showing How He Visited the Insect World and Learned Much Wisdom.* London: Chapman and Hall, 1838.

Bass, Laura R. *The Drama of the Portrait: Theater and Visual Culture in Early Modern Spain*. University Park, PA: Pennsylvania State University Press, 2008.

Bates, Harry. "Farewell to the Master." 1940. Rpt. New Mexico: Sterling Publications, 2012.

Beake, Lesley. *Song of Be*. New York: Henry Holt and Company, 1993.

Beil, Laura. "Surgery for Obese Children?" *The New York Times*. February 16, 2010: D5.

Belkin, Lisa. "Watching Her Weight." *The New York Times Magazine*. July 8, 2001: 30–33.

Belluck, Pam."It's Not So Easy to Adopt an Embryo." *The New York Times*. Week in Review. Sunday, June 12, 2005.

Benjamin, Melanie. *The Autobiography of Mrs. Tom Thumb*. New York: Delacorte Press, 2011.

——. "America's Royal Wedding: General and Mrs. Tom Thumb." *Huffington Post*. April 19, 2011. http://www.huffingtonpost.com/melanie-benjamin/royal-wedding_b_850540.html

Bennet, Cherie. *Life in the Fat Lane*. New York: Bantam Doubleday Dell, 1998.

Berlant, Lauren. *The Queen of America Goes to Washington City: Essays on Sex and Citizenship*. Durham, NC and London: Duke University Press, 1997.

Bierhorst, John. *The Deetkatoo: Native American Stories About Little People*. New York: William Morrow and Co., 1998.

Bindman, David. "The Black Presence in British Art: Sixteenth and Seventeenth Centuries" in *The Image of the Black in Western Art, Vol. III: From the "Age of Discovery" to the "Age of Abolition," Part 1: Artists of the Renaissance and Baroque*. Eds. David Bindman and Henry Louis Gates, Jr. Cambridge, MA: Belknap Press, 2010: 235–270.

Blake, Robin. *Anthony Van Dyck: A Life, 1599–1641*. Chicago: Ivan R. Dee, 1999.

Blyn, Robin. *The Freak-Garde: Extraordinary Bodies and Revolutionary Art in America*. Minneapolis: University of Minnesota Press, 2013.

Bodger, Joan. *How the Heather Looks: A Joyous Journey to the British Sources of Children's Books*. New York: Viking, 1965.

Bogdan, Robert. *Freak Show: Presenting Human Oddities for Amusement and Profit*. Chicago and London: University of Chicago Press, 1988.

Bone, J. J. *Going Native*. New Hope, PA: The Pygmy Press, 1989.

Bosmajian, Hamida. "*Charlie and the Chocolate Factory* and Other Excremental Visions." *The Lion and the Unicorn* 9 (1985): 36–49.

Bowler, Peter J. *Monkey Trials and Gorilla Sermons: Evolution and Christianity from Darwin to Intelligent Design*. Cambridge, MA and London: Harvard University Press, 2007.

Bradford, Phillips Verner and Harvey Blume. *Ota: The Pygmy in the Zoo*. New York: St. Martin's Press, 1992.

Brantlinger, Patrick. "Victorians and Africans: the Genealogy of the Myth of the Dark Continent." *Critical Inquiry* 12 (Autumn 1985): 166–203.

Braziel, Jana Evans and Kathleen LeBesco, eds. *Bodies Out of Bounds: Fatness and Transgression* Berkeley: University of California Press, 2001.

Briggs, Raymond. *The Man*. 1992. London: Red Fox Books (Random House UK), 1994.

Brink, Carol Ryrie. *Andy Buckram's Tin Men*. New York: Viking Press, 1966.

Bristow, Joseph. *Empire Boys: Adventures in a Man's World*. London: HarperCollins Academic, 1991.

Brown, Carol S. *The Tall Tale in American Folkore and Literature*. Knoxville: University of Tennessee Press, 1987.

Brown, Jonathan. *Painting in Spain, 1500–1700*. New Haven and London: Yale University Press, 1998.

Brown, Kenneth D. *Factory of Dreams: A History of Meccano Ltd., 1901–1979*. Lancaster: Crucible Books, 2007.

Brown, P., T. Sutikna, M. J. Morwood, R. P. Soejono, Jatmiko, E. Wayhu Saptomo and Rokus Awe Due. "A New Small-bodied Hominin from the Late Pleistocene of Flores, Indonesia." *Nature* 431. 28 October 2004.

Browne, Thomas. *Religio Medici*. London, 1643.

Brynjolfsson, Erik and Andrew McAfee. *The Second Machine Age: Work, Progress, and Prosperity in a Time of Brilliant Technologies.* New York: W. W. Norton, 2014.

Bühler, Curt. *The History of Tom Thumb.* Evanston, IL: Northwestern University Press for the Renaissance English Text Society, 1965.

Bunyan, John. *A Book for Boys and Girls, Or, Country Rhimes for Children.* London, 1686.

Burgess, Melvin. *The Earth Giant.* 1995. New York: PaperStar, 1999.

Burke, Edmund. *A Philosophical Enquiry into the Origin of our Ideas of the Sublime and Beautiful.* 1757. Edited by J. T. Boulton. London: Routledge and Kegan Paul and New York: Columbia University Press, 1958.

Burrows, Captain Guy. *The Land of the Pigmies.* New York and Boston: Thomas Y. Crowell and Co., 1898.

Byrne, James P. "The Genesis of Whiteface in Nineteenth-Century American Popular Culture. *MELUS* 29 nos. 3/4 (Fall–Winter 2004): 133–149.

Calhoun, Ada."Mommy Had to Go Away For A While." *New York Times Magazine.* April 29, 2012. 31–36.

Campos, Paul. "The Lock-up Diet." July 13, 2004. http://www.spiked-online.com/ Articles/0000000CA5E7.htm.

Carmer, Carl. *The Hurricane's Children.* 1937. New York: David McKay Company, 1965.

Charles, Jim. "Out of the Cupboard and Into the Classroom: Children and the American Indian Literary Experience." *Children's Literature in Education* 27, no. 3 (1996): 167–179.

Checa, Fernando. *Velázquez: The Complete Paintings.* Trans. Donald Pistolesi. London: Thames and Hudson, 2008.

Chemers, Michael M. "Jumpin' Tom Thumb: Charles Stratton Onstage at the American Museum." *Nineteenth Century Theatre and Film.* 31, no. 2 (Winter 2004): 16–27.

——. "On the Boards in Brobdignag [*sic*]: Performing Tom Thumb." *New England Theatre Journal* 12, no. 1 (2001): 79–104.

——. *Staging Stigma: A Critical Examination of the American Freak Show.* New York: Palgrave Macmillan, 2008.

Clarke, Pauline. *The Return of the Twelves.* 1962. New York: Coward, McCann & Geoghegan, Inc., 1963.

Clifton, James A. "The Indian Story: A Cultural Fiction." *The Invented Indian: Cultural Fictions and Governmental Policies,* edited by James A. Clifton. 29–47. New Brunswick, NJ: Transaction Publishers, 1994.

Cohen, Susan and Christine Cosgrove. *See Normal At Any Cost? Tall Girls, Short Boys and the Medical Industry's Quest to Manipulate Height.* New York: Jeremy P. Tarcher/ Penguin, 2009.

Cohen, Jeffrey Jerome. "Preface: In a Time of Monsters." *Monster Theory: Reading Culture,* edited by Jeffrey Jerome Cohen. Minneapolis: University of Minnesota Press, 1996: vii–xiii.

——. "Monster Culture (Seven Theses)." *Monster Theory: Reading Culture,* edited by Jeffrey Jerome Cohen. Minneapolis: University of Minnesota Press, 1996: 3–25.

——. *Of Giants: Sex, Monsters, and the Middle Ages.* Minneapolis and London: University of Minnesota Press, 1999.

Colie, Rosalie L. *The Resources of Kind: Genre-Theory in the Renaissance.* Ed. Barbara K. Lewalski. Berkeley: University of California Press, 1973.

Collett, Anne. " 'Sharing a Common Destiny': Censorship, Imperialism and the Stories of Doctor Dolittle." *New Literature Review* 33 (1997): 81–93.

Collicutt, Paul. *Robot City Adventures: City in Peril!* Somerville, MA: Templar Books, 2009.

Cooke-Taylor, R. W. *The Factory System and the Factory Acts.* London: Methuen and Company, 1894.

Coombes, Annie E. *Reinventing Africa: Museums, Material Culture and Popular Imagination in Late Victorian and Edwardian England.* New Haven and London: Yale University Press, 1994.

Cooner, Donna. *Skinny.* New York: Point Press (Scholastic), 2012.

Cooper, Anthony Ashley (Lord Shaftesbury). "Infant Labour." *Quarterly Review* 67, 1840–41 (December 1840): 171–181.

Cowper, William. *"Tirocinium: or, a Review of Schools.* 1784. *The Poetical Works of William Cowper.* Ed. Robert Southey. 2 vols. London: Henry G. Bohn, 1854.

Craton, Lillian. *The Victorian Freak Show: The Significance of Disability and Physical Differences in 19th-Century Fiction.* Amherst, NY: Cambria Press, 2009.

Cunningham, Hugh. *The Children of the Poor: Representations of Childhood Since the Seventeenth Century.* Oxford: Blackwell, 1991.

Curlin, Jay. "The Evidence of Things Not Seen." *The New Yorker.* July 30, 2012, 77.

Cutler, Jane. *Song of the Molimo.* New York: Farrar Straus Giroux, 1998.

Dahl, Roald. *The BFG.* 1982. Puffin Books, 1997.

———. *Charlie and the Chocolate Factory.* 1964. New York: Alfred A. Knopf, 1973.

Daniel, Carolyn. *Voracious Children: Who Eats Whom in Children's Literature.* New York: Routledge, 2006.

D'Avenant, William. *Jeffereidos, Or The Captivitie of Jeffery.* London, 1630.

David Livingstone. London and Edinburgh: Oliphants Ltd. (American imprint: Grand Rapids, MI: Zondervan Publishing House), 1953.

Desmond, Alice Curtis. *Barnum Presents General Tom Thumb.* New York: Macmillan Company, 1954.

Dickens, Charles. "The Noble Savage." *Household Words.* Vol. 8, no. 168 (Saturday, June 11, 1853): 337–339.

DiDonato, Tiffanie, and Rennie Dyball. *Dwarf: A Memoir.* New York: Plume (Penguin Group USA), 2012.

Dixon, Bob. *Catching Them Young 1: Sex, Race and Class in Children's Literature.* London: Pluto Press, 1977.

———. *Catching Them Young 2: Political Ideas in Children's Fiction.* London: Pluto Press, 1977.

"Doctor Offers Advice to Severely Overweight Child." May 24, 2005. http://abcnews. go.com/GMA.

Dove, Frederick. "What's Happened to Thalidomide Babies?" *BBC News Magazine.* November 2, 2011. http://www.bbc.co.uk/news/magazine-15536544?print=true.

Drimmer, Frederick. *Very Special People: The Struggles, Loves, and Triumphs of Human Oddities.* New York: Amjon Publishers, 1973.

Drum, Kevin. "Welcome, Robot Overlords. Please Don't Fire Us?" *Mother Jones.* May 13, 2013. http://www.motherjones.com/print/223026.

Drury, G. Thorn, ed. *The Poems of Edmund Waller,* Vol. 1. 1686. London: A. H. Bullen and New York: Charles Scribner's Sons, 1901.

Dundas, Judith. "Unriddling the Antique: Peacham's Emblematic Art." *Deviceful Settings: The English Renaissance Emblem and its Contexts,* edited by Michael Bath and Daniel Russell. 55–81. New York: AMS Press, 1999.

Dunn, Katherine. *Geek Love.* New York: Warner Books, 1989.

Earle, John. *Microcosmographie, or a Peece of the World Discovered.* London: Printed by W. S. for Ed. Blount, 1628.

Easton, Nina J. "Stem Cell Vote May Challenge President." *Boston Globe,* May 24, 2005. boston.com

Emery, Alan E. H. and Marcia L. H. Emery. *Mother and Child Care in Art.* London: Royal Society of Medicine Press, 2007.

Ertelt, Steven."Capitol Hill Children's Event Places Spotlight on Human Embryo Adoptions." *LifeNews.com.* September 23, 2004. http://archive.lifenews.com/bio469. html

Fairley, Don. *Hunting Pygmy Hunters.* Orig. pub. date unknown. Findlay, Ohio: Fundamental Truth Publishers, 1980.

Farnsworth, Jane. " 'An *equall*, and a *mutuall* flame': George Wither's A *Collection of Emblemes* 1635 and Caroline Court Culture." *Deviceful Settings: The English Renaissance Emblem and its Contexts,* edited by Michael Bath and Daniel Russell. 83–96. New York: AMS Press, 1999.

Farrell, Amy Erdman. *Fat Shame: Stigma and the Fat Body in American Culture*. New York and London: New York University Press, 2011.

Ferriss, Jim. "Introduction: The Ugly Word" in Michael M. Chemers, *Staging Stigma: A Critical Examination of the American Freak Show*. New York: Palgrave Macmillan, 2008.

Fiedler, Leslie. *Freaks*. New York: Simon and Schuster, 1978.

Field, Genevieve. "Small Comfort." *New York Times Magazine*. March 27, 2016: 46–50, 53.

Fielding, Helen. *Bridget Jones's Diary*. 1996. Rpt. New York: Viking Penguin, 1998.

Fielding, Henry. *Tom Thumb and The Tragedy of Tragedies*. Edited by L. J. Morrissey. Berkeley: University of California Press, 1970.

Findlay, Paula Findlen. "Jokes of Nature and Jokes of Knowledge: The Playfulness of Scientific Discourse in Early Modern Europe," *SRen* 43 (1990): 292–331.

Findling, John E. *Chicago's Great World's Fairs*. Manchester and New York: Manchester University Press, 1994.

Fine, Anne. Introduction to *Mistress Masham's Repose* by T. H. White. 2nd ed. 1998, Rpt. 2002. Ilustrated by Martin Hargreaves. Reprint by G. P. Putnam's Sons and Jonathan Cape Children's Books, 4–5.

Fisher, Ruth B. *On the Borders of Pigmy-Land*. 3rd ed. London: Marshall Brothers, 1905.

Foot, Michael, introduction to *Gulliver's Travels*. Edited by Michael Foot. New York: Penguin Books, 1984.

Ford, Martin. *Rise of the Robots: Technology and the Threat of a Jobless Future*. New York: Basic Books, 2015.

França, Alfeu. *Ota Benga: A Pygmy in America*. Documentary Film. Berkeley, California: University of California Extension Center for Media and Independent Learning, 2002.

Frist Center for the Visual Arts. *Fairy Tales, Monsters, and the Genetic Imagination*. Text by Mark W. Scala. Nashville, TN: Vanderbilt University Press, 2012.

Fuller, Thomas. *The Worthies of England*, edited by John Freeman. 1662. London: George Allen and Unwin, 1952.

Galvan, Astrid. "Teen Taken from Parents Coping With Loss. *Albuquerque Journal*. October 14, 2011.

Gandhi, Leela. *Postcolonial Theory: A Critical Introduction*. New York: Columbia University Press, 1998.

Gandy, Imani. "Roe v. Wade and Fetal Personhood: Juridical Persons and Not Natural Persons, And Why It Matters." *Rewire*. January 3, 2013. https://rewire.news/article/2013/01/03/fetal-personhood-laws-juridical-persons-are-not-natural-persons-and-why-it-matter/

Geil, William Edgar. *A Yankee in Pigmy Land*. London: Hodder and Stoughton, 1905.

George, Robert P. and Christopher Tollefsen. *Embryo: A Defense of Human Life*. New York: Doubleday, 2008.

Gibbs, A. M., ed. "Jeffereidos, Or the Captivitie of Jeffery." *Sir William D'avenant: The Shorter Poems, and Songs from the Plays and Masques*. 37–43. Oxford: Oxford at the Clarendon Press, 1972.

Gillis, John R. "Birth of the Virtual Child: Origins of Our Contradictory Images of Children." *Childhood and Its Discontents*, edited by Joseph Dunn and James Kelly. 31–50. Dublin: Liffey Press, 2002.

Gilman, Sander L. "Defining Disability: The Case of Obesity." *PMLA* 120, no. 2 (March 2005): 514–517.

———. *Obesity, The Biography*. Oxford: Oxford University Press, 2010.

Gilmore, David D. *Monsters: Evil Beings, Mythical Beasts, and All Manner of Imaginary Terrors*. Philadelphia: University of Pennsylvania Press, 2003.

Going, K. L. *Fat Kid Rules the World*. New York: Puffin Books, 2003.

Goldberg, Vicki. *Lewis W. Hine: Children at Work*. Munich, London and New York: Prestel, 1999.

Gombrich, E. H. *The Story of Art*. 1950. London: Phaidon Press, 2006.

Gores, Steven J. "The Miniature as Reduction and Talisman in Fielding's *Amelia*." *Studies in English Literature* 37 (1997): 573–593.

Graff, Lisa. *The Thing About Georgie.* New York: Harper Trophy, 2006.

Greenblatt, Stephan. *Marvelous Possessions: The Wonder of the New World.* Chicago, University of Chicago Press, 1991.

Greenhouse, Linda. "A Never-Ending Story. *NY Times.com.* September 5, 2012 http://opinionator.blogs.nytimes.com/2012/09/05/a-never-ending-story/.

Griffiths, Lucy J. and Angie S. Page. "The Impact of Weight-related Victimization on Peer Relationships: The Female Adolescent Perspective." *Obesity.* Vol. 16, Supplement 2 (November 2008): S39–S45.

Griswold, Jerry. *Feeling Like a Kid: Childhood and Children's Literature.* Baltimore: The Johns Hopkins University Press, 2006.

Gugliotta, Guy. "Were 'Hobbits' Human?" *Smithsonian* 39, no. 4 (2008): 61.

Hade, Dan. "Reading Children's Literature Multiculturally" in *Reflections of Change: Children's Literature Since 1945,* edited by Sandra Beckett. 116–122. Westport, CT: Greenwood Press, 1997.

Halliburton, Richard. *The Famous Adventures of Richard Halliburton.* 1932. Indianapolis: Bobbs-Merrill Company, 1940.

——. *Richard Halliburton's Complete Book of Marvels.* Indianapolis, Indiana: Bobbs-Merrill Company, 1941.

Halliwell-Phillips, James Orchard. *The Metrical History of Tom Thumb the Little, as issued early in the eighteenth century.* Edited by James Orchard Halliwell-Phillips. London: printed for the editor, 1860.

Hamilton, Virginia. *The Planet of Junior Brown.* 1971. New York: Macmillan Publishing, 1991.

Hancock, Susan. *The Child That Haunts Us: Symbols and Images in Fairy Tale and Miniature Literature.* London and New York: Routledge, 2009.

Harris, Dan and Mikaela Conley. "Childhood Obesity: A Call for Parents to Lose Custody." July 14, 2011. http://abcnews.go.com/Health/childhood-obesity-call-parents-lose-custody/story?id=14068280

Harris, Lynn. "Clump of Cells or 'Microscopic Americans?' " *Salon,* February 5, 2005. http://www.salon.com/life/feature/2005/02/05/embryos

Harris, Neil. *Humbug: The Art of P. T. Barnum.* Boston and Toronto: Little, Brown and Co., 1973.

Hearn, Michael Patrick. Preface to *The History of Tom Thumbe.* vii–xxiii. New York: Garland, 1977.

Hearn, Karen. "Van Dyck in Britain", *Van Dyck & Britain* exhibit catalogue. 11–13. London: Tate Publishing, 2009.

Hegi, Ursula. Illus. Giselle Potter. *Trudi and Pia.* New York: Atheneum, 2003.

Heide, Florence Parry. *The Shrinking of Treehorn.* 1971. *Treehorn Times Three.* New York: Dell Yearling, 1992.

Henig, Robin Marantz. "Fat Factors." *The New York Times Magazine.* August 13, 2006 (section 6): 28–33, 52–55, 57.

Hernandez, Daniela. "Enter the Wild West of the Embryo Adoption Industry." *Fusion.* June 10, 2015. http://fusion.net/story/145489/enter-the-wild-west-of-the-embryo-adoption-industry/.

Heywood, Colin. *A History of Childhood: Children and Childhood in the West from Medieval to Modern Times.* Polity Press, 2001.

Hibbard, Caroline. " 'By Our Direction and For Our Use': The Queen's Patronage of Artists and Artisans seen through her Household Accounts." *Henrietta Maria: Piety, Politics and Patronage,* edited by Erin Griffey. 115–137. Burlington, VT and Aldershot, England: Ashgate Publishing, 2008.

The History of Jack and the Giants. Facsimile, n.d. *Classics of Children's Literature, 1621–1932.* Selected by Alison Lurie and Justin G. Schiller. New York: Garland Publishing, 1977.

Hoffman, Daniel. *Paul Bunyan: Last of the Frontier Demigods.* 1952. Lincoln: University of Nebraska Press, 1983.

Holt, Kimberly Willis. *When Zachary Beaver Came to Town.* New York: Henry Holt and Co., 1999.

Horn, Pamela. *The Victorian Town Child*. New York: New York University Press, 1997.
"How To Run a Meccano Club." Liverpool: Meccano Ltd., 1949.
Hughes, Ted. *The Iron Giant*. 1968. New York: Alfred A. Knopf, 1999.
———. *The Iron Woman*. London: Faber & Faber, 1993.
The Iron Giant, directed by Brad Bird (1999; Warner Brothers).
Isaacs, Anne and Paul O. Zelinsky. *Dust Devil*. New York: Schwartz and Wade Books, 2010.
———. *Swamp Angel*. New York: Puffin, 1994.
Itzkoff, Dave. " 'If I Have Offended Anyone, and I'm Sure I Have, I Don't Apologize.' " *New York Times Magazine* January 15, 2012. 24, 26–27, 54.
Jacobson, Mireille and Heather Royer. "Aftershocks: The Impact of Clinic Violence on Abortion Services." *American Economic Journal: Applied Economics* 3.1 (January 2011): 189–223.
Johansen, Bruce E. *Shapers of the Great Debate on Native Americans: Land, Spirit, and Power*. Westport, CT: Greenwood Press, 2000.
Johnson, Kathleen Jeffrie. *Target*. New York: Roaring Brook Press (Macmillan), 2003.
Johnson, Steven. *Future Perfect: The Case for Progress in a Networked Age*. New York: Riverhead Hardcover, 2012.
Kaplan, Paul H. D. "Italy, 1490–1700" in *The Image of the Black in Western Art, Vol. III: From the "Age of Discovery" to the "Age of Abolition,"* Part 1: *Artists of the Renaissance and Baroque*, edited by David Bindman and Henry Louis Gates, Jr. Cambridge, MA: Belknap Press, 2010: 93–190.
Keller, Eve. "Embryonic Individuals: The Rhetoric of Seventeenth-Century Embryology and the Construction of Early-Modern Identity." *Eighteenth-Century Studies* 33, no. 3 (2000): 321–348.
———. *Generating Bodies and Gendered Selves: The Rhetoric of Reproduction in Early Modern England*. Seattle and London: University of Washington Press, 2007.
Kellman, Martin. *T. H. White and the Matter of Britain*. Lewiston/Queenston: Edwin Mellen Press, 1988.
Keplinger, Kody. *The Duff: Designated Ugly Fat Friend*. New York and Boston: Poppy Books, 2010.
Kerr, M.E. *Little Little*. New York: HarperCollins, 1981.
Khorana, Meena, ed. *Africa in Literature for Children and Young Adults: An Annotated Bibliography of English-Language Books*. Westport, CT: Greenwood Press, 1994.
Klieman, Kairn A. *"The Pygmies Were Our Compass": Bantu and Batwa in the History of West Central Africa, Early Times to c. 1900 CE*. Portsmouth, NH: Heinemann, 2003.
Klise, Kate and M. Sarah Klise, illus. *Stand Straight, Ella Kate: The True Story of a Real Giant*. New York: Dial Books, 2010.
Knowles, James. " 'Can ye not tell a man from a marmoset?': Apes and Others on the Early Modern Stage." *Renaissance Beasts: Of Animals, Humans, and Other Wonderful Creatures*, edited by Erica Fudge. 138–163. Urbana and Chicago: University of Illinois Press, 2004.
Kotar, S. L. and J. E. Gessler. *The Rise of the American Circus, 1716–1899*. Jefferson, NC and London: McFarland and Company, 2011.
Kuznets, Lois. *When Toys Come Alive: Narratives of Animation, Metamorphosis, and Development*. New Haven: Yale University Press, 1994.
Lagerlöf, Selma. *The Wonderful Adventure of Nils*. Radford, VA: Wilder Publications, 2009.
Lahr, Marta Mirazón and Robert Foley. "Palaeoanthropology: Human Evolution Writ Small." *Nature* 431, no. 7012 (2004): 1043–1044.
Landau, Paul S. "Empires of the Visual: Photography and Colonial Administration in Africa" in *Images and Empires: Visuality in Colonial and Postcolonial Africa*, edited by Paul S. Landau and Deborah D. Kaspin. 141–171. Berkeley: University of California Press (2002).
Lange, Erin Jade. *Butter*. New York: Bloomsbury, 2012.

Langmuir, Erika. *Imagining Childhood*. New Haven and London: Yale University Press, 2006.

Laqueur, Thomas. *Making Sex: Body and Gender From the Greeks to Freud*. Cambridge, MA: Harvard University Press, 1990.

Lehman, Eric D. *Becoming Tom Thumb: Charles Stratton, P. T. Barnum, and the Dawn of American Celebrity*. Middletown, CT: Wesleyan University Press, 2013.

Lejeune, Clara. "The Story of Tom Thumb." *Human Life Review* 28, nos. 1/2 (Winter/Spring 2002): 78–86.

Lepore, Jill. *The Mansion of Happiness: A History of Life and Death*. New York: Alfred A. Knopf, 2012.

Levy-Navarro, Elena. "*La Monstrua* on PMLA's Cover." *PMLA* 126, no. 3 (2011): 815.

Lewis, C. S. *The Lion, the Witch and the Wardrobe*. New York: Collier Books, 1950.

Lindenmeyer, Kriste. *A Right to Childhood: The U.S. Children's Bureau and Child Welfare, 1912–1946*. Champaign, IL: University of Illinois Press, 1997.

Lipsyte, Robert. *One Fat Summer*. 1977. Rpt. New York: Harper Trophy, 1991.

Lloyd, A. B. *In Dwarf Land and Cannibal Country: A Record of Travel and Discovery in Central Africa*. London: T. Fisher Unwin, 1899.

Lobel, Arnold. *Giant John*. New York: Harper and Row, 1964.

Lofting, Christopher. Afterword. *The Story of Doctor Dolittle*. Centenary Edition. Delacorte Press, 1988.

Lofting, Hugh. *The Story of Doctor Dolittle*. 1920. Toronto: McClelland and Stewart, 1923.

——. *The Voyages of Doctor Dolittle*. 1922. Philadelphia: J. B. Lippincott, 1950.

López-Rey, José. *Velázquez's Work and World*. Connecticut: New York Graphic Society, 1968.

Lurie, Allison and Justin G. Schiller. *Classics of Children's Literature, 1621–1932 : a Collection of 117 Titles in 73 Volumes*. Selected by Alison Lurie and Justin G. Schiller. New York and London: Garland Publishing, 1977.

Lyons, Claire L., John K. Papadopoulos, Lindsey S. Stewart, and Andrew Szegedy-Maszak, eds. *Antiquity and Photography: Early Views of Ancient Mediterranean Sites*. J. Paul Getty Museum, 2005.

Lyons, Claire L., "The Art and Science of Antiquity in Nineteenth-Century Photography" in *Antiquity and Photography: Early Views of Ancient Mediterranean Sites*. *Antiquity and Photography*. edited by Lyons, Clare L., John K. Papadopoulos, Lindsey S. Stewart, and Andrew Szegedy-Maszak J. Paul Getty Museum (2005): 22–65.

McAllister, Peter. *Pygmonia: In Search of the Secret Land of the Pygmies*. St. Lucia, Queensland: University of Queensland Press, 2010.

MacCann, Donnarae. "Hugh Lofting." *Writers for Children: Critical Studies of Major Authors Since the Seventeenth Century*, edited by Jane M. Bingham. New York: Scribner Book Company. 365–371. 1988.

McDonald, George. "The Giant's Heart" in *The Light Princess and Other Fairy Tales*. 67–96. New York and London: G. P. Putnam's Sons, 1893.

McDonald, Margaret Read. *Tom Thumb*. Phoenix, AZ: Oryx Press, 1993.

McEwan, Ian. *Nutshell*. New York: Nan A.Talese/Doubleday, 2016.

McGillis, Roderick. " 'And the Celt Knew the Indian': Knowingness, Postcolonialism, Children's Literature" in *Voices of the Other: Children's Literature and the Postcolonial Context*, edited by Roderick McGillis. 223–235. New York: Garland Publishing, 1999.

Mack, John. *Art of Small Things*. London: The British Museum Press, 2007.

McKinley, Nita Mary. "Ideal Weight/Ideal Women: Society Constructs the Female" in *Weighty Issues: Fatness and Thinness as Social Problems*, edited by Jeffery Sobal and Donna Maurer. 97–115. New York: Aldine de Gruyter, 1999.

McKissack, Patricia and Fredrick. Foreword to *The Story of Doctor Dolittle*. Illustrated by Michael Hague. New York: William Morrow and Company, 1997.

Mackler, Carolyn. *The Earth, My Butt, and Other Big Round Things*. New York: Candlewick, 2003.

Maddy, Yulisa Amadu and Donnarae MacCann. *African Images in Juvenile Literature: Commentaries on Neocolonialist Fiction.* Jefferson, NC: McFarland and Co., Inc., 1996.

Magri, Countess M. Lavinia. "Mrs. Tom Thumb's Autobiography." *New York Tribune Sunday Magazine.* September 16, 1906.

Manduca, Joseph. *The Meccano Magazine, 1916–1981.* London: New Cavendish Books, 1987.

Mark, Joan. *The King of the World in the Land of the Pygmies.* Lincoln and London: University of Nebraska Press, 1995.

Marriott, Roger. *Meccano.* Oxford: Shire Publications, 2012.

Marsh, Katherine. *Jepp, Who Defied the Stars.* New York: Hyperion, 2012.

Marten, James. *Childhood and Child Welfare in the Progressive Era: A Brief History with Documents.* Boston and New York: Bedford/St. Martin's, 2004.

Martinez-Lage, Juan F., Miguel A. Pérez-Espejo, and Marcelo Galarza. "Pediatric Diseases in Juan Carreño de Miranda's Paintings." *Child's Nervous System* 28 (2012): 181–184.

Martinez-Regino, Adela. Editorial. Without Measure. http://www.size-acceptance.org/without_measure/wom_07_2002/

Massingham, H. J. *Fee, Fi, Fo, Fum or the Giant in England.* London: Kegan Paul, Trench, Trubner & Co., 1926.

Mawer, Simon. *Mendel's Dwarf.* New York: Penguin Books, 1998.

Mayer, Robert. "Nathaniel Crouch, Bookseller and Historian: Popular Historiography and Cultural Power in Late Seventeenth-Century England." *Eighteenth-Century Studies* 27, no. 3 (Spring 1994): 391–419.

Medina, Nico. *Fat Hoochie Prom Queen.* New York: Simon Pulse, 2008.

Merish, Lori. "Cuteness and Commodity Aesthetics: Tom Thumb and Shirley Temple" in *Freakery: Cultural Spectacles of the Extraordinary Body,* edited by Rosemarie Garland Thomson. 185–206. New York: New York University Press, 1996.

Microphilus, *The New Yeare's Gift.* London, 1636.

The Mighty, directed by Peter Chelsom (1998; Miramax Films).

Millar, Oliver. *Van Dyck in England.* London: National Portrait Gallery, 1982.

Mintz, Steven. *Huck's Raft: A History of American Childhood.* Cambridge, MA: Belknap Press, 2004.

Mirsky, Reba Paeff. *Thirty-One Brothers and Sisters.* New York: Dell Publishing, 1952.

Mittman, Asa Simon. "The Impact of Monsters and Monster Studies" in *The Ashgate Research Companion to Monsters and the Monstrous,* edited by Asa Simon Mittman and Peter J. Dendle. 1–14. Surrey, England and Burlington, VT: Ashgate Publishing, 2012.

Modica, Andrea. *Barbara.* Tucson, AZ: Nazraeli Press, 2004.

———. *Treadwell.* San Francisco: Chronicle Books, 1996.

———. http://www.andreamodica.com/

Morris, Gary. "The Incredible Shrinking. . . and Expanding Ethnic Minority, or The Racist in the Cupboard." *Bright Lights Film Journal Online.* Issue 15 (November 1995). http://brightlightsfilm.com/15/racist.php#.UxdSafRdVCw

Morwood, Mike and Penny van Oosteree. *A New Human: The Startling Discovery and Strange Story of the "Hobbits" of Flores, Indonesia.* New York: HarperCollins Publishers, 2007.

Moseley, Charles. *A Century of Emblems: An Introductory Anthology.* Aldershot, England and Brookfield, VT: Scolar Press, 1989.

Mundy, Liza. "Souls On Ice: America's Embryo Glut and the Wasted Promise of Stem Cell Research." *Mother Jones.* http://www.motherjones.com/politics/2006/07/souls-ice-americas-embryo-glut-and-wasted-promise-stem-cell-research.

Murdock, Deroy. "The Adoption Option." *National Review online.* August 27, 2001. http://www.nationalreview.com/articles/205006/adoption-option/deroy-murdock

Nandy, Ashis. *Traditions, Tyranny and Utopias: Essays in the Politics of Awareness.* Delhi: Oxford University Press, 1987.

Needham, Joseph. *A History of Embryology.* New York: Arno Press, 1975.

Ness, Patrick. *A Monster Calls*. Somerville, MA: Candlewick Press, 2011.

Neumark-Sztainer, Dianne, et. al. "Issues of Self-Image among Overweight African-American and Caucasian Adolescent Girls: A Qualitative Study. *Journal of Nutrition Education* 31, no. 6 (November/December 1999): 311–320.

——. "Perceived Stigmatization Among Overweight African-American and Caucasian Adolescent Girls. *Journal of Adolescent Health* 23, no. 5 (November 1998): 1–11.

The New Tom Thumb; or, Reading Made Quite Easy. Newcastle: T. Simpson and Sons, 1850.

Newkirk, Pamela. *Spectacle: The Astonishing Life of Ota Benga*. New York: HarperCollins, 2015.

Newman, Karen. *Fetal Positions: Individualism, Science, Visuality*. Stanford: Stanford University Press, 1997.

Newman, William. "The Homunculus and His Forebears: Wonders of Art and Nature" in *Natural Particulars: Nature and the Disciplines in Renaissance Europe*, edited by Anthony Grafton and Nancy Siraisi. 321–345. Cambridge, MA: MIT Press, 1999.

Newport, Frank. "In US, 46% Hold Creationist View of Human Origins." June 1, 2012. http://www.gallup.com/poll/155003/hold-creationist-view-human-origins.aspx.

Ngai, Sianne. *Our Aesthetic Categories: Zany, Cute, Interesting*. Cambridge, MA and London: Harvard University Press, 2012.

Nightlight Christian Adoptions Agency. http://www.nightlight.org.

Nilsson, Lennart. *A Child is Born*. New York: Delta, 1993.

Niven, Jennifer. *Holding Up the Universe*. New York: Knopf, 2016.

Norton, Mary. *The Borrowers*. 1952. New York: Odyssey/Harcourt Brace, 1990.

Nottage, Lynn. *Las Meninas*. New York: Dramatis Play Service, Inc. 2002.

Nussbaum, Felicity. *The Limits of the Human: Fictions of Anomaly, Race, and Gender in the Long Eighteenth Century*. Cambridge: Cambridge University Press, 2003.

Onion, Rebecca. "How Science Became Child's Play: Science and the Culture of American Childhood, 1900–1980." PhD Diss. University of Texas, 2012.

Opie, Iona and Peter Opie. *The Classic Fairy Tales*. London: Oxford University Press, 1974.

Oppenheimer, Jane M. *Essays in The History of Embryology and Biology*. Cambridge, MA and London: MIT Press, 1967.

Orbach, Susie. *Fat Is a Feminist Issue*. New York: Paddington Press, 1978.

"The Original and Celebrated General Tom Thumb, The World-Renowned American Man in Miniature." 1860. Http://chnm.gmu.edu/lostmuseum/lm/212/

Pace, Patricia. "The Body-in-Writing: Miniatures in Mary Norton's *Borrowers*." *Text and Performance Quarterly*. 11, no. 4 (October 1991): 279–290.

Page, Nick. *Lord Minimus: The Extraordinary Life of Britain's Smallest Man*. London: HarperCollins Publishers, 2001.

Parry, Graham. *The Golden Age Restor'd: The Culture of the Stuart Court, 1603–42*. Manchester: Manchester University Press, 1981.

Paul, Lissa. "The Return of the *Iron Man*." *Horn Book* 86, no. 2 (March/April 2000): 218–225.

Pearce, Michelle J., Julie Boergers, and Mitchell J. Prinstein. "Adolescent Obesity, Overt and Relational Peer Victimization, and Romantic Relationships." *Obesity Research* 10, no. 5 (May 2002): 386–393.

Perrault, Charles. "Le petit Poucet," in *Perrault's Fairy Tales*. 1697. New York: Dover Publications, 1969.

Petcheski, Rosalind Pollack. "Fetal Images: The Power of Visual Culture in the Politics of Reproduction." *Feminist Studies* 13, no. 2 (Summer 1987): 263–292.

Philbrick, Rodman. *Freak the Mighty*. New York: Blue Sky Press, 1993.

Picoult, Jodi. *Sing You Home*. New York: Atria Books, 2011.

Piercy, Marge. *He, She, and It*. New York: Fawcett Crest, 1991.

Pieterse, Jan Nederveen. *White on Black: Images of Africa and Blacks in Western Popular Culture*. New Haven and London: Yale University Press, 1992.

Pigot, Richard. Introduction to *Moral Emblems with aphorisms, adages, and proverbs, of all ages and nations, from Jacob Cats and Robert Farlie: with illustrations freely rendered, from designs found in their works*. By John Leighton, translated and edited, with additional material, by Richard Pigot. London: Longman, Green, Longman and Roberts, 1860.

Pilkington, Ed. "Alone in Alabama: Dispatches from an Inmate Jailed for Her Son's Stillbirth." *The Guardian*. October 7, 2015. https://www.theguardian.com/us-news/2015/oct/07/alabama-chemical-endangerment-pregnancy-amanda-kimbrough.

Pinkus, Karen. *Picturing Silence: Emblem, Language, Counter-Reformation Materiality*. Ann Arbor, University of Michigan Press, 1996.

Pinto-Correia, Clara. *The Ovary of Eve: Egg and Sperm and Preformation*. Chicago and London: University of Chicago Press, 1997.

Place, François. *The Last Giants*. 1992. Translated by William Rodarmor, 1993. Chrysalis Children's Books, 1999.

Poignant, Roslyn. *Professional Savages: Captive Lives and Western Spectacle*. New Haven and London: Yale University Press, 2004.

Poliquin, Rachel. "The Visual Erotics of Mini-Marriages: The Appeal of Tiny Nuptials Between Children, Stuffed Kittens, and Other Small, Cute Things." *The Believer*. November/December2007.Http:///www.believermag.com/issues/200711/?read=article_poliquin

Powless, Robert E. "Iroquois Indians," Discovery Channel School. June 28, 2001. http://www.discoveryschool.com/homeworkhelp/worldbook/atozgeography/i/281880.html

Price, Willard. *Elephant Adventure*. New York: John Day Co., 1964.

Probyn, Elspeth. *Carnal Appetites: FoodSexIdentities*. London and New York: Routledge, 2000.

Quick, Catherine S. " 'Meant to be Huge': Obesity and Body Image in Young Adult Novels." *ALAN Review* 35, no. 5 (Winter 2008): 54–61.

R.B. [Nathaniel Crouch]. *Delights for the Ingenious, in above Fifty Select and Choice Emblems, Divine and Moral, Ancient and Modern*. London, 1684.

——. *Choice Emblems, Divine and Moral, Antient and Modern, or, Delights for the Ingenious, in above Fifty Select Emblems, Curiously engraven upon Copper-plates*. 6th ed. London: Printed by Edmund Parker, 1732.

Raatschen, Gudrun. "Merely Ornamental? Van Dyck's Portraits of Henrietta Maria" in *Henrietta Maria: Piety, Politics and Patronage*, edited by Erin Griffey. 139–163. Burlington, VT and Aldershot, England: Ashgate Publishing, 2008.

Rankine, Claudia. "The Meaning of Serena Williams." August 25, 2015. www.nytimes.com/2015/08/30/magazine/the-meaning-of-serena-williams.html.

Reichardt, Jasia. *Robots: Fact, Fiction and Prediction*. London: Thames and Hudson, 1978.

Republican Party Platform 2016. https://prod-cdn-static.gop.com/static/home/data/platform.pdf

Ricker, Jewett E., ed. *Sculpture at a Century of Progress, 1933, 1934*. Chicago, 1934.

Ridley, Matt. *Genome: The Autobiography of a Species in 23 Chapters*. New York: HarperCollins, 1999.

Rivero, Albert J. *The Plays of Henry Fielding: A Critical Study of His Dramatic Career*. Charlottesville: University of Virginia Press, 1989.

"A Robot that Walks, Talks and Smokes: Aluminum Giant with Electric Brain." *The Meccano Magazine*. June 1939: 342.

Rochman, Bonnie. "Should Parents Lose Custory of Their Extremely Obese Kids?" July 13, 2011. http://healthland.time.com/2011/07/13/should-parents-lose-custody-of-their-very-obese-kids/

Rockwood, Roy. *Bomba the Jungle Boy and the Cannibals, or Winning Against Native Dangers*. New York: Cupples and Lion, 1931.

Rodgers, Terence. "Empires of the Imagination: Rider Haggard, Popular Fiction and Africa" in *Writing and Africa*. edited by Mpalive-Hangson Msiska and Paul Hyland. London and New York: Longman, 1997: 103–121.

Roe, Shirley A. *Matter, Life, and Generation: Eighteenth-Century Embryology and the Haller-Wolff Debate.* Cambridge: Cambridge University Press, 1981.

Rothblum, Esther and Sondra Solovay, eds. *The Fat Studies Reader.* New York and London: New York University Press, 2009.

Rowling, J.K. *Harry Potter and The Chamber of Secrets.* New York: Scholastic Press, 1998.

——. *Harry Potter and the Goblet of Fire.* New York: Scholastic Press, 2000.

Russo, Mary. *The Female Grotesque: Risk, Excess and Modernity.* New York and London: Routledge, 1994.

Rydell, Robert W. "Making America (More) Modern: America's Depression-Era World's Fairs" in *Designing Tomorrow: America's World's Fairs of the 1930s,* edited by Robert W. Rydell and Laura Burd Schiavo. 1–21. New Haven and London: Yale University Press, 2010.

——. *World of Fairs: The Century-of-Progress Expositions.* Chicago and London: University of Chicago Press, 1993.

Saguy, Abigail C. *What's Wrong with Fat?* Oxford: Oxford University Press, 2013.

Sampsell-Willmann, Kate. *Lewis Hine as Social Critic.* Jackson: University Press of Mississippi, 2009.

Sanchez, Victoria E. and Mary E. Stuckey. "Coming of Age as a Culture? Emancipatory and Hegemonic Readings of *The Indian in the Cupboard.*" *Western Journal of Communications* 64, no. 1 (Winter 2000): 78–91.

Sánchez-Eppler, Karen. *Dependent States: The Child's Part in Nineteenth Century American Culture.* Chicago: University of Chicago Press, 2005.

Schweitzer, Marlis. "Barnum's Last Laugh: General Tom Thumb's Wedding Cake in the Library of Congress." *Performing Arts Resources* 28, no. 1 (2011): 116–126.

Segal, Harold B. *Pinocchio's Progeny: Puppets, Marionettes, Automatons, and Robots in Modernist and Avant-Garde Drama.* Baltimore: Johns Hopkins University Press, 1995.

Sharpe, Kevin. "Van Dyck, the Royal Image and the Caroline Court." *Van Dyck & Britain* exhibit catalogue. 14–23. London: Tate Publishing, 2009.

Shelley, Mary. *Frankenstein: Or, The Modern Prometheus.* 1818. London: Henry Colburn and Richard Bentley, 1831.

Sikundar, Sylvia and Alison Astill. *Forest Singer.* New York: Barefoot Books, 1999.

Silver, Carole G. *Strange and Secret Peoples: Fairies and Victorian Consciousness.* New York and Oxford: Oxford University Press, 1999.

Skal, David J. "What We Talk About When We Talk About Monsters" in *Speaking of Monsters: A Teratological Anthology,* edited by Caroline Joan S. Picart and John Edgar Browning. New York: Palgrave Macmillan, 2012: xi–xii.

Sketch of the Life, Personal Appearance, Character and Manners of Charles S. Stratton, The Man in Miniature, Known as General Tom Thumb, and His Wife, Lavinia Warren Stratton . . . New York: Printed by Samuel Booth, 1874.

Sketch of the Life, Personal Appearance, Character, and Manners of Charles S. Stratton, the Man in Miniature, Known as General Tom Thumb, and His Wife, Lavinia Warren Stratton; Including the History of Their Courtship and Marriage, With Some Account of Remarkable Dwarfs, Giants, & Other Human Phenomena, of Ancient and Modern Times, and Songs Given at Their Public Levees (New York: Press of Wynkoop & Hallenbeck): paragraph 119, Disability History Museum, http://www.disability museum.org/lib/stills/2077.htm

Sloan, Holly Goldberg. *Short.* New York: Dial Books, 2017.

Sobal, Jeffery. "The Size Acceptance Movement and the Social Construction of Body Weight" in *Weighty Issues: Fatness and Thinness as Social Problems,* edited by Jeffery Sobal and Donna Maurer. 231–249. New York: Aldine de Gruyter, 1999.

Solomon, Andrew. *Far From the Tree: Parents, Children, and the Search for Identity.* New York: Scribner, 2012.

Somashekhar, Sandhya. "Ohio Governor Vetoes 'Heartbeat Bill' but Signs Another Abortion Restriction Into Law." *The Washington Post.* December 13, 2016. https://

www.washingtonpost.com/news/post-nation/wp/2016/12/13/ohio-governor-vetoes-heartbeat-bill-but-signs-into-law-another-abortion-restriction/?utm_term=. dc56b849a129

Sonheim, Amy. "Picture Books about the Golem: Acts of Creation Without and Within." *The Lion and the Unicorn* 27 (2003): 377–393.

"Souls on Ice: America's Human Embryo Glut and the Unbearable Lightness of Almost Being," *Mother Jones*. July/August 2006. http://www.motherjones.com/ politics/2006/ 07/souls-ice-americas-embryo-glut-and-wasted-promise-stem-cell-research

Stabile, Carole. "Shooting the Mother: Fetal Photography and the Politics of Disappearance." *Camera Obscura* 28, no. 1 (Fall 1992): 178–205.

Steedman, Carolyn. *Strange Dislocations: Childhood and the Idea of Human Interiority, 1780-1930*. Cambridge, MA: Harvard University Press, 1995.

Steege, David. "Doctor Dolittle and the Empire: Hugh Lofting's Response to British Colonialism" in *The Presence of the Past in Children's Literature*, edited by Ann Lawson Lucas. 91–97. Westport, CT: Praeger, 2003.

Steig, William Steig, *The Toy Brother*. New York: Michael di Capua Books, HarperCollins Publishers, 1996.

Sterne, Laurence. *The Life and Opinions of Tristram Shandy, Gentleman*. 1759. Mineola, NY: Dover Publications, 2007.

Stevens, Laura M. *The Poor Indians: British Missionaries, Native Americans, and Colonial Sensibility*. Philadelphia: University of Pennsylvania Press, 2004.

Stewart, Susan. *On Longing: Narratives of the Miniature, the Gigantic, the Souvenir, the Collection*. 1984. Durham, NC and London: Duke University Press, 1993.

Swift, Jonathan. *Gulliver's Travels*. 1726. Introduction by Michael Foot. New York: Penguin, 1967.

Szegedy-Maszak, Andrew. "Introduction." In Clare L. Lyons, John K. Papadopoulos, Lindsey S. Stewart, and Andrew Szegedy-Maszak, eds. *Antiquity and Photography: Early Views of Ancient Mediterranean Sites*. J. Paul Getty Museum (2005): 2–18.

Taylor, Rhonda Harris. "*Indian in the Cupboard*: a Case Study in Perspective." *Qualitative Studies in Education* 13, no. 4 (2000): 371–384.

"Thalidomide Apology Insulting, Campaigners Say." BBC News Health. September 1, 2012. http://www.bbc.co.uk/news/health-19448046?print=true

Thomson, Rosemarie Garland. *Extraordinary Bodies: Figuring Physical Disability in American Culture and Literature*. New York: Columbia University Press, 1997.

——. *Freakery: Cultural Spectacles of the Extraordinary Body*. New York City: New York University Press, 1996.

Thone, Ruth Raymond. *Fat: A Fate Worse than Death? Women, Weight and Appearance*. New York and London: Haworth Press, 1997.

Tietze-Conrat, Erika. *Dwarfs and Jesters in Art*. New York: Phaidon Publishers, 1957.

Tingley, Kim. "The Weight." *New York Times* magazine. January 25, 2015. 36–41,48.

Todd, Pamela. *Pig and the Shrink*. New York: Delacorte Press, 1999.

Tuan, Yi-Fu. *Dominance and Affection: The Making of Pets*. New Haven and London: Yale University Press, 1984.

Tyson, Edward. *The Anatomy of a Pygmy Compared with that of a Monkey, and Ape, and a Man. With an Essay Concerning the Pygmies &c. of the Antients. Wherein it Will Appear that They Are All either Apes or Monkies, and not Men, as Formerly Pretended*. 1699. 2nd. ed. London: T. O. Osborne, 1751.

Vaughan, Virgina Mason, Fernando Cioni, and Jaquelyn Bessell, "Introduction" in *Speaking Pictures: The Visual/Verbal Nexus of Dramatic Performance*, edited by Mason, Cioni and Bessell. 11–22. Madison and Teaneck, NJ: Fairleigh Dickinson University Press, 2010.

Vidal, John, "Bones of Contention." *Guardian Weekly*. January 12, 2005. http://www.theguardian.com/science/2005/jan/13/research.science.

Waller, Edmund. *The Poems of Edmund Waller*. Vol. 1. Ed. G. Thorn Drury. 1686. London: A. H. Bullen and New York: Charles Scribner's Sons, 1901.

Walmsley, Leo. *Toro of the Little People*. New York: George H. Doran Co., 1925.

Walpole, Hugh. Introduction to *The Story of Doctor Dolittle*. Toronto: McClelland and Stewart, 1923.

Warner, Marina. "Fee, fi, fo, fum: the Child in the Jaws of the Story" in *Cannibalism and the Colonial World*, edited by Francis Barker, Peter Hulme and Margaret Iversen. Cambridge: Cambridge University Press, 1998: 158–182.

——. *No Go the Bogeyman: Scaring, Lulling, and Making Mock*. New York: Farrar, Straus and Giroux,1998.

Warner, Sylvia Townsend. *T. H. White: A Biography*. New York: Viking Press, 1968.

Watson, Elizabeth See. *Achille Bocchi and the Emblem Book as Symbolic Form*. Cambridge: Cambridge University Press, 1993.

Weiss, Harry B. "Three Hundred Years of Tom Thumb," in *The History of Tom Thumbe*, 157–166. New York: Garland, 1977.

Werthein, Margaret. "Life Begins at 'Want a Cigarette?' " *Alternet,* June 23, 2005. http://www.alternet.org/story/22261

Wheelock, Arthur. "The Queen, The Dwarf and the Court: Van Dyck and the Ideals of the English Monarchy" in *Van Dyck 1599–1999: Conjectures and Refutations*, edited by Hans Vlieghe. 151–166. Turnhout, Belgium: Brepols Publishers, 2001.

White, E. B. *Stuart Little*. 1945. New York: Harper and Row, 1973.

White, T. H. *Mistress Masham's Repose* (1947). 2nd ed. 1998, Rpt. 2002. Illustrated by Martin Hargreaves. Reprint by G. P. Putnam's Sons and Jonathan Cape Children's Books.

Whitney, Geffrey. *A Choice of Emblems, and other Devises: for the moste parte gathered out of Sundrie Writers, Englished and Moralized*. Leyden: 1586.

Wilde, Oscar. *The Birthday of the Infanta*. Illus. by Pamela Bianco. New York: Macmillan Company, 1929.

——. "The Selfish Giant" in the *Complete Shorter Fiction of Oscar Wilde*, edited by Isobel Murray. 110–114. Oxford: Oxford University Press, 1979.

Wilgoren, Jodi. "The Terms of Debate in Kansas." *New York Times*. May 15, 2005.

Wilkin, Karen. "Spain and Picasso." *The New Criterion*. January 2007: 48–52.

Williams, Wes. *Monsters and their Meanings in Early Modern Culture: Mighty Magic*. Oxford: Oxford University Press, 2011.

Wilson, Catherine. *The Invisible World: Early Modern Philosophy and the Invention of the Microscope*. Princeton: Princeton University Press, 1995.

Windle, Bertram C. A. Introduction to *A Philological Essay Concerning the Pygmies of the Ancients by Edward Tyson (1699). Now edited, with an Introduction Treating of Pigmy Races and Fairy Tales*. London: David Nutt, 1894.

Wither, George. *A Collection of Emblemes, Ancient and Moderne*. London: Printed by A. M. for Henry Taunton, 1635.

The Wonders of the Microscope; or, An Explanation of the Wisdom of the Creator in Objects Comparatively Minute: adapted to the Understanding of Young Persons. 1808. London: printed for William Darnton, 1823.

Wood, Audrey and David Shannon, illus. *The Bunyans*. New York: Blue Sky Press, 1996.

Wood, Edward J. *Giants and Dwarfs*. London: Richard Bentley, 1868.

Wooden, Warren. *Children's Literature of the English Renaissance*. Lexington, KY: University of Kentucky Press, 1986.

Wynne, John Huddlestone. *Choice Emblems, Natural, Historical, Fabulous, Moral, and Divine, for the Improvement and Pastime of Youth*. London: George Riley, 1772.

Yamanaka, Lois-Ann. *Name Me Nobody*. New York: Hyperion, 1999.

Yonge, Charlotte. *The History of the Life and Death of the Good Knight Sir Thomas Thumb*. Edinburgh: Thomas Constable and Co., 1855.

Zelizer, Viviana. *Pricing the Priceless Child: The Changing Social Value of Children*. New York: Basic Books, 1985.

Zunshine, Lisa. *Strange Concepts and the Stories They Make Possible: Cognition, Culture, Narrative*. Baltimore: Johns Hopkins University Press, 2008.

INDEX

abortion, opposition to 52–3
abstract, dwarf as 73–4, 79
Abu Ghraib detention center 263–5
Abu Simbel temples 259–64
achondroplasia 57, 121, 124, 268 n. 14
Adelson, Betty M., *Lives of Dwarfs* 118, 289 n. 51, 289 n. 54, 289 n. 58
Africa, in colonial myth 136–40, 143–6
alchemy, and origins of life 17, 33, 35, 37, 38–9, 43–4
Alciato, Andrea, *Emblematum liber* 75–7, 79–80
Aleksander, Igor and Burnett, Piers 208
Allen, Woody 25
Allende, Isabel, *Bosque de los Pigmies/ Forest of the Pygmies* 162–3, 165
Alpers, Svetlana 91, 93, 101
ambition, and size 78, 80, 82–3
anatomy, and science 131–2, 272 n. 31
animalcule 45–7
Anker, Suzanne and Nelkin, Dorothy 11–12
anthropology:
    interest in 107, 139–40
    and pygmies 8, 19, 134–5, 140–2, 144, 163
ape:
    and dwarfs 69–72, 81–4
    and pygmies 131–2, 141–2, 144, 147
appetite, and giants 230–1
Appleton, Victor II, *Tom Swift and His Giant Robot* 212–17
Arendt, Hannah 258
aristocracy:

and dwarfs 100, 248
and exotics 88, 280 n. 15
Arthur, King and Tom Thumb figure 30, 43, 50–1
Astill, Alison 162
Attack of the Fifty-Foot Woman (film) 188

Baden-Powell, Robert 201–3, 213, 215
Ballantyne, R. M. 143
Baltasar Carlos, Prince of Spain 92–7, 99, 106
Banks, Lynne Reid, *The Indian in the Cupboard* 164–73, 175–6, 230
Barbara 12, 190, 250–5
bariatric surgery 238–40, 262
Barnum, P. T. 61
    American Museum 18, 107–10, 114, 138, 288 n. 28, 292 n. 25
    and General Tom Thumb 18, 106–16, 130, 150, 184, 286 n. 5
    and giants 111, 184
    and pygmies 138–9
Barwell, Mrs, *The Novel Adventures of Tom Thumb the Great, Showing How He Visited the Insect World and Learned Much Wisdom* 49
Bass, Lara R. 100
Bassompierre, Marshal François de 63–4
Bates, Harry, "Farewell to the Master" 306 n. 31
beauty, and smallness 21–2
Belkin, Lisa 246
Belzoni, Giovanni Battista 260

Benga, Ota 8, 12, 21, 131, 150, 178, 295 n. 57
and 1904 World's Fair 18, 140–1, 163
and Bronx Zoo 18, 141–2, 144, 160–1
seen as missing link 19, 144, 147
suicide 143, 160–2, 163
Bennett, Cherie, *Life in the Fat Lane* 240–3
Berlant, Lauren 51, 53
Bird, Brad 233
Blake, William 77
Bocchi, Achille, *Symbolicarum Quaestionium de Universo Genere* 85
Bodger, Joan 151
Bogdan, Robert 106, 107, 110, 124, 128
boy culture 189, 193, 209–23
Boy Scout movement 201–3, 209, 211, 212, 220
Bradford, Phillips Verner 139–40
Bradford, Phillips Verner and Blume, Harvey 141, 143
Brady, Matthew 115
Brahe, Tycho 125–6
Briggs, Raymond, *The Man* 173–8
Brink, Carol Ryrie, *Andy Buckram's Tin Men* 216–17
British Empire, and machines 201–3
Brown, Carol S. 227
Brown, Kenneth D. 210
Browne, Thomas, *Religio Medici* 29, 31, 58
Buchan, John 135
Buckingham, George Villiers, 1st Duke 63–5, 68
Bunyan, John, *Divine Emblems* 83, 85–6
Burckhardt, J. L. 260
Burgess, Melvin, *The Earth Giant* 185
Burke, Edmund 6–7, 17, 111, 184–5, 190
Burney, Venetia 62–3
Burroughs, Edgar Rice 143
Burrows, Guy, *The Land of the Pigmies* 133, 141–2
Bush, George W. 54–5
Bushmen 137

capac hucha Inca festival 21–2
Čapek, Karel *Rossum's Universal Robots* 208
"Cardiff Giant" 186
Carreño de Miranda, Juan:
Eugenia Martínez Vallejo ("La Monstrua") 248–50, 254
La Monstrua Desnuda 249–50
Cats, Jacob 79, 80, 83–4
Charles I of England 63–5, 86
Charles II of England 66

Checa, Fernando 93, 98
Chemers, Michael M. 104, 113–14
chiasmus, in painting 88–9
child labor 194–200
childhood:
and colonialism 132–4, 142, 145, 152–6, 173, 175
and dwarf discourse 85–6, 86–102, 111–13, 128, 133
and Industrial Revolution 195–201
and interiority 21
children:
and cuteness 7, 113, 191
dwarf 8, 18–19, 23–4, 71, 118–23, 129
and emblem books 21, 82–6, 94
as food for giants 186–7
and Industrial Revolution 194–8
material culture *see* Meccano
and miniatures 7, 18–19, 21–3, 26, 147, 157, 230, 257
and monsters 182–3, 246–50
and obesity 13, 244–55
and otherness 7
pygmies seen as 133–4, 142, 145–6
sacrifice 21–2
and scale 3, 182–3, 194, 197–9, 253
and science education 209–23
seen as pygmies 196
Snowflake 54–5, 56, 59
and Tom Thumb weddings 116–17, 127, 128
chimera 35
Civil War (English) 65–6
Clarke, Pauline, *Return of the Twelves* 166, 167–8, 175–6
Class:
and alterity xi 4–5, 226
and childhood 128, 177, 211–17, 246, 251–2
and poverty 251–2
and size 1, 72, 173, 176–7, 189
Coello, Alonzo Sánchez, *The Infanta Isabella Clare Eugenia and Magdalena Ruiz* 90
Cohen, Jeffrey Jerome 9, 10, 224, 237, 254–5
Cohen, Percy 183
Coleridge, S. T. 77
Colie, Rosalie L. 77
Collett, Anne 160
Collicutt, Paul, *Robot City Adventures* 221
colonialism:
and childhood 132–4, 142, 145, 152–6, 173, 175
and conversion 132–3, 145–9, 164, 177–8

and giants 156–7
and myths of Africa 136–40, 143–4
and photography 134–5, 259–62
and race 131–2
and size 152–5
comedy, and dwarfs 25
Comenius, Jan Amos, *The Great
    Didactic* 48–9
conception:
    and microscopy 45–6
    and Tom Thumb story 28, 33, 41, 51
conversion, and colonialism 132–3,
    145–9, 164, 177–8
Coombes, Annie E. 138
Cooner, Donna, *Skinny* 239–40
Cowper, William, *Tirocinium* 29, 31, 58
Craik, Dinah Mulock 30
Craton, Lillian 107, 129
Crouch, Nathaniel (R. B.), *Delights for the
    Ingenious* 79, 80–4
Cunningham, Hugh 195
Curlin, Jay 57–8
cuteness 7, 113, 191
Cutler, Jane, *The Song of the Molimo* 163,
    169, 173, 178

Dahl, Roald:
    The BFG 182, 188
    Charlie and the Chocolate Factory 13,
        159, 160, 163, 173
Dahmer, Jeffrey 9
Daniel, Carolyn 230
Darwin, Charles 5, 22–3, 57, 134–5, 266 n.
    3, 291 n. 9
daumerling 30
Davis, Warwick 128
De Castelet, Laurens 39
De Graaf, Regnier 46
Dickens, Charles:
    and littleness 129
    and Noble Savage concept 135
DiDonato, Tiffanie 24
difference:
    and anxiety 60–1, 85, 94, 258
    as otherness 3, 4–6, 23–8, 106, 130,
        257–8, 263
Digital Revolution 219–20
dime museums 26, 104, 138
Dinklage, Peter 105
Disability:
    and performance 104
    and size 308 n.4, 308 n. 5
diversity, and size 8
Dr Dolittle *see* Lofting, Hugh
Droeshout, Martin 73, 79
Drum, Kevin 220

Du Camp, Maxime 259–61, 262–5
Dunn, Katherine, *Geek Love* 44–5
dwarf discourse:
    and age 90
    and childhood 85–6, 86–102, 111–13,
        128–9, 133
    and emblems 7, 21, 74–89, 106
    and Hudson 63–74, 111
    and performance 103–29, 175
dwarfs 8, 23–5, 33, 60–102
    and anxiety of difference 60–1, 85,
        94, 106
    and apes 69–72, 81–4
    celebrity 104–10, 127, 128
    and children 8, 18–19, 23–4, 71, 93–6,
        118–23, 129
    in children's literature 13, 103, 105,
        118–29, 155
    as comedic 25
    court 17–18, 21, 78, 93–5, 98–102, 105,
        112, 119–21, 125–6, 297 n. 3
    as cultural sign 60
    in emblem books 21, 74–89, 94, 106
    as exotic other 69–70, 71, 90, 118
    female 86–9, 95–6, 99–102
    and Flores hominins 27
    and limb-lengthening surgery 24, 262
    and *multum in parvo* 61, 73, 83, 85,
        102, 111
    in portraiture 78, 87–90, 92–4, 96, 100,
        285 n. 83
    proportionate 64, 74, 105, 108, 111,
        114, 130
    and sexuality 116
    textual 61–3, 66–7, 78, 82
    as tragicomic 66, 82, 127–8
    visual 61, 67, 78, 82

Earle, John, *Microcosmographie* 19
emblem books, and dwarfs 21, 74–86,
    94, 106
emblems:
    and metaphor 77–8
    and painting 101–2
embryo:
    and homunculus 38, 40, 60
    and preformationism 46–7, 56
    rights 53–4
    and stem cell research 32, 34, 52–3,
        54–6
embryo adoption 32, 34, 54, 56, 59
embryology 275–6 n. 74
Emery, Alan E. H. and Emery, Marcia
    L. H. 250
epigenesis 46
epitome, dwarf as 73–4, 78–9, 111

ethics:
and assisted reproduction 32
and children's literature 150–8
and stem-cell research 55–6
Evans, William 73, 184
evolution:
and debates over 267–8 n. 11
and childhood 132–3
and education 22–3
and human dwarf species 27
and missing link theory 19, 144, 147, 150, 174
and pygmies 132–5, 137, 139–40, 141–3
exceptionalism, human 5–6
exotics, and aristocracy 88

fairies, and pygmies 133–4, 137
The Famous History of Tom Thumb 42
Fantasy Island (TV series) 105
Farrell, Amy Erdman 236–7
fat acceptance 238, 245–6, 252, 310 n. 33
Fat Studies 311 n. 34
Father Cats 79
femininity:
and giants 185, 222–3, 224–30
and miniatures 20, 113, 181, 229–30
and obesity 189–90, 225–6, 236–43, 248–55
Ferris, Jim 104
fetal photography 276 n. 75
fetus:
and dwarfs 271 n. 21
personhood 52–4
and politics of size 51–6, 58, 253
Fielding, Helen, Bridget Jones's Diary 240–1
Fielding, Henry, The Tragedy of Tragedies; or the Life and Death of Tom Thumb the Great 30, 42–3, 49
film, dwarf actors 105
Fisher, Ruth B. 134
Flaubert, Gustave 260, 264
folklore:
and giants 186
and homunculi 40, 42
and the miniature 23, 28, 132
and thumblings 30–1, 34–5
Fore, Devin 259
Frankenstein, Victor 9, 182–3, 186
freak shows:
and dwarfs 44–5, 104–5, 107–11, 127
and giants 111, 183–4
and obesity 232, 249
and pygmies 133, 134, 137–9

Fuller, Thomas, Worthies of England 66, 184
future perfect 193, 201, 207, 212–13, 217, 219–22

Galen 131
Game of Thrones (TV series) 105
Gandhi, Leela 161
Garnett, Amaryllis 151
Geil, William, A Yankee in Pigmy Land 133–4, 136, 138
gender:
and dwarf discourse 86–9, 95–6
and giants 181, 189–90, 225–6, 226–43, 254
and mechanical bodies 192
and miniaturization 171–3
and scientific utopianism 10–11
General Tom Thumb see Stratton, Charles S.
genetics, and size 11, 35, 37, 43–5, 47, 51
Gervais, Ricky 128
giants:
and appetite 230–6
in children's literature 186–9, 212, 225–6, 226–43, 231–2
and colonialism 156–7
display 111, 183–4
as eating children 186–7
and femininity 185, 222–3, 224–6, 226–43, 309 n. 13
friendly 188, 255
giant robots 189, 192–3, 205–9, 211–23
as lacking intelligence 185
and miniatures 9, 157, 184–6
as monstrous 9, 181–90, 191, 217, 225, 236–7, 246, 255
obese females as 189–90, 225–6
in sport 229
as violent 186–7
Gillis, John R. 54
Gilman, Sander 225
Gilmore, David 182
Giordano, Luca 98
Godzilla figure 186, 242
Goffman, Erving 104
Going, F. L., Fat Kid Rules the World 233–4, 237
Goldberg, Vicki 197, 198–9
Goldsmith, Oliver 83
Golem 182, 187
Gombrich, E. H. 67
Goodrich, Carter 247
Gordon, James H. 142
Gores, Steven J. 169

Graff, Lisa, *The Thing About Georgie*
    121–2
Griswold, Jerry 266 n. 5, 285 n. 81
Gulliver's Travels (Swift) 5–6, 36–8, 40, 45,
    64, 150–1, 156, 158

Hade, Dan 167
Haggard, H. Rider 143–4
Hague, Michael 160
Halliburton, Richard 146–50, 156,
    158–60, 173, 177
Hamilton, Virginia, *The Planet of Junior
    Brown* 233
Hancock, Susan 27–8, 301 n. 141
Handler, Chelsea 127
Harris, Neil 111, 118
Hartlib, Samuel 48
Hartsoeker, Nicolaas 47
Harvey, William 46
Headrick, Daniel 134
Hearn, Karen 68
Hegi, Ursula, *Trudi and Pia* 121, 122–3
Henrietta Maria, Queen 63–72, 86,
    128, 150
Henty, G. A. 143
Herodotus 6, 134
hESC research *see* human embryonic
    stem cell (hESC) research
Heth, Joice 106
Heywood, Thomas 73
Higgs boson 58, 279 n. 97
Hine, Lewis 197–200
hobbits 27
Holt, Kimberly Willis, *When Zachary
    Beaver Came to Town* 232–3
homunculus 33, 35, 37–47, 60
    and masculinity 47
    and spermist preformationism
        46–7, 56
    and Tom Thumb figure 47–59
Honey, I Blew Up the Kid (film) 247
Hooke, Robert, *Micrographia* 1, 57
hormonal treatment for children 308 n. 4
Hornby, Frank 209–10
Hudson, Jeffrey 8, 12, 18, 21, 63–74, 128,
    296 n. 78
    banishment 66
    death 66
    as emblem 73–4, 74–86, 111–12
    exile 65–6
    as gift to Henrietta Maria 64–5, 66, 72,
        86–7, 150, 184
    humiliation 64, 126, 128
    in poetry 72–3, 79
    portraits 65, 67–71, 85, 86–7, 94,
        96, 128

Hughes, Ted:
    The Iron Man/Giant 188, 217–19, 221,
        233, 254, 296 n. 89
    The Iron Giant (film) 303 n. 28
    The Iron Woman 185
human embryonic stem cell (hESC)
    research 32, 34, 52–3, 54–6, 262
humanity:
    and giants 191–3, 212
    and human measure 258–65
    and machines 193–203, 207–8
    and missing links 19, 144, 147, 150, 174

idealism, scientific 205–6
identity:
    and body image 231, 238, 240
    and normality 11
    and performance 56, 103, 105,
        118, 129
    and reproduction 32, 41, 44, 60
    and size 1, 24, 29–30, 32, 39, 51, 257
    spoiled 104, 118
The Indian in the Cupboard (film) 298 n.
    108, 300 n. 124
Industrial Revolution:
    and adults and machines 200–3, 220
    and children and machines 193–201,
        211–12
inferiority, and smallness 131–6
interiority:
    and childhood 21
    and Tom Thumb tale 28
The Iron Giant (film) 188–9
Isaacs, Anne and Zelinsky, Paul O.,
    Swamp Angel 228–9, 254
Isabella of Bourbon 92
Isabella Clara Eugenia, Archduchess
    86–9, 125, 290 n. 69

"Jack the Giant Killer" 185
Jeffers, Susan, *Brother Eagle, Sister
    Sky* 167
Jepp 125–6
Johnson, Richard, *The History of Tom
    Thumbe* 30
Joyce, William 247

Kasich, John 53
Kellman, Martin 152
Kerckring, Theodor 32, 46
Kerr, M. E., *Little Little* 121, 123–5
Kimbrough, Amanda 52
King Kong figure 158, 186
Kipling, Rudyard 161
Klieman, Kairn A. 25–6
Knowles, John 70, 72

Kuznets, Lois 175, 298–9 n. 109, 299 n.
117, 299 n. 120, 300 n. 129

Lagerlöf, Selma, *The Wonderful
Adventure of Nils* 296–7 n. 90
Landau, Paul S. 134–5
Lange, Erin Jade, *Butter* 234–5, 237
Langmuir, Erika 100
Laqueur, Thomas 46–7
Lazarus, Emma, "The New Colossus" 222
Lebesco, Kathleen and Braziel, Jana
Evans 226
Leeuwenhoek, Anton van 45–6
Lehman, Eric D. 109
Lejeune, Jérôme 52
Leopold II of the Belgians 133, 140, 156
Lewis, C. S., *The Lion, the Witch and the
Wardrobe* 187
Lezcano, Francisco 99, 284 n. 76
The Life and Death of Tom Thumb 42
Life's Too Short (TV series) 128
Lipsyte, Robert, *One Fat Summer* 231
literature, tall tale 226–9
literature for children:
and dwarfs 13, 103, 105, 118–29, 155,
290 n. 60
and emblem books 21, 82–6
and giants 186–9, 212, 225–6, 226–43,
302 n. 15, 303 n. 21
and miniatures 13, 19–21, 26, 143–4,
150, 158–73, 230
and obesity 226–43, 310 n. 18
and racialized other 131–3, 136,
143–50, 151, 156, 158–73, 173–7,
292 n. 23, 292 n. 24, 301 n. 136
revision 158–73, 175
and robots 212–23
and Tom Thumb figure 47–51
little man figures 17–28, *see also*
homunculus; Tom Thumb figure
Little People, Big World (TV reality
show) 127
Livingstone, David 136–7
Lobel, Arnold, *Giant John* 188
Lofting, Hugh, Dr Dolittle series 143–6,
147, 156, 159–60, 163, 173, 175
López-Rey, José 99, 102, 104, 285 n. 79
Lowell, Percy 62–3
Ludwig, David 246–7
lusus naturae 150–8, 183
Lyons, Claire L. 261

MacCann, Donnarae 144
MacDonald, George, "The Giant's Heart"
186–7
machines:

and adults 200–3
and children 193–201, 211–12
see also robots
Mack, John 22, 57, 275 n. 60
McKinley, Nita Mary 236, 241
McKissack, Patricia and Frederick 160
Mackler, Carolyn, *The Earth, My Butt,
and other Big Round Things*
237–8, 242
Madan, Falconer 62
mandrake 39–40
Margarita Theresa of Spain 97, 98, 100
Maribárbola (court dwarf) 99–102, 313 n.
63
Marsh, Katherine, *Jepp, Who Defied the
Stars* 121, 125–6
Martagh, Lindsey 246–7
Martinez-Regino, Adela 244, 246
Martinez-Regino, Anamarie 244–7,
250–2, 254
masculinity:
and Charles Stratton 112–14
and the gigantic 181, 231–5
and machines 201–3, 209
and mechanical bodies 192–3, 211–12,
215–16, 221–2, 224
and the miniature 20–1, 36–7, 181
and obesity 231–5
and Tom Thumb trope 35–7, 42–3, 47,
49–51
Mason, Keith 52
Mawer, Simon, *Mendel's Dwarf* 44–5, 57
Mazo, Juan Bautista del 99
Meccano 209–11, 212
Meccano Guild 210–11
Meccano Magazine 210
Merish, Lori 7, 113, 287–8 n. 26
microscopes and microscopy 1–2, 8, 31,
48, 131, 269 n. 3
and conception 45–6
and preformationism 46–7
midgets 114
midget villages 117–18
Mignon 19–20
miniatures:
and children 7, 18–19, 21–3, 26, 147,
157, 230, 257
in children's literature 13, 19–21, 26,
143–4, 150, 158–73
and cuteness 7, 113
and emblems 70–1, 83
and femininity 20, 113, 181
and giants 9, 157, 184–6
and little men 17–28
and masculinity 20–1, 35–7, 42–3, 47,
49–51, 112–14, 181

racialized 8, 13, 25–6, 130–6, 143–7,
    151, 156–73,173–7
  and resistance and subversion 173–8
  and Tom Thumb figure 34
  see also dwarfs; pygmies; Tom Thumb
    figure
minstrels, pygmies as 13, 137–8, 145, 161,
    175, 177–8
minstrelsy 300–1 n. 136
missing links 19, 144, 147, 150, 174
Mittmann, Asa Simon 225
modernity, and spectacle 138
Modica, Andrea 190, 250–2, 254–5
monkey, and dwarfs 69–71, 90
monsters 8–10
  and children 182–3, 246–50
  giants as 181–90, 191, 217, 225
  and obesity 225, 236–7, 241–3, 246,
    248–50, 254–5
  and other 10–11
  terrorists as 10
Montenay, Georgette de, Emblems ou
    Devises Chrestiennes 75
Morra, Sebastián de 93
Morris, Gary 172–3
Moseley, Charles 75–7
Mulan (film) 186
multum in parvo:
  and dwarfs 61, 73, 83, 85, 102, 111
  and Tom Thumb trope 33, 36
Mytens, Daniel, Charles I and Henrietta
    Maria departing for the Chase 68,
    69–71

Nandy, Ashis 133
National Child Labor Committee (US)
    197
Native Americans, in children's literature
    26, 135–6, 164–73, 230
Ness, Patrick, A Monster Calls 182
The New Yeare's Gift by Microphilus 73–4,
    78–9
Newman, William 47
Ngai, Sianne 288 n. 32, 303 n. 1
Nightlight Christian Adoptions Agency
    54
Noble Savage concept 135–6, 156, 161,
    163, 165–6
Norton, Mary, The Borrowers 13, 19–20,
    36, 158, 296 n. 81, 301 n. 138
Nottage, Lynn, Las Meninas 296 n. 87
Nussbaum, Felicity 6

Obama, Barack 55
obesity:
  and bariatric surgery 238–40, 262

  and body image 303 n. 30
  childhood 13, 244–55
  and ethnicity 310 n. 32, 313 n. 58
  and femininity 189–90, 225–6, 236–43,
    248–50
  and genetics 312 n. 49
  as industry 312 n. 54
  and masculinity 231–5
  ogres 35–6
Oompa-Loompas 13, 159
otherness:
  and children 7
  and difference 3, 4–6, 23–8, 106, 258,
    263
  and dwarfism 23–4, 69–70, 71, 90,
    104–5, 118, 130
  and monsters 10, 11
  and race 6, 25–6, 130–6, 140–7, 156,
    158–73
  and Tom Thumb trope 34
Owen, Robert 195–6

Pace, Patricia 19–20, 36
Page, Nick 66
painting, and emblems 101–2
Paley, William, Natural Theology 57
Paracelsus, De Natura Rerum 39–40, 56
Parr, Thomas 73
Parry, Graham 68
Parsons, Walter 184
Peel, Sir Robert 195–6
performativity:
  and dwarf body 103–5, 111–18,
    119–20, 121–5, 127–9, 175
  and pygmies 138, 145, 146, 150, 178
Perrault, Charles, Le petit Poucet 35–6,
    40, 50
Personhood USA 52–3
Pertusato, Nicolas (court dwarf) 99
Philbrick, Rodman, Freak the Mighty 185
Philip IV of Spain and Portugal 90–2,
    94, 97–8
photography:
  and colonialism 134–5
  and human measure 260–5
  and obesity 190, 250–5
  and social change 197–200
Pieterse, Jan Nederveen 136, 177
Pigot, Richard 83
Pinkus, Karen 101
Place, François, The Last Giants 155–8,
    163, 167, 173, 175, 177, 219
Pliny the Elder (Gaius Plinius
    Secundus) 6
Pluto (planet) 61–3
Poignant, Roslyn 138

Poliquin, Rachel 116
politics:
  of identity 11, 60
  and size 13, 51–6, 58, 124
  postcolonialism, and revision and erasure
    158–73, 175
Pourbus, Frans the Younger, *Archduchess
    Isabella Clara Eugenia and her
    Dwarf* 86–9
power and size 3, 6, 9, 25, 35–6, 72, 79–80,
    96, 177, 184, 187, 207, 220, 250
  and robots 207, 213
Prader-Willi syndrome 249–50
preformationism 46–7, 52, 56
Prichard, Troy 246
primitivism 6, 22, 130, 138, 143, 150
progress:
  and colonialism 132, 134, 138, 140,
    161, 261
  and technology 13, 138, 193, 201,
    203–9, 211–12, 215, 222
Prometheus 76
proportion and size 7, 17, 48, 50, 72,
    191, 248
  dwarfs 64, 74, 105, 108, 111, 114, 130
  and Gulliver 37–8
Pupin, Michael 206
pygmies 8, 25–7, 131–6
  children seen as 196
  in children's literature 159–73
  display 133, 134, 137–8, 140–3
  in evolutionary theory 132–5, 137,
    139–40, 141–3
  as minstrels 13, 137–8, 145, 161, 175,
    177–8
  in postcolonial discourse 158–73
  and resistance and subversion 173–8
  seen as apes 131–2, 141–2, 144, 147
  seen as children 133–4, 142
  seen as sport of nature 150
  see also Benga, Ota

Quick, Catherine S. 238

R. B. *see* Crouch, Nathaniel
race:
  and otherness 6, 25–6, 130–6, 140–7,
    156, 158–73, 173–8
  and size 6, 8, 13, 18, 25–6, 130–6
Ray, Charles, *Family Romance* 11–12
Ray, John, *Wisdom of God in the
    Creation* 57
reduction *see multum in parvo*
religion, and science 31–2, 48, 57–9
reproduction:
  assisted 32, 34, 45, 57, 60

  and the miniature 32
  and Tom Thumb trope 33–6, 38,
    41–2, 47, 52
Reynolds, Joshua 84
Richardson, James, "Big Scenes" 256, 265
Ridley, Matt 249
Right-to-Life movement 51–2
robots 10–11, 13, 181–2, 189–90,
    193–203, 205–9, 211–23
Roloff family 127
Rowling, J. K. 272 n. 27, 301 n. 142,
    302 n. 18
Rubens, Peter Paul 91, 99
Russo, Mary 236
Rydell, Robert W. 204–5, 208–9

Saguy, Abigail C. 225
Sampsell-Willmann, Kate 197
Sánchez-Eppler, Karen 304 n. 4, 304 n. 13
Sasquatch (Bigfoot) 186
scale:
  and children 3, 182–3, 194, 197–9,
    253–4
  and human measure 258–65
  and Industrial Revolution 193–203, 219
  and the norm 1–3, 12, 37–47, 61, 191
science:
  and anatomy 131–2, 138
  and business 203–6
  and children 209–23
  and progress 13, 138, 193, 201, 203–9,
    211–12, 215, 222, 262
  and religion 31–2, 48, 57–9
  scientific idealism 205–6
Science Advisory Committee 205–6
Scott, Walter, *Peveril of the Peak* 66
servants, black 69–70
sexuality:
  and children 230
  and dwarfs 116
  and the gigantic 230
  and race 158
Shaftesbury, Anthony Ashley Cooper, 7th
    Earl 195–7
Shelley, Mary Wollstonecraft,
    Frankenstein 9, 182–3, 186
Sikundar, Sylvia, *Forest Singer* 161–2,
    163, 173
Silver, Carole G. 133
size:
  and diversity 8
  genetics 11, 35, 37, 43–5, 47, 51
  as marker of difference 1–3, 4–8, 60–1,
    178, 257–8
  politics 13, 51–6, 58
  and textuality 61–3

Skal, David J. 10, 225
slavery 146–9, 158, 163
Slepian, Barnett 53
smallness:
    and beauty 21–2
    and inferiority 131–6
    see also dwarfs; miniatures
Smith, Susan 236
Snowflake children 54–5, 56, 59
Solomon, Andrew 3, 8, 23–5
spectacle:
    and modernity 138
    and obese females 236
sperm, as animalcule 45–7, 60
sport, and female giants 229
Statue of Liberty 222–3, 224
Steedman, Carolyn 19–20, 21
Steege, David 146
Steig, William, The Toy Brother 43–4, 45
Stern, Howard 127
Sterne, Laurence, Tristram Shandy 41–2,
    43, 45, 53
Stevens, Laura M. 135–6
Stewart, Susan 19, 25, 28, 37, 111, 117,
    172, 183, 187, 270 n. 9, 288 n. 45
stigma, and performance 104–5, 118
Stowe, Harriet Beecher, Uncle Tom's Cabin
    147–8
Stratton, Charles S. 8, 12, 20–1, 37
    and childhood 111–12
    as General Tom Thumb 18, 104,
        105–6, 106, 108–18, 128, 130,
        150, 286 n. 5
    marriage 114–17, 127, 128
sublimity, and size 6–7
Swift, Jonathan, Gulliver's Travels 5–6,
    36–8, 40, 45, 64, 150–1, 156, 158,
    168, 173

tall tales 226–9
Tavernor, Robert 258–9
Taylor, John 73
Taylor, Rhonda 170–1
technology:
    and business 203–6
    and progress 13, 138, 193, 201, 203–9,
        211–12, 215, 222
telescopes 1
television:
    dwarf actors 105
    reality shows 127
terrorism, and monsters 10
textuality, and size 61–3
Thackeray, William Makepeace 5
thalidomide 45
Thaumlin (Little Thumb) 30

theatricality, and dwarf body 103–4,
    117–18
Thomson, Rosemarie Garland 183,
    289 n. 50
Thone, Ruth Raymond 241
Thumbelina 20, 36, 152, 242
thumblings 13, 28, 30, 60, 105–6, 60,
    see also homunculus; Tom
    Thumb figure
Tiller, George 53
Tom Thumb figure 18, 27–8, 29–32, 64
    in children's literature 47–51
    and multum in parvo 33, 36
    as phallus or fetus 33–6, 42–4, 49
    redactive tradition 34, 36, 47–9
    and reproduction 33–6, 38, 41–2,
        47, 52
    Tom Thumb weddings 116–17,
        127, 128
    as trickster 35, 36, 155
    as trope 32–7, 273 n. 46
    see also homunculus; Stratton,
        Charles S.
Tom Thumbe, His Life and Death 42
Tombaugh, Clyde W. 62
Tomling, Sven 30
Trimmer, Sarah, The Oeconomy of
    Charity 196–7
Trump, Donald J. 222–3
Tuan, Yi-Fu 25
Turner, Herbert Hall 62
Tygesdatter, Magdalene 126
Tyson, Edward, The Anatomy of a
    Pygmy 131–2, 142

utopianism, scientific 13, 189, 193, 207–8,
    211–14, 217, 219
    and gender 10–11

Van de Venne, Adrian 83–4
van Dyck, Anthony
    Charles I and Henrietta Maria with
        their two eldest children, Prince
        Charles and Princess Mary 68
    as court painter 67–8
    The Five Eldest Children of Charles I
        71, 91
    Queen Henrietta Maria with Sir Jeffrey
        Hudson 18, 21, 67–71, 85, 86–7,
        94, 96
Velázquez, Diego 61, 86, 90–2, 104
    Don Baltasar Carlos with a Dwarf
        94–7, 99–100
    Las Meninas 93, 95, 97–102, 249
    Prince Baltasar Carlos in the Riding
        School 92–4, 96

Verner, Samuel Phillips 139, 140–1, 142–3, 150
Vesalius, Andreas 131
Villechaize, Hervé 105

Walpole, Hugh 144, 159
Warner, Marina 23, 182, 297 n. 92, 302 n. 1
Warren, Lavinia 20, 37, 105, 114–17, 287 n. 23, 289 n. 48
Watson, Elizabeth See 77, 85
weight, ideal 236–7, 240–1; see also obesity
White, E. B., *Stuart Little* 7
White, T. H., *Mistress Masham's Repose* 151–5, 165, 167, 173, 175–8
Whitney, Geffrey, *A Choice of Emblemes* 75–7, 80
Wilberforce, William 195–6
Wilde, Oscar:
"The Birthday of the Infanta" 25, 119–21, 123
"The Selfish Giant" 187
Willy Wonka and The Chocolate Factory (film) 159
Wilson, Catherine 48
Windle, Bertram C. A. 132, 133
Wither, George, *A Collection of Emblemes* 80–1

The Wizard of Oz (film) 105
women:
in tall tale literature 227–9
see also femininity; gender; giants
The Wonders of the Microscope 48, 50
Wood, Edward J., *Giants and Dwarfs* 66
Woodruff, Louise Lentz 207
World's Fairs293 n. 30
Chicago 1933–4 193, 204–8, 215, 219–20, 304 n. 2
New York 1939 306 n. 32, 306 n. 33
St Louis 1904
and indigenous peoples 139–40
and pygmies 140–1, 163
Texas 1936 306 n. 32
Wright, James, *History and Antiquities of the County of Rutland* 66
Wynne, John Huddlestone, *Choice Emblems* 82–3

Yates, Andrea 236
Yonge, Charlotte 144
The History of Sir Thomas Thumb 28, 30, 49–51

Zip 106, 111
Zunshine, Lisa 306 n. 31